Foundations of Modern
Historical Scholarship

Language, Law, and History

in the French Renaissance

Verbi certa fides vt mundo augustior esset
principe francisco nobilitata fuit ¡

Guillaume Budé: De l'institution du Prince (Lausanne,
Bibliothèque Publique et Cantonale, MS E. 497, p. 15)

Foundations of Modern Historical Scholarship

Language, Law, and History
in the French Renaissance

Donald R. Kelley

Columbia University Press

New York and London, 1970

Preface

IN LOOKING back over the history of this history of history, I must say
that my interest in the subject is considerably older than my professional commitment to Renaissance studies in particular. It derives in
part from a curiosity, first provoked by the writings of Herbert Butterfield and R. G. Collingwood, about this outlandish way of looking at
the world called historical mindedness, and in part from a growing
belief in the need to subject historical thought to the kind of critical
re-examination which E. A. Burtt and others have applied to scientific thought. It has been confirmed by my long-standing fascination
with Ernst Cassirer's studies in epistemology, which touch upon every
mode of thought except the historical, and with Wilhelm Dilthey's
projected but unrealized "critique of historical reason"—though one
need not be a neo-Kantian, I hope, nor even a historian of ideas, to
see the value of a critical understanding of history.

But my most substantial debts are personal, and I should like to
acknowledge the most essential of these. First in point of time was my
undergraduate encounter with the "sense of history" in Myron Gilmore's seminar in historiography, which has enticed more than one
unsuspecting student into this field. I learned much, too, from my
teachers at Columbia, especially the late Garrett Mattingly, Paul O.
Kristeller, and J. H. Mundy. More recently acquired are my debts to
Hans Baron, Eugene Rice, Aldo Scaglione, Peter Gay, A. A. Schiller,
Ralph Giesey, Dorothy Thickett, and Guido Kisch. For many kindnesses
and provocations I should also like to thank several of my contemporaries, among whom I count those with whom I can argue without
reservation or undue remorse, especially Samuel Kinser, George Huppert, Julian Franklin, L. R. Shelby, Sanford Elwitt, Joseph Levine,
Stuart Prall, Edward Mahoney, and Charles Schmitt. I hope that I have

sufficiently disguised, if not distorted, what I have stolen from all these mentors and friends. I am only sorry that I have not been more receptive to their experience and advice, and that I cannot rely more heavily upon their authority.

Some of the most obvious deficiencies of this study, I prefer to think, are inseparable from the questions which provoked it in the first place. In particular, I have not been able to examine as thoroughly as I should have liked any single author or theme, although the subject of any one of the principal chapters deserves, I think, an entire book. At the same time I have had to venture into a number of technical fields where I can claim no special competence—particularly the history of philosophy, classical scholarship, and three separate branches of law—civil, canon, and feudal. But it is my hope that the scope of the inquiry is appropriate to the questions posed, and it is my belief that whatever value this book may possess is largely the result of my poaching, unlicensed as it has been, upon such alien preserves.

Some of the material on which this book is based has been published as follows: *"Historia Integra:* François Baudouin and his Conception of History," *Journal of the History of Ideas,* XXV (1964), 35-57; *"De Origine Feudorum*: The Beginnings of an Historical Problem," *Speculum,* XXXIX (1964), 207-28; *"Fides Historiae*: Charles Dumoulin and the Gallican View of History," *Traditio,* XXII (1966), 347-402; "Legal Humanism and the Sense of History," *Studies in the Renaissance,* XIII (1966), 184-99; "Jean du Tillet, Archivist and Antiquary," *Journal of Modern History,* XXXVIII (1966), 337-54; and "Guillaume Budé and the First Historical School of Law," *American Historical Review,* LXXII (1967), 807-34.

I must also express my gratitude to several institutions, especially to the Fulbright Commission, the American Philosophical Society, the Newberry Library, and the American Council of Learned Societies, for making possible three expeditions to Europe and extensive research in many libraries and archives on both sides of the Atlantic.

Most essential of all has been the support of my wife Nancy and my chief critic John Reed. They are the ones who have really kept things in perspective.

London, April 1968   D. R. K.

Contents

Note on Documentation

THIS is a work of interpretation and synthesis, and so citations have been given in a rather general form. It has not been possible to include texts in the original languages; but since much of the secondary literature for this subject is either unfamiliar or hidden in works pertaining to other disciplines, it has seemed useful to make the notes a kind of cicerone for relevant biographical, historical, and technical studies, as well as for the most significant printed and manuscript material. A comprehensive bibliography would require a volume at least the size of the present book.

Here is a list of the most common abbreviations used in the footnotes:

Allen	P. S. Allen (ed.), *Opus Epistolarum Des. Erasmi Roterodami* (12 vols., Oxford, 1906-58)
Aubert	H. Aubert, E. Aubert, H. Meylan, A Dufour (eds.), *Correspondance de Theodore de Bèze* (5 vols., Geneva, 1960-68)
[B]HR	*[Bibliothèque d'] Humanisme et renaissance*
BN MSS	Bibliothèque Nationale, Manuscrits
BSHPF	*Bulletin de la Société de l'histoire du protestantisme français*
Barni	G. L. Barni (ed.), *Le Lettere di Andrea Alciato giureconsulto* (Florence, 1953)
Bayle	Pierre Bayle, *Dictionnaire historique et critique*
CR	*Corpus Reformatorum*, ed. K. G. Brettschneider (87 vols., Halle, 1834-1900)
Cioranesco	A. Cioranesco, *Bibliographie de la littérature française du seizième siècle* (Paris, 1959)
D	Digest

De Thou   J. A. de Thou, *Histoire universelle* (11 vols., The Hague, 1740)

Haag   Eugène and Émile Haag, *La France protestante* (10 vols., Paris, 1846-59)

Hartmann   A. Hartmann (ed.), *Die Amerbachkorrespondenz* (5 vols., Basel, 1942-58)

Heineccius   J. G. Heineccius (ed.), *Jurisprudentia romana et attica*, I (François Baudouin, *Opuscula omnia*) (Lyon, 1737)

Isambert   F. Isambert (ed.), *Recueil général des anciennes lois françaises* (29 vols., Paris, 1821-33)

JHI   *Journal of the History of Ideas*

L'Estoile   Pierre de l'Estoille, *Journal pour le règne de Henri III (1574-89)*, ed. L. Lefèvre (Paris, 1943), and *Journal pour le règne de Henri IV*, ed. L. Lefèvre (3 vols., Paris, 1958-60)

Mesnard   P. Mesnard (ed.), Jean Bodin, *Œuvres philosophiques* (Paris, 1951)

Migne   J. P. Migne (ed.), *Patrologia Latina* (221 vols., Paris, 1844-80)

[N]RHDFE   *[Nouvelle] Revue historique de droit français et étranger*

Recueil   Jean du Tillet, *Recueil des Roys de France, leurs couronne et maison* (Paris, 1607)

SR   *Studies in the Renaissance*

Scaligerana *Scaligerana, Thuana, Perroniana, Pithoeana, et Colomesiana* (2 vols., Amsterdam, 1740)

Tractatus   *Tractatus universi juris*, duce et auspice Gregorio XIII (15 vols., Venice, 1584)

Wolf   J. Wolf (ed.), *Artis historiae penus octodecem scriptores* (2 vols., Basel, 1579)

ZSSRG   *Zeitschrift der Savigny-Stiftung für Rechtsgeschichte*

Foundations of Modern
Historical Scholarship

Language, Law, and History

in the French Renaissance

CHAPTER 1

Introduction: The Prehistory
of Historicism

Le dottrine debbono cominciare da quando co-
minciano le materie che trattano.

Vico, *La Nuova scienza*, CVI, 314

"AMONG THE APHORISMS of the ancients . . . the most remarkable was
that of Chilon, one of the seven sages . . .: Know thyself. Now this
knowledge depends upon history, sacred as well as profane, universal
as well as particular."[1] So wrote a learned French jurist of the sixteenth century. This statement contains, of course, the oldest of com-
monplaces, but like other ancient formulas revived in the Renaissance,
it took on a somewhat different meaning in its new environment. For
Montaigne it was an invitation to autobiography; for Gaillard it suggested also that man needed to understand the past of his civilization
in order to understand himself. Implicitly, the observation offers the
basis for a more profound conception of man. It represents him not
merely as a creature with certain unique attributes but as a creator,
learning as well as living in time. The idea is analogous to Pico's view
of the "human condition," which also had ancient roots, except that
here the emphasis is not upon the philosophic attribute of freedom but
upon the human fact of accumulated and inherited cultural experience.
In a sense, man is defined not as a rational or a political animal but as

---

[1] Pierre Droit de Gaillard, *Methode qu'on doit tenir en la lecture de l'histoire* (Paris, 1579), p. 1, and "De Utilitate et ordine historiarum praefatio," in
Bap. Fulgosii factorum dictorumque memorabilem libri IX (Paris, 1578),
f. a ii^r.

a remembering animal, not as *homo sapiens* but as *homo historicus*. This awareness of the indelibly historical nature of man, which furnishes perhaps the most fundamental motive for the modern study of history, is the point of departure of this book.

Some Questions

What is history? Men often ask this question but, like Pilate, seldom stay for an answer. Answers we have, of course, but most of them seem to concern rather different questions. What ought history to be? Or what would one like history to be? Or what must history be in order to preserve one preconception or another. The trouble is that the question has usually been asked by the wrong people. It has been asked by philosophers, who are often barely tolerant of, if not actually disgusted by, the everyday work of the practicing historian. It has been asked by social scientists, who have hopes of fitting it into their own scholarly schemes. It has been asked by theologians, who really have their sights fixed upon more transcendent problems. Occasionally it has been asked by historians, but normally as an opportunity for self-justification or autobiography. Almost never has it been asked with much respect for a historical point of view. Yet if history is a means to self-understanding, as many men, from Gaillard to Collingwood, have believed, what better way can we proceed than to turn the method of history upon itself? In order to understand what history is, we must first ask: What has history been?

What is history? For the past two thousand years few literate men would have had difficulty in giving an answer. History is the memory of human words and deeds without which, as Cicero put it, men would remain forever children. Unfortunately, this leaves us as puzzled as before. What is the precise nature of this "memory," we ask, how is it acquired, and how may it be expressed? It would be too much to expect Cicero to recognize the methodological and epistemological difficulties involved in this question, but it is distressing to think how long it has taken historians to see these problems, not to speak of making provisions for resolving them. This neglect accounts for the difference between even the best of ancient and medieval historical writing, which approached sources of information with naïve trust or skepticism, and the critical and synthetic scholarship of modern times. Only in the past two centuries, according to Collingwood, was "scissors-and-paste history" superseded by the attempt to restore the past by criticizing and controlling various and perhaps conflicting sources.[2] With this attitude has come the realization that the "past" in question is not directly accessible but must be in some sense reconstructed by the historian. The inference is that history must be understood not simply as a branch of knowledge but as a mode of thought—as "an intellectual form," as Huizinga put it, "for understanding the world."[3]

What is the sense of history? Everyone is aware of the past, but not everyone takes it seriously. Some people regard it as a legacy to be exploited, others as a burden to be thrown off. Some few look upon it as an experience to be relived. It is in this sense that history seems to be one of the distinguishing characteristics of Western civilization. If the achievements of historical studies have not been as sensational as those of natural science, is this not perhaps because they have not served man's animal needs so directly, while at the same time they have so disappointed his moral demands? Clearly, history has been as effective as science in broadening intellectual horizons—and in subverting conventional values. Indeed, the sense of history has not only widened the range of human experience, it has also promoted a psychological transformation, a veritable Copernican revolution in man's attitude toward his culture, hence toward his own being. It has provided man not only with a deepened perspective but also with a more intense awareness of the plenitude, variety, and instability of human nature. These are some of the reasons for suggesting that there has been a historical as well as a scientific revolution.

---

[2] Collingwood, *The Idea of History* (Oxford, 1945), p. 33. The survey of historical writing on which this famous work rests has little independent value, nor has Croce's *Theory and History of Historiography*, trans. D. Ainslie (London, 1941), which follows Fueter's manual uncritically. There is no satisfactory study of pre-nineteenth-century historical writing.

[3] J. Huizinga, "A Definition of the Concept of History," *Philosophy and History*, eds. R. Klibansky and H. Paton (Oxford, 1936), p. 5. On the fortunes of the term "history" down to the sixteenth century see K. Keuck, *Historia, Geschichte des Wortes* (Emsdetten, 1934).

What is "historicism"? For one thing, it is a much-abused and often pejorative term which historians, unlike many students of literature, sociology, and philosophy, seem reluctant to accept.[4] Yet there is no better way of identifying the intellectual phenomenon just outlined; and it hardly seems necessary, even if it were possible, to banish the word simply because of certain regrettable overtones deriving from nineteenth-century German thought or from more recent fictions devised by positivists, "logical" and otherwise, who are still haunted by Hegelian ghosts and by La Place's demon of determinism. The fact is that the term "historicism" has been applied with increasing frequency to a distinguishable set of traits in modern thought that have had a life quite independent of the particular ideological manifestations of the nineteenth and twentieth centuries. It is a word which serves not only to designate the conceptual basis of the historian's quest but, more important, to emphasize the deep-rooted and continuing traditions of historical scholarship.

Understood in this neutral but, it seems to me, historically meaningful sense, "historicism" refers to a group of correlative principles or tendencies which seem to be minimum requirements for understanding the past. These may be termed, broadly and without specification, humanism, individuality, pluralism, relativism, and mutability. In other words, "historicism" refers to that cast of mind which, consciously or not, turns not to nature but to the world of man's making; which seeks out not the typical but the unique; which emphasizes the variety rather than the uniformity of human nature; which is interested less in similarities than in differences; and which is impressed not with per-

---

[4] This is not the place to enter into the debate over the various "historicisms" and "historisms" of twentieth-century invention. The classic study of the standard nineteenth-century view is Friedrich Meinecke, *Die Entstehung des Historismus* (Munich, 1959), and *Zur Theorie und Philosophie der Geschichte* (Stuttgart, 1959), pp. 216 ff. Karl Popper's famous attack, *The Poverty of Historicism* (Boston, 1957), is quite without relevance either to the subject of Meinecke's book or to the present study. The most meaningful use of the term, it seems to me, is that of such literary historians as Vittorio Rossi (see ch. II, n. 59), Ernst Curtius, and Erich Auerbach (see ch. XI, n. 1), and this approximates my usage. No direct notice of this is taken in the otherwise useful survey by D. Lee and R. Beck, "The Meaning of 'Historicism,'" *American Historical Review*, LIX (1954), 569-77.

manence but with change. This rather awkward and, at this point, empty idealization does not entail particular ideological values, theories of causation, models of explanation, or political goals, which are themselves the products of particular temperaments or historical circumstances. Nor is it suggested as a desirable or even attainable point of view. Rather it is offered as a generalization identifying a particular scholarly syndrome that, it seems to me, distinguishes historical scholarship from other intellectual enterprises.

When did the modern study of history and this historicist attitude begin? Historians have always celebrated the coming-of-age of their muse—or the establishment of their science—but they have never quite agreed upon the date. The commonest view would trace modern historical scholarship to the romantic movement of the nineteenth century.[5] There is some plausibility in this, but not much; it depends upon taking the romantic historians entirely at their own estimate. It is true, of course, that the reaction to eighteenth-century rationalism and more especially to Jacobinism and to Bonapartism provided impetus to and an ideological basis for concerted historical investigation. The tools and methods of the German historical schools, however, had already been fashioned by scholars in other branches of learning, and so were many of the basic concepts of historical interpretation. Niebuhr was trained as a philologist, it may be recalled, and Savigny as a jurist. What was most novel about these nineteenth-century historicists was the fusion of these techniques and ideas with a peculiar organistic and nationalistic theory of civilization—a theory which itself, it should be added, had its roots in other fields. At the most it may be said that historicism reached a new peak of self-consciousness and organization in the early nineteenth century.

That historicism was not simply a byproduct of the *Freiheitskriege* was already apparent to some alumni of the German historical schools in the nineteenth century. There were indeed, as Lord Acton noted, brave men before Agamemnon.[6] Even if the historians of the Enlighten-

---

[5] Characteristic is the enthusiastic statement by Lord Acton in his famous inaugural lecture in *Lectures on Modern History* (London, 1950), p. 14, that this movement was "deeper and more serious than the revival of ancient learning."

[6] John Acton, "German Schools of History," in *Historical Essays and Studies*

ment were as shallow and uncritical as some observers pretended (and this was a view increasingly difficult to maintain) one could always point to such apparent anomalies as Herder and Vico to suggest that eighteenth-century scholarship was not wholly without perspective and sophistication. If nothing else, the eighteenth-century climate of opinion permitted the survival of a few "precursors" of historicism.

This is about as far as historians have cared to go. There has been nearly universal agreement that the seventeenth century, ridden with Baconian distrust and racked with Cartesian doubt, was a poor field for the cultivation of history, except for technical accomplishments in the so-called auxiliary sciences. The result was a kind of war between two cultures—between those "two great scholarly creations of the modern world," as Troeltsch called them, naturalism and historicism.[7] It was hardly an equal fight. Mathematics became the new logos, and to a man like Galileo the word "historian" was an epithet to be flung in the teeth of his obscurantist enemies.[8] Not only did the idea of a mathematical or mechanical universe seem to eliminate the need for history, but the language of the "new philosophy" tended, as Karl Vossler said, to drive the senses, God, the soul, and finally man himself out of the world.[9] In the relentless quest for absolute certainty, history seemed at best a featureless conveyor of "examples," at worst a part of that antiquated scholastic baggage to be thrown out altogether.

(London, 1919), p. 344, referring to F. X. von Wegele, *Geschichte der deutschen Historiographie* (Munich, 1885), which celebrates many of these "brave men." On the eighteenth-century antecedents of the historical schools the classic statement is that of Wilhelm Dilthey, "Das achtzehnte Jahrhundert und die geschichtliche Welt," *Gesammmelte Schriften*, III (Munich, 1927). See also Ernst Cassirer, *Philosophy of the Enlightenment*, trans. Koeller and Pettigrove (Princeton, 1951), pp. 197 ff; Ernst Troeltsch, *Der Historismus und seine Probleme* (Tübingen, 1922), p. 11; Herbert Butterfield, *Man on His Past* (Cambridge, 1955); and most recently A. Kraus, *Vernunft und Geschichte* (Freiberg, 1963).

[7] Ernst Troeltsch, *Der Historismus*, p. 104. Cf. Collingwood, *Idea of History*, p. 59, remarking that Descartes "did not believe history to be, strictly speaking, a branch of knowledge at all."

[8] Galileo Galilei, *Dialogue concerning the Two Chief World Systems*, trans. S. Drake (Berkeley, 1953), p. 113.

[9] Karl Vossler, *The Spirit of Language in Civilization*, trans. O. Oeser New York, 1932), p. 164.

If it was Boileau who cut the throat of poetry, so this argument runs, it was Descartes who emasculated history.

Yet even this view does not seem altogether satisfactory. Besides exaggerating the effects of the scientific revolution upon the study of human culture—and, conversely, ignoring the mythical character of historical thinking—it quite overlooks the continuing tradition of humanist scholarship that linked the Enlightenment with the Renaissance. The "geometric spirit" may well have cast a blight upon the study of history, but the effects were far from fatal, as the work of Bayle or even of Leibniz makes clear. The case of Giambattista Vico, though it has been the source of much confusion, is most instructive of all. Was he a man far in advance of his time or far behind it? A founder of European historicism or, in the words of a recent author, "the last great philosopher who had an immediate contact with the humanist tradition"?[10] In the perspective of this book he was both. For it was Vico's profound and prolonged immersion in the literary and legal works of humanist scholarship that led him to turn viciously—or as Joyce would have said, vicously—against the dessicated method of Cartesianism, which for a time had claimed his allegiance, in favor of a historical philosophy. This is only the most conspicuous illustration of the much-neglected truth that historical thought was not simply anti-Cartesian but to a large extent pre-Cartesian, and had its roots in the rich soil of Renaissance scholarship. Vico was not so much the creator of a "new science" as the preserver of an old science, the science of philology. In this sense, he did not so much found historicism as inherit it.

Who, then, were the first "historicists"? Whether or not the term seems convenient, it seems clear that, at least in the context of European civilization, the humanists of the Renaissance were the first men to make a conscious and concerted effort to revive a dead past with some appreciation of temporal perspective and willingness to examine antiquity in its own terms. To a man like Luis Vives, for example,

[10] E. Grassi, "L'origine des sciences de l'esprit dans l'humanisme," in H. Bédarida (ed.), *Pensée humaniste et tradition chrétienne* (Paris, 1950), p. 114. On Vico and historicism see Meinecke, *Historismus*, and Auerbach, *Literary Language and its Public in Late Latin Antiquity and in the Middle Ages*, trans. R. Manheim (New York, 1965), pp. 7 ff, as well as Vico's *Autobiography*, trans. M. Fisch and T. Bergin (Ithaca, New York, 1944), pp. 113 ff.

history was not simply the celebration of national tradition but the "image of truth."[11] To be sure, the motives of humanists were not always entirely pure. In the attempt to establish a splendid and heroic classical ancestry they tended to devote themselves to a myth-making rather than a historical impulse. Yet the remoteness and alien character of antiquity gave an unusual quality even to their idealizations. They created a new kind of myth which, it may be argued, lies at the roots of historicism. Ultimately, as Mircea Eliade has written about Western civilization, "it seeks to discover, 'awaken,' and repossess the parts of the most exotic and most peripheral societies. . . . The goal is no less than to revive the entire past of humanity."[12] In this unique intellectual enterprise there were many forces at work, including the renewed familiarity with ancient Greek learning beginning in the twelfth century and the cultural shock produced by the geographical discoveries of the fifteenth and sixteenth centuries. But it was in the context of humanist thought, with its fundamentally intercultural and time-conscious orientation, that the "vertiginous widening of the historical horizon" occurred.

Some Assumptions

History may always be contemporary in a sense, but it should not content itself with mere ancestor worship. This is a lesson which, curiously enough, has been learned more quickly by historians of science than by historians of history. For more than a generation, scholars have been uncovering the roots of scientific thinking underlying the sensational achievements of the seventeenth century. Rejecting the old positivist, or Baconian, view of science as a consistent and cumulative advance toward truth, historians of science have begun to examine more closely the actual circumstances of scientific discovery and to appreciate the role of hypothesis and even creative error in the emergence of new patterns of thought necessary for further discovery.[13] Historical scholar-

---

[11] "De Causis corruptarum artium," ch. VI, *Opera omnia* (Valencia, 1785), V, 106.

[12] Mircea Eliade, *Myth and Reality* (New York, 1963), p. 136. In general, see the valuable discussion by J. G. A. Pocock, "The Origins of Study of the Past," *Comparative Studies in Society and History*, IV (1961-62), 209-46.

[13] See J. Agassi, *Towards an Historiography of Science* (*History and Theory*, Beiheft II, 1963), and especially the work of Thomas Kuhn (see ch. II, n. 58).

ship, too, since it involves the interpretation as well as the collection of evidence, must be viewed as a human enterprise. History has not been simply the product of a relentless progression toward truth, objectivity, and a critical attitude, but the passionate and often partisan assault upon an alien and refractory past. Like nature, history must be, in Bacon's metaphor, "put to the question," and like nature may lie to the very end. It has not been an easy process, nor have the questioners and their methods always been above reproach. It is difficult to avoid seizing upon those ideas and discoveries which we retrospectively favor, but we should recognize that the circumstances of these discoveries and the pedigree of these ideas are not always as reputable as we might like.

Recent interpretations of the history of science have suggested another principle affecting the strategy of this work. "All decisive advances in the history of science," as Arthur Koestler put it, "can be described in terms of mental cross-fertilization between different disciplines."[14] This observation seems even more appropriate for modern historical thought, which owes its very existence to the encounters between philology and other branches of knowledge. Indeed, philology stands in somewhat the same relation to historical scholarship as mathematics stands to natural science.

The first problem has been how to trace in concrete terms the effects of philological methods upon historical scholarship. This might be done through a number of disciplines, including classical literature, Biblical studies, or even philosophy. For a number of reasons (not including any predilection on the author's part) the choice has fallen upon the field of law. In the first place, no other field is so closely tied to history with respect both to content and to method. Second, it was largely the influence of legal studies that revolutionized the theory of history, that is, the so-called art of history, in the sixteenth century. Third, it so happens that the lawyers contributed more than any other social or professional group to historical scholarship, and their preoccupations were decisive in shifting attention from drum and trumpet history to institutional, social, and cultural studies. Finally,

---

[14] Arthur Koestler, *The Act of Creation* (New York, 1964), p. 230.

the marriage of legal and historical studies in the sixteenth century
provided one of the most enduring elements in the continuity of historicism from that age down to the present.

At this point, however, a crucial qualification must be registered.
Pervasive as was the influence of classical humanism, we should not
overlook the subtle but substantial effects of medieval scholarship,
which not only persisted into the sixteenth century but enjoyed a kind
of revival. Like the romantic historians, the humanists should not be
taken quite at their own estimate; for it was their philological achievements, not their rhetorical claims, that made the most enduring contribution to history. In various medieval legal traditions there were
ideas and techniques of vital importance for historical scholarship. Not
only did medieval jurists have certain insights about the nature of
society and its relation to law, which humanists learned only with difficulty, but they developed ideas about the nature of time, especially
with regard to the problems of continuity and tradition, and even a
kind of cult of fame, which is usually associated with the humanists.
"Perhaps this trail, too," Ernst Kantorowicz remarked, "was first
trodden by the jurists."[15] It is unfortunate—and for present purposes
most inconvenient—that medievalists have not pursued such investigations beyond the no-man's-land of the fifteenth century. If civil and
canon law were fertile fields for the investigation of human society,
the sixteenth century represents in many respects the harvest time.

The study of history has always thrived upon the soil of national
culture, and it has seemed convenient to focus in particular upon the
French intellectual scene. The choice could have fallen on Italy, where
modern philology was born, or on Germany, where the assault upon
medieval history began, or even England, though the "historical revolution" there was a late stage and a peripheral case of a much
wider-ranging phenomenon.[16] It was in France, however, that medieval
and Renaissance traditions mingled most freely, and it was in France
that the central problems of European history—the conflict of church

---

[15] Ernst Kantorowicz, *The King's Two Bodies* (Princeton, 1957), p. 277.
See ch. VI and VII.

[16] See the informative if rather insular work of F. S. Fussner, *The Historical
Revolution, English Historical Writing and Thought 1580-1640* (New York,
1962), and F. J. Levy, *Tudor Historical Thought* (San Marino, 1967).

and state, feudalism, and the growth of national monarchy—were confronted most directly. Faced with the somewhat degrading fact of a mixed and multiple heritage, French scholarship also seems to represent a kind of mean, cultural as well as geographical, between Roman and Teutonic extremes. Avoiding the Italian emphasis upon classical antiquity and literary values on the one hand, and German absorption in ecclesiastical history and religious polemic on the other, French scholars were able to project their researches on a broader scale and to acquire a more balanced appreciation for the manifold inheritance of European civilization and a deeper consciousness of the diversity and mutability of human nature. This is one reason why, despite their suspicions of foreign influence in general, they were so extraordinarily receptive to the ideas and achievements of foreign scholarship—and why I have devoted so much attention to their borrowings, especially from Italian and German authors.

In examining the history of historical scholarship, it would be a great error to neglect the social context and the political pressures of the time. If the sense of history in general was the product of Renaissance humanism, the specific forms and interpretations of history were shaped in particular by the upheavals of the Reformation and by national rivalries. This was not altogether a misfortune. It is true that partisanship often distorted historical perspective and protected certain legends, but it served also to give impetus, organization, and direction to historical investigation and to discredit various errors. The exposure of most myths, it seems, was made in the name of honor or faith rather than of truth, and the search for new sources of information was seldom disinterested. The achievements of historical scholarship should be restored to their ideological context even though eventually they survived it.

In general, history is not something which, like poetry, is recollected in tranquillity. On the contrary, it is precisely in times of crisis, in times of self-doubt and self-searching, that men begin most intensely to question their antecedents and to seek the reasons for their plight.[17] Such have been the motives of many historians from Thucydides to

---

[17] See E. R. Curtius, *European Literature and the Latin Middle Ages*, trans. W. Trask (New York, 1953), pp. 3 ff. Some cases in point have been discussed

Machiavelli, and from Machiavelli to Friedrich Meinecke. Such were the motives, too, of the great French historians of the sixteenth century. Between them and Machiavelli, however, there was one crucial difference: their purpose was not simply to locate discrete causes or to affix guilt but rather to review their entire heritage.[18] For the formative crisis of French historical thought was not just a political or a military confrontation but a veritable *Weltanschauung*-clash which, accompanied by bitter civil wars, shook society to its foundations. Men like Pithou and Pasquier, who were concerned with the totality of French culture, could not be satisfied with the sharply focused and starkly political history written by Machiavelli or Guicciardini. Their purpose, put briefly, was not analytical and causal but synthetic and descriptive.

There is another reason for omitting this kind of historical writing which usually figures so prominently, or indeed exclusively, in discussions of Renaissance historical thought. This is the appearance of what may be called the transcendent impulse, which constitutes one of the most clearly marked boundaries of historicism in general and of this work in particular. By the "transcendent impulse" I mean the ever-present urge to rise above the letter to the spirit of a text, or to replace universal with particular history, or to go beyond history altogether in search of a science of society, a philosophy of culture, or some comparable metahistorical system. This is not the historian's way.

> "Men's curiosity searches past and future
> And clings to that dimension. But to apprehend
> The point of intersection of the timeless
> With time, is an occupation for the saint—" [19]

In this sense Machiavelli, whose interest in history was largely subordinated to his search for eternal principles of political behavior, was

---

by F. Chatelet, *La Naissance de l'histoire* (Paris, 1962), H. Baron, *The Crisis of the Early Italian Renaissance* (Princeton, 1966), and R. von Albertini, *Das Florentinische Staatsbewusstsein* (Bern, 1955), p. 299 ff.

[18] That these two kinds of historical writing may be treated in isolation is indicated by almost all discussions of Machiavelli, including Felix Gilbert's recent *Machiavelli and Guicciardini* (Princeton, 1965), which presents an excellent analysis of "the humanist concept of history" but without any attention to the kind of historical scholarship considered here.

[19] T. S. Eliot, "The Dry Salvages," V.

more "saintly" than the most pious monastic chronicler. The same may be said of Bodin, who likewise owed much of his influence—and likewise his somewhat diabolical reputation—to his transcendant claims. The ideas of these men were certainly better suited to the tastes of a more scientific age, and they gained further renown as apparent anticipations not only of Montesquieu but of Durkheim and of Pareto. Yet it is precisely the "sociological" tendency that alienated them from the mainstream of humanist learning and of historicism, as the term is used here. This distinction is by no means intended to be invidious; on the contrary, the workaday historian should be grateful for as well as wary of the work done by his colleagues in the social sciences. The point is simply that the transcendent impulse, the tendency to impose premature and procrustean patterns upon the past, operates as a limit upon strictly historical investigation, and so it is of peripheral significance here.

The approach of this study, then, is unfamiliar but not, I hope, unreasonable. It concentrates not upon formal historiography or the philosophy of history but upon the concrete investigation of laws, institutions, society, and culture. It rests upon the proposition that many of the important insights and breakthroughs in the interpretation of history were made not by the grand figures of historical narrative or of political philosophy but by pioneers laboring in relatively obscure and technical fields of scholarship and concerned more with the texture than with the structure of history. That Budé had as much to offer as Bodin, or Pasquier as Machiavelli, may seem to us an eccentric view, but it would have been eminently sensible to a literate gentleman of the sixteenth—or for that matter the eighteenth—century. This view is submitted here as a useful, perhaps even an enlightening anachronism, which may help to correct the rather unbalanced view of Renaissance historical thought derived from the study of popular (and mainly vernacular) writings.

There is another eccentricity in this book. Although it deals with the history of ideas and with the political context of these ideas, it is not aimed at conscious ideological positions assumed on the grand issues of political or historical thought, such as Constitutionalism, Toleration, or the Idea of Progress, which may relate to political or temperamental bias rather than to a particular reading of history. Instead, it is concerned with the somewhat intangible phenomenon of historical mindedness—"the intellectual form," as Huizinga put it, "in which a civilization renders account to itself of its past."[20] Just as it no longer suffices intellectual historians to follow the dictum of Hegel that the thought of an age is best expressed in philosophic systems like his own, so it is not enough for them merely to report the differences of opinion about traditionally formulated topics. On the contrary, as Whitehead once warned,

When you are criticizing the philosophy of an epoch, do not chiefly direct your attention to those intellectual positions which its exponents feel it necessary explicitly to defend. There will be some fundamental assumptions which adherents of all the various systems within an epoch unconsciously presuppose. Such assumptions appear so obvious that people do not know what they are assuming because no other way of putting things has ever occurred to them.[21]

This advice seems to me even more appropriate for historical thought, which is not ordinarily disposed to examine its own presuppositions and arguments. Consequently, the focus here is upon those authors who have inquired into, rather than pontificated about, history; and the emphasis is more upon their language and scholarly practice than upon their ideological preferences and theoretical pronouncements. Particular attention will be paid to vocabulary, especially to topoi, metaphors, and legal formulas, which form so much of the substance of historical scholarship in the sixteenth century. It seems only fair to apply to history, which itself emerged from the humanities, the methods of philology and literary criticism.

Otherwise my plan is straightforward. It is to present a survey of the major features of modern historical thought in its relation to the study of law and institutions in sixteenth-century France. In order to provide depth as well as breadth and some coherence, the strategy is to concentrate upon certain representative scholars whose careers and work best illustrate the major themes and at the same time to preserve a semblance of chronological order both in the sequence of chapters

[20] Huizinga, "A Definition of the Concept of History," p. 9.
[21] A. N. Whitehead, *Science and the Modern World* (New York, 1948), pp. 49-50.

and within each chapter. The story begins, necessarily, with the Italian background, then moves on to a number of distinguishable, yet closely related, French scholarly traditions, and ends with that remarkable antiquarian renaissance of the later sixteenth century. This episode is at once the meeting point of all the previous traditions and, in a longer perspective, the culmination of the first stage of European historicism.

PART ONE

Italian Beginnings

CHAPTER II

The Sense of History: Lorenzo Valla Reveals
the Grounds of Historical Knowledge

Tenenda praeterea est omnis antiquitas, exem-
plorumque vis; nequum legum, aut juris civilis
scientia neglegenda est.

Cicero, *De Oratore*, I, v, 18

"THE DISCOURSE of historians exhibits more substance, more practical
knowledge, more political wisdom . . . , more customs, and more learning of every sort than the precepts of any philosophers," declared
Lorenzo Valla. "Thus we show that historians have been superior to
philosophers."[1] Since Valla also held that "the mother of history is
the oratorical art," one would have to be unusually obtuse to miss the
intent of this argument: it was quite flagrantly to promote his own
profession, that of rhetoric, above conventional philosophy. This was
clearly academic subversion, and yet except for its pointed expression,
the attitude was by no means peculiar to Valla. Indeed, it may be taken
as emblematic of the humanist movement as a whole, whose accomplishment it was to raise the *studia humanitatis*, basically grammar and
rhetoric, and in their company history itself, to the level of an independent discipline. This discipline, which humanists themselves
came to call "philology," drew other arts and sciences into its orbit
and became the center of one of the profoundest intellectual revolutions of modern times.[2] By the fifteenth century this revolution, which

---

[1] Lorenzo Valla, *De rebus a Ferdinando Hispaniarum rege et majoribus ejus
gestis*, "proeemium," in *Opera omnia*, ed. E. Garin (Turin, 1962), II, 6.
[2] By "philology," a term which received wide currency in the sixteenth

LAVRENTII VALLA ROMANVS

Defuncto Valla Musis plorantibus inquit
Phœbus, hic antistes nostri Hiliconis erit

LORENZO VALLA (T. de Bry, *Icones et
effigies virorum doctorum*) Courtesy of the
Bibliothèque Nationale, Paris

demands to be called the "historical revolution," had acquired a sense both of identity and of direction. Nowhere was this illustrated so vividly or, paradoxically, explained so philosophically as in the work of Valla. Since it was also to have a forceful, in several cases a formative, impact upon sixteenth-century scholarship, this work provides an ideal point of departure for an examination of the rise of modern historical thought.

Humanism and History

History was the centerpiece of the humanist world view. To Petrarch and his followers most formal philosophy seemed an unearthly creation which, though it promised consolation, offered no tangible reward. History, on the other hand, seemed superior to systematic thought precisely because of its conceptual limitations, because instead of pretending to transcend time and the human condition, it provided concrete knowledge and a specific perspective. Even Pico, who had no sympathy for such a timid view, based his overreaching philosophy upon an exhaustive investigation of the cultural past. At first, no doubt, humanist devotion to history had overtones of nostalgia and naïve ancestor-worship; and so Petrarch could, at least in a rhapsodical moment, identify history with "the praise of Rome."[3] Yet with the growth of a professional spirit, humanists ultimately came to adopt a more critical and a less parochial attitude. In effect, men who prided themselves on being "philologists" came to regard history as an independent form of knowledge with its own standards and goals, indeed as the methodological foundation of their own "encyclopedic" discipline. Reciprocally, history itself, with the help of humanist educational reforms, was given a methodical organization and so raised to

century, I mean the scholarly aspect of the *studia humanitatis* as they apply to scholarship and textual criticism. For this purpose I find most convenient the interpretation of P. O. Kristeller, as presented, e.g., in his *Studies in Renaissance Thought and Letters* (Rome, 1956), pp. 561 ff. The only attempt to assess the significance of philology for the history of ideas is A. Bernardini and G. Righi, *Il concetto di philologia e di cultura classica* (Bari, 1953).

[3] See T. E. Mommsen, *Medieval and Renaissance Studies*, ed. E. Rice (Ithaca, New York, 1959), p. 122.

the status of a "science," if not the "source of all disciplines" and the key to wisdom itself.[4]

Between humanism and history there were also more formal ties, arising from the very nature of the *studia humanitatis*. In the first place, grammar was based upon an "historical" method—that is, a literal mode of interpretation (*sensus historicus sive grammaticus*) that was the essence of the historian's craft. Just as the grammarian had to beware of the enticements of allegory, so the historian had to be on his guard against the distortions of theory. Fidelity to the letter and to fact—both virtues were located by the topos "faith of history" (*fides historiae*)—became a cardinal rule of the historical method.[5] Still closer, indeed (recalling Valla's remark) almost incestuous, were the relations between rhetoric and history. Among other things, each relied upon the faculty of memory, each was designed to move men by referring them to concrete experience, and each needed a continuous prose style in order to show cause and effect. In their attitude toward truth, perhaps, they diverged a bit, but not enough to invalidate Cicero's dictum that history was the business of the rhetorician (*munus oratoris*). Finally, even between history and the third member of the *trivium,* dialectic, at least the reformed dialectic of the humanists, there was a growing cordiality on the basis of a common standard, utility, and in the face of a common enemy, scholastic logic. It is difficult to conceal the "trivial" origins of the modern study of history.[6]

---

[4] P. Droit de Gaillard, *Methode qu'on doit tenir en la lecture de l'histoire* (Paris, 1579), p. 552, 1. See the discussion in chapter V.

[5] In classical times *fides historiae* implied historical truth as distinguished from various kinds of literary distortion. So Cicero, *Ad Quintum fratrem*, I, 1, 23; Pliny, *Epistolae*, IX, 19, 5; Aulus Gellius, *Noctes Atticae*, II, 16, 8. Modern use of this term by humanist and by Reformation authors will be noted in later chapters. See also M. P. Gilmore, *Humanists and Jurists* (Cambridge, Mass., 1963), pp. 111-15.

[6] See especially Cicero, *De Oratore*, II, xii-xv, and Quintilian, *De Oratore*, X, 1. The relation of grammar and history is particularly evident in the field of Biblical studies, as shown by S. Berger, *La Bible au seizième siècle* (Paris, 1879), and W. Schwarz, *Principles and Problems of Bible Translation* (Cambridge, 1955). For rhetoric the best study is H. Gray, *History and Rhetoric in Quattrocento Humanism* (Harvard doctoral dissertation, 1956), while the medieval career of the rhetorical view of history has been traced by M. Schulz, *Die Lehre von der historischen Methode bei den Geschichtschreibern des Mittel-*

But if this seems faintly degrading, it should be recalled that this was one condition for the long and fruitful collaboration between philology and history.

Philology was a creation, or at least a recreation, of Renaissance humanism. True, there was a distinguishable tradition of medieval humanism which had preserved a grammatical method, but this tradition lacked the self-awareness and the ideological impetus to constitute an intellectual movement in any significant sense.[7] Nor did it possess an eponymous hero like Petrarch, who gave coherence and direction to Italian humanism as much through the legend he fashioned as through his actual accomplishments. Petrarch's disciples were much more than a school; they formed a militant party which rebelled quite consciously against the values of the academic establishment. This party gained further identity through a commonly accepted, though differently construed, program calling for a repudiation of scholastic method and for a return to original sources (*ad fontes*) and to human reality (*ad res*) in order to find, for whatever purpose, particular models of behavior. Even when professed humanists renewed their interest in such scholastic monopolies as philosophy and law, they clung to their "trivial" approach and to their literary values. It was conscious alienation from the pedantic and pedagogical conventions of scholasticism that provided humanists with a sense of identity and so, given the nature of their program, with a "sense of history."

The point is that Renaissance humanism represented not merely new knowledge of and new appreciation for classical antiquity—that is an old story—but a major reorientation in thought.[8] What happened, in

---

alters (Berlin, 1909). As for dialectic, see especially P. Joachimsen, "Loci communes," *Luther Jahrbuch*, VIII (1926), 27-97, and W. Ong, *Ramus, Method and the Decay of Dialogue* (Cambridge, Mass., 1958).

[7] One aspect of this forms the subject of two books by B. Smalley, *The Study of the Bible in the Middle Ages* (Oxford, 1952), including an excursus on Roman law by H. Kantorowicz, and *English Friars and Antiquity* (Oxford, 1960). See also H. Hailperin, *Rashi and the Christian Scholars* (Pittsburg, 1963), and P. Lehmann, *Erforschung des Mittelalters*, I (Stuttgart, 1959).

[8] The classic modern expression of this view is G. Voigt, *Die Wiederbelebung des classischen Alterthums* (first edition 1859), a work unfortunately and unreasonably overshadowed by that of Burckhardt published the next year; its ultimate source is the Petrarch legend. On this subject see F. Simone,

brief, was that the mere problem of gaining access to the past began to supersede the problem of how to make use of it. Increasingly, scholars were struck by the distance and the disparity between themselves and men of former ages. To some moderns, in fact, a widening perspective and knowledge of alien societies suggested that wisdom itself needed to be grounded in historical understanding. Even those humanists who, beguiled by nostalgia or national sentiment, tended to idealize antiquity could not avoid the fact of historical change, so conspicuously reflected in the vicissitudes of literary style, social customs, and religious practices. This was especially obvious to hellenists, who had to make sense of a civilization not only remote in time but practically devoid of ancestral associations. Wrestling with this anthropological dilemma (still one of the fundamental problems of historical thought) led them toward what was, in effect, a principle of cultural relativity. It was a significant step in the development of historical studies when the instability of human nature became not merely an occasion for lamentation but an object of investigation.

Most remarkable of all, though it is not widely recognized by historians, Italian humanism provided for the first time a philosophical—or should we say anti-philosophical?—justification for historical scholarship. Once again philology was the key, and once again history was placed in its debt. In their intoxication with words—and to some extent in self-defense—humanists established a new logos upon the assumption that language reproduced, if it did not actually create, the configurations of reality. "It was precisely the 'philologists' of the Renaissance," as Ernst Cassirer put it, "who through their deepened knowledge of language demanded a new 'theory of thought'"[9]—a theory resulting from a new esteem for particular facts and for original sources, that is, for descriptive historical scholarship. Admittedly, the final product was a somewhat make-shift epistemology, serving rather to rationalize the often trivial concerns of the grammarian than to broaden the aims of humanistic studies. Yet it marks the basis for the

---

Il Rinascimento francese (Turin, 1961), as well as W. Ferguson, *The Renaissance in Historical Thought* (Boston, 1948).

[9] Ernst Cassirer, *The Philosophy of Symbolic Forms*, I, *Language*, trans. R. Manheim (New Haven, 1953), p. 127.

claims of philology, and implicitly those of history, to be a self-contained and self-conscious discipline. Here, if anywhere, is the birthplace of modern historical thought. And here is where Lorenzo Valla comes in.

Valla was the *enfant terrible* of philology. Behind a façade of pedantry and polemic he concealed one of the acutest minds of modern times. He never allowed his readers to forget that, by profession and by conviction, he was a rhetorician (*mea professio . . . est ars oratoria*).[10] He was a master of words, a judge of style, and it is in his conception of language that we must look for the essence of his historical thinking. Yet for this very reason we must proceed by indirection; for many of Valla's crucial ideas, if they are articulated at all, are disguised by hyperbole or hidden beneath the issue of the moment. It would be an error to exaggerate the ambiguities and contradictions which abound in his writings or to put questions to him as we might to such a systematizing thinker as Pico. Because of his fidelity to a particular method and to his chosen mission, Valla's ideas have an underlying unity in the midst of his most violent invectives and doctrinal reversals. Whether chastising the papacy for betraying Roman ideals or praising it for helping to preserve Latin civilization, Valla never lost sight of his calling, which was to spread the "word" and, regardless of transitory ideologies, to defend a certain style of thought. He pursued the same goals in his philological as in his philosophical works. These were, as Cassirer has said, "clarity, simplicity, and purification of language, which, in turn, will immediately lead to neatness and purity of thought."[11] Ultimately, then, Valla's allegiance was not to a particular doctrine, whether philosophical or political, but to a particular set of scholarly values.

[10] Lorenzo Valla, *Antidoti in Poggium*, II (*Opera*, I, 286). Cf. *Elegantiae latinae linguae*, IV, 81, and "Oratio . . . habita in principio sui studii" (*Opera*, I, 148-49, and II, 281-86). Useful discussions of Valla's work include G. Gentile, *La Filosofia*, II, *L'Umanesimo* (Milan, 1915), 266 ff; G. Saitta, *Il Pensiero italiano*, I, *L'Umanesimo* (Bologna, 1949); F. Gaeta, *Lorenzo Valla* (Naples, 1955); and most recently, Jerrold E. Seigel, *Rhetoric and Philosophy in Renaissance Humanism* (Princeton, 1968), pp. 137-69, though none of these pays much attention to the philological implications.

[11] Cassirer, *The Individual and the Cosmos in Renaissance Philosophy*, trans. M. Domandi (New York, 1965), p. 160.

In general, the work of this arch-philologist forms a locus of practically all of the themes of humanist historical thought. Assuming leadership in the campaign against school philosophy, Valla became an effective spokesman for what was most profound and original in humanist thought, that is, the philosophy of language and of culture. Many of his views about historical method and the study of ancient literature will re-appear, though seldom so dogmatically asserted, in the work of his successors, especially the French, who took him at his own estimation as the "restorer of the Latin language."[12] In his criticism of ecclesiastical tradition, too, Valla contributed to the re-evaluation of European history which was carried out principally in the next century. Most important, as a founding father both of legal and of Biblical humanism, he had an almost incalculable impact upon a wide range of sixteenth-century scholarship. In his posthumous career, spurred by the invention of printing which just predated his death (in 1457), Valla left as deep an impression upon that age as he had upon his own generation. In some respects, indeed, he spoke even more directly to men of the sixteenth century.

Valla's life, too, was a pattern for ambitious scholars of a later age.[13] Moving from university to university, from court to court, from issue to issue, he preached his philological cause, engaged in murderous polemical duels, placed his talents in the service of various interests, and in general led the life of a restless scholar errant. At first his enterprises were literary, but increasingly he moved into more controversial areas, including law, philosophy, and theology. His major work, *Elegancies of the Latin Language,* was one of the most influential books of the Renaissance, not only as a textbook of classical usage but as a handbook of literary criticism and of historical method.[14] Both in this book and its ill-tempered companion piece, *A Rem-*

---

[12] Pierre Paul Viellot in the first Paris edition (1471) of Valla's *Elegantiae.*

[13] The principal biography, G. Mancini, *Vita di Lorenzo Valla* (Florence, 1891), should be supplemented by R. Sabbadini, "Cronologia documentata . . .," reprinted in *Opera,* II, 353-454. On Valla's polemical battles, see C. Nisard, *Les Gladiateurs de la république des lettres* (Paris, 1860), pp. 195 ff.

[14] Garin says there were about 60 editions of the *Elegantiae* before 1543 (there were many more afterwards); 33 were by Guillaume Budé's publisher, as indicated by P. Renouard, *Bibliographie . . . de Josse Badius Ascensius* (Paris,

edy for Poggio, and in his letter to Pier Candido Decembrio attacking the scholastic jurist Bartolus, Valla entered with his customary iconoclasm into the field of Roman law, to the scandal of generations of lawyers. Still more upsetting, though it is difficult for us to appreciate the passions awakened, was his scattered work as a textual critic—not only his critique of Roman law and the Donation of Constantine but his emendations of Livy and of the New Testament. Was no authority sacred? contemporaries asked. Sacred perhaps, but none was beyond question, was Valla's answer, especially in view of the inherent complexity and corruption of human "tradition." Besides, he added, even Homer nodded.[15] In this way, too, philology was independent. It was only natural that Valla should turn his weapons against that most corrupt of traditions, Aristotelian philosophy, which, at least as represented in the schools, seemed to exclude everything he held dear. In his *Dialectical Disputations* Valla expressed most clearly his underlying philosophy and his justification of historical scholarship.

To historiography itself Valla's contribution was most undistinguished, but it serves at least to show that even on the most commonplace level history ranked high in Valla's personal hierarchy of learning. For a nation as well as for an individual it was a mark of adulthood (*memoria temporum gentiumque sine quibus nemo non puer est*). Contradicting the Aristotelian dictum, Valla asserted that history was superior to poetry and philosophy precisely because it was founded upon literal truth (*fides historiae*) and because, as Cicero had pointed out, it was prior in time. Certainly, being full of learning and wisdom (*doctrinae sapientiaeque plena*), it was more useful; and unlike moral philosophy it did not simply exhort men to virtue by precept, it moved them to virtue by example.[16] But such formal and Ciceronian praise of the art of history does not go very far in showing Valla's attachment to a historical point of view except in that it adds lustre to the

---

1908), pp. 325 ff. An interesting sixteenth-century commentary (on Dolet's edition, 1541) has been published in F. Mugnier, *Les Gloses latino-françaises de Jacques Greptus* (Paris, 1893).

[15] Valla, "Confutatio prior in Benedictum Morandum Bononiensem," (*Opera*, II, 5-6).

[16] These commonplace views appear in *Ferd. Hispan.*, "proeemium" (*Opera*, II, 5-6); the phrase *fides historiae* is in a letter to Flavio Biondo (II, 119).

related arts of grammar and rhetoric. It was not as a branch of knowledge or a genre of literature but as a mode of thought, as an ally of philology, that history was best served by Valla.

The Arch-Philologist

Language was the alpha and omega of Valla's world. It formed the basis of his interpretation of history, his critique of Roman law and of theology, his conception of culture, and his theory of knowledge. His fascination with words also opened the way to his revolutionary new philosophy. It was not as revolutionary, perhaps, as Valla would have his readers believe. There were certain traditional elements in his thinking, derived in particular from terminist logic and of course from humanism itself, as shown by the works of such men as Leonardo Bruni and Catone Sacco. Yet Valla stood quite consciously—indeed defiantly—apart from any school (*mihi qui nullae sectae me addixi*).[17] Even toward the classics he adopted a remarkably independent attitude and did not hesitate to criticize such "authorities" as Cicero and Livy. He had, it is true, an idealized picture of antiquity, but it was his own reconstruction. In short, he recognized no man as his master. Only philology itself was sacred, and only to its service did Valla remain faithful. It was in this way that Valla was able to achieve his philosophic purpose, which was nothing less than to remake the world in his own image and that of his profession.

If Pico seemed almost to identify himself with God, Valla took the part of a kind of destructive demiurge. In the beginning, he assumed, was the word, the "logos," whose primary meaning was not abstract reason (*ratio*) but human discourse (*oratio*).[18] Only through the word could one hope to attain wisdom, he believed, while alienation from it had been the ruin of true philosophy. "Philosophy and dialectic," he argued, "should not recede from the most usual style and from the common fashions."[19] Affecting to soar above the liberal arts, he charged, philosophers had fallen into the most elementary errors. De-

---

[17] Valla, letter to Serra (*Opera*, II, 393).
[18] *Dialecticae disputationes*, I, 9 (*Opera*, I, 663)
[19] *Ibid.*, I, 3 (I, 651).

parting not only from common usage (*usus humanitatis*) but from common sense (*sensus naturalis*), they had conjured up imaginary and inhuman problems. "O that peripatetic tribe," lamented Valla," destroyer of natural meaning!"[20] Much better to descend to a popular form of speech (*melius populus quam philosophus loquitur*); best of all to be an orator, a leader of society (*dux populi*), a master of correct usage and so of correct thinking. Unlike the pholosopher, whose thought was basically non-social (*domesticus et privatus*), the orator was concerned with the public interest.[21] To this extent Valla's apology for rhetoric rests upon the premises of "civic humanism" as well as upon a desire for a restoration (*repastinatio*) of true philosophy.

In order to bring about this reformation Valla found it necessary to establish a useful science of language (*scientia sermocinans*), and this in turn led him to a radical critique of Aristotelian thought, especially as interpreted by "recent" philosophers, that is, by the "scholastic doctors." The first of these, Boethius, Valla chose as the most convenient scapegoat.[22] School philosophy, built upon the ruins of Latin eloquence, or rather dancing upon its grave, had neither intellectual nor social value, according to Valla. By proliferating abstractions and superfluous distinctions, scholastic philosophy had lost contact with concrete reality. It had cut men off from meaning, hence from their own humanity. Valla's philosophy, on the other hand, emphasized precisely these standards—concreteness, utility, and humanity. This was in accord both with his admiration for history and with the Ciceronian topos, so ironically popular with humanists, placing the value of things above words (*res non verba*). Indeed, a return to reality (*redire ad res*) may be taken as the slogan of Valla's entire philosophy.

Yet it was through words, after all, that Valla expected to obtain this noble objective. His first step was to secure the concept "thing"

---

[20] *Ibid.*, I, 12 (I, 673).

[21] *Ibid.*, I, 17, and II, "praefatio" (I, 685 and 693).

[22] *Ibid.*, I, *passim* (I, 645-93). This aspect of Valla's thought has been analysed by E. Cassirer, *Das Erkenntnisproblem in der Philosophie und Wissenschaft der neueren Zeit*, I (Berlin, 1906); by C. Prantl, *Geschichte der Logik im Abendlande*, IV (Leipzig, 1870), 161-67; by Saitta and Gaeta (see n. 10); and especially by C. Vasoli, "Le 'Dialecticae disputationes' del Valla . . .," *Rivista critica di storia della filosofia*, XII (1957), 412-33.

as the foundation of his metaphysics. He therefore banished five of the six so-called transcendentals (*ens, aliquid, unum, verum, bonum*), keeping only the catch-all category *res*.[23] The *Ding an sich,* in short, was "king" of the natural world. Then, much in the fashion of William of Ockham, who had a similar aversion to arbitrary abstraction, Valla proceeded to show that the rejected terms could all be resolved into concrete things: "the good" into "good things," "the true" into "true things," and so on. As for "being" (*ens*), Valla argued not only that it was hollow and unreal but that, except as applied in a transcendental and theological sense to God Himself, it was poor usage since classically "being" was a participle. Although by analogy with Greek it might be used as a noun, it was reducible to "thing that is"; and it seemed nonsense to speak, with Aristotle, of being as being (*ens quatenus ens*), as if a thing that is might somehow not be. Similarly, Valla rejected such monstrous terms as *entitas* or *identitas* or *Platonitas*, since logic and the rules of grammar required that names ending in -*itas* be derived from adjectives. All of these arguments were designed to show, directly or indirectly, that the objective world—the "real" world—was sufficiently accounted for by the category "thing."

Next Valla moved into the subjective realm. He eliminated seven of the ten "predicaments" (*quantitas, relatio, ubi, quando, situs, habitus, passio*), retaining only "substance," "action," and "quality." "Substance," in the best authors, was equivalent to essence and needed no auxiliary concepts like form and matter, a distinction useless to make and impossible to imagine. "Action" included all kinds of change, and again Valla ridiculed such meaningless terms as "potency." More complicated was the concept "quality," and here Valla found it necessary to make a few distinctions himself in order to account for different levels of human cognition. Yet every variety of human judgment—from the simplest perception, such as heat, to the most exalted concept, such as political power—could be reduced ultimately to this category. Such, according to Valla, was the tripartite structure of human experience.[24] What is most important to note is that this three-fold division corresponds to the principal parts of speech—to nouns, verbs, and

[23] Valla, *Dialecticae disputationes,* I, 2-4 (I, 646-52).
[24] *Ibid.*, I, 6, 16, 13-14 (I, 656, 673-81, 673-77).

adjectives or adverbs, which is to say, to the "categories" of the grammarian. The inference is, though Valla did not quite draw it, that the world, its structure and its transformations, was a facsimile of human discourse, understood in its historical sense.

In general, for Valla as for most humanists, it was the letter and not the spirit that gave life. Understanding proceeded from literal meaning and not from any figurative construction; and so with his usual uncompromising logic he insisted that there be an unequivocal relation between words and things. Properly speaking, words were signs, and meaning was essentially signification—in terms, of course, of the predicaments and the rules of grammar. At times Valla sounds more like a contemporary semanticist than a Renaissance rhetorician; certainly, he had the same gift for tautology. "When a noun does not signify a thing," he warned, "do not ask, 'what does it signify!'" With great relish he pointed out the absurdity of trying to determine if there was a time when 'time' was not, or of arguing that since "a man is, therefore 'being' is." Deplorably perhaps, but not unexpectedly, Valla had no use for mathematical fictions, such as infinitesimals, because they fell outside the range of ordinary human experience and so did not fit his grammatical scheme. Like Ockham, Valla was almost unutterably literal-minded, and he tended to regard philosophy as the science of terms, not things. Like Ockham, too, he had a principle of economy, a grammatical kind of "razor": "No things should be construed as diverse that are not diverse" (*nihil pro diversis ponens quae diversae non sunt*).[25]

What Valla actually did was to extract from Aristotelian philosophy a simple and yet ingenious epistemology based upon a radical dualism: on the one hand, an objective "reality" composed of discrete and discernible things, and on the other, a set of subjective categories through which these things and their relationships could be understood. In short, Valla had what may be regarded as a copy theory of knowledge, except that for him the structure of the world conformed not to an artificial logical or mathematical model but to the patterns of conventional speech. Consequently, whether he realized it or not, his arguments applied mainly to the world of man's making—to

[25] *Ibid.*, I, 16, and III, 14 (I, 680 and 751).

society rather than to nature, which was little more than a backdrop for the human drama. In view of this limitation and of Valla's general indifference to natural philosophy, it might be more appropriate to call him a "grammaticist" than, as has so often been done, a naturalist. Certainly, it seems in agreement with his own estimation, if not with his choice of terms. According to Valla it was the forms of grammar that gave meaning to reality, and it was through the conventions of speech that human cognition was possible. What is more, it was not logic but usage that governed speech itself (*usus hominum . . . verborum est autor*).[26] The conclusion was inescapable: the man in the best position to understand the world was not the dialectician or the philosopher but the grammarian—or rather, since rhetoric included grammar, the orator.

In this chain of reasoning there was still another step, and Valla did not hesitate to take it. As a man devoted rather to public life than to private speculation, the orator was also in the best position to *shape* the world. At this point we may think that Valla has gone too far in his claims for the power of words and for the dignity of his profession. To honor the orator as a maker of public opinion was a commonplace; to take him seriously as a creative thinker was practically a solepsism. Yet, given his intense devotion to rhetoric, Valla's egocentric epistemology should occasion no surprise; for he took his values and views of reality not from nature (to use another classical formula) but from convention, which ideally meant from the judgment of men of eloquence and learning, that is of men like himself. Such were the conditions of Valla's radical subjectivism. Sometimes he seemed to argue that qualities were nothing more than the construction which men placed upon reality, that reality was the product of verbal formulation, which in the final analysis was a social act. At other times he preferred to make his point in Platonic terms, holding that qualities are revealed to men by the light of reason just as colors are revealed by the light of the sun. In any case, reality appeared as a human construct, and the only approach to it was through self-knowledge. "Therefore in our minds," Valla concluded, "is truth and falsity."[27] Here is

---

[26] Valla, *In eundem Poggium libellus primus*, "praefatio" (I, 385).
[27] Valla, *Dialecticae disputationes*, I, 2 (I, 649).

the heart of his "anti-philosophy" and, implicitly, the epistemological basis of his philological method.

The significance of Valla's rhetorical nominalism, as it might be called, was not in its effect on philosophy—how could it be, given his scorn for the preoccupations of this profession? Rather it was in providing a considered justification for the menial tasks of humanists, not only for the special pleading of the orator but also for the apparently unfocused and purposeless pedantry of the philologist. It cannot be held that the great figures of sixteenth-century historical scholarship were in conscious agreement with Valla's arguments; it is not even likely that many took the trouble to read his *Dialectical Disputations*, although his rhetorical and critical works came to have almost canonical authority. Yet it must be inferred that the bulk of their work rested upon unconscious premises that would have been expressed—if anyone had taken the trouble to express them—in much these terms. Valla's critique is the closest thing we have to a philosophy of humanist scholarship.

The Anti-Philosopher

Whatever the cogency of Valla's arguments, one obvious effect was to exalt the world of history above that of nature. Language was no doubt natural as well as conventional, since in a primordial sense words were sounds (*voces, soni*); but functionally they were conventions, that is signs (*signa*), hence historical products. "Signification," as Valla put it, "is derived from custom" (*ab institutione* or *ab artifice*).[28] It was, consequently, the job of the grammarian or the rhetorician rather than the natural philosopher to determine the signification of terms, which were the conventional "images" of things. It was a job demanding the most encyclopedic knowledge, the most consummate scholarship. There were some standards, of course, especially the rules of grammar, but again these rules came from usage rather than from logic—"not from reason but from example, not from a law of speech but from observation."[29] In this sense, Valla's philosophy was grounded in an ex-

---

[28] *Ibid.*, I, 14 (I, 676).
[29] Valla, *Antidoti in Poggium*, IV (I, 387).

treme—indeed in a lexicographical—sort of empiricism. What is more significant, it implied a very fundamental sort of historical relativism.

It was custom, then, that governed human discourse (*consuetudo vero certissima loquendi magistra*). To the grammarian this might mean vulgar, even vernacular usage. To the orator, however, it meant that "the propriety, force, signification and interpretation of Latin words consist not in reason but in the authority of ancient writers."[30] Not that Valla really valued literary standards above truth, even if he could conceive of a conflict between the two. It was simply that he had committed himself to a theory of knowledge that assumed an organic relation between form and content, between eloquence and doctrine. Just as in his psychology he refused to divorce body and spirit, just as in his ethics he refused to divorce pleasure and virtue, so in his epistemology he refused to separate truth and elegance—"that Latin elegance," he remarked, "without which learning is blind" ("especially," he added, "in civil law").[31] For there was no such thing as the naked truth; truth had always to be dressed in words, and of course Valla preferred the most splendid costume. Yet if classical antiquity represented an ideal for Valla, it was a specific ideal created at a particular time and in particular circumstances, hence amenable to a historical method.

The key to Valla's philosophy is to be found in his conception of style (*stilus, usus, consuetudo* or *modus loquendi, verborum proprietas*, and other expressions). He was not satisfied with mere grammatical correctness, that is, with the minimum standards of that "mediocre" triumvirate, Donatus, Priscian, and Servius. Without being a doctrinaire Ciceronian, he was willing to settle for nothing less than a humanist style (*usus humanitatis*), that is, the "higher style" established by the Roman orators, especially that "Achilles among heros," Quintilian.[32] Rhetoric, being to elocution what grammar was to locution, was thus both superior to and dependent upon the more elementary

---

[30] *Ibid.*, II (I, 288). Cf. the famous formula stated in *Elegantiae*, III, 17 (I, 92): "With regard to elegance I accept as law whatever pleases the great authors."

[31] Valla, *Elegantiae*, III, "praefatio" (I, 80).

[32] *Ibid.*, I, 13, and *Dialecticae disputationes*, I, 20 (I, 19 and 693). In a youthful work Valla expressed his preference for Quintilian even above Cicero.

art, for it involved not merely artificial rules but the learned usage of the past (*melius esse Latine quam grammatice loqui, hoc est, ex consuetudine peritorum quam ex artis analogia*).[33] If the grammarian's task was "historical" in the sense that it required literal interpretation, the rhetorician's task was historical in the subtler sense that it required the reconstruction of a departed style of thought and way of life. In this sense Valla had to be a redeemer as well as a demiurge. No wonder he had an almost religious enthusiasm for Latin eloquence (*Latini sermonis sacramentum*) and for his own calling (*munus oratoris*), which was that of a historian not only in a formal sense but, more profoundly, in his life work of resurrecting the elegance of antiquity.

Style, as we have been told only too often, is the individual man. But style is also, we should remind ourselves, the individual culture. This is an idea which was quite familiar to the ancients and which in modern times was promoted by the growth of civic humanism. Valla knew that linguistic usage was not a private but a public creation, the expression of a group, whether the vulgar speech of a whole people or the elegant discourse of Valla's elite (*hic noster cultus*). He believed also that a cultural style embraced such non-literary arts as painting, sculpture, and architecture, although he did not doubt that language was the primary measure, if not the vehicle of cultural growth.[34] Classical eloquence was simply the first voice in that "chorus of muses" which Petrarch had first heard and which Valla celebrated in his "golden age." It was not easy, of course, to make out these harmonies in the dissonant society of fifteenth-century Europe. Valla realized that the recovery of antique style had to be accomplished within a modern context. In spite of his uncompromising classicism, he had the his-

[33] Valla, *Antidoti in Poggium*, IV (I, 385).

[34] Valla, *Elegantiae*, I, "praefatio," and "Oratio ... habita in principio sui studii" (I, 4, and II, 284). In general, see E. Panofsky, *Renaissance and Renascences* (Stockholm, 1960), p. 16; and A. Buck, *Das Geschichtsdenken der Renaissance* (Krefeld, 1957), p. 26. The term *aureum seculum* (from Vergil, *Ecl.* 4, 39) appears in *Antidoti in Poggium*, III (I, 321); *chorus musarum* in "De reciprocatione sui et suis" (I, 249), having been used earlier by Petrarch, according to P. de Nolhac, *Petrarque et l'humanisme* (Paris, 1892), p. 45, and later to be used by Budé.

torical insight to understand that ancient culture could not be reproduced exactly; and so he recommended the emulation, not the literal
imitation of antiquity. To this extent he belonged to the party of the
moderns.

It was through his reflections on language and on style, too, that
Valla's idea of history emerged. It is no exaggeration to say that Valla's
conception of culture was a deduction from his view of language. Thus
the Roman Empire was ultimately neither a political nor a religious
society but, in Valla's often quoted phrase, "wherever the Roman language was spoken"—an attitude which Valla shared, incidentally,
with the civil and canon lawyers he so despised.[35] More characteristically humanist was his conviction that eloquence, together with other
civilized arts, was bound up closely with political dominion. In the
widest sense *Latinitas* included not only language but all the arts of
war and peace, and Valla believed that the trajectory of Roman political fortunes paralleled the rise and fall of oratory and jurisprudence.
But the conquests of the Roman language, unlike those of the imperium, were enduring—having been preserved, as Valla came to acknowledge in his mellower years, by the Roman church. If Rome was
eternal, this was due not to military prowess but to literary excellence
and to the Christian religion: *Latina litteratura aeterna*.[36]

Yet Valla had few illusions about the permanence of language, especially such a learned tongue as the Roman, which was the most
polished species of Latin. Indeed, it is precisely in his awareness of
the progressive "corruption" of Roman style, paralleling that of Roman
morals and politics, that Valla's sense of history appears in its most
conspicuous form. Not only did he recognize the historical transformations of literary style, he had a rudimentary notion of periodization.
Following classical distinctions but applying them in a chronological
rather than an invidious fashion, he defined several stages of Latin

---

[35] Valla, *Elegantiae*, I, "praefatio," and repeated and discussed at greater
length in *Antidoti in Poggium*, II (I, 3 and 295-97). S. Mochy Onori, *Fonti
canonistiche dell'idea moderna dello stato* (Milan, 1951), p. 174, cites this
formula from the *Summa Lipsiensis*: "Praeterea, quicunque utuntur lingua
latina dicuntur romani ... et ideo romani his intelleguntur omnes latini. Unde
et hoc jure omnes latini astringuntur."

[36] "Oratio ... habita in principio sui studii" (II, 285-86).

style, including an early period (*vetustissima aetas, veteris stilus Romanis*), the ages (*secula*) of Cicero and Quintilian, of the classical jurists (especially Ulpian), and of the grammarians (Donatus and the rest).[37] Beginning with Boethius and Isidore of Seville, Valla's sense of discrimination diminished as his disgust grew; and down to the barbarous and "Gothic" style of recent writers he saw only decline (*degeneravit ab illa prisca*) and the disintegration of vulgar Latin into vernacular tongues. On the other hand, Valla admitted that barbarism was the fault not so much of men as of the evil times they had fallen upon (*non nostra sed temporum culpa*).[38] More generally, he seemed to be aware of the inexorable process of change and discovery to which language was subject (*nova res novum vocabulum flagitat*).[39] These judgments, commonplace in themselves, are indications of Valla's sense of historical relativism. They illustrate another aspect of the conceptual basis of history which Valla was helping to construct.

It was through his interest in stylistics, finally, that Valla was able to perfect those techniques of historical criticism which were to have so profound an impact upon modern scholarship. Close attention to texts—to vocabulary, to form, and to historical context—allowed Valla to make invaluable contributions to the science of philology and to the understanding of the classical tradition. The range and sophistication of Valla's scholarship are well shown in his translation of Thucydides (which Seyssel was to use for his French version) and in his emendations of Livy, which include everything from straightforward paleographical and factual correction to the boldest sort of conjectural emendation.[40] Such intuitive criticism could easily be abused and frequently

[37] This temporalized conception of style is fundamental to Valla's method, and innumerable examples might be drawn from the *Elegantiae*—e.g., II, 42, 49, and especially III, "praefatio" (I, 71, 74, 79-80). On this subject, see E. Norden, *Die Antike Kunstprosa* (Stuttgart, 1958), II, 767 ff; R. Sabbadini, *Storia del Ciceronianismo* (Turin, 1885); I. Scott, *Controversies over the Imitation of Cicero* (New York, 1910); and E. Auerbach, *Literary Language and its Public*, p. 10.

[38] Valla, *Antidoti in Poggium*, II (I, 297). Cf. Budé's use of this formula in the next chapter.

[39] Valla, *In Barptolomaeum Facium Ligurem invectiva* (I, 504), the significance of which was pointed out by P. Monnier, *Le Quattrocento* (Paris, 1920), p. 282.

[40] On this crucial aspect of Valla's thought see the discussions of R. West-

was abused both by Valla and his still more self-confident successors; but given the condition of manuscripts and many printed books, it was a necessary technique for the authentication and restoration of primary texts. This method was the most radical form of historical criticism; it was also the ultimate test of the philologist.

Valla's discoveries and methods were passed on to the sixteenth century by three primary channels, separate but connected at certain points. First, there was Biblical scholarship, in which he showed both the importance of Greek and the priority of grammar to theology.[41] In the sixteenth century this work was carried on by Erasmus, Guillaume Budé, and others. More sensational was Valla's critique of canon law, especially of that cornerstone of papal supremacy, the Donation of Constantine, which was to play a leading role in Reformation controversies over ecclesiastical history and in the elaboration of Gallican tradition in particular. The significance of Valla's declamation was neither in applying philological criteria, for Petrarch and others, including canonists, had taken this step, nor in denying the authenticity of the document, which had already been placed in doubt; rather it was in exhibiting the whole array of humanist weapons—polemic and personal vituperation as well as criticism stemming from grammar, logic, geography, chronology, history, and law.[42] Finally, and

gate, "The Text of Valla's Translation of Thucydides," *American Philosophical Society, Trans. and Proc.,* LXVII (1936), 240-51, on Valla's collation of manuscripts; R. Valentini, "Le 'Emendationes in T. Livium' di L. Valla," *Studi italiani di filologia classica,* XV (1907), 262-302; and above all G. Billanovich, "Petrarch and the Textual Tradition of Livy," *Journal of the Warburg and Courtauld Institutes,* XIV (1951), 137-208, representing Valla as "the champion of conjectural criticism" (p. 172). This was a function of Valla's classicist tastes, not a contradiction of them, as C. Thurot seems to have believed: "Notices et extraits de divers manuscrits latins pour servir à l'histoire des doctrines grammaticales au moyen âge," *Notices et extraits des manuscrits de la Bibliothèque Impériale,* XXII (2) (1868), 491 ff.

[41] Besides W. Schwarz, *Principles and Problems,* pp. 133-39, and P. Mestwerdt, *Die Anfänge des Erasmus* (Leipzig, 1917), see A. Morisi, "La filologia neotestimentaria di Lorenzo Valla," *Nuova rivista storica,* XLVIII (1964), 35-49, and S. Garofalo, "Gli umanisti italiani del secolo XVe e la Bibbia," *Biblica,* XXVII (1946), 338-75.

[42] That Valla made a critical study of canonist texts appears from his "Pro se et contra calumniatores ... apologia" (I, 795), where he remarks the "scriptura Gratiani corrupta" and a misquotation from Isidore of Seville. In

more relevant to the immediate discussion, came Valla's presumptuous
studies in Roman law, in which once again he was a pioneer, indeed
a kind of godfather to the new historical school of jurisprudence that
in the next century came to reside in France. For these various reasons,
Valla may be regarded—especially from the perspective of sixteenth-
century France—as one of the founding fathers of modern historical
scholarship.

Legal Humanism

Valla's encounter with civil law was inevitable. Civil law, especially
the Digest, which was the major repository of clasical jurisprudence,
represented the most characteristic aspect of Roman civilization and
the most impressive system of practical philosophy achieved by any
society.[43] Yet no part of the legacy of antiquity had been more roughly
handled by those modern barbarians, the scholastic doctors. Valla's
aim was to rescue this remnant of *Romanitas* from the dead hand of
the schools and, as always, to assert the ascendancy of the *studia
humanitatis*. To Valla Roman law was a golden science (*disciplina
aurea*), an ideal synthesis of eloquence and doctrine worthy of the
company even of rhetoric, with which indeed it had fraternal ties,
though Valla in effect claimed the seniority of his own discipline.[44]
In general, the parallels between law and language were striking. Like
language, law arose from custom and, in its most sophisticiated form,
depended upon learned authority (the *responsa prudentium*). Valla

general, see G. Laehr, "Die konstantinische Schenkung in der abendländischen
Literatur des ausgehenden Mittelalters," *Quellen und Forschungen aus italie-
nischen Archiven und Bibliotheken*, XXIII (1931-32), 120-81; G. Antonazzi,
"Lorenzo Valla e la donazione di Costantino," *Revista di storia della chiesa in
Italia*, IV (1950), 186-234; C. Colman, *Constantine the Great and Christianity*
(New York, 1914), pp. 188 ff, and his introduction to *The Treatise of Lorenzo
Valla on the Donation of Constantine* (New Haven, 1922); and for background
D. Maffei, *La Donazione di Costantino nei giuristi medievali* (Milan, 1964).

[43] For general orientation, the most useful books are P. Koschaker, *Europa
und das römische Recht* (Munich, 1948); F. Schulz, *History of Roman Legal
Science* (Oxford, 1953), and *Principles of Roman Law*, trans. M. Wolff
(Oxford, 1936); and H. F. Jolowicz, *Roman Foundations of Modern Law*
(Oxford, 1957). The best introduction to legal humanism is D. Maffei, *Gli
Inizi dell'umanesimo giuridico* (Milan, 1956).

[44] Valla, *Antidoti in Poggium*, II (I, 286).

admired the classical jurists (*prisci illi jurisconsulti*) for their almost Ciceronian eloquence, remarkable, he added, in view of their remoteness from that pristine age. In its own way, moreover, law was a kind of linguistic science, and Valla recalled the dictum of Quintilian that it consisted either in the interpretation of words or in the discrimination between good and bad. Finally and most impressively, law, like language, reflected the unity of Roman culture: *una lex, una est lingua Romana.*[45]

Such at least was the ideal, but as Valla well knew, the legacy of Roman law had not been acquired intact. Like the Latin language, Roman law had undergone a long process of corruption and displacement. The original sources survived only in a Byzantine anthology which itself had been transmitted imperfectly to Western scholars. Thus the Digest, which was a striking illustration of the destructive effects of time and an uncomprehending posterity, provided an ideal target for the new techniques of historical criticism which Valla had helped to create. The first problem was that the Digest was the work of men who had not only abridged the classical texts but had altered them without acknowledgment, introducing various anachronisms and contradictions. Who was to blame for this? Like his friend Maffeo Vegio, Valla was inclined to suspect not Justinian, who "knew neither laws nor Latin letters," but his chief editor Tribonian, whose infidelity in religious matters was well known.[46] How could one return to the "fathers of jurisprudence," as Petrarch had called them?[47] Only, Valla believed, through a critical examination of the Digest in terms of classical Roman style and legal practice. In this way, Valla heralded the theme of "anti-Tribonianism," which was to play so crucial a role in legal and historical scholarship.

But this was not all. If the Digest had been defaced by the Greeks, it was positively defiled by the barbarians of more recent times. If

[45] Valla, *Elegantiae*, I, "praefatio" (I, 4).

[46] *Ibid.*, VI, 35 (I, 216). On this anti-Tribonianist tradition, which will be taken up in the next three chapters, see the excellent book of L. Palazzini Finetti, *Storia della ricerca delle interpolazione nel corpus iuris giustinianeo* (Milan, 1953).

[47] Petrarch, *Epistolae de rebus familiaribus*, ed. Fracasetti (Florence, 1863), III, 18.

the Byzantine compilers had mixed Greek with Latin, the scholastic interpreters introduced a "Gothic" language which, Valla complained, "turned his stomach." Besides introducing various barbarisms (such as *guerra* for *bellum*), they had combined civil law with the corrupt canonist tradition (*jus pontificum . . . ex maxima parte gothicum est*).[48] What is more, they had inflicted upon civil law the same kind of atrocities which their Aristotelian brethren had inflicted upon philosophy. With their quibblings and their quiddities, they had detached Roman law from common sense as well as from historical context; they had dehumanized a "human science." For this flock of philistines, who preferred the company of such "geese" as Bartolus and Accursius to the "swans" of ancient jurisprudence, Valla had nothing but scorn. Needless to say, this was returned with interest by the professionals.

Valla approached Roman law, as he approached everything, in the role of philologist; and as in his critique of dialectic, his fundamental nominalism makes itself evident from the beginning. He had no patience with useless debates over classification, such as which of the two terms for a donation (*munus* and *donum*) was the species and which the genus. He preferred to read the words in a common rather than a technical sense, and he concluded that "neither species nor genus is to be found in the two names."[49] Nor was he willing to accept arbitrary identifications made for legal purposes, such as *pignus* and *hypothecus*, one a Latin, the other a Greek term, because of their different origins and connotations. What was more disconcerting to lawyers, he seemed perversely receptive to the notion of contradictions (*antinomiae*, the lawyers called them) in the Digest, although Justinian had expressly outlawed them and scholastic jurists had spent much effort in reasoning away the most obvious difficulties.[50] But Valla was not one to concern himself with the niceties of legal science or the requirements of a legal system. To him the *antinomiae* were the

[48] Valla, *In Bartoli de insigniis et armis libellum* (I, 633). Cf. *Elegantiae*, III, "praefatio," and IV, 64, and *Antidoti in Poggium*, I (I, 80, 144 and 273).

[49] Valla, *Elegantiae*, VI, 39 (I, 218) (D, 50, 16, 18, and 20, 5, 1). Reference is always to the Mommsen-Krueger edition of the Digest.

[50] *Ibid.*, VI, 59 (I, 232), pointing out the differing interpretations of veteran and novice slaves by Venuleius and Ulpian, and choosing the latter's (in terms not of length of service but of condition) (D, 21, 1, 65).

natural products of human error and of history. And in general, Roman law was to be judged in terms not of the authority of Justinian or of the law schools but of the "authority of antiquity."

Thus Valla transformed the study of Roman law. Yet beyond promoting the cause of legal humanism and identifying its enemies, his contributions to legal scholarship were not impressive. They were limited to the elucidation (not always correct) of a few words taken largely from the famous title of the Digest on the meaning of terms (*De verborum significatione*), which was to become so popular with humanists.[51] In general, his procedure was to pick out difficult or ambiguous terms; to illustrate the usage of jurists (Ulpian was his favorite); then to compare this with that of other authors, such as grammarians or poets, sometimes introducing related Greek terms; and finally to resolve the problem through the authority of the major classical writers, that is, Quintilian and Cicero. The word for women (*mulier*), for example, was applied to an unmarried woman by Gaius but not by Ulpian, and Valla decided in favor of the latter on the basis of Ciceronian usage.[52] Valla's assumption that the style of the Roman jurisconsults never strayed far from classical usage was not very sophisticated; indeed it entailed, as sixteenth-century critics were to point out, a kind of unhistorical fallacy which blinded men to the development within classical jurisprudence. But at least it served well enough in the most rudimentary stages of the task of separating Roman from Byzantine law.

One problem of particular interest to Valla was that of etymology, especially since it involved questions of historical origin and linguistic change. The word volume (*volumen*), for example, he preferred to derive from the word for "roll" (*volvo*, instead of *volo*) because it corresponded to the form of early written books. He ridiculed the goperisms of Isidore of Seville and other grammarians regularly cited

[51] *Ibid.*, VI, 35-64 (I, 216-35). These passages have been published in C. A. Duker, *Opuscula varia de latinitate jurisconsultorum veterum* (Leiden, 1711), together with the criticisms of Andrea Alciato (see chapter IV), Francesco Florido Sabino, and a certain anonymous "defensor." The first commentary on this title, that by Valla's friend Maffeo Vegio, was first published by Sassi in *Historia literario-typographia mediolanensis* (Milan, 1745).

[52] *Elegantiae*, VI, 38 (I, 217-18) (D, 50, 16, 13).

by lawyers. Deriving "testament" from the word for mind (*mens*), for example, as if it meant "a testifying or witnessing of the mind" (*testamentum . . . quod testatio mentis est*), was ludicrous and appalling in its implications.[53] Should *mens* also be associated with "ornament," Valla asked, or to "cement"? "The etymology found in Donatus, Servius, and Isidore," he continued, "seems no less inept, that 'oration is said to be the mouth's reason'" (*oratio dicta est quasi oris ratio*). What about "aratio," "operatio," and a thousand others? For such medieval word-play, for such violation of historical sense, even when sanctioned by the books of law, Valla had only contempt. His general conclusion constituted another rule of historical method: "When the etymology is false, the definition will be false."[54]

Even in so technical a field as Roman law, then, there were no substitutes for classical learning and for philological methods. It was by working on this assumption that Valla helped to lay the foundations of the sixteenth-century historical school of law. His critical techniques, applied with characteristic abandon, became the center of passionate controversy in later generations. He was acclaimed—or denounced—almost universally as the apotheosis of the new learning. In general, his work in this field marked not only an act of aggression by philology against the academic establishment but a crucial stage in the convergence of legal and historical scholarship. It was the locus classicus of legal humanism, and many of the themes assembled there will reappear in various forms throughout the following chapters.

The Historical Revolution

Propagandist, critic, anti-philosopher—each of these roles was simply an extension of Valla's vocation as a rhetorician, which encompassed and transcended that of grammarian.[55] It was under this "trivial" ban-

[53] *Ibid.*, VI, 36 (I, 217) (Inst., 2, 10). The topic is taken up again in *Antidoti in Poggium*, II (I, 293). The English rendering is by Henry Swinburne, *A Brief Treatise of Testaments* (London, 1590), p. 3.

[54] Valla, *Elegantiae*, VI, 52 (I, 228).

[55] Valla, *In eundem Poggium . . .*, II (I, 385): "Discourse in a Latin, not merely a grammatical, fashion is required of orators and scholars. Discourse in a Latin fashion is therefore placed among the virtues of rhetoric, since what grammar is to locution Latinity is to elocution."

ner, indeed, that Valla took part in that historical revolution brought about by Renaissance scholarship. His obsession with eloquence should not obscure the fact that his thoughts about investigating the past were by no means superficial or unscholarly. As a philologist he had considered problems of anachronism and historical change more deeply than had writers of history, including even so astute an antiquarian as Flavio Biondo, who was also a serious student of Roman law and who was to make a great impression upon sixteenth-century learning.[56] As a legal scholar Valla helped not only to humanize Roman law but to bring it into fruitful contact with historical studies. As a philosopher, finally, he was perhaps more pragmatic than profound, but for this very reason he had more to offer the study of human civilization as such. His rejection of scholasticism served him much as the rejection of Cartesianism was to serve Vico or, in a more restricted way, as the rejection of natural-law philosophy was to serve Savigny —to mention only two historians who took Roman law as their point of departure. Precisely because of his trivial concerns, it seems, Valla was able to address himself to aspects of historical thought neglected by formal philosophy, and so was able to provide historical and literary studies with a simple yet solid epistemological foundation. Whether or not they would agree with—or even understand—Valla's theory of knowledge, most Renaissance philologists worked largely in accordance with his principles.

"It is the belief in the autonomy of the word," a great philologist of the present century has written, "which made possible the whole movement of Humanism, in which so much importance was given to the word of the ancients and of the Biblical writers."[57] From this point of view and from that of historical thought, Valla seems to be the very incarnation of humanism, or rather of that scholarly aspect of humanism which has been identified as philology. Going a step further—entering, in fact, that speculative realm which Valla himself regarded so suspiciously—it may be suggested that Valla represents, in

[56] Especially Flavio Biondo, *De Roma triumphante* (Basel, 1531), III and IV, and *De militia et jurisprudentia*, in *Scritti inediti e rari*, ed. B. Nogara (Rome, 1927).

[57] Leo Spitzer, *Linguistics and Literary History* (Princeton, 1948), p. 21.

terms of the sciences of culture, the emergence of a new "paradigm" in much the sense that Thomas Kuhn has applied this term to scientific revolutions.[58] For by establishing a method and an epistemology, Valla promoted philology to the level of a science and gave it philosophic justification. Like Copernican astronomy, then, it became the basis for a new perspective of the world and man's place in it. What is more, philology too was transformed into a "coherent tradition of scientific research," which possessed a similar consensus of scholarly values and techniques. Pursuing the specific goals of this tradition, an activity which Kuhn calls "normal science," such as the restoration of Roman law, was the business of less venturesome scholars who, though they were trained in this school, took the "historical revolution" for granted and did not care to inquire into its sources or structure. No doubt it is going too far to call Valla the Copernicus of historical thought; his discoveries were not that unique nor his method that well formulated, and his exaggerated view of rhetoric was distasteful to many sixteenth-century philologists. Yet he came closer than any other author to expressing the attitudes, presumptions, methods, and goals of historical scholarship as it would be practiced for centuries.

What was this paradigm which Valla helped to create, though he never quite gave it explicit formulation? Passing over Valla's particular brand of classicism, since it was not an integral part of the "normal science" of philology and since later philologists would bring quite different personal and political prejudices to their work, here is a somewhat schematic summary. First, as we have seen, Valla demanded a return to human "reality," for he was convinced that knowledge could be attained only through the examination of particular things. Not, of course, that Valla abstained from all generalization. On the contrary, it is obvious that his empirical studies, that is, his literary and lexicographical studies, were aimed at the reconstruction of one

---

[58] Thomas Kuhn, *The Structure of Scientific Revolutions* (Chicago, 1962). This "historical revolution," which is a fundamental transformation of thought and perspective encompassing several generations, might be represented by other authors, such as Petrarch; this in fact is the view of Seigel, *Rhetoric and Humanism*, p. 223. I have chosen Valla because of his scholarly influence, his philosophic justification of his position, and especially his contributions to the "science" of philology.

highly intangible facet of a cultural configuration which was hypostasized by such rhetorical abstractions as *Latinitas* or *antiquitas*; but
such human categories were in violation neither of elegance nor of
history. In the second place, Valla called for a return to original sources; for style was an organic part of doctrine, and antiquity had to
be allowed to speak in its own, ultimately inimitable, accents. Implicit in this argument was the acknowledgment of the uniqueness of
cultural achievement and the irreversibility of historical change. Lastly,
and inevitably, Valla adopted an attitude that was both pluralistic and
relativistic. Every age had literally to be understood in its own terms,
and truth could no more be separated from its cultural environment,
or from its cultural style, than form could be separated from matter.
Thus Valla's method was fundamentally comparative as well as historical.

Valla's historical thought was founded, in short, upon the recognition of a principle of individuality, of a determinable process of
temporal change, and of a kind of cultural relativism. These are the
makings of that intellectual revolution which, coinciding roughly with
the emergence both of the science of philology and of the printed
book, was to transform completely man's conception of himself. As
Vittorio Rossi once remarked, Valla's work marked the transition
"from empiricism to historicism." [59] Because of the essential continuity
of the philological tradition there seems to be no more appropriate
way of characterizing Valla's significance: he represents a form, perhaps an early stage, of European "historicism."

From Valla to Budé

After Valla the philological tradition, spurred by the need to prepare

---

[59] Vittorio Rossi, *Il Quattrocento* (Milan, 1933), p. 78 (appearing for the
first time in this, the 3rd edition). It is an excessively narrow—and unhistorical—view of humanism to oppose it to "historicism," as does Bernardini (*Il Concetto di filologia*, p. 56), "l'umanesimo contro lo storicismo,"
referring to Muret; and Schulz (*Roman Legal Science*, pp. 278 ff), contrasting
"historicism" with "juristic classicism" and "the shackles of humanism" because he regards it as incompatible with his "palingenetic research" into the
changes of Roman law *between* the classical and Byzantine periods—although

accurate texts for the printed page, was carried on with great fidelity by Italian, and especially by Florentine, humanists of the late fifteenth century. In general, growing reverence for the printed word reinforced the concentration of scholars on the purely historical sense and intensified interest in the prosaic tasks of textual criticism, which represented perhaps the most basic part of the "normal science" of philology. Among the first major works in this genre was Ermolao Barbaro's commentary on Pliny's *Natural History*, which was a model for sixteenth-century scholars. Like Valla, Barbaro had frequent recourse to intuitive corrections made on the basis of classical style (*ex Latina loquendi consuetudo*), and his work gave further celebrity to the practice of conjectural emendation.[60] In a famous interchange with Pico, Barbaro also came to the rescue of rhetoric against the tyranny of philosophy. He reaffirmed Valla's principle of the inseparability of eloquence and wisdom, though apparently without his awareness of the epistemological problems involved.[61] Nevertheless, his point of view, if not his somewhat frivolous line of argument, was preserved and enriched by such sixteenth-century scholars as Melanchthon and Budé.

Of all Valla's successors the most significant was Angelo Poliziano, who at the same time was the most effective advocate for the intellectual revolution brought about in his century—"the wonderful faith of history reborn," as he referred to it, "the wonderful second dawning of Rome."[62] He was also conscious of the particular and relative character of history, whose elements he declared to be "person, cause, place, time, custom, means, material, and thing," and whose style, since it was designed for description and explanation, he required to

---

it seems clear that Valla's approach, if it fell short of twentieth-century standards of philological discrimination, was a necessary first step in clearing away Byzantine interpolations and purely textual corruptions.

[60] Ermolao Barbaro, *Castigationes ... in Plinium* (Venice, 1495), k ii[v]. In general, see A. Ferriguto, *Almorò Barbaro* (Venice, 1922).

[61] Barbaro, *Epistolae, orationes, et carmina*, ed. V. Branca (Florence, 1943), II, 68, 70-71 (pp. 84-87, 100-9). Melanchthon's letter in support of Barbaro, together with Pico's letter, appears in *CR*, IX (Melanchthon, *Epistolae ...*), col. 678-703); translation and discussion of these documents by Q. Breen in *JHI*, XIII (1952), 384-426; analysis also by Bernardini, *Il concetto di filologia*, ch. II.

[62] Angelo Poliziano, *Opera omnia* (Basel, 1553), p. 621.

be continuous (*stylus in historia fusus et continuus*).[63] But like Valla, Poliziano made his major contributions to historical scholarship as a philologist—or, as he preferred to say, as a "grammarian." These appear above all in his seminal *Book of Miscellanies*, although he left a large amount of manuscript notes as well. Like Valla, too, he must be regarded as one of the founders of legal humanism; for he was the man who really began the systematic study of the Digest through the legendary Florentine manuscript, which had come into the hands of the Medici in the fifteenth century and which was to be one of the primary targets of modern scholarship.[64] Until the sixteenth century it was regarded not only as essential for the restitution of the Digest but as literally "ancient," a physical link with the sixth century, and so it became the symbol of legal humanism.

Poliziano was clearly superior to Valla as a classical scholar, especially in the study of Greek, and his contribution to the interpretation of Roman law was more substantial. He also had a more elaborate conception of philological method. He insisted that the historical critic have an "encyclopedic" knowledge not only of the humanities and philosophy "but of jurists, physicians, dialecticians, and whoever else make up that circle of learning which we call 'encyclia.' "[65] Even more clearly than Valla he illustrates, as one modern scholar has observed, "a fundamental historicism replacing a fundamentally monistic view of the world."[66] Yet in epistemology and in the conceptual basis

[63] Poliziano, *Panepistemon* (*Opera*, p. 468), where the phrase *fides historiae* appears again.

[64] Poliziano, *Liber miscellaneanorum* (*Opera*, pp. 213 ff), chapters 41, 78, 82, 93, and 95 being devoted to the "restitution" of the Digest. Poliziano left other unpublished notes, used by Pietro Crinito, Lodovico Bolognini, Budé, and others, which were finally published by A. Bandini, *Ragionamento istorico sopra la collazioni delle Fiorentine Pandette* (Livorno, 1762). On the use of the Florentine manuscript, see H. Brenkmann, *Historia pandectarum* (Utrecht, 1722); P. F. Girard, "Les préliminaires de la renaissance du droit romain," *RHDFE*, sér. 4, I (1922), 5-46; F. Buonamici, *Il Poliziano giureconsulto* (Pisa, 1863); and the articles of L. Sighinolfi on Poliziano and Bolognini in *La Bibliofilia*, XXIV (1922), 165-202, and *Studie e memorie per la storia dell'Università di Bologna*, VI (1921), 187-308.

[65] Poliziano, *Liber miscellaneanorum* (*Opera*, p. 229).

[66] A. Scaglione, "The Humanist as Scholar and Politian's Conception of the *Grammaticus*," *SR*, VIII (1961), 50. On Poliziano's relations to philology see also *Il Poliziano e il suo tempo* (Atti del IV Convegno internazionale di studi

of philology Poliziano apparently had little interest. His discussion of dialectic, for instance, was quite old-fashioned and detached from his historical method. Caught up in his many critical and literary activities and untouched by any need for self-justification, Poliziano seems to be a typical practitioner of "normal science."

Poliziano's friend and beneficiary, Pietro Crinito, was the last survivor of the Florentine school. Crinito preserved some of Valla's views, such as identifying his humanist ideal (*honestas*) with Romanism (*Romanitas*), but he did not feel obliged to react to the hostility of philosophers or lawyers, nor did he display a pioneer's aggressiveness. Instead, he devoted himself complacently to "all those things which pertain to human life and to ancient learning" (*ad usum vivendi eruditionemque antiquitatis*), or more specifically to those things "which make up civil and canon law and others which pertain to the institutions of the ancients and to the humanities" (*ad institutiones veterum et humaniores disciplinas*).[67] Like both Valla and Poliziano, he gave careful consideration to the problem of style and its role in historical criticism. Following Varro, he distinguished four stages of style (*priscum, Latinum, Romanum, mistum*), and he lamented the inexorable decline of eloquence, pointing in particular to the age of Ulpian as the beginning of stylistic "deformity" and "depravity."[68] With the same presumptions as Valla and Poliziano and with the same distrust of Accursius, that unfortunate child of a "rude and illiterate age," Crinito addressed himself likewise to that fundamental task of "normal science," the reconstruction of classical Roman law.

With Crinito ended the first, the Italian, phase of the historical revolution. It did not literally end, of course, since in the next generation there were still major Italian contributors to philology and to legal humanism, such as Andrea Alciato and Alessandro d'Alessandro, who

---

sul rinascimento, Florence, 1954), especially the articles by Garin (pp. 17-39) and A. Mancini (pp. 57-67), and I. Maïer, *Ange Politien* (Geneva, 1966). An interesting but little known defense of Poliziano's views is Claudio Tolomei's *De corruptis verbis iuris civilis dialogus* (Siena, 1517), a dialogue between Poliziano and (representing the old school) Giasone del Maino.

[67] Pietro Crinito, *De Honesta disciplina*, ed. C. Angeleri (Rome, 1955), XXV, xii (p. 485); also p. 59.

[68] *Ibid.*, III, iii (pp. 105-6).

shared the values and goals of Valla, though they rejected his excesses. There was a widespread feeling, however, that Italian predominance was on the wane with the coming of the "barbarians" after 1494. Poliziano as well as Valla had felt the exhilaration of belonging to a "golden age"; Crinito lived to see not only the political collapse of Italy but the almost simultaneous deaths of his great friends, Poliziano, Barbaro, and Pico. To him this seemed to herald an emigration of the muses (*quasi musarum secessus*).[69] This legend, too, became part of the consensus of the philological tradition and added to the self-confidence of the northern humanists. It was not difficult, then, for French humanists in particular to conceive of themselves as the true successors of Italian humanism—the children of the historical revolution. "The Italians will surrender easily in Greek and Latin letters," predicted one French scholar in 1507, "and will finally give them up to the French."[70] And so, with this latter-day "translation of studies," we come to the second phase—in a sense to the fruition—of Renaissance philology.

[69] *Ibid.*, XV, ix (p. 317). Another book in this tradition is the *Genialium dierum libri sex* (1522) by Alessandro d'Alessandro, who however disassociated himself from Valla's cult of rhetoric because of his arrogant and excessively literary attitude toward the law, and (like Alciato, as discussed in chapter IV) favored the more neutral views of Barbaro and Poliziano. See the analysis of this work, D. Maffei, *Alessandro d'Alessandro* (Milan, 1956).

[70] Tissard's *Gnomagyricus*, cited by H. Gillot, *La Querelle des anciens et des modernes en France* (Paris, 1914), p. 25.

PART TWO

Philological Tradition

CHAPTER III

The Science of Philology: Guillaume Budé
Begins the Restoration of Roman Law

Omnes artes, quae ad humanitatem pertinent,
habent quoddam commune vinclum, et quam
cognatione quadam inter se continentur.

Cicero, *Pro Archia*, 1

"ONCE AN ORNAMENT," remarked Guillaume Budé, "philology is today the means of revival and of restoration."[1] Thus Budé identified
the crucial role which philology was playing in Renaissance scholarship, while at the same time recognizing its rhetorical pedigree. Philology was not only the most effective tool of historical method, however,
it was also the source of certain ideas essential for interpreting the past
and the changing configurations of culture. Just as language was the
most sensitive indicator of historical change, so the science of language
was most fruitful in providing explanations for this change. Unfortunately, historians were, as always, slow in discovering the poten-
tialities of philology. Students of more specialized and better-defined
subjects such as law and the Bible soon recognized these possibilities
and began to develop them in the sixteenth century. While historians
like Paolo Emilio and Polydore Vergil and even their vernacular successors worried over the formal problems of historical narrative and
value judgments, philologists like Budé and Erasmus were breaking
new ground in the study of classical and Christian antiquity and even
of the European middle ages. And it was their work—and that of
their vernacular successors—that was to transform historical writing.

[1] Guillaume Budé, *De Philologia* (Basel, 1533), p. 217.

Sol Juris Graij et latij sermonis ocellus
Nocte sepulturæ funera lustro meæ.

GUILLAUME BUDÉ (T. de Bry, *Icones
et effigies virorum doctorum*) Courtesy of the
Bibliothèque Nationale, Paris

It is no exaggeration to say that the tap root of modern historical scholarship was not conventional historiography but philology. Nowhere is this illustrated more clearly than in the seminal researches of Budé in Roman law and institutions.

The Arch-Philologist of France

Philology came late to France. To most humanists, northern as well as southern, the Alps presented a cultural as well as a geographical barrier which could never be passed without leaving something behind, but the new learning lost nothing except its Italian chains. Nobody believes today—did they ever?—that Italian culture was brought to France in the knapsacks of Charles VIII's troops, but there is something to be said for the thesis that philology became fashionable in France as a result of the intensified contacts of the Italian wars. True, there were signs of "good letters" in France even before Valla was born (in 1407), while just a year after his death (in 1458) the study of Greek was introduced into the University of Paris by Gregorio Tifernas. Enthusiasm for "eloquence and doctrine" was still more conspicuous a dozen years later, when Guillaume Fichet and his younger colleague Robert Gaguin, later to be France's first humanist historiographer, began to promote the study of the best authors, especially Valla, whose work was among the first to be published by the press set up in 1470 in the basement of the University. Not long afterwards that much-abused teacher of Greek, George Hermonymus, arrived in Paris; and a growing stream of visiting Italian humanists had a certain catalytic effect on French literary society. Yet it was not until the turn of the century that the philological tradition invaded French intellectual circles in full force.[2] It was Guillaume Budé whom French men of letters, correctly or not, honored as the bearer of the humanist message and of that light which was to issue from philology. Consequently, it is Budé whom we must honor as the patriarch of historical thought in France.

[2] The standard work is still A. Renaudet, *Préréforme et humanisme à Paris pendant les premières guerres d'Italie* (Paris, 1953). See also L. Thuasne's introduction to his edition of Robert Gaguin's *Epistole et orationes* (Paris, 1904).

Budé was born in 1468 of a prominent Parisian *famille de robe* and received a conventional education, first at the University of Paris and then at the law school of the University of Orleans.[3] His student years, to hear him tell it, were idle and undirected; he did, at any rate, acquire a few unproductive habits which he never lost—love of good society and good wine and of such diversions as the hunt. Then something very like a religious conversion changed his life: he discovered philology and put away the things of youth. He devoted himself with exorbitant zeal to the new learning, though he could not pursue it in good conscience until the death of his father, who had planned a sensible legal career for his eldest son. Budé began his serious studies by 1490 and his assault on Greek by 1494, some six years before Erasmus. From the beginning he placed Greek culture (*attica illa paedia*) above Latin and, as his admitedly graceless style showed, doctrine above eloquence. Although he published nothing until 1505, and then only a few minor translations from Greek, he had gained a certain scholarly reputation by 1496, when Fausto Andrelini dedicated a book to him. Like Erasmus, his "rival in the love of philology,"[4] Budé served a long apprenticeship and by the age of forty had still not begun his major work.

Then in 1508, within the space of a few months, Budé wrote and published his *Annotations on the Pandects*, which established him as the apostle of humanist scholarship in France.[5] This book was revo-

---

[3] L. Delaruelle, *Guillaume Budé, les origines, les débuts, les idées maîtresses* (Paris, 1907), is excellent but does not go beyond 1520. Other general studies include Jean Plattard's brief *Guillaume Budé et l'origine de l'humanisme français* (Paris, 1923), and A. Tilley, *Studies in the French Renaissance* (Cambridge, 1922). See also H. Omont, "Notes sur la collection de manuscrits de Jean et Guillaume Budé,"*Bulletin de la Société de l'histoire de Paris*, XII (1885), 100 ff, and "Papiers de Guillaume Budé à la Bibliothèque de Brême," *BHR*, XXX (1968), 155-83, by G. Gueudet, who is preparing a thesis on Budé's works.

[4] Budé, *Epistolae posteriores* (Paris, 1522), f. 119ᵛ. Budé's autobiographical remarks appear in *De Philologia*, pp. 89 ff, as well as in many of his letters, for which the essential guide is Delaruelle's supplementary thesis, *Répertoire analytique et chronologique de la correspondance de Guillaume Budé* (Paris, 1907). A Latin translation of Budé's Greek letters was published by A. Pichon (Paris, 1574). See now the translation of the letters between Budé and Erasmus by M. de la Garanderie (Paris, 1967).

[5] Budé, *Annotationes... in quatuor et viginti Pandectarum libros* (Paris,

lutionary in its own curiously haphazard fashion. It did for Roman law what eight years later Erasmus' New Testament was to do for Biblical studies: it introduced a new method of criticism into one of the major professional domains in order to begin a reformation—a reformation not only of a university discipline, but, by restoring the purity of ancient doctrine, contemporary society in general. Surely no book as technical, formless, and unreadable has ever had a greater impact upon historical scholarship.

Budé's next work, no more original but with a broader popular appeal, gained him admittance, along with Erasmus and Vives, into the great "triumvirate" of sixteenth-century learning.[6] This was his book on Roman coinage, *The As and its Parts* of 1514, in which he showed the value of philology for more general kinds of antiquarian investigation. Budé also promoted his calling through his correspondence, which ranged over a quarter of a century and included an array of friendships and discipleships second only to Erasmus', and through two well-known manifestos, the *Study of Learning* (1527) and *Philology* (1530). Most important of all was his *Commentaries on the Greek Language* (1529), which has been the foundation of Greek lexicography down to the present century. Finally, because of a decade-long publicity campaign, Budé was widely credited with inspiring Francis I to subsidize regius professorships in the classical languages.[7] These chairs, established in 1530 and forming the nucleus of the future Collège de France, represent the institutional fulfillment of the philological ideal. Such were the major sources of Budé's image as France's answer to Erasmus—as "the greatest Greek in Europe," in the words of the younger Scaliger, the ultimate judge in such matters.[8]

Like Petrarch, to some extent like Valla, Budé created his own

---

1535), the first edition to be published by Budé's son-in-law Robert Estienne. A revised edition had been issued by 1517, in 1526 a supplementary commentary on the last four books of the Digest.

[6] This invention of Claude Chansonette was acknowledged by Budé in 1519 in *Epistolae*, f. 37ᵛ.

[7] *Ibid.*, f. 19ʳ (to Jacques Toussain, 20 Nov. 1520) and preface to *Commentarii linguae graecae* (Paris, 1529). See A. Lefranc, *Histoire du Collège de France* (Paris, 1893), and "Les commencements du Collège de France," *Mélanges Pirenne* (Brussels, 1926), 291-306.

[8] *Scaligerana* (Amsterdam, 1740), II, 145-46.

legend. Identifying himself, under the sponsorship of the king, with "rebirth of letters" in France, Budé dramatized his role and taught his disciples to disregard that false dawn before the reign of Francis I. His first biographer was merely echoing the great man's own disparaging remarks when he called Hermonymus, Budé's first teacher, a humble man of mediocre learning.[9] Budé granted more credit to Janus Lascaris, but in general he took pride in being self-taught. He proclaimed his membership in the Italian school of philology, but he was conspicuously independent in his judgments and, like Valla, never hesitated to oppose conventional views. In the field of hellenic studies in particular, he claimed to be a true pioneer ($K\alpha\theta\eta\gamma\eta\tau\dot\eta\varsigma$).[10] Contemporaries thought so, too. Seconding the opinion of Erasmus himself, both Vives and Cuthbert Tunstall compared his work in the renaissance of letters (*ad instaurandas litteras*) to that of Valla, Poliziano, and Barbaro, precisely the models selected by Budé.[11] Even Ulrich Zasius, his rival as a legal scholar, would not declare Budé inferior to his devoted friend Erasmus. The publication of Louis le Roy's eulogistic biography in the year of Budé's death (1540) set a formal literary seal upon his reputation as the arch-humanist of France and upon the complementary legend of Francis I as "father of the muses." In the next generation this was to be taken as an official episode in the history of the French monarchy. Thus, in political and scholarly terms, Budé was canonized.

The Gallican

From the beginning Budé was as anxious for national glory as he was for personal fame. This was only to be expected—not only because in the well-established tradition of civic humanism Budé assumed a

---

[9] Louis le Roy, G. *Budaei viri clarissimi vita* (Paris, 1540), p. 11; cf. Budé, *Epistolae*, f. 116ʳ. In general, see F. Simone, *La Coscienza della rinascita negli umanisti francesi* (Rome, 1949), pp. 108 ff.

[10] Budé, *Epistolae*, f. 3ᵛ (to Christophe de Longueil, 15 Oct. 1519). In general, see E. Egger, *L'Hellenisme en France* (Paris, 1869), and D. Rebitté, *Guillaume Budé* (Paris, 1846).

[11] Allen, IV, 274 (from Luis Vives, 4 June [1520]); II, 539 (from Cuthbert Tunstall, 15 Apr. 1517); and Hartmann, II, 179 (Zasius to Bonifacius, 16 Aug. 1519). Cf. Allen, II, 460 (to Budé, 15 Feb. 1517).

natural connection between philology and public service, but because Budé's own fortunes were bound up with those of the monarchy. Much of his adult life he spent in the king's service, acting several times as envoy for Louis XII as well as for Francis I. In 1522 he was rewarded with the charges both of *maître des requêtes* and of *bibliothécaire du roi* (by courtesy first librarian of the Bibliothèque Nationale).[12] He made conventional complaints about the burdens of office and the vanity of court life, but in fact he made good use of his public position. He had access not only to the royal library established at Fontainebleau but, through a family sinecure, to the royal archives (the *trésor des chartes*); and his diplomatic missions allowed him to extend his scholarly contacts as well as to make the Italian pilgrimage expected of every humanist. It was as a representative of the crown, too, that he tried to entice Erasmus to France. Nothing came of the attempt since that cautious scholar feared to offend his sovereign, Charles V, and no doubt had some suspicions of Budé as well.[13] The fact is that solicitude for national honor did not improve Budé's already somewhat arrogant disposition. Criticism of his countrymen, such as Erasmus' attack on Lefèvre d'Etaples, he took almost personally; affronts to himself might constitute an international incident, as in the case of Erasmus' punning comparison of him (Budaeus) with his publisher (Badius).[14] He could not have been as mean as his portrait represents him—small-eyed, large-nosed, sour-looking—but it is clear that his sense of humor did not match his sense of dignity.[15]

To the glory of the monarchy Budé sacrificed not only his public energies but the bulk of his private researches. His *Annotations on the*

[12] G. du Bellay, *Fragments de la première Ogdoade*, ed. V. L. Bourrilly (Paris, 1904), p. 4, and *Catalogue des actes de François Ier*, VII (Paris, 1896), 490.

[13] Budé, *Epistolae*, f. 124v, and Allen, II, 443 (5 Feb. 1517).

[14] Allen, II, 268 (from Budé, 12 Apr. [1518]), and VI, 478, to Budé, 23 Mar. 1527); Erasmus' jest about Badius appeared in the *Ciceronianus* of 1527. On the touchy question of plagiarism Budé had disagreements both with Alciato (*Epistolae*, f. 56r, to Longueil, 21 Feb. 1520) and with Zasius (*ibid.*, f. 37v, to Chansonette, 17 July 1519).

[15] There is a portrait in the Metropolitan Museum of Art in New York. Portraits of many of the scholars discussed in this book (Valla, Poliziano, Budé, Alciato, Zasius, Cujas, and Hotman) may be found in T. de Bry, *Icones et effigies virorum doctorum* (Frankfurt, . . . 1645, text by J. J. Boissardo).

Pandects, filled with tributes to French institutions, represented a conscious attempt to transfer leadership in the new humanist jurisprudence to France. Admitting the cultural supremacy of Italy in former times (*Italia omnium gentium magistra*), Budé came to believe that the lamp of learning (*lampadem*) was passing to more capable hands.[16] This was a prominent theme of the *De Asse,* which contained still more aggressive vindications of the cultural independence of France. It seems that the politics of the intervening years, especially the conflict with the papacy over the Council of Pisa, had given a polemical edge to Budé's views. Although he had little sympathy with the kind of reform advocated by Lefèvre, his intense Gallican convictions led him to bitter attacks against Rome and the corruption of justice as well as against those traitors (*misopatrides*) who undervalued their own country. In 1519 he was so carried away with national enthusiasm that, for the first and only time, he composed a work in the vernacular.[17] The result was his *Institution of the Prince,* in which he played Aristotle to Francis I's Alexander. Budé's last service to the monarchy was a Gallican defense of the king's repressive measures against the Sacramentarian "rebels," who in 1534 had staged the notorious affair of the placards. This *Transition from Hellenism to Christianity,* which made up for its obscurantism by helping to provoke Calvin's *Institutes of the Christian Religion,* was an indication at once of Budé's subservience to royal policy and of his growing disillusionment with the Italianate science of philology.[18]

This needs a word of explanation. Budé's attraction to philology had a religious quality, but a marital analogy might be more appropriate,

[16] Budé, *De Asse et partibus ejus* (Paris, 1532), f. 169ᵛ. Cf. *Annotationes,* f. 100ᵛ: "For we shall see the light of Latin letters, which within the memory of our fathers began from Italy to shine on this side of the Alps, appearing through those barbarous shadows."

[17] Budé, *De l'Institution du prince* (Paris, 1547), also appended to C. Bontems et al, *Le Prince dans la France des XVIᵉ et XVIIᵉ siècles* (Paris, 1966). There is a useful discussion by M. Triwunatz, *Guillaume Budé's de l'Institution du prince* (Munich, 1903), containing parallels with Erasmus' and Machiavelli's "princes," but it must be corrected by the remarks of Delaruelle, *Guillaume Budé,* pp. 119 ff.

[18] Budé, *De Transitu Hellenismi ad Christianismum,* ed. and trans. D. F. Penham (unpubl. diss., Columbia, 1954). On this aspect of Budé see J. Bohatec, *Budé und Calvin* (Graz, 1950).

especially since he himself suggested it. If we can judge by his letters, Budé's deepest passions and tensions attached themselves less to his wife, who was over twenty years younger than he, than to his "other spouse" (*altera conjux*) philology. In any case, Budé's affair with philology, though it lasted for a half-century, was stormy and guilt-ridden. From the beginning he had displayed a certain ambivalence toward the worldly wisdom offered by classical literature. He was mildly critical of the meanderings of scholastic logic (*ambulationes peripateticorum qui tanta vim differendi in nugis consumpserunt*),[19] but unlike Valla he never rejected conventional philosophy altogether nor the sempiternal knowledge it affected to possess. Yet even philosophy Budé regarded with some suspicion, representing it sometimes by the overreaching figure of Prometheus, sometimes by Pandora. He continued to believe that there was a natural connection, a "golden chain," leading from pagan learning to theology, or, as he called it, "major philology"; but increasingly he grew fearful of the "error of Hellenism."[20] Like Erasmus, it seems, he did not want to grow old in secular studies.

About the study of history he felt similar inhibitions. He distrusted the "mythistorical" view of the Greeks, who lacked a knowledge of "sacred and incorruptible history" and who thus believed in the eternity of the world. "The knowledge of ancient history," he warned, "is to be sought not from the Greeks but from the Egyptians and the Chaldeans," who had entrusted this knowledge to the priests.[21] Much as he loved philology, Budé could not help wanting to transcend language and to pursue the logos in its supernatural form—to pass beyond the historical world and to devote himself to things of the spirit. Even in his textual criticism he suggested the superiority of the figurative to the literal sense (*vagina est historia, gladius est litteraturae spiritus*).[22] After 1520 this attitude was intensified by a growing consciousness of his own mortality and of the ephemeral

[19] Budé, *De Asse*, f. 181ʳ.

[20] Budé, *De Transitu*, p. 7 ("praefatio"), 59, *passim*.

[21] Budé, *De Asse*, f. 118, going on to recommend the recently forged history of "Berosus." Cf. Josephus, *Against Apion*, I, 1.

[22] Budé, *De Transitu*, p. 715.

nature of human life, first expressed in his *Contempt of Fortuitous Things* (1525). Increasingly, his thought turned from secular learning (*doctrina secularis, externa philosophia*) to a higher kind of wisdom (*transita ad sanctiorem philosophiam; doctrina Christi*) which he called "philotheory" (*philotheoria qui culmen est columenque philosophiae et theologiae*).[23] Such was his symbolic "transition from Hellenism to Christianity."

Here is a good example of what I have referred to as the transcendent impulse, which tends to inhibit purely historical understanding. Torn between "esoteric" and "exoteric" wisdom, Budé seem to illustrate the epistemological puzzle identified by Karl Vossler.[24] "On the one hand language is thought to be error and illusion, a veil hiding truth, self-deception; on the other it is looked upon as the first and most important educator of our thought, even as thought itself." Like St. Jerome, Budé felt remorse about being more of a Ciceronian than a Christian. Yet in Budé's case, too, it seems clear that the transcendent impulse was peripheral to his real achievement. There can be no doubt that his true calling was "minor philology" and that his gift was a sense of history. If "philotheory" represents the endpoint in Budé's intellectual development, it represents also a betrayal of those ideals which give him so distinguished a place in the history of classical scholarship and in any discussion of Renaissance historicism.

In spite of his doubts, in spite of his reservations about Italian influence (*Italismus*), Budé remained throughout life a member in good standing of the philological tradition (*natio* or *ordo philologorum*). With Petrarch and Valla he rejoiced in that "chorus of muses" which graced his "golden age"; and his writing was replete with all the Renaissance imagery (*instauratio antiquitatis, ad litteras cum Latinas tum Graecas in integrum vitae instituendas, literas vitae restitutas postliminio*, and many other such phrases) which had become the hallmark of humanist rhetoric. "Restitution," indeed, is the key label of his individual textual emendations as well as the justification for his scholarship in general. Budé may have fancied himself a theolo-

---

[23] *De Studio litterarum* (Basel, 1532), pp. 62, 37 ff.

[24] *Ibid.*, p. 59. Cf. Vossler, *The Spirit of Language in Civilization*, trans. O. Oeser (New York, 1932), p. 1.

gian; his disciples saw in him the successor to the great Italian philologists, especially to Valla, Poliziano, and Barbaro (with honorable mention to Crinito, Beroaldo, Sabellico, Biondo, and Perotto). Herein lay his contribution to historical scholarship.

Encyclopedic Humanism

Between Budé's youthful enthusiasm for the Italian avant-garde and his last years as a pious and reactionary Gallican lay one of the most revolutionary half centuries in European history. It is not surprising that Budé, who already shared St Jerome's qualms about classical learning, was depressed by the turn of events. Yet he could never change his old ways entirely, and what has been said about Valla applies also to him. Budé shared most of Valla's fundamental assumptions about the nature of human culture, starting with the conviction that eloquence and doctrine were inseparable. He agreed, too, that words reflected reality (*verba rerum imagines*) and that the contours of the historical world were revealed only through the close study of language.[25] It was only natural that he should have turned increasingly from translation to textual criticism and thence, though without discarding his historical method, to lexicography. In this way Budé pushed historicism to its logical—and methodological—extreme.

In Budé's interpretation of historical change, again, the concept of style figured most prominently. He assumed that each national group and each age had its own morphology, its characteristic style in the broadest sense, of which literature was the most sensitive indicator and learned opinion (*consensus eruditorum*) the final judge. Budé was following ancient convention when he characterized particular ages (*Ciceronis aetas, Ulpiani tempus, Accursiani seculum,* and so on) and when he distinguished between "classical" and "proletarian" writers.[26] Like Valla, however, he went further by adding a sense of progressive stylistic change, even suggesting a periodization equiv-

[25] Budé, *Annotationes*, f. 8ʳ.

[26] *Ibid.*, f. 38ᵛ. On the classical-proletarian distinction (Aulus Gellius, 19, 8, 15), see *ibid.*, f. 95ʳ and 102ʳ; in *Epistolae*, f. 20ᵛ, Budé modestly placed himself in the latter category. See also *Annotationes*, f. 118ᵛ.

alent to the later ancient-medieval-modern convention, which in a way was implicit in his conception of philology. A sense of history is displayed also in his digressions on national culture, which was hypostasized by such expressions as *genius* or *Minerva Franciae*; for he saw a basic correlation between cultural achievement and political success, arising from prosperity and the patronage of great princes, and between social custom and literary style.[27] More generally, he plotted a life-cycle of civilization beginning with childhood (*secula infantiae*), filled with superstition and poetry; then adolescence, characterized by learning and eloquence, that is, history and philology; and finally a period of decline, due to moral corruption and the vicissitudes of time (*inclinationes temporum*).[28] Such was the shape of history as seen through the eyes of a philologist.

For Budé, then, philology represented a new world view. Like Valla he had nothing but contempt for the educationists of that day, those "scholastic doctors" who dominated the schools, including the University of Orleans, where Budé had acquired his initial distaste for law. Yet in a sense Budé shared the bias of these guildsmen (*sectatores*, he called them), for what he wanted was not so much to topple the medieval hierarchy of learning as to promote philology to the level of the older disciplines. In agreement with Erasmus, he regarded philology as a true "science" based upon the *studia humanitatis*. This ideal had ancient roots, of course, especially in Cicero's view of the liberal arts and in the "encyclopedia" of Quintilian and Vitruvius; but more directly, it was a combination of the art of grammar according to the famous definition of Poliziano and the art of rhetoric according to the notorious views of Valla. In short, philology involved the historical interpretation of texts in the light of the humanist encyclopedia, which by the sixteenth century had come to encompass not only the liberal arts but such disciplines as philosophy, law, and medicine. In particular, philology depended upon eloquence, which "binds together this cycle of learning . . . like a living body."[29] Without this, Budé added

[27] Budé, *De Asse*, "praefatio," f. 52ᵛ, and *De Philologia*, pp. 158 ff. Cf. Valla, *Elegantiae*, I, "praefatio" (*Opera*, I, 4).

[28] Budé, *De Studio*, p. 33 ff.

[29] Budé, *De Asse*, f. 179ʳ⁻ᵛ. Cf. Quintilian, *De Oratore*, 1, 10, 1; Vitruvius, *De Architectura*, 1, 1; also Poliziano, *Liber miscellaneanorum* (*Opera*, p. 229).

in Valla's words, "learning is blind, especially in civil law." As a literary ideal, philology stood above history, a possession of all the ages (*dicendi facultas ars . . . omnium tenporum et locorum*).[30] By the sixteenth century, however, it had been reduced to the monopoly of a scholarly cult; it had become a "cornucopia" of classical learning and a historical method.

For the study of history in a formal sense Budé had great respect, although he had little to say beyond the tired topoi of humanist rhetoric, rehearsed all too often by Valla and others. The function of history was doubtless commemorative and didactic (*exemplorum eventuumque memorabilem plena est historia*), and in order to survive it needed to be "written expertly . . . by a good orator." He advised the king to take history rather than any school teacher as his mistress (referring to the Ciceronian *historia magistra vitae*). "In this way," Budé concluded, "a wise prince can resemble Janus, who is represented with two faces seeing equally well forwards and backwards."[31] What is much more significant, Budé recognized the common methodological basis of history and philology. He associated the truthfulness of narrative history, that is, with the literalness of the grammatical method, celebrating both as the "faith of history" (*fides historiae*).[32] The inference is that Budé conceived of history in the most fundamental sense not as a literary genre but as an independent mode of thought. His own purpose, certainly, was not the fashioning of a narrative line but the investigation (*indagatio*) and the restoration (*restitutio*) of ancient culture through philology.

Budé's most celebrated effort of reconstruction was his study of Roman coinage, a subject which had been the despair of such scholars as Biondo, Poliziano, and Barbaro.[33] In the course of unearthing relevant material, Budé displayed not only an encyclopedic knowledge of clas-

[30] Budé, *De Philologia*, p. 81.

[31] *Ibid.*, p. 232; cf. *Annotationes*, f. 94ᵛ ("plena est exemplorum vetustas, plena sententiarum"). The relevant passages in *Institution du prince* are pp. 43, 45, 65.

[32] *Ibid.*, p. 126, and *De Asse*, f. 38ᵛ. Cf. *De Transitu*, p. 713, referring to to the four methods of interpretation and adding that one access was "through history, which establishes the truth of deeds" (*per historiam, qui fidem rerum gestarum facit*).

[33] Budé, *De Asse*, ff. 397, 26, 154, 46.

sical sources but a unique grasp of the principle of "controlling" sources by external criticism. Like Valla, he did not hesitate to question classical authors; they were only, he said, men like ourselves. In this book, Budé claimed, he did not confine himself to a single discipline but aimed at "the interpretation of antiquity in general" (*in universum pertinentem ad antiquitatis interpretationem*). When he was not launched into one of his chronic digressions, his ostensible subject was determining the names and values of ancient moneys, which he claimed to be the first man in over eight-hundred years to understand. From here he moved to the larger question of the economic basis of the Roman empire. He compared its wealth to modern Europe as well as to other ancient societies; and he discussed in detail such topics as usury, the beginnings of coinage, and the incomes of various professions, observing incidentally that formerly scholars had been much better rewarded for their labors. He had no doubt that the splendor of Rome depended largely upon the wealth—and the ideas—wrested from other peoples, and that its political and cultural degeneration was tied to economic factors, as suggested by the progressive devaluation of currency. This awareness of the economic foundations gave a dimension to Budé's view of antiquity that was lacking in that of his Italian forebears. This was another necessary ingredient for a really comprehensive kind of cultural history.

Roman Law

It was in the field of Roman law that the quality of Budé's scholarship appeared most clearly and that his historical method was applied to best advantage. Like Valla, Budé regarded Roman law as one of the most impressive monuments of ancient culture, as the most effective system of social organization ever created, and, since it belonged to moral philosophy, as a significant part of the classical encyclopedia. More than that, it was virtually a species of wisdom, as in fact it was defined by the Digest (*notitia rerum divinarum humanarumque*).[34] It

---

[34] **D**, 1, 1, 1, and *Annotationes*, f. 3ᵛ. This theme parallels the discussion of wisdom in a more general sense (*scientia rerum humanarum et divinarum*) which has been described by E. Rice, *The Renaissance Idea of Wisdom* (Cambridge, Mass., 1958).

pleased Budé, too, that the Roman principle of equity was based upon a distribution of law (*isonomia*) which was proportional but not equal in terms of class structure—republican perhaps but democratic never. He endorsed the idea of absolutism (*princeps legibus solutus*), though with certain natural and institutional limits which no Frenchman could fail to acknowledge. In many respects the social and political ideals of Roman law seemed to correspond to those of France. Finally, Budé commended Justinian's edict against further interpretation; for such commentary—and here Budé was obviously thinking of the scholastic tradition—was always the source of strife (*alimentum litium*).[35] At first glance, them, Budé's conception of Roman law appears to be that of a faultless monolith, a system of jurisprudence to be studied for the edification which might be derived from it.

Yet Budé's approach was not really that static and uncritical. In fact, he was attracted to Roman law not as "written reason" (*ratio scripta*) but as a battered relic, as a locus of the most fundamental problems confronting the historian. The effects of foreign influence, especially of Greek philosophy, the extent of historical change as reflected in social and stylistic variations, the detection of interpolations, the value of legal sources for history—such questions as these made the Digest an incomparable challenge to the historical imagination. Budé took up the task exactly where it had been left by the two greatest of Italian philologists, that ideal critic Lorenzo Valla, who had begun the exegesis of the Digest from a literary point of view, and that "man of excellent doctrine" Angelo Poliziano, who had begun the restoration of the text as a paleographer, that is, by means of the Florentine codex. This closely guarded manuscript had come to be regarded with a respect bordering on idolatry. "It was protected as a holy and precious relic," one jurist later remarked, "and shown only by torch-light, as mystagogues formerly showed their sacred treasures."[36] Budé himself, during one of his Italian trips, had enjoyed

[35] Budé, *Annotationes*, f. 58ᵛ and 34ᵛ. The reference is to Justinian's constitutions "Tanta" and "Deo auctore."

[36] François Hotman, *Antitribonian* (Paris, 1603), p. 124. This manuscript, still preserved in the Laurentian Library, was published by Lelio Torelli (Florence, 1553); and in this century it was reproduced photographically, *Justiniani Augusti Digestorum seu Pandectarum codex Florentinus olim Pi-*

the rare honor of seeing this manuscript, but only briefly and "through a grating." So like most scholars before 1553 he had to rely on the notes and commentaries of Poliziano.[37]

Budé treated Roman law with reverence, but it was the reverence of a priest of the muses (*sacerdos musarum*) rather than of a priest of the laws (*sacerdos legum*). He saw the Digest not as a book of authority, which in Gallican France it could not be anyway, but as a historical monument, as an "image of antiquity" (*effigies antiquitatis*). Like Erasmus three or four years earlier, Budé had received his inspiration from Valla. It was the *Elegancies of the Latin Language*, Budé tells us,

> that led me to read the Digest more carefully, wherein I found many things partly corrupted and partly mutilated, and so I turned my attention to many words of good and ancient coinage transformed by the ignorance of the times into foreign usage. Moved by this indignity, I undertook a little while ago, by chance and without counsel, to spread among my friends what I had done in order that the Pandects could be read more correctly and intelligently.[38]

His hastily compiled *Annotations*—"neither perfect nor complete," he admitted, "but somewhat perfunctory"—consisted of random notes on the first twenty-four of the fifty books of the Digest, mainly philological but swollen by digressions, literary and philosophical as well as legal and lexicographical in character. His purpose was both to improve the text and to elucidate certain passages that offered special difficulties to the modern reader.

In order to accomplish this task Budé found it necessary to discard both the standards and the traditional topics of medieval jurisprudence. He did not gloss over but positively insisted upon the fundamental social changes reflected in Roman law. "By the time of Ulpian," he remarked of the imperialist formula, *princeps legibus solutus,* "nothing remained of that original civic spirit [*prisca civilitas*], everything

---

sanus phototypice expressus . . . (Rome, 1902-10). Like Poliziano, Budé regarded this as an "ancient" manuscript; the first scholar to reject this notion is the subject of F. de Zulueta's biography, *Don Antonio Agustín* (Glasgow, 1939), p. 40. Budé counted 37 (there are 39) authors in the Digest.

[37] Budé, *Annotationes,* f. 36v-37r, where Budé mentions his visit to Crinito and his knowledge of Poliziano's unpublished notes (see ch. II, n. 64).

[38] *Ibid.,* f. 7v. The phrase *effigies antiquitatis* was applied to the Twelve Tables by Cicero, *De Oratore,* I, xliii, 193.

being ruled by the will of the prince."[39] Along with Zasius and other like-minded contemporaries, Budé was drawn particularly to that indispensable but unusually corrupt summary of legal history attributed to Pomponius, which epitomized the transmutations of law and language and which had suffered cruelly at the hands of medieval commentators. What was most offensive to jurists of the old school, Budé insisted that historians and poets as well as lawyers should be granted authority, since they were cited in the Digest and were obviously necessary for its understanding. The result was that in his desire to offer "obiter dicta relating to the restoration of the Latin language"—another echo from Valla—he actually substituted for the authority of civil law the "authority of antiquity," a literary concept and, if only potentially, a historical standard.[40]

Like Valla again, but still more aggressively, Budé took up the anti-Tribonianist theme, repeating Suidas' charges of Tribonian's illiteracy and infidelity. The editorial work of this "analphabetic" man and his collaborators was literally an atrocity. "In the manner of brutal surgeons cutting into living flesh," Budé lamented, "they gave us a Digest not assembled but rather dissected."[41] A famous example of a Tribonianism was the substitution of "annua die" for Ulpian's conventional legal phrase "annua bima trima die," which was unknown to medieval lawyers but which Valla had explained.[42] One title in particular, Budé pointed out, contained many passages "written by Greek authors and so left by Tribonian, as may be seen by the style, which is sordid and obscure compared to that of the classical jurists, and which was not so much translated as twisted from the Greek without

---

[39] *Ibid.*, f. 37ᵛ (D, 1, 3, 31).

[40] *Ibid.*, f. 28ʳ (D, 1, 2, 2—"De origine juris"), echoing Valla, *Elegantiae*, I, "praefatio" (*Opera*, I, 4). Elsewhere (f. 113ᵛ) Budé remarks, "It is evident to even the most ignorant that [the law] concerns philosophers, since the science of law, as we have said before, is part of civil science, which itself is part of moral science; and finally moral science is the third part of philosophy.... Moreover, it is clear that philosophy is attendant upon that circle of learning we call the encyclopedia...."

[41] Budé, *Annotationes*, f. 8ᵛ (D, 1, 2, 2); cf. especially f. 145ʳ, and the article "Tribonianus" in *Suidae Lexicon* (Cambridge, 1705).

[42] *Ibid.*, f. 100ᵛ (D, 13, 7, 8), referring to Valla, *Elegantiae*, IV, 80 (*Opera*, I, 148).

knowledge of either language." "Nor," he remarked elsewhere," is the skill greater in many laws of the Code, as the style bears witness."[43] Technical and marginal as this problem of interpolation may appear, it provided a powerful impetus to the development of historical criticism.

Normally, Budé preferred to follow the most reliable texts; and so he made the fullest use of Poliziano's reconstructions based upon the Florentine manuscript, especially for Greek terms, which in earlier editions of the Digest, if they appeared at all, were often ludicrously mangled (*themelici* and *sexustici* for *thymelici* and *xystici*, for instance, and a host of others).[44] But Budé was by no means a slave to textual authority. At one point he even departed from the Florentine manuscript, mistakenly, "lest I should be subject to Poliziano in everything." Nor, like Valla, had he scruples about exposing the "hallucinations" even of classical authors, or at least their copyists. Thus he rebuked Pomponius for confusing his Tarquins and his Scaevolas, as could be shown by reference to Livy.[45] This practice of controlling sources, which was noted earlier, was a permanent feature of Budé's method and of legal humanism in general. It was a lesson learned late indeed by historiographers.

When history was silent, when manuscript authority was lacking, Budé resorted to a technique more precarious and at the same time more characteristic, that is, to a kind of higher criticism based upon his sense of style. He was suspicious of the intuitions of other scholars; "to divine is not to emend," he once scolded Barbaro. Yet Budé himself, once again following Valla's lead, never hesitated to make

[43] *Ibid.*, f. 117ᵛ (D, 18, 1, 1); cf. f. 31ᵛ.

[44] *Ibid.*, f. 72ʳ (D, 3, 2, 4). Cf. *ibid.*, f. 71ʳ (D, 2, 13, 8); f. 64ʳ (D, 1, 16, 6); f. 68ᵛ (D, 1, 16, 12), changing a passage to read, "The legate has [instead of does *not* have] legislative authority in his jurisdiction." In these three passages Budé follows Poliziano, but in f. 70ᵛ (D, 2, 11, 2) he rejects Poliziano's "diem diffissum" (Mommsen: "diem diffisum") for "diem diffusum," by analogy with Livy's usage. The corresponding commentaries are Poliziano, *Liber miscellaneanorum*, ch. 93, 95, 78, 41 (*Opera*, p. 305, 306, 287, 260).

[45] *Ibid.*, f. 15ʳ (D, 1, 2, 2), showing that the son of Demaratus was Tarquinius Priscus not Superbus, and f. 32ᵛ, replacing P. M. by Q. M. Scaevola. About the "De origine juris" in general Budé remarked that (f. 16ᵛ) "many words have become depraved and in order to understand them one must refer to Livy's history.

conjectural emendations of passages that seemed to him "depraved" or "mutilated." He could not conceal his pride in his own successful "restitutions," and he entered with great relish into that increasingly popular humanist sport, the hunt for interpolations.[46] Typically, he would remark (here on the use of *quanti* instead of *quanto*) that a term "was not a Latin construction, that is, alien to the style of the ancient jurists and especially abhorrent to Ulpian." Or again (substituting *venditio res mansisset* for *venditiores mansisset*) that "neither the authority nor the examples of Accursius will persuade me that Ulpian would speak so ineptly."[47] Budé offered many such corrections—some comic (*aedilitas*, aedileship, for *edulitas*, hunger), some interpolations in their own right (*pastillatum* for *pusillatum* instead of, correctly, *pusulatum*), some merely misprints (*indico* for *iudico*, and the like).[48] The significant thing about Budé's emendations was not their quality or correctness—it was the method which they sanctioned and publicized.

No less striking were the various contradictions in which Tribonian might be "caught napping," as Budé put it. Such was the irreconcilable pair of definitions of "veteran" and "novice" slaves, first noticed by

[46] *Ibid.*, f. 62^r (D, 1, 13, 1): "... 'argentum decoctum ochetae.' Which place I have been the first to restore, I think. In all copies one reads 'argentum et edoctum tetechae.' " Cf. f. 104^v, where he reprimands Barbaro for confusing "polluctores" with "pollinctores," and *De Asse*, f. 40^r ("divinare est non emendare").

[47] *Ibid.*, f. 121^r (D, 19, 1, 11) and f. 143^v (D, 19, 1, 25).

[48] *Ibid.*, f. 106^r (D, 16, 2, 17), about which Accursius' remark had been, "Edulitatis, id est famis"; f. 133^v (D, 19, 2, 31); and f. 152^r, where many more errors are listed. Budé's effect on modern scholarship has been slight. Mommsen accepts but one of Budé's many suggestions for "quanti" instead of "quanto" (f. 120^v, on D, 18, 1, 75); accepts "injuriosam" for "incuriosam" (f. 148^r, on D, 22, 1, 33) but credits it to Haloander, first humanist editor of the Digest (1529); accepts without comment "illuvie" for "ingluvie" (f. 140^r, on D, 21, 1, 12), "sequiores" for "deteriores" (f. 71^r, on D, 2, 15, 8), and "praeceptae" for "receptae" (f. 76^r on D, 4, 3, 11); and notes, without accepting, Budé's suggestion of "referre" instead of "deferre in commentarios" (f. 80^r, on D, 4, 6, 32), made on stylistic grounds, and "causa" for "casu" (f. 92^v, on D, 10, 4, 8), again attributed to Haloander. A good nineteenth-century editor would be forced to regard many of Budé's emendations as themselves "interpolations." Yet Mommsen's own notice of interpolations is very imperfect, according to P. Bonfante, *Storia del diritto romano* (Milan, 1959), II, 137.

Valla.[49] Ostensibly forbidden by Justinian, these *antinomiae* were practically unavoidable because of that "Trojan horse" of classical jurisprudence which until the sixth century admitted certain judicial opinion (the *responsa prudentum*) as a source of law. Before the coming of legal humanism this problem, too, had been neglected. The reason for this was not only because, as Budé argued, "many *antinomiae* cannot be understood without knowing many things of which Accursius was ignorant," but because medieval commentators, with their divinatory and desultory method (*interpretatione illa ariolatrice et desultoria levitate*), glossed over these differences with sophistry.[50] Budé, on the other hand, looked upon the *antinomiae* not as "dissonances" to be harmonized but as challenges to historical insight—and incidentally as evidence of the historical mutability of Roman law.

If Budé was critical of Tribonianism, he was outraged at Accursianism (*Accursianitas*). On this subject he adopted the bad manners as well as the bias of his philological forebears, which had the effect at least of enlivening his rather pedantic style. In the first place the glossators had violated Justinian's edict against interpretation (*contra enarratores*) which provided that henceforth there would be only brief "paratitles." What was worse, they were in his opinion the very incarnation of anti-intellectualism (*verborum contemptores, Priscianomastiges, obtrectatores humanitatis*). He denied these "barbarians" any claim to philosophy, "unless we call philosophers those who have mastered no philosophy, who are accustomed to forbid themselves and their students all those arts which show no immediate profit, and who thus have a minimal knowledge of all the authors."[51] (Listen to the resonant echo of this in the cry of one of Budé's admiring correspondents against "those fools who have studied less philosophy than a mule . . . , who have as much knowledge of the classics as a toad has feathers, although the law is full of those subjects and cannot be understood without them.") As a result, Budé continued, Roman laws "were propagated by men ignorant of Latin, and so it is not sur-

---

[49] *Ibid.*, f. 144v (D, 21, 1, 65); cf. Valla, *Elegantiae*, VI, 59 (*Opera*, I, 232).
[50] *Ibid.*, f. 17v.
[51] *Ibid.*, f. 3v. Cf. Rabelais, *Pantagruel*, II, 10, and Valla, *Antidoti in Poggium*, I (*Opera*, I, 273). See n. 35.

prising that they have been covered by many layers of errors, some permanent . . . , others correctible, unless one believes that the authority of Accursius is sacrosanct, which I, as a disciple of the ancient jurists and as a grammarian, am not accustomed to do."[52] The Digest in particular had become an intricate palimpsest which only the most skilled philologist could decipher.

Despite such freewheeling invective, it was in the critique of the scholastic reshaping of the Digest, especially as expressed in the Accursian Gloss, which was required reading for every law student, that Budé's historicism was most conspicuously displayed. The point is that while Budé lamented the "degeneration of jurisprudence from its ancient purity," he repeatedly argued that the deficiencies of medieval scholarship were, after all, the fault of the times rather than of the men (*temporum magis quam hominum ignorantia; ignorantia Acursii vel seculi potius Accursiani*).[53] Just as he admitted that his own achievement was due, at least in part, to the excellence of his "golden age," so, like Valla, he had the historical sensitivity to recognize scholastic jurisprudence as a cultural rather than an individual infirmity. Commonplace as such an admission may seem, it indicates an important feature of Renaissance historicism—the replacing of a narrow and unhistorical classicism by an attitude of relativism.

To forgive all, however, was not to understand all; and Budé did not let his compassion interfere with the job of clearing away the deposit of error left by the Accursian Gloss. This deposit was profuse, but in general it may be reduced to two types—errors of grammar and errors of fact, thus corresponding to the two faces of "history" itself.

---

[52] *Ibid.*, f. 151ᵛ (D, 22, 3, 28). There is no point in multiplying examples of such polemics against the Accursians which run all through the *Annotationes*, especially since they have been quoted so often by historians of legal humanism.

[53] *Ibid.*, f. 5ʳ, 40ʳ; *De Studio*, p. 16; *De Philologia*, p. 119. Cf. *Annotationes*, f. 58ᵛ: "Those whom I call Accursians are not such able men as Accursius, Bartolus, and others, who, men of singular industry if they had only lived in a more fortunate time, failed rather through the ignorance of the time than through their own, but those more stupid men who, ignorant of their authors, want their interpretations of the most involved passages of the Pandects to be believed blindly."

In the first place, classical vocabulary seemed quite beyond Accursius' ken. Defining *sella* as chariot instead of magistrate's chair, *exhedra* as window instead of attic, and *camera* as bedchamber, "which meaning Ulpian never knew," Budé added—these were only a few of his misconstructions. Nor was he much more familiar with "ancient legal terms," such as *legis actio* or *servitutem recipere*. Still more deplorable were Accursius' absurd etymologies, such as deriving the word for a legal claim (*vindiciae*) from the man Vindicius mentioned in the same passage or *metropolis* from measure (*mensura*), which had come to Accursius from Isidore of Seville by way of Gratian.[54] Like Valla, Budé objected to Accursius' arbitrary and artificial distinctions. From classical usage he showed, for example, that Ulpian's famous definition of law (*ars boni et aequi*) was really derived from a single concept, corresponding to the Greek equity (*epieikeia*).[55] As for the field of history itself, Accursius appeared to be utterly without bearings. His neglect of chronology led him to such misconceptions as confusing the senate with the centumviral court, his indifference to it to such inappropriate identifications as the Roman and pontifical colleges. Budé also exploded the legend, sanctified by canon law and perpetuated by the Gloss, about the Greek wise men who, coming to give laws to the Romans, made a gesture signifying the Christian trinity.[56] In almost every possible way, it seemed, Accursius had strayed from the historical sense.

From this it is clear that Budé's philological method required not only encyclopedic learning but a sense of anachronism. Far from being

[54] These are just a few characteristic examples: *Annotationes*, f. 88ʳ (D, 8, 3, 7), 91ᵛ (D, 9, 3, 5), 133ʳ (D, 19, 2, 19), 39ʳ (D, 1, 7, 4), 88ᵛ (D, 8, 4, 5), 18ʳ (D, 1, 2, 2), 64ʳ (D, 1, 16, 4). As Budé himself remarked, f. 133ʳ, "There are six hundred and more such [errors], which we do not think worth mentioning. For it is childish not to know them, not because of the predominance of learned men but because of the felicity of our times."

[55] On the subject of *epieikeia* see Guido Kisch, *Erasmus und die Jurisprudenz seiner Zeit* (Basel, 1960), presenting a critical edition of *Annotationes*, f. 1ʳ-10ᵛ (D, 1, 1, 1). Cf. (f. 76ᵛ) Budé's criticism of Accursius' "fourfold" interpretation of "allegat" (D, 4, 4, 18).

[56] Budé, *Annotationes*, f. 51ᵛ (D, 1, 1, 8), while Accursius had said, "Quasi centumviri, id est senatores" (D, 5, 2, 17; Code, 3, 31, 12, and 6, 28, 4); f. 5ᵛ; and f. 17ᵛ. The significance of the second passage was pointed out by E. Kantorowicz, *The Kings Two Bodies* (Princeton, 1957), p. 121.

an innovation of Renaissance scholarship, however, this was an essential feature of Roman legal science, which was obliged to classify certain laws, such as the Twelve Tables, as antiquated. While proclaiming his respect for antiquity (*antiquitatis reverentia*), Justinian had specifically instructed Tribonian not to include laws that had fallen into disuse (*in desuetudinem*).[57] Budé, too, recognized that some laws were obsolete (*de prisca nimis et obsoleta antiquitate*), but as usual he set this problem in a broader cultural context. The same process of obsolescence occurred in language, he suggested, and only the historian could do much to arrest it. "Those who collect old and unused words," he remarked, "are called antiquarians . . . , or, by the Greeks, philarchaists."[58] According to Pomponius, this kind of anachronism appeared in the writing of the jurist Tubero; in modern times, said Budé, it had been affected by such scholars as Theodore Gaza—and, he might well have added, by himself.

Budé's obsession with the vicissitudes of language, the true basis of his historicism, becomes most apparent in his discussion of Ciceronianism, which in spite of Erasmus' suspicions was not a doctrine that claimed his allegiance—he was not an "ape of Cicero"—but simply an issue that attracted his interest. It was also, which is more important, a standard of historical judgment. "Many words and phrases came into currency after Cicero," Budé observed at the beginning of one digression, "some of which I shall set down as they occur to me." So he recalled, for example, that "Quintilian and his contemporaries say 'praesumere,' while Cicero and his age say 'praecipere'"; or again that "it was only after the time of Cicero that the term 'fisc' acquired the meaning which it has today." Other words survived only in attenuated form, such as *justus*, which Leonardo Bruni had taken to mean exact but which had other connotations as well (true, full, etc.). "There are many old words," Budé concluded, "whose usage today should be multiple for those who want to recover the ingenuity of antiquity and restore it to our practice."[59] In general, Budé realized

[57] Again the reference is to Justinian's two edicts prefacing the Digest.

[58] Budé, *Annotationes*, f. 18ᵛ (D. 1, 2, 2). In general, see E. H. Gombrich, "The Debate on Primitivism in Ancient Rhetoric," *Journal of the Warburg and Courtauld Institutes*, XXIX (1966), 24-38.

[59] Budé, *Annotationes*, f. 110ʳ, 103ᵛ. Budé's Ciceronianist digressions may

that the transformations of vocabulary, archaisms as well as neologisms, constituted the most concrete evidence of historical change. His documentation of this point was to have a profound effect upon later scholarship, historical as well as legal and philological.

Medieval Studies

At one point Budé departed significantly from the Italian tradition of philology. This was in his adoption of a comparative method, which was to be characteristic of French scholarship throughout the century. In a deeper sense, no doubt, a comparatist point of view was inherent in French thought, since French society was the product of a confluence of alien cultures that had not quite lost their identities; but Budé's approach was much more self-consciously assumed. He followed Valla in accepting a Latin standard (*norma latina*), but in practice he made this a historical measure rather than a literary ideal. He despised modern jargon—he would have been horrified, for example, at being called a "humanist"—and yet he was fascinated with the vulgar counterparts of ancient terms. Like Valla he was disgusted at the Accursian practice of introducing barbarisms (such as *guerra* for *bellum*), and yet he continually made parallels between ancient institutions and those of modern France (*apud nos, hodie, ut nunc loquimur, vulgo* or *lingua vernacula dicimus*...).[60] This was the subject of his posthumously published *Forensia* as well as numerous asides in his *Annotations*.

---

be found in f. 26r-28v (D, 1, 2, 2) and f. 76v ff (D, 4, 4, 18). See Erasmus, *On Copia of Words and Ideas*, trans. D. B. King and H. D. Rix (Milwaukee, 1963), ch. XII (pp. 24-25), "The Words Peculiar to Different Ages." Notice that Budé, too, fancied himself a Biblical critic, and he pointed out a number of Nicolas of Lyra's "hallucinations" as he had done for Accursius. He had no more patience than Erasmus with those who regarded the Vulgate as superior to the Greek original. This was like saying of a tree that "the branches were superior to the trunk from which they sprang" (f. 31v)—or that the text of the Gloss was superior to the Florentine manuscript. So he tended to agree with Erasmus that the Bible in its present Latin form could hardly be attributed to Jerome. In 1516 he offered his notes on the New Testament to Erasmus (Allen, II, 227-33) and later inserted them in the revised edition of his *Annotationes*, especially f. 31v and 141v.

[60] *Ibid.*, 118r (D, 18, 1, 1), complaining about the use of such "sesqui-

In these discussions of comparative law and institutions Budé never found a wholly consistent point of view; that is, he could not quite decide (as a modern) what his relation to antiquity was—or (as a Frenchman) what it ought to be. Sometimes, when his religious or political convictions were not at stake, Budé pretended to recognize in contemporary society certain "vestiges of ancient custom." It was with this in mind that he compared the Roman *gentilitas* with the French *noblesse*, *mancipium* with *seizin*, *insignia* with *arma*, *formula* with *stilus*, *praefectus* or *tribunus militum* with the *marechal* (though he was aware of the Germanic root of the word), and the ancient *colonus* with the villein.[61] Unfortunately, in his distaste for barbarism Budé sometimes fell into a kind of anachronism the reverse of Accursius', that is, replacing vulgar terms with their supposed classical equivalents. In this way he tried to disguise feudal law, that eyesore of European society which medieval jurists persisted in honoring as "Roman." After making a superficial analogy with the ancient *patrocinium*, Budé concluded that feudalism (*nostra feudorum consuetudo*) "arose from the relation of client to patron, wherefore I usually apply the Latin term 'clients' to those called vassals and 'clientele' to that relation and ceremony called 'homage.'"[62] This surrender to classicist bias, which at the same time was a violation of the philological method, was one of the rare instances in which Budé came under fire by the next generation of legal scholars.

For the most part, however, Budé was protected from the fallacies of classicism by his nominalist cast of mind and by his Gallican ideology. He borrowed Valla's philological tools, in short, without accepting his monolithic Romanism. He shared his love of elegance without agreeing with his apotheosis of antiquity. It was natural that Budé, as a spokesman for French culture and as a declared foe of those

---

pedalian" words as "legista," "canonista," and "ultramontanus"; and f. 7ᵛ, referring to Valla, *Elegantia*, IV, 64 (*Opera*, I, 144). That the *Forensia* (Paris, 1544), devoted to such discussions of comparative legal terminology, was Budé's has been shown by E. Armstrong, *Robert Estienne* (Cambridge, 1954), p. 113, in spite of Delaruelle's doubts.

[61] *Ibid.*, f. 20ʳ ff.

[62] *Ibid.*, f. 146ʳ (D, 21, 2, 63). On this see my "De Origine Feudorum," *Speculum*, XXXIX (1964), 218, and ch. VII.

renegades (*Francomastiges, Gallomastiges*) who turned against their own heritage, should have stood with the moderns in their age-old quarrel with the ancients.[63] Not only did he reject the mindless mimesis of the rigid Ciceronians, but he was suitably impressed by two of the three principal exhibits of the modernist party. He does not seem to have been interested in the new geographic discoveries (which after all reflected little honor upon the French monarchy), but he celebrated the "unheard-of" developments in military science (*res inauditas . . . ut machinas belli*) and in book-making (*l'invention des impressions, qui est l'instauration et perpetuation de l'antiquité*), which, as he later told his son, had made such great advances in his own lifetime. What pleased Budé most was the prospect for learning. "Since we see in our age letters restored to life . . . ," he asked, "what prevents us from expecting to see among us new Demosthenes, Platos, Thucydides, Ciceros, and other contemporaries, not only imitators but emulators of these?"[64] This view constitutes not only one of the roots of the "idea of progress" but one of the most prominent signs of Renaissance historicism.

Given Budé's perspective, it is not surprising that he often took a greater interest in French institutions than in their ancient counterparts. The roman *praetor*, for example, reminded him of the French chancellor, and he went on to trace this office from its "most ancient" (that is, twelfth-century) origins down to modern times. He took up also one of the favorite topics of historians, the peers of France, which he compared to the Roman patricians; and discussion of the word *libellus* led him to consider the French *arrêt* and the office of *maître des requêtes,* which he later came to hold. His comments on the Roman *scrinium* introduced the subject of the royal *trésor des chartes,* of which his family had long held the charge and of which Budé himself was one of the first to make critical use. In these monographic digressions Budé relied not only on his administrative experience but also on historians, including Paolo Emilio and the chronicles of St. Denis, and on archival records, especially in the *trésor des chartes.* Ex-

---

[63] Budé, *De Asse,* f. 141r, 170r, *passim.*

[64] Budé, *De Philologia,* pp. 226 ff, and *Institution du prince,* p. 63. Cf. *Epistolae,* f. 44v (to Dreux Budé, 8 May 1519).

amining these documents and puzzling over their "ancient script" aroused Budé's antiquarian instinct. He referred to one of them, the journal of Pierre Barrière, as an "image of antiquity," the same phrase he had applied to the Twelve Tables.[65] In fact, Budé treated the monuments of the French monarchy with the same archeological enthusiasm—and some of the same philological acumen—as he did the Digest itself.

Perhaps the most interesting of Budé's essays in comparative institutional history was his discussion of the parlement of Paris, to which he was led in the course of his commentary on the Roman senate and centumviral court and on Accursius' careless confusion of the two. This was to be one of the primary targets of historical research in the sixteenth century. Budé compared the French and Roman courts and the Greek areopagus in terms of composition, jurisdiction, and procedure and then went on to present a voluminously documented study of the parlement, its original constitution, and its later development. Although Budé believed that the parlement had the same origin as other French councils, that is, the king's *curia,* he insisted that the parlement was unique. "It has everything," he argued, "that is in the senate and the centumvirate as far as jurisdiction and power are concerned." Except for "accidental resemblances," however, he concluded that it was an error—an anachronism—to identify the parlement of Paris with either of the Roman institutions.[66] In general, Budé assumed that most institutions, ancient and modern, were unique if not autochthonous. Here is another axiom of Renaissance historicism.

In this rather haphazard fashion Budé began to apply the new science of philology to the vulgar and vernacular problems of medieval history. The result was not only to widen the range and to deepen the perspective of historical inquiry but, through the insistence on encyclopedic preparation, to improve historical method. Budé's researches —his pioneering work in the history of French institutions as well as his classical studies—were fully appreciated by later generations of philologists, jurists, and historians. So were his views on philology

---

[65] Budé, *Annotationes,* f. 59ᵛ (D, 1, 11, 1), 52ᵛ (D, 1, 8, 8), 67ʳ (D, 1, 16, 9), and 68ʳ (cf. n. 38).
[66] *Ibid.,* f. 40ʳ ff (D, 1, 9, 12).

and his defense of modernism. Budé provided not only a model but a valuable lesson for his successors—that whatever aid might be derived from classical scholarship, modern society had to be investigated and interpreted in its own terms. The nature of any culture, ancient or modern, he taught, could be grasped neither through philosophic categories nor even classical parallels, but only through an intense effort of encyclopedic learning and historical understanding. The proper attitude, consequently, was one of temporal and cultural relativism. In these various ways, while remaining faithful to the legacy of Valla, Budé helped to lay the foundation of medieval studies.

From Budé to Le Roy

In the sixteenth century Budé's influence was profuse and pervasive. His work was respected by Protestants as well as Catholics, by propagandists as well as philologists. Aside from jurisprudence, he left a significant imprint upon Roman antiquities, especially numismatics, on the study of French institutions, and on Greek lexicography. His criticisms of the papacy and of judicial corruption were widely cited, and so were his advertisements for French culture. Above all, he was identified with the new science of philology and the promises it held out for the future of humanity. The focus here has been upon the contribution made by Budé to legal humanism. But before resuming this central theme, it will be appropriate to suggest in a more general fashion the effects of Budé's views upon historical thought and to anticipate some of the transformations which the philological tradition would undergo in the less fortunate but more sophisticated age of the later sixteenth century. The most economical way of going about this, one of the most illuminating as well, is to consider the work of one of Budé's most faithful disciples, who preserved many of the master's ideals and attitudes but at the same time adapted them to the new problems and new intellectual climate of his own age. This disciple was Louis le Roy, who was at once the heir to and the chronicler of the ideal of encyclopedic humanism.[67]

[67] Suffice it now to refer to W. Gundersheimer, *The Life and Works of Louis de Roy* (Geneva, 1967), and the bibliography there cited.

Between Budé and Le Roy there was a barrier not only of class but of two generations and a whole world of experience; yet there were a number of striking ties. At about the age of thirty Le Roy began his literary career with a biography of Budé (1540) and ended (in 1577) as professor of Greek in the College Royal which Budé reputedly had helped to found. Like Budé he had attended the University of Paris and had studied law before turning to philology. No legal scholar himself, Le Roy fully appreciated Budé's role as "the first man to uncover civil law," and he later noted his preference for the humanist method of his friend Connan over the scholastic approach of his teachers at the University of Toulouse. Like Budé, too, he concentrated on Hellenic studies, especially on that "noble" but neglected science of politics. Besides translations from Plato and Aristotle and (at the request of Charles IX) part of Budé's *Philology*, he wrote various pamphlets in response to the challenge of the civil wars, defending Gallicanism and the principle of monarchy. But Le Roy's masterpiece was his last, hardly finished book, which a modern scholar has called "the first treatise devoted to the history of civilization," his *Vicissitude or Variety of Things in the Universe* ("and," the title continues, "the concurrence of arms and letters by the first and most illustrious nations of the world since civilization began until the present").[68] This work, which sums up Le Roy's conception of history, reverberates with echos of Budé's discussion of human culture—and indeed may be taken as a popularization and continuation of it.

Toward history itself Le Roy ostensibly took a naïvely utilitarian view, expressed by the Ciceronian (and Budaean) representation of history as a repository of examples (*historia plena exemplorum; histoire plein d'exemples*). "The memory and knowledge of the past," Le Roy declared, "is the instruction of the present and the warning of the future."[69] As early as 1559 he thought of turning his hand to this subject, and not long after that he was given a commission by Catherine

---

[68] A. Lefranc, "Le traité 'De la vicissitude ou variété des choses' de Louis le Roy et sa véritable date," *Mélanges Lanson* (Paris, 1922). Le Roy's *Traité de la venerie* (Paris, 1861) is a translation of part of book II of Budé's *De Philologia*.

[69] Louis le Roy, *La Vicissitude des choses* (Paris, 1584), f. 247^r, 254^r.

de' Medici, though he never went beyond a perfunctory "design," arranged according to the chief institutions of the monarchy and displaying the influence of Seyssel. The fact is that Le Roy, like Budé, looked at history less as a branch of knowledge than as an approach to human culture in general. Thus he opened his pamphlet on the *Differences and Troubles of Men due to the Diversity of Opinions in Religion* with a historical sketch of the Reformation; he prefaced his translation of Plato's *Phaedo* with a short history of ancient philosophy and his translation of Aristotle's *Politics* with a survey of the history of political philosophy.[70] It was only natural, then, that his major book should attempt to place human culture in general in historical perspective. What for Budé had been the basis for an historical method, namely the "encyclopedia," became for Le Roy the very substance of history.

Le Roy lived much of his life during the fratricidal conflicts of the religious wars, and his work is filled with lamentations about these. Like Budé he noted that scholarship was not nearly so well rewarded as it had been in antiquity, a conclusion reinforced in his case by years of poverty. Yet he never lost Budé's euphoric feeling of belonging to a uniquely blessed age. "What prevents us from expecting to see new Demosthenes, Platos . . . ," Budé had asked; and Le Roy's answer was given without hesitation—"nothing." [71] In his opinion "the restitution of languages and of all disciplines" had begun in the early fifteenth century, but the harvest time was his own age. The two greatest names were Budé and Erasmus, equal in stature, though the

---

[70] Le Roy, *Consideration sur l'histoire françois et l'universelle de ce temps* (Paris, 1568), and "Project ou dessein du royaume de France, pour en representer en dix livres l'estat entiere," in *Exhortation aux françois pour vivre en concorde* (Paris, 1570), outlining a wide-ranging institutional history of France (ancient Gaul, the Frankish kingdom, "police," the Gallican church, the court, ceremonies, offices, economic basis, jurisdiction, and the nobility constitute the ten topics); *Des differens et troubles advenans entre les hommes par la diversité des opinions en la religion* (Paris, 1562); "L'origine, progres et perfection de la philosophie . . .," in *La Phedon de Platon* (Paris, 1553); and *De l'origine, antiquité, progres, excellence, et l'utilité de l'art politique* (Paris, 1567). To Le Roy, it seems, the historical form came naturally.

[71] Le Roy, *Le Phedon*, p. 14; cf. Budé, *De Philologia*, p. 226. In general, see H. Baron, "The *Querelle* of the Ancients and the Moderns as a Problem for Renaissance Scholarship," *JHI*, XX (1959), 3-22.

former was devoted more to utility, the latter to delectation. As for the future, Le Roy had still more extravagant hopes than Budé, believing that the plenitude of nature guaranteed that the moderns would continue to surpass the ancients. This was more than a prediction, it was a moral imperative. "It is necessary to do for posterity," Le Roy wrote, "what antiquity has done for us."[72]

According to Le Roy, however, the sixteenth century was only one of a number of "heroic ages"—a term applied by Cicero (and again by Budé) to fifth-century Athens.[73] Given a certain economic level to provide leisure for study and given a certain political success, every nation could attain comparable excellence; indeed, in Le Roy's reading of history, sooner or later every nation did. If there had been a "translation of empire," there had been a translation of virtue as well, and it followed precisely the same course—from the Medes to the Persians, Greeks, Romans, and finally to France, Spain, Germany, England, and other modern nations. Arms and letters, Le Roy assumed, always tended to rise and fall together; Minerva, in Budé's fanciful terms, was accompanied by Mars. Like Budé, Le Roy had a primitive notion of culture, in which arts and letters had a kind of organic unity and a recognizable style. He assumed, too, that each nation had a unique character (*chacune nation a ses graces et singularitez particulieres*) and changed according to a biological pattern, corresponding to human development through infancy, adolescence, maturity, and old age. This was so at least with Rome, England, and France, as shown respectively by Seneca, Polydore Vergil, and Seyssel.[74] Out of such conventional notions Le Roy assembled something resembling a theory or morphology of cultural history.

In some quarters Le Roy has had a reputation as a herald of the

[72] Le Roy, *La Vicissitude*, f. 255ʳ, and also *La Phedon*, p. 16. On the comparison of Budé and Erasmus, see *Vita Budaei*, p. 29.

[73] *Ibid.*, f. 61ᵛ; cf. Budé, *De Studio*, p. 10.

[74] *Ibid.*, f. 20ʳ. Cf. *Exhortation*, p. 12: "Virtue had its first seat in Assyria, whence it was transported to the Medes, then to Persia and to Greece, finally . . . to Rome; and if after the fall of the Roman empire it seemed not to have lasted very long . . ., in recompense it was extended into different places, such as France, Spain, Germany, England, Poland, Muscovy, and the empire of the Turks. . . ." This is clearly an adaptation of the idea of *translatio imperii.* Cf. H. Levin, *The Overreacher* (Cambridge, Mass., 1952), p. 33.

Baconian conception of progress. Certainly, he placed great emphasis upon the novelties of his age—"new seas, new types of men, manners, laws, customs . . . ," and he was confident that further novelties would appear in the course of time.[75] What is most remarkable about his arguments, however, is not their originality but the intensity and conviction with which he defended the superiority, or at least the uniqueness, of the modern age. Like Budé he opposed the "slavery" of literal imitation of the ancients, and he celebrated the invention of printing and (with reservations) of the new techniques of war. But Le Roy went further. Moved by the vernacularist enthusiasm of the mid-sixteenth century, he paid direct homage to his national tradition by writing—and even lecturing at the university— in French (*a la decoration de la langue françoise*). Indeed, while he helped to spread knowledge of antiquity, he expressed some doubt about the desirability of spending a lifetime, as he and Budé had done, in ancient languages. Nowadays, he warned, it was no longer possible to master even a single discipline, not to speak of a whole "encyclopedia." In any case, he added, practical experience was quite as important as book-learning.[76] Was it not precisely this which set the modern apart from the ancients?

Yet whether or not Le Roy actually espoused an "idea of progress" no longer seems as crucial for his historical thought as it did two generations ago. More significant than his expectations for the future was his conception of the process of change to which civilization was subject. His topic, after all, was not "the advancement of learning" but "the vicissitude and variety of things"; and the dominant feature of his work was not optimism, which represented only one mood and applied to only one phase of the development he traced, but rather his sense of cultural variation and change. "There is nothing under the eternal heavens that has a beginning that does not have an end," he declared, "nothing that grows that does not diminish, being subject to corruption and mutation according to the time ordered by the course of nature . . . This instability is found also in provinces,

---

[75] *Ibid.*, f. 215^r.

[76] *Ibid.*, 251^r. The celebration of "experience," one of the leading themes of Le Roy's work, appears also in the autobiographical passages of *Le Sympose de Platon* (Paris, 1559), p. 180.

cities, manners, laws, empires, republics, principalities, lordships, families, arts, and languages."[77] Although Le Roy represented this process in the conventional terms of Aristotelian philosophy, he organized his analysis along comparative and historical lines. He lacked Bodin's transcendent impulse: he was interested less in finding a universal pattern than simply in exhibiting the plenitude and vitality of civilization.

Le Roy was encouraged by his theme and method to adopt an attitude of relativism which, reinforced by the tragic events as well as the discoveries of his age, quite surpassed that of Budé. His vision of history was, indeed, dialectical. "Everything down here is full of contradiction," he remarked. "What is good in one time is bad in another; what is holy here is profane there . . . ; the corruption of one thing is the generation of another."[78] Le Roy's reaction was to assume a kind of historical tolerance very similar to that of Bodin or of Montaigne. Of the ancients, for example, although they were clearly inferior to the moderns, he conceded that "they knew all that it was possible for them to know in their time." He allowed for geographic variation, too, and like Bodin hoped to understand "the diversity of things in terms of the difference of places."[79] In these various ways Le Roy's work represents a most conspicuous illustration of Renaissance historicism.

Yet it was not Le Roy who carried on most fruitfully the original work to which Budé had contributed so heroically. At best he provided a popular expression—literally a vulgarization—of the ideals of philology and the intersection with historiography. It was left to other scholars, reacting a bit from Budé's literary values and yet in closer agreement with his philological goals, to push further his pioneering investigations in classical and medieval studies. Among these the most prominent were a group of jurists, contemporary with Le Roy, who inherited the tradition of legal humanism and who may be regarded as the first historical school of law.

---

[77] Le Roy, *Les Politiques d'Aristote* (Paris, 1600), p. 377; cf. *La Vicissitude*, f. 47r, and Claude de Seyssel, *La Monarchie de France*, ed. J. Poujol (Paris, 1961), p. 108.

[78] Le Roy, *Des differens*, p. 12.

[79] Le Roy, *La Vicissitude*, f. 15r and 121v.

Andreas prisco reddit sua jura nitori ,
Consultosque facit doctius inde loqui .

ANDREA ALCIATO (T. de Bry, *Icones et effigies virorum doctorum*) Courtesy of the Bibliothèque Nationale, Paris

The Historical School of Roman Law: Andrea Alciato and His Disciples Discover Legal History

> Necessarium itaque nobis videtur, ipsius juris originem atque processum demonstrare.
>
> Pomponius, *De Origine juris civilis*
> (Digest, 1, 2, 2)

"IT HAS BEEN my honor," boasted Andrea Alciato, "to teach civil law in a Latin manner for the first time in a thousand or more years, and by my example I have drawn others after me." [1] An exaggeration, no doubt, and yet it indicates well enough the role, whether actual or symbolic, which this Italian jurist played in the founding of the historical school of law in sixteenth-century France. Alciato was neither as original as Budé nor as learned as Jacques Cujas, but as the man who introduced the historical method into university education, he was as influential as either. The significance of his accomplishment was twofold. First, he took a step toward the reconciliation of philology and the legal profession, which was to be essential for the future of legal scholarship. Second, he helped to indoctrinate a whole new generation with the ideals and the methods of the new "reformed jurisprudence." It was largely the intellectual progeny of Alciato in France—"the new sect of Alciato," as one hostile observer called it—that introduced legal humanism into the study of history

---

[1] Andrea Alciato, *Paradoxa juris civilis*, "proeemium," in *Opera omnia* (4 vols., Frankfurt, 1617), IV, col. 1.

itself.[2] This transition from the historical study of law to the investigation of legal and institutional history forms the subject of the present chapter.

The History of Law

As a form of public memory, law appeared to be historical by its very nature; men did not have to read Budé to suspect this truth. But professional lawyers tended to look upon their texts as expressions of, or at least approximations of, a single unchanging code of ideals, and so it was left up to humanist jurists to begin tracing the actual development of laws and institutions. In a general way this arose from the humanist fascination with origins and with the "first begetters of things." According to Polydore Vergil, the reason for this was partly commemorative and partly didactic—"partly that no one should be unjustly praised and partly that those who wish to follow examples should know whom to imitate."[3] More specifically, as we have seen, humanist interest in the history of law was a reaction to the utilitarian values and categorical judgments of scholasticism. This attitude may be traced all the way back to that archetypal humanist, Petrarch himself, who acquired his distaste for medieval jurisprudence at the University of Bologna. "The majority of our jurists," he later complained, "caring little or nothing for the origins of law and the first fathers of jurisprudence, or anything except professional gain . . . , did not believe that knowledge of the arts and of literature would be of use. . . ."[4] Such was the challenge taken up by philologists of the fifteenth and sixteenth centuries.

---

[2] Alberico Gentili, *De Juris interpretibus dialogi sex* (London, 1582), p. 4 ("Scaevola"). An early sympathetic account of this school is "De Jurisprudentiae dignitate" (1578) by Le Douaren's student, Nicolas Cisner, in his *Opuscula* (Frankfurt, 1611), pp. 536-45.

[3] Polydore Vergil, *De Rerum inventoribus* (Basel, 1536), "praefatio."

[4] Petrarch, *Epistolae de rebus familiaribus*, III, 18. On the "precursors" of the historical school in general, see P. F. Girard, "Les préliminaires de la renaissance du droit romain," *RHDFE*, sér. 4, I (1922), 5-46, and D. Maffei, *Gli Inizi dell'umanesimo giuridico* (Milan, 1546), as well as Dante dal Re, *I Precursori italiani di una nuova scuola di diritto romano nel secolo XV* (Rome, 1878), and the classic summary in the last volume of Savigny's *Geschichte des römischen Rechts im Mittelalter*.

The philological assault upon Roman law illustrated at once the expansion of humanism beyond its original literary confines and one aspect of what has been called civic humanism. Among the precursors of legal humanism were Ambrogio Camaldolese, who showed a strong preference for the elegance of ancient jurists over the ignorance of modern commentators, and his friend Niccolò Niccoli, who was interested enough in the Digest to have copied out certain Greek passages. More important was Valla's friend Maffeo Vegio, who reversed the classic pattern of Petrarch by turning from poetry to the study of law and who wrote the first in a long series of humanist commentaries on the Digest title "on the meaning of words" (*De verborum significatione*). Carrying on the same enterprise but in a different category were the antiquarians, who studied Roman law mainly as a source for ancient history. "As the soul is superior to the body," declared Pomponio Leto, "so history is superior to other bequests, and claims for itself the mightiest part of wisdom."[5] Leto's work on the "Magistrates, priests, jurists, and laws of the Romans" was, in Savigny's opinion, the first book that deserves to be called a legal history. A similar work, *On the Power of the Romans,* was written by his Florentine contemporary Andrea Fiocchi. Best known of all, however, was Flavio Biondo, who wrote on this subject both in his *Rome Triumphant* and in his essay, "Warfare and Jurisprudence." Long before the sixteenth century, then, humanist scholarship had begun to consider Roman law from a historical point of view.

But the true starting point of legal history was not merely a vague appreciation for classical jurisprudence or a passing interest in Roman offices and institutions. It was, to be precise, that corrupt and fragmentary title "On the origin of law" (*De origine juris*) taken from the work of Pomponius. Indeed, what was nominally the first history of Roman law, published by the French jurist Aymar du Rivail in 1515, was little more than an elaboration of this title, controlled to

---

[5] Pomponio Leto, letter to Francesco Borgia prefacing his "Romanae historiae compendium," in *Opera ... varia* (Mainz, 1521), f. 2ʳ; his "De Romanorum magistratibus, sacerdotiis, jurisperitis, et legibus" appears in ff. 55ʳ-70ᵛ. Cf. Fiocchi, *De Potestate Romanorum libri II* (Antwerp, 1561), in whose prefatory letter the phrase *fides historiae* once again appears, and the work of Biondo (cited ch. II, n. 56).

some degree by Livy's history. Du Rivail organized his book with the help of Aristotle's threefold division of constitutional forms, arranged to parallel the major sources of law. First came a discussion of the laws of the Roman kings. Next he took up the "timocratic" period, beginning with the expulsion of Tarquin, the laws of the people, and the plebiscita. "Thirdly," he continued, "the Roman republic accepted the rule of the Senate over the city because of the difficulty of convening the whole people, and so arose the third species of government under control of the optimates, which Aristotle called democracy," and which saw the creation of the pretorian edicts and the *senatusconsulta.* Lastly, there was the Empire and the imperial decrees, including also the decisions of the great jurists.[6] Although Du Rivail had few of the tools and none of the graces of humanism, his work does provide a clear illustration of the "historicization" of law in the sixteenth century.

Du Rivail's work is a curiosity. Much more significant were the humanist exegeses of the Digest, shapeless and pedantic as they were. The most comprehensive commentary "On the origin of law" was written by Budé's contemporary Zasius, who followed the spirit and sometimes (as Budé himself complained) the letter of Budé's *Annotations.* Unlike Budé, Zasius wrote as a professional jurist and even followed the old Bartolist style of commentary, though by no means sticking to their opinions. Yet he had quite obviously learned the lessons of legal humanism. He indulged in the conventional praises of philology and in the equally conventional denouncements of Tribonian and of Accursius. Like Budé he discussed the problem of anachronism, giving additional examples from classical authors, and he made even more extensive use of historical information (*fides historiarum*). Perhaps the most fundamental principle of Zasius' method was his concern with the "origin of law," which again he construed in a historical rather than a legal sense. Great rivers often flowed from very small sources, he explained and so it was with law, which gradually emerged from practice (*lex ex facto oritur*).[7] This, too, suggests a shift from a

---

[6] Aymar du Rivail, *Historia juris civilis* (Mainz, 1530), pp. 2-3, 15, 26, 247, and 321. This work was republished in *Tractatus,* I, f. 3r-25v. On this see E. von Moeller, *Aymar du Rivail, der erste Rechtshistoriker* (Berlin, 1907).

[7] Zasius, *Paratitla,* in *Operum omnium* (2 vols., Lyon, 1550), I, col. 17 (on

philosophic point of view, in which the "source" of law was reason itself, to a historical point of view, in which law arose from specific human customs.

The study of customary law, which was to play so important a part in the field of legal history, was pursued by Zasius most directly in his monograph on feudalism. Like Budé he answered the question of feudal origins by pointing to the ancient clientele, and he found the link with European society in the Roman *militia*. But even here Zasius seems to have recognized the individuality of European customs, for he added that fiefs "emerged in the course of time, which transcends all."[8] In general, this question of the "origin of fiefs" remained on the frontiers of legal scholarship, waiting to be explored by a younger and somewhat more open-minded generation. What is significant is that Zasius helped to open this question to the techniques of philology.

In promoting this, Zasius was joining forces not only with Budé, who had preceded him, but with a man who was at once the third member of the great "triumvirate" of legal humanism and the primary link with the next generation of scholars. This was Andrea Alciato, who in 1518, when he was just twenty-six and Budé fifty years of age, made his entry both into the republic of letters and into French academic society. At this point he becomes the protagonist of our story.

Humanist Jurisprudence

If Guillaume Budé was the Columbus of the historical exploration of Roman law, he was also, like that rather uncertain navigator, soon surpassed in his achievements. Yet Budé left not only a legend but a

---

"De Origine juris"). In his monumental *Commentaria* on this title (*ibid.*, col. 270-363) Zasius' dependence upon Budé is made clear, as in his criticism of the legend about the trinity (col. 279) perpetuated by Accursius, in his attack on Tribonian (col. 308), and in his criticism of Accursius' error of identifying "fasces" and "menses" (col. 302), though in the latter case Zasius failed to given credit to Budé (cf. *Annotationes*, f. 68ᵛ). Zasius agreed with Budé (col. 297) that "a jurist should have a knowledge not only of universal civil law . . . but also of philosophy, especially moral, dialectic, oratory, and above all Latin style . . ."; but it should be noted that Zasius subordinated the "encyclopedia" to the science of law. See also the "Epilogus historiae de origine et progressu iuris . . .," in Johannes Oldendorp's commentary on this same title (Lyon, 1551), p. 108 ff.

[8] Zasius, *Usus feudorum epitome* (Lyon, 1556), pp. 3-4, and *Commentaria*,

legacy of considerable proportions. By the time of his death in 1540 the methods and attitudes which he had made famous had inspired a new school of legal scholarship. This was shown both in the infiltration of certain law faculties by philology and in growing cries of dismay from the Bartolist camp, beginning with Matteo Gribaldi's *Method of Studying Law* (1541) and culminating in Alberico Gentili's *Interpreters of Law* (1582). Besides rejecting Budé's vaunted encyclopedia and denying the value either of Greek or of the Florentine manuscript, Gentili, in his dialogue "Pomponius," criticized at length the historical interpretation of law.[9] In France, too, legal humanism had its critics; and Étienne Forcadel, with a professional arrogance hardly in keeping with his modest accomplishments or with his literary affectations, set the "patricians" of the old school above the "plebean" grammarians.[10] By the second half of the sixteenth century, in short, philology had become a real threat to the profession of law. How had this come about?

Although Budé shared some of the blame, in fact the "French method of teaching law"—the *mos gallicus juris docendi* as distinguished from the old-fashioned *mos italicus*—was none of his doing. A promoter, even a prophet, he may have been; a teacher he was not. Nor, despite the urging of friends throughout Europe, did he ever manage to finish his work on the Digest. Growing "a bit disgusted" with the subject and with secular learning in general, Budé decided to leave the task to a younger generation. One scholar in particular caught his eye, as he told Vives and Longueil in 1520. The next year Budé wrote directly to this scholar and informed him of his commission:

---

col. 273-74. On Zasius in general, see G. Kisch, *Humanismus und Jurisprudenz* (Basel, 1955), and R. Stinzing, *Ulrich Zasius* (Basel, 1857).

[9] Alberico Gentili, *De Juris interpretibus,* pp. 73, 92, 157, *passim*. Gribaldi's "De Methodo ac ratione studiendi in jure" may be found in N. Reusner (ed.), *Cynosure juris* (Speyer, 1588), pp. 110-17. In general, see G. Astuti, *Mos italicus e mos gallicus nei dialoghi "De juris interpretibus" di Alberico Gentili* (Bologna, 1937).

[10] Etienne Forcadel, *Sphaera legalis* (Lyon, 1569), p. 71. See P. Mesnard, "Un rival heureux de Cujas et de Jean Bodin: Etienne Forcadel," *ZSSRG,* Rom. Abt., LXVII (1950), 440-58. Forcadel was also the author of a fanciful history of France (Trojan origins and all), *De Gallorum imperio et philosophia* (Paris, 1579).

I perceive that you are capable of equalling and surpassing what I have begun in this century, the revelation of the corrupt and hidden meaning of the Pandects. . . . At the same time I am encouraged by the oath and testimony of the most eminent men, who grant you by merit many excellent and singular talents. If you have all these, then I desire the glory of this task for you.[11]

The man addressed by Budé was the young Italian jurist Andrea Alciato, whom Budé had met only two years before. Alciato was very conscious of belonging to a new school of jurisprudence. He gave credit to certain teachers, especially to Giasone del Maino, and praised Poliziano as the one who "first restored the Digest to light";[12] but his main inspiration came from elsewhere, above all from Erasmus and from such German humanists as Beatus Rhenanus and the Amerbachs. Although he later broke with the cause of religious reform, for a time he fought the same good fight as these men. He was also aware of his debts to Budé, yet he was far from being a docile disciple. Like Erasmus he was somewhat put off by Budé's vanity and by the insufferable French attitude that "none but Budé had a knowledge of literature." [13] The factor of plagiarism, a perennially explosive issue among fame-hungry philologists, also created ill-feeling between the two scholars, each charging the other with having leaned a bit too heavily upon his published works (Alciato upon Budé's *De Asse* as well as the *Anno-*

[11] Budé, *Epistolae*, f. 66ᵛ (to Alciato, 17 Mar. 1521). Cf. f. 97ʳ (to Tunstall in 1517), f. 10ʳ (to Vives in 1520), and f. 55ᵛ (to Longueil in 1520). Budé had expressed doubts (f. 19ʳ) about continuing his work as early as 1511, in a letter to another legal humanist, Nicolas Bérault.

[12] Andrea Alciato, *Praetermissa*, II, and *Parerga juris*, V, 26 (*Opera*, IV, 227, 368-69). The best biography is still P. Viard, *André Alciat 1492-1550* (Paris, 1926), but it must be supplemented by the recent studies of G. L. Barni and especially of R. Abbondanza (see his bibliography in *Dizionario biografico degli italiani*). Also important is Barni (ed.), *Le Lettere di Andrea Alciato giureconsulto* (Florence, 1953), but it must be corrected by the reviews of Abbondanza in *Annali di storia del diritto*, I (1957), 467-500, and of G. Kisch, in *Tijdschrift voor Rechtsgeschiedenis*, XXIV (1956), 222-26.

[13] Hartmann, III, 407 (1 Mar. 1529). Budé's complaints of unacknowledged borrowings appears in *Epistolae*, f. 56ʳ (to Longueil, 21 Feb. 1520); Alciato defended himself in a letter of 21 Dec. 1520 (Barni, pp. 18 ff), and later presented his own grievances (Hartmann, III, 288, 26 Dec. 1527). In general, see D. Bianchi, "L'Opera letteraria e storica di Andrea Alciato," *Archivio storico lombardo*, XX (1913), 5-130, and G. Gueudet, "Une lettre inédite de Budé à Alciato," *Moreana*, 19-20 (1968), 70-90.

tations, and Budé, in his revised *Annotations*, upon Alciato's commentaries). Still, Alciato did not deny Budé's pioneering role, and at the
end of his life he was proud to claim a position between those "men
of eternal fame," Erasmus and Budé.[14]

Alciato's own scholarly credentials were most impressive. Erasmus
saw in him the most complete synthesis of eloquence and learning
since Cicero's friend Crassus, who had become a kind of symbol of
legal humanism.[15] Having shown his inclination toward philology in
1515 with his *Annotations on the Code* and having taken his doctorate
the following year at Bologna, Alciato made a spectacular debut into
the world of humanism with three critical miscellanies in the tradition
of Poliziano and Crinito. These were the *Paradoxes of Civil Law,*
dealing with a number of conventional and controversial topics; the
Dispunctiones, devoted to the restitution of the Digest, following the
trail blazed by Poliziano and Budé; and the *Praetermissa*, treating
various linguistic questions in the law. As a result, he was called that
year to the University of Avignon, where he began his great commentary "On the meaning of words" (*De verborum significatione*) and
where he encountered Budé. Ten years later, at the height of his fame
and perhaps through the good offices of Budé, he came to the University of Bourges, where he began another of his fundamental philological works, the *Parerga*. In France he was looked upon not only as
a distinguished guest but as a prize taken from the Emperor. One of
his lectures was attended by the King himself, who could boast of
few successes in those years.[16]

By this time Alciato was widely regarded as the leader of the new
school of jurisprudence. Not only did he display most of the characteristics of legal humanism which we have come to recognize, but to
judge from some of his writings, notably his youthful history of Milan
and his letter in praise of history (*encomium historiae*), he had a

[14] Alciato, "Ad P. Jovium epistola," (1549), in Giovio's *Historiae sui temporis* (Venice, 1553). This letter, which does not appear in Barni, was reconstructed by Giovio, according to V. Cian, "Lettere inediti di Andrea Alciato
a Pietro Bembo," *Archivio storico lombardico*, VII (1890), 829-844.

[15] Erasmus, *Ciceronianus*, in *Opera omnia* (Leiden, 1703), col. 1010.

[16] Alciato, "Oratiuncula, cum Christianissimus Gallorum rex Franciscus Va-
lesius lectionis suas adesset, habita," in *Opera*, IV, col. 870-71.

deeper interest than Budé in formal history, which he once referred to as "the most certain philosophy." [17] What is more, he joined this interest to his legal studies and at one point planned to write a constitutional history of the Roman empire. Though he never completed this project, he did write a brief survey of the "forms" of the empire from Augustus down to his own sovereign "Carolus Augustus", and later he published a study of the magistrates of Rome as an introduction to his pioneering edition of the *Notitia Dignitatum*. Like Budé, however, Alciato was concerned with analysis rather than narrative, with *eruditio*, as he put it, rather than *historia*. He made his own valuable contributions to the search for interpolations and to the correction of the Gloss. Finally, through his unpublished but widely known collection of inscriptions, he helped to create one of the auxiliary sciences of history. "Alciato not only reformed jurisprudence," Mommsen wrote, "he laid the foundations of epigraphy." [18]

With all of his antiquarian projects Alciato never finished the specific assignment which Budé had given him, that is, "cleansing the Augean stables of law." [19] This was a bigger job than anyone had expected, and anyway Gregory Haloander anticipated him in producing a critical edition of Justinian's corpus, though still without adequate use of the Florentine manuscript. Yet Alciato did something which in the eyes of contemporaries was just as significant: he brought philol-

---

[17] Alciato, "Encomium historiae" (Barni, p. 222), first published as the preface to his annotations on Tacitus. The *Rerum . . . patriae . . . libri IIII* (Milan, 1625) appeared posthumously. In spite of the use of inscriptions this is not a particularly critical work, nor is the *De Formula Romani imperii libellus* (Basel, 1559), where (pp. 20-21) the story of the Trojan origin of the Franks is repeated.

[18] Theodor Mommsen, *Corpus Inscriptionum Latinarum* (Berlin, 1877), I, 624. Alciato's work in epigraphy, which gives him a place in the tradition of Renaissance antiquarianism, is related also to his famous emblem book, which cannot be discussed here. Cf. Budé's discussion of "emblemata" in *Annotationes*, f. 92^r (D, 10, 4, 7).

[19] In the phrase of Amerbach (Hartmann, III, 442, 31 Aug. 1529). Like Haloander, Alciato did not have direct access to the Florentine manuscript, but he did use the notes of Poliziano and Bolognini and a certain "old manuscript" (*Dispunctiones*, "proeemium," in *Opera*, IV, 143), which has been discussed by Barni, "Notizie del giurista et umanista Andrea Alciato: su manoscritti non glossati delle Pandette," *BHR*, XX (1958), 25-35.

ogy into the classroom. Yielding to the demands of his students, he unlocked his "hidden treasures." He dispensed with the old-fashioned practice of reciting the interminable opinions of the Bartolists and substituted the humanist method of *explication de texte*, which in effect meant returning to the method endorsed by Justinian himself.[20] True, his students were probably attracted as much by the economy as by the elegance of the method, but this did not detract from his achievement. The story was told, and few disbelieved it, that in 1529 at the University of Bourges Andrea Alciato established a new school of humanist jurisprudence. Such were the origins, partly legendary as they may have been, of the "French method," which was to have a profound impact not only upon the profession of law but upon historical research.

The most formidable weapon in Alciato's scholarly arsenal was of course philology (his usual term was *studia humanitatis*), and he never doubted that the jurist had first of all to be a literary critic. In terms recalling the epistemological principle underlying the whole philological tradition, he warned against the semantic trap which had claimed so many jurists of the old school: "Words signify, things are signified."[21] Problems of style fascinated him, and since he did not have access to the Florentine manuscript, he was, like Budé, forced sometimes to resort to conjectural emendations—"restitutions"—on the basis of ancient style (*veteris loquendi ratio*). This was a way, too, of differentiating between ancient and medieval law, between "the Latin and elegant jurists," for example, and the canonists, "who do not care much for correct style."[22] Alciato kept a sharp eye out for neologisms and interpolations, and many of his corrections (more than those of Budé) made their way into Mommsen's edition. He continued the criticism

---

[20] Louis Raynal, *Histoire du Berry* (Bourges, 1844), III, 377, 173, and Q. Breen, *John Calvin: A Study in French Humanism* (Grand Rapids, Mich., 1931), pp. 43 ff.

[21] Alciato, "De verborum significatione," *Opera*, I, 1025-26, except (he added) for hieroglyphs, which signified even though they were ideograms (emblems) and so "things"—or so Alciato, in agreement with all Renaissance scholars, assumed.

[22] Alciato, *In aliquot primae Digestorum . . . titulos commentaris* (*Opera*, I, 14). Cf. *Dispunctiones*, e. g., I, 5 (*Opera*, I, 145 ff).

of the Accursian Gloss, pointing out, for example, that *castratus* referred not to a natural condition, but, as classical usage indicated, to a eunuch; and he carried on the humanist campaign against ludicrous etymologies, such as the erroneous derivation of "metropolitan" which Budé had noted.[23] In the interpretation of texts, he believed, nothing should interfere with the historical sense.

Alciato had a high regard for eloquence, but on the whole he did not allow his classical training to obscure his understanding of European society. Even the old proverb, "When in Rome do as the Romans," he recited in order to reinforce the notion of geographic and social relativity.[24] Moreover, partly through his reading of such German historians as Beatus Rhenanus, he was led to state a rule of prime importance for medieval studies: "All peoples are accustomed to take their words from their own rather than from a foreign idiom, and so . . . they err who are led to ascribe Latin roots to barbarian words"— such as the word "German" itself or "Lombard", which were of foreign derivation (*ex Celtico sermone deducta*).[25] Like Budé he tended to assume that barbarian institutions as well as their terminology were indigenous and had to be understood not by analogy but by empirical, that is, by philological, investigation.

Yet there was one significant point at which Alciato differed from Budé. He had no intention of raising philology, admirable as it was, above its subordinate status; and, conscious of his professional obligations, he admonished those *litteratores* (Budé himself, he recalled, was only a master of arts) who failed to show respect for the science of law. Worst of all was Valla, who though he may have been "emperor of the grammarians" was the despair of the lawyers, and who, at least in Alciato's eyes, was the embodiment of all the literal- and literary-minded excesses of philology. Besides objecting to his amateurism and arrogance—"Valla, who once spared no one, is stilled," he recited,

[23] Alciato, *Praetermissa*, I, and *Dispunctiones*, II, 23 (*Opera*, IV, 217, and 170); cf. Budé, *Annotationes*, f. 62ᵛ.

[24] Alciato, "De Verborum significatione," *Opera*, I, 935, remarking that "one who observes a certain form according to the custom of one place will not be accepted if he goes elsewhere since, as it is commonly said, 'Cum Romae fueris, Romano vivito more' " (originally referring to religious practice).

[25] Alciato, *Parerga*, V, 12 (*Opera*, IV, 356).

"now all he does is bite the dust"—Alciato attacked in detail his emendations of Roman law.[26] Sometimes Alciato seemed to score a point, as in resolving one of the so-called *antinomiae* discovered by Valla (the apparent disagreement about identifying *hypotheca* and *pignus*) by distinguishing between customary (*de usu*) and proper usage (*de proprietate*). Sometimes he seemed to play the quibbler himself, as in arguing against Valla's criticism of the *testamentum* derivation ("quod testatio mentis est") because "Justinian adduces not an etymology but an allusion, which grammarians call *paranomasis* . . . [and which] refers not to the origin of the word but to the similarity of the sounds."[27] He even went so far as to dismiss Valla's critique of the Donation of Constantine on the grounds that it touched merely upon a historical question and did not affect the legal claims of the pope. "Although the document itself was not mentioned by contemporary historians such as Eusebius," he argued, "nevertheless the common opinion received by men is that the donation was made by Constantine."[28] He was unwilling, in short, to let historical fact override legal principle.

In general, Alciato was skeptical about Valla's uncompromising historicism, believing that a critic had to take into account the intention (*voluntas* or *mens*) as well as the words of an author. Like Erasmus he hoped to pass from the letter to the spirit of a text—ultimately, indeed, to the "spirit of the laws" (*mens legum*). It was an error, for Valla no less than for Accursius, to reduce things to present-day standards (*ad nostri temporis normam*).[29] Thus, by curbing the excesses of

[26] Alciato, *Dispunctiones*, IV, 7 (*Opera*, IV, 201). Alciato's extensive and relentless criticisms of Valla appear in his commentary "De verborum significatione" (*Opera*, I, 1025 ff) and again in Duker, *Opuscula* (see ch. II, n. 51). For such reasons it seems better to call Alciato a "humanist jurist" than a "legal humanist," but custom precludes this.

[27] C. A. Duker, pp. 234 and 24; cf. Valla, *Elegantiae*, VI, 57 and 37 (*Opera*, 231, 217).

[28] Alciato, *Praetermissa*, VII, 19 (*Opera*, IV, 403).

[29] Alciato, *Dispunctiones*, IV, 21 (*Opera*, IV, 208). Yet Alciato was well aware of the ambiguities in Justinian's collection (*Justiniani inconstantia in condendis legibus*), and he carried on the anti-Tribonianist tradition. On Erasmus' view of textual criticism and its relation to history, see P. Bietenholz, *History and Biography in the Work of Erasmus* (Geneva, 1966).

literal interpretation, Alciato helped to give maturity and further perspective to the philological method.

This does not mean that Alciato was above bias, or even that he was as cosmopolitan in outlook as his friend Erasmus. On the contrary, he came to be a partisan of both of those universal institutions in which an Italian might take pride. He defended the principle of papal supremacy, which in his view "was most subtly explained by Boniface VIII, who taught the Biblical law that the two swords belonged to the pope." The tradition of imperial Rome he celebrated still more enthusiastically, arguing that the Franks as well as the Gauls had been subject to the empire. As for the present French king, Alciato concluded, "I hold the opinion of Bartolus as closest to the truth, that the King of France recognized the Emperor as superior in law." The Gallican formula which contradicted this he rejected as merely a de facto rule. Alciato's general interpretation of history was perhaps best summed up in the famous legal maxim that he liked to elaborate upon, that Rome was the common fatherland (*Roma communis patria*).[30] Like Valla, whom he otherwise loathed, Alciato had a political as well as a philological commitment to Rome.

Ideologically, Alciato could not have felt at home in France. Certainly his political views were an abomination to any good Gallican. There is some evidence of his alienation, too, in the reactions of his French students, including Jean Calvin and François Connan, who objected to his arrogant treatment of Pierre de l'Estoile, his rival at the University of Orleans.[31] In any case, Alciato left Bourges in 1532, having been recalled by the Duke of Milan, or so he excused himself. Yet in spite of such differences Alciato's scholarly influence, the result

[30] Alciato, *Praetermissa*, VII, 21; *Dispunctiones*, I, 21-22; and *Commentaria* ("De justitia et jure"), in *Opera*, IV, 404, 165-68, and I, 10. Cf. F. Schulz, *Principles of Roman Law*, trans. M. Wolf (Oxford, 1936), p. 109. The Gallican formula, "the king recognizes no superior in temporals," is from Innocent III's "Per venerabilem," in Gregory IX, *Decretals*, IV, 13, 17.

[31] Barni, pp. 154-55 (to Jean de Boyssonné, 22 Aug. 1534). See A. Lefranc, *La jeunesse de Calvin* (Paris, 1888), pp. 72-79, Breen, *John Calvin*, pp. 43 ff, and Bohatec, *Budé und Calvin*, p. 439. Calvin's first printed work was a dedicatory letter, addressed to François Connan, for Nicolas Duchemin's *Antapologia* (Paris, 1531), which was a counterattack against Alciato on behalf of L'Estoile.

of a bare four years at Bourges, represented practically a second infusion of Italian humanism. For the rest of the century the law faculty
of this university was, despite professional squabbles and bitter ideological conflict, the home of the "reformed jurisprudence." It was
very largely the *Alciatei* who made up the historical school of law of
the sixteenth century.

Alciato's New Sect

During the mid-1540s Michel de l'Hôpital, then chancellor of Marguerite of Navarre, Duchess of Berry, paid a visit to his mistress' favorite institution, the University of Bourges, to see for himself the
reasons for the splendid reputation of the law faculty. The story goes
that he attended a class of the first professor of law, Eguinaire Baron.
Impressive with his gray beard and taffeta robe, Baron put on a special
show for his distinguished auditor and gave a colorful description of
the new jurisprudence. "He began by describing Justinian's prohibi-
tions against interpretations of civil law, remarking . . . that when a
dog has pissed somewhere, there is no cur . . . that will not come to
lift his leg and piss with his fellows. So when Bartolus, Baldus, or
another lawyer discusses a point in some passage, no matter how long
or irrelevant, the whole tribe of doctors will come to befoul the same
passage with conclusions, limitations, reasons pro and con, amplifica-
tions, explanations, repetitions, and other professional apparatus."[32]
Such were the "Augean stables" of law which Budé and Alciato had
set out to clean. And such was the principal target of the academic
revolution which the historical school of law intended to bring about.

At this time the University of Bourges was a center of avant-garde
ideas in more ways than one. As early as 1525 Lutheran doctrines had
made their appearance in the town and were infiltrating the school.
According to some scholars, Calvin himself was converted to a reformed faith during his stay at the university (1530-31). Given the
ideals and pretentions of the humanist movement, it was only natural
that the reformed jurisprudence should be welcomed there, too, and
that there should be a certain cordiality between the two movements.

---

[32] *Contes et discours d'Eutrapel*, in N. du Fail, *Œuvres facétieuses* (Paris,
1874), I, 263.

Legal humanism had, after all, been associated all along with the notion of reforming society and its institutions, ecclesiastical as well as civil; for as Budé himself had argued, a "purified jurisprudence" implied moral improvement. Thus Christian and legal humanism reinforced one another, and at Bourges in particular, under the approving eyes of Marguerite of Navarre, they flourished together. All of the members of the historical school of law, at least in their younger years, sympathized with the "so-called reformed religion." It was an exciting place. No wonder Rabelais enrolled Pantagruel in this school, or that it began to rival Orleans as the quasi-official law faculty for the University of Paris, where the teaching of civil law was technically forbidden. By the 1550's, then, the University of Bourges was not only the principal center of the *mos gallicus*, it was a leading Protestant refuge; it sheltered the progeny not only of Alciato but of his one time student Calvin.[33]

In this way Bourges was transformed into an intellectual battleground that prefigured in a remarkable fashion the bloodier conflicts to come. Alciato's followers will be found on both sides of the struggle, which indeed they did their share to intensify. Students were involved, too, and at least one was killed in the accompanying disorders. Even the parlement became annoyed at the goings on, or rather at the heretical overtones. Yet the trouble had all started, apparently, with a faculty squabble. The established group within the law school was "the partisans of Le Douaren," who constituted not only a faculty clique but a kind of crypto-Calvinist club.[34] Besides François le Douaren himself, this group included Hugues Doneau and several German students,

---

[33] See N. Weiss, "La Réforme à Bourges au XVIe siècle," *BSHPF*, LIII (1904), 307-15, and P. Imbart de la Tour, *Les Origines de la Réforme*, III (Paris, 1914), 407-8.

[34] Preface of Louis le Caron's edition of Zasius, *Catalogus legum* (Paris, 1555), and the "De Jurisprudentiae dignitate" of Cisner, who was a leader of the student group which, in the name of the German nation, protested against the enemies of Le Douaren, including Baudouin. The best general accounts of the law faculty are still A. Eyssell, *Doneau, sa vie et ses écrits*, trans. Simmonnet (Dijon, 1860); E. Jobbé-Duval, "François le Douaren (Duarenus) 1509-1559," *Mélanges P.-F. Girard* (Paris, 1912); and L. Raynal, *Histoire du Berry*, III, 372 ff, and *De l'enseignement du droit dans l'ancienne université de Bourges* (Bourges, 1838).

such as Nicolas Cisner; it was supported from afar by François Hotman (who joined the faculty in later years) and eventually by Calvin. In the opposite camp, or at least excluded from this party, were two equally distinguished jurists, François Baudoin and Jacques Cujas, who also sympathized with the cause of reform as they understood it. It was Cujas who, after Le Douaren's death in 1559, became the acknowledged leader of the historical school of Roman law. The period down to his death in 1590, coinciding roughly with the bitter years of civil war, was the golden age of Roman law scholarship in France. It was also—and not accidentally—the dawning age of medieval studies.

These men constituted the intellectual posterity, at least in France, of Alciato and to a degree of Budé. Like Alciato, they were professional-minded and were careful to avoid the extremes of philology, adopting instead a moderate position between the legalistic approach of Bartolus, though without his present-mindedness, and the grammatical approach of Valla, though without his radical classicism. Their pedagogical views were particularly conservative; Cujas even recommended the Gloss for beginning students.[35] What is more, some of them began to adopt the same kind of systematizing method that Budé had tried to discredit. They became involved in schemes of legal reform on the basis, whether directly or indirectly, of Roman law; and increasingly they became interested in "method" in the sense of logical arrangement. Here, incidentally, is where Ramist influence becomes significant. This tendency is apparent in Le Douaren's commentary on the Digest, "interpreted methodically," and still more conspicuously in the works of Doneau and Calvin's old friend Connan, who seemed to be more disturbed by the chaotic arrangement of the Digest than by its textual condition. This attitude pointed in two directions: first, toward the creation of a native French "code," a goal which, though it was not to be attained for two and a half centuries, and then only after a cycle of violent revolution, was to have a detectible effect upon

---

[35] J. Flach, *Cujas, les glossateurs et les bartolistes* (Paris, 1883). The classic discussion of humanist jurisprudence is still R. Stinzing, *Geschichte der deutschen Rechtswissenschaft*, I (Munich, 1880), 367 ff, emphasizing the influence of Ramist logic and tendencies toward legal "reform."

historical scholarship; and second, toward a systematic science of politics, which presumed to direct and even to supersede historical scholarship and which reached its culmination in that sixteenth-century "summa" of social thought, Jean Bodin's *Republic*. This is another example—perhaps the most impressive and intimidating example—of the "transcendent impulse" which threatened, though at the same time it served to inspire, the study of history. It is not denying the importance of such developments to suggest that they were of only peripheral significance for philology and for historical scholarship.

Yet, for all these expeditions into professional and philosophic territory, the disciples of Alciato did not forget the original goals of legal humanism. They carried on the restoration of the texts of Roman law, though more cautiously and more methodically than Budé, as befits those who follow a course already charted. They began their own pioneering operations into the field of pre-Justinianian law, and what is most interesting, they began the serious investigation of medieval law and institutions. This major phase of legal humanism, which will bring us to the threshhold of modern historical scholarship, may best be summarized by considering some of the key contributions of four of these scholars—Le Douaren, Hotman, Cujas, and (in the next chapter) Baudouin. In several characteristic but quite different ways, they illustrate the manifold links between law and the study of history.

François le Douaren

Le Douaren was, according to Pierre Bayle, "the first of the French jurists to chase barbarism from the chairs of law." As a young man he had been so attracted to philology that his father, fearing that he was neglecting his legal studies, appealed to Budé. Though he had done precisely the same thing in his youth, Budé, now an old man, warned Le Douaren against this.[36] In his later work Le Douaren did not forget to pay tribute to Budé as well as to Alciato. It was in 1542 that he first came to teach at Bourges, but a dispute with his elder colleague Eguinaire Baron—"Baron in name but Varro in learning," he had remarked impertinently (*baro* means stupid in Latin)—over the inter-

[36] Published in Le Douaren, *Opera omnia* (Lucca, 1765-68), IV, 387-88.

pretation of *imperium* led to his departure.[37] In 1550, however, upon the death of Baron and with the backing of the Duchess of Berry and of Michel de l'Hôpital, he returned to become the dominant figure on the faculty until his own death in 1559. Even then he was unable to avoid controversy, although from this time on it centered upon ecclesiastical issues. It was precisely in this period that legal humanism began to be concerned with problems of church and state, and Le Douaren was one of the first to make this transition.

Le Douaren's point of departure was, in general, the program set forth by Budé. This he made quite explicit in his "Method of legal study" (1544), one of the earliest and best-known manifestos of the French historical school, which was later to be followed by similar statements from Hotman, Cujas, and Baudouin, among others. For the proper understanding of Roman law, Le Douaren argued, three things were needed: repudiation of the opinions of those "barbarous doctors" who subscribed to the *mos italicus,* a knowledge of correct and elegant Latin, and a method of interpretation founded upon historical analysis as well as a familiarity with the law. Tribonian himself, he added, had recognized the fundamental importance of history by placing the fragment from Pomponius at the beginning of the Digest.[38]

Le Douaren's business was to teach civil law, but because of this emphasis upon history he seemed often to be interested more in the stages of development leading up to Justinian's compilation than in the *corpus juris* itself. It was his view that the law of Rome, private as well as public, was the product of long-standing usage (*jus publicum ex consuetudine, jus hominis privati ex praescriptione nascitur*). He recognized eleven "sources" of law (several more than Pomponius himself), beginning with custom and ending with judicial interpreta-

---

[37] Le Douaren, "Epistola ad Andream Guillartum . . . de ratione docendi, discendique juris conscripta," *Opera*, IV, 363-71, and in Reusner (ed.), *Cynosura juris*, 17-37, which contains also the "methods" of Baudouin, Hotman, and Baron. See also his interesting letter to Baudouin (*Opera*, IV, 371-78, Jan. 1549), where he refers to the "conjunction of grammar and jurisprudence" and recommends as models Budé and Poliziano. On the controversy between Baron and Le Douaren, see M. P. Gilmore, *Argument from Roman Law in Political Thought 1200-1600* (Cambridge, Mass., 1941), p. 77.

[38] *Ibid.*, *Opera*, IV, 363.

tion (the *responsa prudentum*), all of which were of course obsolete by the time of Justinian except for imperial legislation.[39] One of Le Douaren's primary goals was discriminating between "old" and "new" law, that is, classical and Byzantine, and in determining the chronological sequence of laws. "Although the compilers of the Pandects placed the names of the ancient jurisconsults at the head of the individual chapters . . . ," he pointed out, "nevertheless many things in these writings were added or subtracted, so that we cannot tell for sure which opinions were from the books of the ancients."[40] Le Douaren, too, addressed himself to the problem of anachronism—to "Tribonianisms" and to the *antinomiae*.

About textual criticism in general Le Douaren had very pronounced ideas. While recognizing the value of a grammatical approach, like Alciato he could not accept the extreme views of Valla. It was necessary to take into account the inner meaning as well as the literal formulation of laws (*scire leges non hoc esse verba earum tenere: sed vim et potestatem*).[41] He also rejected a rigid classicism on principle because it prevented a correct understanding of medieval society. Here he was in agreement both with Budé and with Erasmus, who in a letter to Alciato had exclaimed: "What is more inappropriate in this wholly new age than to hear religions, empires, magistracies, names of places, edifices, cults and manners discussed as Cicero would have discussed them? If brought back to life, Cicero would have laughed at this sort of Ciceronian."[42] As Le Douaren put it, "We could not live if we could not attach new names to things." Even for Cicero, he added, "new things were permitted to produce their own designations," while Livy, to give a concrete example, had referred to Carthaginian magistrates not as "consuls" but as "suffetes."[43] In this way anti-

[39] Le Douaren, "In primam partem Pandectarum, sive Digestorum, methodica enarratio," *Opera*, I, 17 (D, 1, 2, 2).

[40] *Ibid.*, I, 2, commenting on Justinian's prefaces.

[41] *Ibid.*, I, 10 (D, 1, 3, 17), in the words of Celsus.

[42] Allen, VI, 336 (to Alciato, 6 May 1526); cf. *Ciceronianus* (*Opera*, I, 993). In general, see M. P. Gilmore, *Humanists and Jurists* (Cambridge, Mass., 1963), pp. 102 ff, and the works of Sabbadini and Norden.

[43] Le Douaren, *De Sacris ecclesiae ministeriis ac beneficiis libri octo* (*Opera*, IV, 195 ff). Cf. Valla's formula (ch. II, n. 39).

Ciceronian arguments, reinforced by those of the moderns in their quarrel with the ancients, intensified the historicist tendencies of legal humanism.

In his own investigations of medieval law, canon as well as feudal, Le Douaren put these precepts into practice. Each of these legal traditions, he believed, had to be understood in its own terms, not as offshoots of civil law, which seemed to be the position of the Bartolists. Le Douaren regarded ecclesiastical institutions from a historical point of view, and he presented one of the first historical sketches of canon law (Du Rivail's was only an outline) from Gratian's Decretum through the "degeneration" of recent centuries.[44] In the case of feudal law, which he took up for the benefit of his German students, his knowledge of history led him to break with the Romanist bias which even Budé and Alciato had retained. His conclusion was that "fiefs probably take their origin from Lombard rather than from Roman law."[45] The study of medieval law, possessing its own traditions and developing in its own context, must be treated independently. Nevertheless, as Le Douaren's work shows, it did come within the compass of legal humanism and was shaped accordingly. In general, the investigations of Le Douaren and his younger colleagues at the University of Bourges represent not only the expansion of the historical school of law but also the characteristic shift of interest of French scholars, already foreshadowed by Budé, from classical antiquity to the European middle ages.

François Hotman

A man with still stronger leanings toward medieval studies was that volatile and versatile scholar, François Hotman. This may have been encouraged by his own Germanic heritage (his family was Silesian in origin), but it was due mainly to his Protestant sympathies and his political involvements. Having fallen under Calvin's spell, he left

---

[44] *Ibid.*, "praefatio" (*Opera*, IV, 191 ff). Du Rivail's minute *Historia juris pontificalis* appeared at the end of his *Historia juris civilis*. This subject is resumed in ch. VI.

[45] Le Douaren, *Commentarius in consuetudines feudorum* (*Opera*, II, 314). This subject is resumed in ch. VII.

France to teach rhetoric and dialectic at Lausanne for five years (1550-55) before resuming his legal career. Hotman had studied civil law at Orleans with L'Estoile at a very early age and had given his first public lecture in 1546 at the University of Paris. Throughout his later life he taught civil law at various universities—Strasbourg (where he received a position through the good offices of Calvin), Valence, Bourges (where he came as Cujas' replacement in 1566), Geneva, and finally Basel, where he died in 1590. Despite his innumerable activities and misfortunes civil law was a subject which never lost its fascination for him, and in his last months he was giving lessons on the government of the Roman republic.[46]

To begin with, Hotman professed much the same scholarly ideal as his friend Le Douaren, and in his *Jurisconsult* of 1559 he made a ritual condemnation of scholastic lawyers, "those practitioners [*pragmatici*], not jurists but rather merchants . . . , whom Cicero called mean and mercenary."[47] He had a profound appreciation for history, for which he found many uses, both polemical and scholarly, and for a time he even held the post of royal historiographer. Besides numerous philological works, he composed a commentary on the Twelve Tables, a study of Roman coinage (following and criticizing that of Budé), and a sketch of the history of Roman law, including an account of its twelfth-century revival, which he attributed to the recovery of the Florentine manuscript.[48]

Yet, for various reasons besides his general contrariness, Hotman became increasingly suspicious of the study of Roman law. During the religious wars, in fact, he came to attribute many of the ills of French

[46] The best life of Hotman remains the studies published by Dareste between 1850 and 1908, though they must be corrected by the articles of J. Pannier and H. Vuilleumier; for these works and other bibliography on Hotman and the French scholars discussed in the present chapter, see Cioranesco. There is much manuscript material pertaining to Hotman, particularly correspondence, in French, German, and especially Swiss libraries and archives, on the basis of which I am preparing a full scale biography.

[47] François Hotman, *Jurisconsultus, sive de optimo genere juris interpretandi* (Basel, 1559), p. 34; reprinted in Reusner, *Cynosura juris.*

[48] Hotman, "Ex indice universae historiae," "De Re nummaria," and "Commentatio in leges XII tab.," in *Operum* (Geneva, 1599-1600), I, col. 1067 ff, and III, 369 ff. By 1558 Hotman was in correspondence with Cujas (letter to Amerbach, 10 May, Basel, Universitätsbibliothek, MSS G. II, 19, f. 120r).

society to the reception of Roman law, and in much the same tone as Rabelais he derided those pettifoggers (*chicanourrois*) who came out of the schools of law and swarmed over the courts, both lay and ecclesiastical.[49] Canon law he scorned from the beginning, having attacked it in his earliest polemical work; civil law he found guilty by association. Taken together they constituted, in Hotman's opinion, one great syndrome of legal corruption, for which there is no better term than "Romanism." In France this corruption was especially severe in the provinces of written law (*pays du droit écrit*), where civil law was taken as common law. At Valence in 1566 Hotman lamented:

We are less occupied in teaching civil law than in overturning the sophistical inventions of the practitioners and, as it were, with sweeping out the Augean stables. Since our Dauphinois have long employed, under cover of Roman law, certain rules of chicanery borrowed from Italian custom, we are forced to consider questions considered in their courts, such as those taken up in the decisions of Guy Pape, not a Delphic but only a Delphinal Apollo. The Bishop urges this study with all his might.[50]

More and more Hotman came to associate the study of Roman law with the corruptions of Italian society; and like many French jurists he believed in a golden age of French law, before the coming of "written law," when judgments were simple, morals were pure, and litigation was at a minimum. This was a myth similar in function to that of the "primitive church" and, for Hotman, part of the same general program of reform.

---

[49] Hotman, *Antitribonian* (Paris, 1603), p. 70. He attacked not only public law (pp. 13-18), which he thought irrelevant to French government, but also private law, especially testamentary succession (p. 45), which he regarded as "the source and nursing mother of suits and chicaneries in the so-called provinces of written law." On the significance of this book, see J. Baron, *Franz Hotmann's Antitribonian* (Bern, 1888), discussing the attempts to establish a French "code"; P. Mesnard, "François Hotman (1524-1590) et le complexe de Tribonien," *BSHPF*, CI (1955), 117-37; E. Fournol, "Sur quelques traités de droit public du XVIe siècle," *NRHDFE*, XXI (1897), 298-325; and above all, R. Giesey, "When and Why Hotman Wrote the Francogallia," *BHR*, XXIX (1967), 581-611, which amply demonstrates the connections between this work and the *Anti-Tribonian*. See also R. Marichal, "Rabelais et la réforme de justice," *BHR*, XIV (1952), 176-92.

[50] Hotman, Letter to Henri de Mesmes, ed. Dareste, in *RHDFE*, I (1853), 495.

What is more remarkable, however, is that Hotman began to have doubts also about the value of legal humanism, again because of its ties with Italian culture. Not only did he mock the "pure philologists" (*grammariens purifiez*), but he turned against the very use of the Latin language, which he thought intensified the confusions and corruptions of justice in France. Hence he applauded the ordinance of Francis I (1539) which made the use of French mandatory in civil suits.[51] But this was only a beginning. Always a reformer, Hotman developed subversive ideas not only about the ecclesiastical establishment in France but also about education and the legal profession. Finally, he came to reject the view that Roman law served any significant purpose in French schools—neither for the study of ancient history nor (as such jurists as his friend Doneau seemed to believe) as a basis for a uniform body of laws. As a creation of a particular people at a particular point in time in particular circumstances, Roman law had little more than an antiquarian value.

Such was the train of thought—inherent, indeed, in legal humanism from the beginning—which led to the most radical of all works issuing from the historical school of law. Hotman's *Anti-Tribonian,* composed at the request of Michel de l'Hôpital in 1567, when Hotman was professor at the University of Bourges, was a worthy descendant of Valla's work. The book was at once a monument to and an obituary for legal humanism, and it was one of the most remarkable examples of Renaissance historicism.

[51] Hotman, *Anti-Tribonian*, p. 120; cf. *Franco-Gallia* (Frankfurt, 1665), p. 23. *Anti-Tribonian*, pp. 104-6: "Now if the emperors were careful to have doctors and professors of their civil law in their schools, so the popes for their part were not lax in attracting from all areas men of acute and quick wits to profess their canons . . .; and so there has arisen that stupid and barbarous custom . . . of composing all acts and public instruments in the Latin language." And on the other hand, pp. 118-19: "We must speak of . . . the many debates and contentions which exist today among doctors of a more sophisticated learning, nourished and exercised by good letters, who call themselves professors of pure jurisprudence. Who does not see that most of their contentions are founded only upon disputes of Latin grammar?" And he endorsed Alciato's rejection of Valla's hypercritical remarks about the relation between "testamentum" and "testatio mentis," which was included in the Digest as explanatory and not as a true etymology: *Commentarius verborum juris* (Basel, 1558), and *supra*, n. 27.

Like most devotees of the French method, Hotman was sensitive to "Tribonianisms" (*emblemata Triboniani* he called them in his scholarly work). "In Diocletian's time," he pointed out in his observations on civil law, "there was no law, I think, which made a mother give her daughter's dowry, and so I am easily persuaded that this law was written and added by Tribonian."[52] In his *Anti-Tribonian,* written in the vernacular, he made more serious charges. "Since the time good letters opened the eyes and understandings of men," he remarked, "it has been discovered that Tribonian falsely mixed in not merely three or four words but whole pages and even whole sections, such as the 'Origin of law,' which is obviously fables and reveries added by Tribonian and falsely placed under the name and title of Pomponius." Over twelve years before he had come to this conclusion on the basis of stylistics as well as history (*cum ex styli dissimilitudine tum ex historiae veritate*).[53] In general, he recognized seven types of alteration: the abolishment of previous law, changes in style, illogical arrangement, abridgment of passages, inclusion of later terminology, and retention of anachronisms, such as the extreme formalisms of ancient law. For these reasons, Hotman concluded, "the books of Justinian contain a complete description neither of the democratic state nor of the true Roman empire nor of Constantinople, but only a collection of different bits and pieces of each of these three forms."[54] To investigate ancient society, Hotman argued, it was much better to have recourse to the historians.

In all of this, of course, there was hardly anything new: nothing in denunciations of Tribonian's scholarly and religious failings, little in his specific detections (which often derived from Valla), little even in his sense of the mutability of Roman law. After all, as Hotman himself recalled, "the ancients often said that laws changed according to the seasons and mutations of the manners and conditions of a people."[55] Yet Hotman did something more than merely gather the

[52] Hotman, *Observationum et emendationum in jure civile libri XIII* (*Operum,* I, col. 80). See also his *Justiniani imperatoris vita* (Strasbourg, 1556), on the "circumcized and amputated" texts of the Digest.
[53] Hotman, *Anti-Tribonian,* p. 96, and *Africanus* (Strasbourg, 1555), f. 8ᵛ.
[54] Hotman, *Anti-Tribonian,* pp. 21-22.
[55] *Ibid.,* p. 12.

insights of his humanist predecessors. He introduced a new emphasis by denying the relevance of Roman law for French society and by documenting this denial in terms of the various kinds of law—laws of persons, of things, of succession, of contracts, and of procedure. Roman law had no roots in France, Hotman argued, nor had there been any so-called reception under Charlemagne. The recent infiltration, therefore, was all the more to be resisted, for "the laws of a country should be accommodated to the state and form of a government and not the government to the laws."[56] In a conventional physical analogy, Hotman likened legislation to the prescription of a doctor, since laws, like medicine, had to suit the "complexions and humors" of a people. No legal system, the inference is, could be quite relevant except within the social context in which it was created.

Hotman's thesis, which amounts to a principle of cultural relativity, had not only a philological and a legal but also a philosophical foundation, and once again we are reminded of the legacy of Valla. It was not simply the old argument that laws designed for a democratic or aristocratic government were inappropriate for a monarchy. "There is more," Hotman claimed, "for all monarchies are not governed always and everywhere the same. Some have a power and authority more absolute, some more limited; some have a greater extent and dominion, others smaller and more resctricted; some have more military, others more civil offices."[57] For much the same reason that Valla had rejected the categories of Aristotelian logic, that is, because of their alienation from human reality, Hotman rejected the categories of Aristotelian politics. In his view they did not correspond to, let alone exhaust, historical reality. This is as clear and direct a statement of historical relativism as one can find in the sixteenth century.

This was not the end, it was only the most crucial phase of Hotman's train of thought about the relations between law and society and about the nature of legal history. It does mark the point, however,

---

[56] *Ibid.*, p. 6. Similar medical conceits were employed by the "Solon" to whom Hotman had dedicated his work: Michel de l'Hôpital, *Traité de la réformation de la justice*, ed. P. Duféy (Paris, 1825), I, 12, which registers similar complaints about Italian influence and the evils of written law.
[57] *Ibid.*, p. 8.

where he shifted emphasis from Roman to medieval law and institutions. Here begins a new stage of Hotman's thought which will be examined independently in a later chapter.[58] This turning point coincides with that watershed of the religious wars, the Massacre of St Bartholomew, which disrupted so many lives (when it did not destroy them) and which helped to crystallize the anti-Romanist views of many Gallicans as well as Huguenots like Hotman. Consequences of this included the formation of the party of the politiques and the search for a more secure Gallican ideology, both of which contributed to the formulation of a new interpretation of French history. For Hotman this disaster was decisive both in ideological and in personal terms. Besides sending him into permanent exile, it confirmed his repudiation of Romanism, toward which he had been moving for two decades, and it led him to a radical reassessment of history. Although Hotman's historical thought may seem to be more of a caricature than a paradigm, his intellectual transformation does illustrate one of the points of contact between the historical school of law and the search for a general interpretation of history.

Jacques Cujas

In Alciato's "new sect," Hotman was unquestionably the most sensational figure. Yet in the final analysis the most positive contribution to scholarship was made by a man who hardly ever strayed from the confines of philology and who managed for the most part to avoid both the pleasures and the risks of controversy. Jacques Cujas, Hotman's predecessor at Bourges, was not a legal reformer but a legal antiquarian; he was interested not in systematic jurisprudence but in the history of law.[59] He agreed, to be sure, that the Digest was in disarray, but it was his sense of anachronism rather than his sense of

---

[58] *Infra*, ch. VII.

[59] Jacques Cujas, *Observationum et emendationum libri XXVIII*, published between 1556 (first preface) and 1598. Cujas' first work was the *Ulpiani fragmenta cum notis* (Toulouse, 1554), based upon a manuscript discovered by the Bishop du Tillet (see ch. VIII). The basic biography is still Berriat-Saint-Prix, *Histoire du droit romain suivie de l'histoire de Cujas* (Paris, 1821), though it must be supplemented by more recent studies, such as P. F. Girard, "La Jeunesse de Cujas," *NRHDFE*, XXIX (1916), 429-504, 590-627; in general, see Cioranesco.

order that was disturbed. From the beginning he showed a deep interest in pre-Justinianian law, and while still at Toulouse, where he had begun teaching in 1547, he published a work of Ulpian based upon a recently discovered manuscript. He also studied the Theodosian Code, of which he later published a pioneering edition. Whenever possible he worked from manuscripts, and he was fortunate that the Florentine codex of the Digest was published in time (1553) for him to make use of it. In 1556, during the first of three periods at the University of Bourges, he began his most important work—his massive *Observations and Emendations*, which was in every respect a worthy successor of Budé's *Annotations* and one of the few products of sixteenth-century scholarship which still retains its value.

Cujas was the scholar's scholar, causing even Scaliger to fall under his spell and for a time to desert literature for the law. He gloried in the epithet "grammarian," derogatory as it sounded in some circles.[60] He had the good fortune also to live in the heroic age of classical scholarship when many of the essential tools of historical criticism were being perfected. The first handbook of textual criticism, which appeared in 1561, gives an indication of the sophistication and methodical basis of mid-sixteenth-century scholarship. Like Budé, Francesco Robortello emphasized the importance of encyclopedic nowledge (*eruditio*) and historical accuracy (*fides*) and pointed to Poliziano in particular as a model of these virtues.[61] In great detail he discussed the problems of textual criticism, especially of conjectural emendation, and he listed eight modes of such criticism, stylistic as well as paleographic. Such were the methods employed by classical scholars to manuscripts as well as to printed books. Nowhere were these methods applied more successfully than to Roman law, and no one was more responsible for this success than Jacques Cujas.

---

[60] *Scaligerana*, I, 285, where Cujas' student François Pithou remarked: "When people wanted to disparage M. Cujas they called him 'grammarian,' but he did not mind and said they were jealous of not being such themselves." See "Lettres inédites de Cujas et de Scaliger," ed. S. de Ricci and P. F. Girard, *NRHDFE*, XL (1917), 403-24.

[61] Francesco Robortello, *De Arte sive ratione corrigendi antiquorum libros disputatione*, in Scioppus, *De Arte critica* (Amsterdam, 1662), p. 119, adding, "Quanta fides, Dii immortales, in Politiano?"

Following and elaborating upon the methods established by Valla, Poliziano, and Budé, and canonized by Robortello, Cujas became not only the final authority in the interpretation of classical jurisprudence but also one of the most pertinacious and successful of the interpolation-hunters. His corrections ranged from the simplest textual errors (such as *in matrimonium* for the abbreviation *in manum*) to anachronistic substitutions (such as *traditio* for *mancipatio* or *pignus* for *fiducia*). In general, Cujas attributed the "Tribonianisms" embedded in the Digest to the necessity of "adapting a matter to the court practices of Justinian's age" (*cum rem accommodaret ad usum fori, qui obtinebat aetate Justiniani*).[62] Through an unparallelled knowledge of Tribonian's style (*stilus, genus scribendi*), or as he sometimes put it, his "incompetence in Latin," Cujas was able to make numerous emendations of Justinian's collection. This, and the job of indexing the citations, led up to a correct "interpretation" of the texts and finally, hopefully, to the "resurrection" of classical jurisprudence in all its pristine splendor. In this way Cujas hoped to understand Roman law in terms of its historical development. Because of this fundamentally archeological point of view and the refinements of his method, one scholar had concluded that, "with Cujas, the history of law was born."[63]

There was another reason for Cujas' prominence: his enormous academic influence, which exceeded that of Alciato and extended far beyond the legal profession. Indeed, Cujas' most distinguished students were never included in that group derisively labelled "Cujacians" by Gentili. In some ways Cujas was untypical, especially from his notorious aloofness from the political controversies of his times (though his Protestant sympathies are beyond doubt). Except for excursions

---

[62] Cujas, *Opera omnia* (Prato, 1837), V, col. 169-70; cf. IV, col. 875; also VIII, col. 46, where he added, "which words are by Tribonian, as are many others in the Digest, just as Gratian added to the Decretum." On Cujas' method, see P. Mesnard, "La Place de Cujas dans la querelle de l'humanisme juridique," *RHDFE*, sér. 4, XXVIII (1950), 521-37; E. Albertario, "I Tribonianismi avvertiti dal Cuiacio," *ZSSRG*, Rom. Abt., XLIV (1910), 158-75; C. W. Westrup, "Notes sur Cujas," *Studi in onore di Pietro Bonfante* (Milan, 1930), III, 131-49; and Palazzini Finetti, *Storia della ricerca delle interpolazioni*. Cf. J. G. Heineccius, "De Secta Tribonianomastigum," *Operum* (Geneva, 1748), III, 171 ff.

[63] P. Mesnard, "La Place de Cujas," p. 534.

into canon and feudal law,[64] moreover, he restricted himself to classical Roman law. Nevertheless, Cujas contributed greatly to historical scholarship both through his scholarly example (incomprehensible as the substance of his work must have been to many of his admirers) and through the students he inspired and encouraged—a number of whom we shall encounter in later chapters. Cujas was the mentor and the model—practically the patron saint—of the first great generation of French antiquarians who, trained in civil law but converted to medieval studies, carried on their researches throughout the civil wars in France and, in spite of political commitments, managed to preserve their scholarly ideals. It was characteristic that the man who taught a whole generation of medievalists should have been a classical scholar; it was crucial that he should have been a jurist as well. Cujas' students, true alumni of the historical school of law, though they shared neither his way of life nor his hostility to politics, revitalized and reshaped historical and social thought with the help of legal humanism.

Of all the disciples of Alciato the most original, though least understood, was François Baudouin, who alone of this group deserves a place in the tradition of historiography proper. His work not only provides a link between humanist jurisprudence and historical scholarship, it also seems nearly to recapitulate the development of the study of legal history. Although Baudoin remained a member in good standing of the historical school of law, much of his work moved far beyond the confines of this movement, and so it needs to be examined separately and in a rather different context.

---

[64] See *infra* ch. VII and (for Cujas' disciples) chs. IX and X.

CHAPTER V

The Alliance of Law and History:
François Baudouin Defines the Art of History

Nescire autem quid ante quam natus sis acciderit, id est semper esse puerum.

Cicero, *Orator*, 120

"HISTORICAL STUDIES must be placed upon a solid foundation of law," François Baudouin declared, "and jurisprudence must be joined to history."[1] This formula not only expressed the basic doctrine of the historical school of law, it forecast the future trend of legal humanism, which was increasingly away from the professional study of law and toward the growing fields of legal and institutional history. What is more, this statement, made in 1561, signaled the first serious attempt in France to formulate a definition of history—indeed, to promote history from an art to a science by organizing it in a methodical way. As the title indicates, this key work of Baudouin's career endorses and illustrates the convergence of legal and historical studies and, in a sense, furnishes a new life for each. Baudouin's book was both a descendant of the Italian "arts of history" and a forerunner of the French "methods of history." Yet it was superior to both in that is was concerned neither with the literary questions of historical narrative nor with the construction of a political philosophy but rather with the concrete problems of historical scholarship. It was a summary of legal humanism and at the same time a prophecy of the course which historical studies would take in the next generation. For these

---

[1] François Baudouin, *De Institutione historiae universae et ejus cum jurisprudentia conjunctione*, ΠΡΟΛΕΓΟΜΕΝΩΝ *libri II*, in Wolf, p. 668.

FRANÇOIS BAUDOUIN (Emile
Doumergue, *Jean Calvin*, Vol. II) Courtesy of the Newberry Library, Chicago

reasons Baudouin and his conception of "integral history" occupy a pivotal position in this book.

The Legal Humanist

Long before coming to the University of Bourges Baudouin had been an enthusiast of the new jurisprudence. In his very first work, a study of Justinian's agricultural legislation published in 1542, he applied himself to the "restitution" of texts, and he referred to the work of Alciato and of Haloander.[2] His historical point of view was made still more apparent three years later when he produced what was perhaps the first history of Roman legal science, whose "origin, progress, fall, and vestiges" he traced down to his own day. Beginning with a survey of ancient jurisprudence, he went on to describe its eclipse in medieval times and its partial survival in barbarian codes. He retold the story of the miraculous recovery of the Florentine manuscript and the first "renaissance" of Roman law under Frederick Barbarossa. He described and deplored the "degeneration of jurisprudence" which had begun with Accursius, and finally he celebrated the second "renaissance" of the fifteenth century, inaugurated by Valla and completed by Alciato.[3] This was Baudouin's own point of departure, both as a philologist and as a successor of Alciato at Bourges, to which he came in 1548.

For the next decade Baudouin carried out investigations over the whole range of Roman legal history. Most essential, of course, was the Digest, and Baudouin lamented its condition in typically humanist fashion. "I can never read without great sadness the old jurists, so miserably mangled by Tribonian that today we see merely a shadow . . . , but so much the more do I want to assemble these scattered pieces and to rescue the holy relics so that we may learn how great and majestic

---

[2] Baudouin, *Justiani de re rustica* (Louvain, 1542), f. ii^r. There is no study of Baudouin's legal scholarship, although Westrup, "Notes sur Cujas," p. 133, has pointed out Baudouin's priority in seeking "elements of continuity in the evolution of Roman law."

[3] Baudouin, "Praefata de jure civile" (1545), Heineccius, col. 3-16. A fuller, more up-to-date account was given later by Le Douaren's student, V. Foster, *De Historia juris civilis* (Basel, 1565).

was the splendor of ancient jurisprudence."[4] In this critical field Baudouin was quite as much a pioneer as his learned "successor" at Bourges, Jacques Cujas, and indeed had preceded him into the wilderness of early legal history. Naturally enough, Baudouin began with the Twelve Tables, "which holds first place in Roman law and in the study of antiquity." In this partially unearthed monument Baudouin saw, among other things, a striking example of Greek influence, and he pointed out that "Justinian did not hesitate to refer the origins of civil law to the Lacedemonians and to the Athenians." Adapting the aphorism of Thucydides, he remarked that Athens was the school not only of Hellas but, through the agency of Roman law, of the whole civilized world. Baudouin's essay of restitution, one of the first such to be written (1550), was intended to be a contribution to universal history as well as to philology.[5] This work was carried on by Cujas, Hotman, and Baudouin's student Louis le Caron, whom we shall encounter later as one of the leading medievalists of the next generation.

After this Baudouin turned to a study of the Scaevola family and its accomplishments, which he augmented through the use of inscriptions, and of a wide range of early Roman legislation. These researches confirmed Baudouin's attachment to the French method. "The more I consider the condition of Roman jurisprudence . . . ," he wrote, "the more I realize that what is necessary is history, not dialectic or rhetoric."[6] So was philology, although like Alciato he avoided the extreme views of Valla. What he favored was a "conjunction of grammar and jurisprudence," that is, an approach which would take into account the

---

[4] Baudouin, *Scaevola, sive commentarius de jurisprudentia Muciana* (1558) (Heineccius, col. 437-38). This work has received high praise from a modern scholar, G. Lapointe, *Quintus Mucius Scaevola* (Paris, 1926), p. 4.

[5] Baudouin, *Commentarius de legibus XII tabularum* (Heineccius, col. 59 ff), also in *Tractatus*, I, f. 226ʳ. He refers here (f. 228ʳ) to Cujas as "jurisconsultus doctissimus et successor in Gallia meus." In his own essay (*Tractatus*, I, f. 268ᵛ ff) Le Caron praised Baudouin for his elegant restorations of laws of the Twelve Tables (*eleganter restitutas et explicatas*). On Le Caron's later work see *infra* ch. X. The earliest discussion is in Johannes Oldendorp, *Juris naturalis gentium* εἰσαγωγή (Antwerp, 1539).

[6] Baudouin, *Ad leges de jure civile . . . commentarii* (1559) (Heineccius, col. 174). Cf. *Scaevola* (Heineccius, col. 435-36), referring to the "De origine juris."

intention of the author (*voluntas*) as well as the rules of language (*verba*). In general, Baudouin concluded, there were three subjects indispensable for the understanding of civil law, each prescribed by a seminal title of the Digest. Just as the title "On natural law" required the study of philosophy, so that "On the meaning of words" required philology, and that "On the origin of law" required history.

On this foundation Baudouin began his major effort of historical reconstruction, his *Justinian, or the New Law* of 1559. This book, although no one has paid much attention to it, was the first comprehensive essay on the anti-Tribonianist theme—anticipating and in some ways going beyond Hotman's more sensational but less scholarly work written eight years later. Baudouin's basic premise was that Roman law could not be understood properly without separating fact from law, that is, what had only antiquarian interest from what had legal authority. In the Twelve Tables there was obviously "more fact than law," for example, while even in the Digest "many laws pertained rather to the history of the times than to civil law as we know it."[7] Consequently, Baudouin concluded, "the memory of ancient law is necessary for the knowledge of new law." This formula could easily be reversed for the benefit of historians, of course, as Baudouin well knew. In fact, it was not long before he took this step himself and shifted emphasis from the legal to the antiquarian aspect of the question.

About the problems posed by the Digest, Baudouin was in general agreement with Hotman and Cujas. In the transferrence of the empire (*translatio sedis imperii*) "from the Roman forum to the Constantinopolitan palace," he argued, the empire "changed not only its seat but its form and face, having a different jurisdiction, a different religion, different customs, and a different government."[8] Abandoning pagan superstition, Constantine had likewise abandoned the Roman speech and way of life. By Justinian's time the estrangement was com-

---

[7] Baudouin, *Justinianus, sive de jure novo* (1559) (Halle, 1728), pp. 2, 275, 379. Of the philological method Baudouin wrote (p. 310): "To jurists grammar pertains not only to the correct use of words but to their intent and meaning."

[8] *Ibid.*, p. 201. He also remarked (p. 126) that "the Greeks were accustomed not merely to change Latin legal terms but to make them conform to their own usage."

plete. Here was the real source of Tribonian's crime (*culpa—crimen* Bodin called it more severely—*Triboniani*). Given his ignorance of law and history, which allowed such anachronisms as having Papinian cite a law of Diocletian, and given the restrictions of Byzantine law, it was no wonder that he made a mess of things, "a stew mixed by an incompetent cook."[9] Like Budé, Baudouin was fond of seizing upon those *antinomiae* where Tribonian was "caught napping." Most deplorable, however, were the uncounted interpolations which Cujas was already busy uncovering, often involving tighter constructions, such as changing Ulpian's "usually" to "always" or the famous distortion of "annua die" already pointed out by Budé.[10] In most cases these arose from Justinian's desire "to accommodate the Pandects to the usage of his age and his courts." Hence the "new law." Yet at the same time Tribonian's "inconstancy" unaccountably left certain absurd "vestiges of antiquity" untouched, such as the obsolete ritual of three symbolic sales which a father had to make in order to emancipate his son. It was a puzzling business.

At any rate, the task of the modern scholar was clear: "to determine what is whole and what is diminished, what is old and what is new . . . , for often what in a particular passage is said to be Ulpian's . . . is actually Justinian's or Tribonian's."[11] For analogous reasons jurists had to establish the chronology of laws with great care. "Since later law abrogates or derogates from earlier law," he argued, "it is obviously necessary to determine the sequence of laws and so to use *fasti*, annals, *diaria*. . . ." And vice versa: soon after this, Baudouin was wondering "whether history received more illumination from the books of jurisprudence or jurisprudence from histories."[12] This was the train of thought which led Baudouin to

[9] *Ibid.*, p. 265.
[10] *Ibid.*, pp. 170-71 (D., 13, 7, 8); cf. ch. III, n. 42. "An antinomia," Baudouin said, "is what most ancients called a conflict of two laws not by nature but in terms of a certain case; but Justinian called laws naturally in conflict antinomiae. . . ." The worst of these, Baudouin thought (p. 131, *passim*), were those cases where Tribonian derogated from the imperial majesty by including laws already contradicted by Justinian's "new" legislation.
[11] *Ibid.*, pp. 4, 203. Besides his own researches Baudouin used also Cujas' edition (1554) of "Ulpian's uninterpolated fragments" (p. 212).
[12] Baudouin, *De Institutione*, 688-69. Cf. *Scaevola* (Heineccius, col. 435-

his thesis that a permanent alliance ought to be formed between law and history, to the mutual advantage of both. Each of these disciplines had been revived in modern times, as witnessed the achievements of Alciato and Paolo Giovio. Why not fuse them together into a single cultural science, especially since the development of law and customs formed the very substance of history? Here is one of the cornerstones of what Baudouin came to call "integral history."

The Christian Humanist

Yet there is another, perhaps more direct, approach to Baudouin's conception of history. For Baudouin was not only a legal humanist after the model of Alciato, he was a Christian humanist in the style of Erasmus. Like Hotman, he combined his scholarly ideals with a program of ecclesiastical reform, designed to remedy the political as well as the religious ills of the age. Although he inherited the values and the apparatus of philology, his specific views about history were fashioned in the heat of controversy and shaped by various political pressures. His extraordinary experiences intensified his attachment to history and led him to modify the naïve humanist view with which he began. Indeed, it was the religious crisis into which he threw himself on the eve of the civil wars that provided the occasion for—and to some extent the context of—his reflections upon the nature and method of history. In Baudouin's case, therefore, it is essential to understand the social and political background of his scholarly work.[13]

---

36), remarking that "I recognize the perpetual conjunction . . . of history and Roman jurisprudence, such that I feel the two to be indivisable parts as of a single body."

[13] Baudouin's first biographer was his disciple Papire Masson, *Elogium Francisci Balduini* (Paris, 1573), who also wrote lives of Cujas, Dumoulin, and Pierre Pithou, and who became a determined foe of Hotman (see *infra* ch. VII). The best biography is still J. Heveling, *De Francisco Balduino jurisconsulto* (Arras, 1871), to which A. Wicquot, *François Balduin d'Arras* (Arras, 1890), adds little. See also J. Duquesne, "François Bauduin et la réforme," *Bulletin de l'Académie delphinal*, sér. 5, IX (1917), 55-108, and the article in Haag. There are a number of unpublished letters of some interest from Baudouin to Amerbach in Basel, Universitätsbibliothek, MSS, G. II. 15, f. 10r ff, and a few from Le Douaren, G. II. 16, ff. 262r-274r; G. II. 15, f. 252r; Fr. Gr. VI. 1, f. 92r. A new biography is now planned by Michael Erbe.

Baudouin came to Paris for the first time in 1540 at the age of twenty. It was too late to make the acquaintance of Budé, but he did meet the great jurist Charles Dumoulin and, through him, Hotman. It was a fateful encounter. The careers of these three men were to intertwine and interact in a most remarkable fashion for the next twenty years. For a time Baudouin acted as Dumoulin's secretary and no doubt, like Hotman, derived from him some interest in French legal history. In his native Artois Baudouin had already received a good humanist education at Louvain, which had one of the first trilingual colleges, and had come into contact with the Erasmian tradition. In Arras he not only practiced law but wrote about Artesian history and customary law. In 1546 Baudouin began his teaching career at the University of Paris, that is in the faculty of canon law, where lectures on civil law were permitted. Once again he crossed paths with Hotman, who was giving classes on the same days. So reported one young student, Etienne Pasquier, who the next year was to travel to Toulouse to hear the first lectures of Cujas as well.[14] This is another point of contact between the historical school of law and the study of French antiquities, of which Pasquier was to be one of the leaders.

Like both Hotman and Dumoulin, Baudouin was an early enthusiast of the "so-called reformed religion" of Calvin. It was on these grounds, in fact, that he had been banished from Arras in 1545. By this time he was already carrying on a pseudonymous correspondence with Calvin, whom he looked upon as his spiritual "father." To indicate the solidity of his allegiance to the Genevan faith (*consuetudo*) he called himself "Petrus Rochius," and he acknowledged his intention of coming to join Calvin.[15] In his letters Baudouin discussed a wide range of current topics, including the state of religion in France and that menacing weapon of "Neptune" (the Tridentine Council). He remarked upon the doings of such mutual friends as Johann Sturm,

---

[14] Pasquier, *Les Lettres* (Paris, 1617), II, 501.

[15] There are 22 letters from Baudouin to Calvin preserved in Calvin's *Epistolae* in *CR,* vols. XXXVIII-XLIX, extending from March or April 1545 to May 1556, that is, just before his break with "Calvinolatry." On his banishment from Arras, see C. Paillard, *Le Procès de Pierre Brully* (Paris, 1578), pp. 158 ff.

whom Baudouin visited in Strasbourg, and his countryman Jean Crespin, the future author of the first Protestant martyrology. He also indicated that, besides his work on civil law, he had begun to study Eusebius and to acquire an interest in ecclesiastical history.[16] In this way he prepared himself for his later examination of church-state relations in the early Christian empire, while at the same time he acquired a perspective from which he could assess Calvinism itself.

Until at least 1548 Baudouin was a devoted follower of Calvin and for a time acted as his secretary.[17] So did Hotman, who by this time was corresponding with Calvin in a still more filial fashion. Between these confessional brothers, however, there was already a growing dislike, arising mainly from jealousy. At this point their paths diverged sharply, and never again would Hotman have a kind word to say about the man with whom he shared so many scholarly values.[18] While Hotman joined Beza at the Calvinist academy in Lausanne, Baudouin took a position as professor of law at the University of Bourges, having received his doctorate the previous year and having ingratiated himself by dedicating a work on Justinian's novels to Le Douaren. But the man Baudouin most admired on the faculty was Le Douaren's rival, Eguinaire Baron, whom he regarded as Alciato's true successor and whose works he later edited. Baudouin himself plunged into the study of early Roman law. Thus launched upon his career, Calvin's "integrus Rochius" became less and less interested in returning to Geneva to

---

[16] See especially Baudouin's letters of Dec. 1545 and Nov. 1546 (*CR*, XLI, col. 231, 430-32).

[17] Baudouin translated M. de Falais' *Apology*; Hotman translated Calvin's treatise against astrology, as well as taking down various letters and sermons. See also E. Doumergue, *Jean Calvin* (8 vols., Paris, 1899-1927), III, 594 ff.

[18] As early as 1547 Hotman had had a scholarly dispute with Baudouin (see letter from Baudouin to Calvin, 28 Nov., *CR*, XLI, col. 432) and had been provoked to publish his first book, *De Gradibus cognationis et affinitatis libri duo* (Paris, 1547). The next year he wrote Calvin (27 Aug. 1548, *CR*, XLII, col. 21), "Unlike Baudouin I do not respond coldly but audaciously according to my conscience, and I freely proclaim [the faith]." Cf. Baudouin's letter of 5 Dec. 1552 (*CR*, XLIII, col. 407). Baudouin also referred to a controversy with certain "quondam friends" (meaning Hotman) over the interpretation of usury, in *Justinianus*, p. 66, in which he took sides with Dumoulin. The work which Baudouin had dedicated to Le Douaren was *Breves commentarii in praecipuas Justiniani Imp. novellas* (Lyon, 1547).

work in Calvin's shadow, though he felt guilty enough to offer excuses and to protest against those who suggested that he was made of wax rather than stone (*ceram potius quam petram*). On the other hand, Hotman, contrasting his loyalty with the coldness if not "nicodemitism" of Baudouin, rejoiced in the charismatic basis of Calvinism and resigned himself to several years of teaching grammar, though with growing impatience. Until 1555, though they remained on friendly terms with Dumoulin, their estrangement grew—as did their reputations and involvements.

During his residence at Bourges Baudouin became increasingly independent in his ecclesiastical views and disillusioned with Calvinism. Then in 1550 Baron died and Le Douaren came back to replace him. Faculty squabbles are never easy to reconstruct, but somehow Baudouin antagonized the "partisans of Le Douaren." Personal rivalry, irregular attendance at classes, and student agitation all had something to do with it, but at bottom there was always the religious issue.[19] In any case, Baudouin left the university early in 1555, ostensibly because of idolatry, and was shortly replaced by Cujas. After visits to Geneva and to Montbéliard, he passed on to Strasbourg, carrying a letter of recommendation from Dumoulin (though not from Calvin). As usual Baudouin did nothing to help his own cause. He took occasion to attack Le Douaren directly, first in his inaugural lecture and then in a book which included Hotman in the condemnation, though not, as yet, Calvin. In his legal writings, too, Baudouin's alienation from Calvinism was increasingly clear.[20] In that same year (1556) he published his *Constantine*, which was dedicated to the cause of what he called "Christian jurisprudence" and to religious reconciliation. This Calvin took to be heresy as well as betrayal.

---

[19] See ch. IV, n. 34, and—for the canonist controversy of the years 1551-56 in which Baudouin, Hotman, Le Douaren, and Dumoulin all figured—the following chapter. Already in Sept. 1554 Baudouin wanted to leave Bourges and its "idolatry" (letter of Dumoulin to Bullinger, *CR*, XLII, col. 225), and by the next February was visiting Dumoulin at his request in Montbéliard (Dumoulin to Bullinger, 5 Mar. 1555, Zurich, Zentralbibliothek, MSS. S. 84, f. 201ʳ, and to Amerbach, Basel, Universitätsbibliothek, MS, G. II, 21, f. 113ʳ).

[20] Baudouin's lecture appeared as *Juris civilis schola Argentinensis* (Strasbourg, 1555), followed by *Responsio Christianorum jurisconsultorum ad Fr.*

The counteroffensive was begun by Hotman, who reported Baudouin's lecture directly back to Bourges and who had been keeping up a continuous attack in his letters. Baudouin must have answered in kind, for in a letter to Calvin in March Hotman exclaimed, "Does he want to burn me in effigy and have my patrimony confiscated?" Yet at that very time it seems that Hotman was planning something hardly more pleasant for Baudouin. Less than four months later, with the combined help of Calvin and Sturm, Hotman took the position of his former friend.[21] Here at Strasbourg, for eight years, Hotman became an increasingly belligerent supporter of the Huguenot cause and opponent of reconciliation. These were some of the circumstances which led Baudouin to his final break with what he came to regard as "Calvinolatry" and the fanaticism it seemed to entail. This was the context, too, of Baudouin's re-examination of church history, toward which his legal studies had been inclining for some time. Like his friends Melanchthon, Castellio, and George Cassander, Baudouin was searching for his own answers to religious conflict; and like them he found himself turning back to patristic "tradition."

Baudouin's next position was at the University of Heidelberg, where he taught during four of the most crucial years of his life—the formative period of his historical thought. This was when, along with Hotman and so many others, he was swept into the maelstrom of ecclesiastical politics. Not that he tried to avoid it, for after all it was

---

Duareni commentarios de ministeriis atque beneficiis (Strasbourg, 1556), copies of which were sent to both Hotman and Calvin. They were appalled: see *CR*, XLIV, col. 172-73 (Calvin to Hotman, 24 May 1556) and 81-83 (Hotman to Calvin, 26 Mar. 1556). "I have never read anything more inept," wrote Hotman to Bullinger (*ibid.*, col. 84). For Le Douaren's reaction see his letter (July 1555) in Calvin's *Responsio ad Balduini convicia* (s. l., 1562), pp. 55-69. Hotman had also let it be known that Baudouin was negotiating for a position at Heidelberg (see letter to Bullinger, 20 Jan. 1555, in Basel, Universitätsbibliothek, MS, G. II, 19, f. 112r).

[21] Hotman to Amerbach, 20 April 1556 (Basel, MS, G. II, 19, f. 116r). In July 1555 Hotman had come to Strasbourg with a letter from Calvin to Johann Sturm (16 July, *CR*, XLIV, col. 687), and just a year later Peter Martyr reported (14 July 1556, *CR*, XLV, col. 197), "Hotman has Baudouin's position." Cf. Aubert, I, 167 ff. Baudouin was officially engaged on 25 March 1555 and Hotman on 24 June 1556: M. Fournier, *Les Statutes et privilèges des universités françaises*, IV (Strasbourg) (Paris, 1894), pp. 64, 67.

part of the jurist's calling (*homo politicus, hoc est, jurisconsultus*).[22] The Lutheran atmosphere of this school, recently "reformed" by Melanchthon, Baudouin found congenial to his doctrinal tastes and to the program of religious pacification which he was beginning to develop. At the Colloquy of Worms in 1557, Baudouin found himself in agreement with Melanchthon and Cassander and saw in their moderate position a means of ending religious strife in France.[23] Henceforth, he supported the program of the irenic party, which was to establish an Erasmian reconciliation on the basis of the Augsburg Confession. For him and for Cassander, the ideological leader of the movement, this came to mean a rejection of Calvin's intolerance and a return to "Catholic tradition." Within France itself, there seemed to be some sympathy for this plan, not only from Antoine of Navarre and such Gallicans as Jean de Montluc but also from Catherine de' Medici and the Cardinal of Lorraine, whom Hotman was to denounce shortly as the "tiger of France." The last hope of the Irenic Party was the Colloquy of Poissy, where the French Catholics, in the person of the Cardinal, and the Calvinists, in the person of Theodore Beza, finally confronted each other.

The problem faced by the French monarchy at this point, insoluble as it seems in retrospect, was clear enough : how to steer between the Roman Scylla and the Genevan Charybdis—how to remain independent against encroachments of two foreign menaces, the ultramontane papacy, which was threatening to recall the Council, a threat which had almost caused a schism ten years before, and international Calvinism, which was equally intransigent and opposed in principle to any *via media.* In France itself party lines, though obscured by political interests and by Gallican traditions that affected both sides, were largely determined by these external forces. Yet for the time being, while these two groups were in equilibrium, there was room for a third party to maneuver even though it had no power fulcrum itself.

[22] Baudouin, *Scaevola,* p. 31.

[23] Baudouin, *Responsio altera ad Joannem Calvinum* (Cologne, 1562), 109. Cf. F. Buisson, *Sébastien Castellion* (Paris, 1892), II, 118. As early as 1550 Beza had expressed his opposition to a "middle way" (*medium iter*), in a letter to Claude d'Espence (*Aubert,* I, 64), who was later to push the Cardinal of Lorraine in that direction. See H. O. Evennett, "Claude d'Espence et son 'Discours du Colloque de Poissy,' " *Revue historique,* CLXIV (1930), 40-78.

In the summer of 1561, then, with the unthinking optimism which scholars can sometimes summon, Baudouin threw himself into the irenic movement. As Cassander's representative, he undertook various missions into France and Germany to drum up support.[24] His goal was not only to preserve Gallican unity in France but, through a theological consensus, or at least toleration, to restore and to reform the *respublica Christiana* as a whole.[25]

It was under the spell of these irenic ideals that Baudouin composed his greatest work, the *Institution of Universal History and its Conjunction with Jurisprudence,* which he hopefully dedicated to those "moderatores" Antoine of Navarre and Michel de l'Hôpital. This book expressed many of the basic themes of his philosophy as well as his hopes for the moment. The theme of universal history was a reflection of his ecumenical ecclesiology, that of a reformed jurisprudence was a reflection of his plans for a more civilized religious organization, and that of an alliance between law and history was a reflection of his hopes for a union of the real and the ideal—of custom and morality. It is in the light of Baudouin's passion for integral Christianity, in short, that his conception for integral history must be understood.

---

[24] Baudouin's activities may best be followed through the account of H. O. Evennett, *The Cardinal of Lorraine and the Council of Trent* (Cambridge, 1930), pp. 235 ff, and in Aubert, I and II (Geneva, 1963-65). The work which disturbed the Calvinists (and which they mistakenly attributed to Baudouin) was Cassander's *De Officio pii viri,* in *Opera omnia* (Paris, 1616), pp. 781-97, which Baudouin brought to Paris in August 1561 just before the Colloquy opened. In general, see M. Nolte, *Georgius Cassander en zijn oecumenisch Streven* (Nijmegen, 1951); P. Bröder, *Georg Cassanders Vermittlungsversuche* (Marburg, 1931); J. Lecler, *Histoire de la tolérance au siècle de la réforme* (Paris, 1955), II, 267-71; and, most relevant to this discussion, P. Polman, *L'Élément historique dans la controverse religieuse du XVIe siècle* (Gembloux, 1932), pp. 168, 202, 385.

[25] Letter to the Duke of Württemberg (10 Aug. 1561) in *Briefwechsel zwischen Christoph, Herzog von Württemberg und Petrus Paulus Vergerius,* ed. E. von Kausler and T. Schott (Tübingen, 1875), p. 280. Hotman was writing to the Duke at the very same time (Dareste, "François Hotman," pp. 31-32) on behalf of the Calvinists. Contemporary accounts include the Genevan *Histoire ecclésiastique,* ed. P. Verron (Toulouse, 1882), I, 348; Beza's *Vie de J. Calvin,* ed. A. Franklin (Paris, 1864), p. 146; and, more favorable, Pierre de la Place, *Commentaires de l'estat de la religion et republic* (1566), ed. Buchon (Paris, 1836), pp. 192-93; cf. also La Popelinière, *Histoire de France* (La Rochelle, 1581), f. 269r.

The Idea of History

Baudouin's *Institution of Universal History,* based upon lectures given at the University of Heidelberg in 1561, was both a manifesto of legal humanism and a "method" of history.[26] It combined, in a sense, the *mos gallicus* with the *ars historica.* In the sixteenth century the "art of history" referred to didactic treatises on the reading and writing of history analogous to the *artes poetica* and *rhetorica.* Precedents for such works may be found both in antiquity, such as Lucian's *How to Write History,* and in the middle ages, such as Isidore of Seville's chapters on the utility of history and on the first historians; but basically this genre, too, was a creation of Italian humanism. In general, the "praise of history" was an immensely popular topic in Renaissance literature and may be found in a number of guises. Besides dialogues, lectures, and letters too numerous to mention, it appears in encyclopedias, such as Polydore Vergil's *Inventors of Things* and Barthélemy de Chasseneuz' *Catalogue of the Glory of the World*; in pedagogical works, such as Vives' *Teaching of the Disciplines* and Budé's *Institution of the Prince*; and in prefaces, such as those of Valla and Alciato already referred to and later those of Luther, Melanchthon, and Grynaeus. Finally, it took the form of such treatises as Giorgio Valla's *Writing of History,* Christophe Milieu's *Writing of Universal History,* and Francesco Robortello's *How to Write History,* to mention three of the earliest.[27] Many of these arts of history, including Baudouin's, were collected and published by Johann Wolf in 1576.

[26] Particularly prominent was the influence of Melanchthon, whose views about universal history closely paralleled those of Baudouin, as shown in his preface (1558) to the *Chronicon Carionis* (*CR,* XII, col. 705 ff); see H. Brettschneider, *Melanchthon als Historiker* (Insterburg, 1880). It was also Melanchthon who first introduced a chair of history into the University of Heidelberg in 1557, the very year that Baudouin arrived: E. Scherer, *Geschichte und Kirchengeschichte an den deutschen Universitäten* (Freiberg, 1927), p. 51. On Baudouin's career at Heidelberg, see J. F. Hautz, *Geschichte der Universität Heidelberg* (Mannheim, 1862), I, 428, 437.

[27] Polydore Vergil, *De Rerum inventoribus* (Basel, 1536), pp. 46-49, "Qui primis historiam condiderunt"; Chasseneuz, *Catalogus gloriae mundi* (Geneva, 1517), pp. 394-95, "Laus historicorum"; Vives, "De tradendis disciplinis," *Opera omnia* (Valencia, 1785), VI, 388 ff. Luther's letter was published as the preface to Robert Barnes' *Vitae Romanorum pontificum* (Basel, 1535) and Grynaeus'

The rhetorical roots of Baudouin's conception of history are only too obvious. Once again he rehearsed the formulas of Cicero and Quintilian, representing history as the business of the orator (*munus oratoris*) and the embodiment of his most essential faculty, which was memory. Once again he sang the praises of truth, which constituted the "first law of history" and which distinguished it from every other form of prose narrative. History was set apart from other literary forms, too, in being concerned with things not words (*res non verba*) and from philosophy in being concerned with man rather than nature (*res humanae*, not *res naturales*).[28]

And yet if Baudouin built upon the literary tradition of the Italian *artes*, he was by no means bound by it. History was concrete and literal no doubt, but it was also, as Polybius had taught, a kind of scientific enterprise. If the mother of history was the oratorical art, as Valla had asserted, its sister was political science, as Casaubon later claimed. "The ancients called that history 'pragmatic,'" Baudouin wrote, "which narrates and usefully explains not only the events but the causes and which describes the consequences as well as the policies."[29] Because of this "pragmatic" function and because of the emphasis on utility not pleasure (*utilitas non voluptas*), history had to be arranged in chronological order (*ordo temporum*). All of this reinforced Baudouin's central point that the major value of history was not private but public, not moral but political and legal. In the tradition of civic humanism Baudouin regarded history not as a literary

---

"De utilitate legendae historiae" appeared in *Justini ex Trogo Pompeio historia* (Basel, 1539) and Valla's "De Scribenda historia" in his *De expendis et fugiendis rebus opus* (Venice, 1501). Milieu's *De Scribenda universita rerum historia* (Basel, 1551), which has interesting parallels with Baudouin's work, was reprinted in Wolf's collection; so were Grynaeus', Robortello's, Pontano's, Lucian's, Dionysius of Halicarnassus' (*Criticism of Thucydides' History*)—as well as Bodin's and others later than Baudouin's. In general, see my "François Baudouin and his Conception of History," *JHI*, XXV (1964), 35-37, and the literature there cited.

[28] Baudouin, *De Institutione*, p. 602: "The history of the nobler animals, that is, of man, is much more admirable than that of other things." Cf. pp. 609, 621, 640, *passim*.

[29] *Ibid.*, pp. 618, 677. Cf. Isaac Casaubon, letter to Henry IV in *Polybii . . . historiarum qui supersunt* (Paris, 1609), f. 6ᵛ, concluding (f. 9ᵛ) that Polybius ranked as a philosopher.

form but as a human—that is, a social and political—science. Indeed, it was the most direct route, at least in secular terms, to wisdom itself.[30]

Here, then, was Baudouin's accomplishment: the transformation of the loose and literary praise of history into a comprehensive theory. His *Institution* was a handbook of historical method, perhaps the first to be written; and it was in this form that the "art of history" was to take root in France. Baudouin's personal contribution to this revitalized tradition was the novel use which he made of specifically legal ideas and techniques. Not only did he want to enrich legal education through the study of history (which after all was the goal of every legal humanist), he wanted the historian to have a thorough training in law.

Already there were parallels between the two occupations. Like the lawyer, for example, the historian had to concern himself with precedents and the problem of "origins"; and he was coming to prize laws and institutions above military exploits: *arma cedant togae*. But Baudouin was discovering still more fundamental connections. "I have become aware," he wrote, "that law books are the product of history and that historical monuments evolve from the books of law."[31] Here he returned to the thesis of his *Justinian*, that "certain laws have more fact than law and therefore are conjoined to history, and they neither can nor should be separated." It was natural that Baudouin should emphasize the value of legal sources, especially of public records. The admirable practice of the ancient church, "whose clerks . . . by public authority diligently and faithfully . . . kept its monuments uncorrupted in the archives, which were open to all," contrasted pitifully with the secrecy and dishonesty of the sixteenth century. If this practice were reversed, he added, it would be revealed that "the noblest and fullest material of this sort would be . . . the records of the kingdom of France and the court of the parlement of Paris."[32] (At that very

[30] Baudouin, *De Institutione*, p. 609: "I say that [history] is the one way and means by which we can ascend to that knowledge of divine and human things which may reflect our haughty spirits as in a mirror, from which we may have some perspective on [circumspiciamus] what has been done in the world . . . which may be worthy of our investigation and memory." Jurisprudence, too, he recalled (p. 668), was "the knowledge of things divine and human."

[31] *Ibid.*, pp. 669 ff.

[32] *Ibid.*, p. 653.

time, as we shall see, these records were being ransacked for the very purpose which Baudouin suggested.)

More remarkable were Baudouin's views on historical criticism. Here again, while clinging to rhetorical formulas, he resorted to legal devices. He made a fundamental distinction between eye-witness accounts (*testes*) and written authorities (*testimonia*), though he recognized public documents as equivalent to the former. The hardest job of all, as Polybius had pointed out long before, was assessing the value of historical writing. "I prefer those witnesses who describe what they have taken part in . . . , while those who give hearsay evidence are only indirect witnesses, which are always rejected by the jurists."[33] In such legal terms Baudouin transformed the commonplace judgment that, in the words of Montaigne, "the only good histories are those written by men who themselves conducted affairs," into a rule about what we should call "primary sources." "The latest and most recent account of events," he concluded, "is usually the least reliable." This was certainly the lesson which a critical study of the Digest taught.

It was always to the primary sources (*primi autores*), not to secondary authorities (*rivuli deducti*), that the historian must turn. If certain old texts, such as Homer or Herodotus, contained a mixture of truth and error, it was not the historian's job to cast doubt upon the whole work in Pyrrhonist fashion, but rather, by a combination of mythology and archeology, to purge history of fable.[34] He had also to determine the "good faith" of the author and the authenticity of the text, for falsifications and interpolations ever threatened the unwary historian. Baudouin stayed on the alert for both and warned against the use of pseudo-Berosus as he had against relying too closely on Tribonian. He was even less tolerant of modern alterations, such as the invention of harangues. "The testimony of the ancients should be presented without any interpolations, nor should new material be added nor any words be substituted for theirs . . . , lest one seem not so much to adorn history as to make it faulty and mendacious." "As

---

[33] *Ibid.*, pp. 653 ff, referring to the Digest title "De fide instrumentum." See the discussion of J. Franklin, *Jean Bodin and the Sixteenth-Century Revolution in the Methodology of Law and History* (New York, 1963), ch. VIII.

[34] Baudouin, *De Institutione*, p. 626, discussing the topos *fides historiae*.

for the validity and reliability of documents," he added, "jurists are not satisfied with copies but require *authentica,* or originals."[35]

Another point in common between history and law was the reliance upon chronological order. Both were to be studied in the same sequence, Baudouin urged, "from the earlier to the later so that by a proper arrangement the latter issue from the former."[36] This was one reason why Baudouin was so sensitive to anachronisms and devoted space to some particularly striking examples. As complementary forms of public memory, moreover, the two disciplines had similar patterns of development; just as history emerged from fable and folklore into literary narrative, so law progressed from custom to written law. The lack of written history or law was a sure sign of barbarism, of cultural childhood. Barbarians were reputedly too busy fighting to bother with written records; these belong to a more reflective—and a more litigious—age. It was to repair this neglect that many humanists turned to the writing of local history. Alciato had contributed to this enterprise in his youth, and so had Baudouin, not only in his *Chronicle of Artois* but in his commentary on the Artesian custom.[37] This, too, was a way of restoring the "integrity" of history.

Baudouin's conception of "integral history" was the product partly of his reading of Polybius and Eusebius and of Melanchthon but most directly, again, of his study of Roman law. "If we desire the true and integral knowledge of things human and divine," he wrote, "we must study universal history. That wise and prudent author Polybius advises us that history must be (in his words) catholic, for it is like a body whose members may not be divided."[38] The past, especially as reflected in the growth of laws and in the relations between different societies, such as Greece and Rome, had a kind of organic unity which it was the scholar's job to reconstruct. The fact that classical and medieval historians tended not only to repeat one another but also to continue one another led Baudouin to hope for a history that had continuity and indivisibility (*individuitas*)—just as he hoped to restore

---

[35] *Ibid.*, pp. 637-38.

[36] *Ibid.*, p. 684; cf. *Justinianus*, pp. 4, 140.

[37] Baudouin, *Chronique d'Arthois* (Arras, 1856), p. 1.

[38] Baudouin, *Scaevola* (Heineccius, col. 437-38). Cf. *De Institutione*, pp. 614, 617.

the seamless cloak of Christianity. After all, history, like the church itself, contained all of humanity. It was Baudouin's conclusion, then, that the story of mankind should be described not merely *ab urbe* but *ab orbe condita*; indeed, in view of its organic character it should be described *ab ovo*.

History was to be universal in geographic as well as temporal terms. "Diodorus Siculus . . . ," recalled Baudouin, "attacked ancient historians who wrote the history only of a single nation because they were writing not history but only a certain disconnected piece of history." If the history of Polybius was "catholic" because it dealt with the Roman empire, the history of Eusebius was catholic in the more profound sense that it included, or at least pretended to include, all human creation. As Melanchthon put it, history was a "portrait of the human race."[39] For Baudouin's generation this meant including the new world, too—"those distant parts of the earth which were once hidden and now are known." Thus Baudouin came to recommend an alliance between geography and "perpetual history," so that the past could be understood in terms not only of chronology (*ratione temporum*) but of environment (*ratione regionum*). Bodin was not alone in his geohistorical constructions, though he pushed them much further than Baudouin.[40]

Finally, Baudouin urged that the universality of history be reflected in its subject matter. In particular, this meant including ecclesiastical as well as military affairs—combining, in a sense, the orientation of ancient with that of medieval history. "We only progress," he wrote, "if we pursue sacred as well as civil history, not confusedly but joined together." One reason that the Greeks had fallen short of universal history was their neglect of this subject, as contrasted with such Christian writers as Optatus.

I say that if we are rightly and wisely to examine the history of the world, we should observe the condition of the church and of religion, for

---

[39] *CR*, XI, col. 1076 and col. 862 ("integrum corpus historiae mundi").

[40] Baudouin, *De Institutione*, p. 665. Cf. A. Meuten, *Bodins Theorie von der Beeinflussung des politischen Lebens der Staaten durch ihre geographische Lage* (Bonn, 1904), and M. J. Tooley, "Bodin and the Mediaeval Theory of Climate," *Speculum*, XXVIII (1953), 64-83; also E. Fournol, *Bodin prédécesseur de Montesquieu* (Paris, 1896).

we should not forget the necessity of understanding that principle of human society, lest we neglect not only the head but the heart and soul of history. Thus when I speak of history, I mean integral and perfect history. So the history of our pontiffs, emperors, and kings should be joined as if practically one.[41]

Thus Baudouin's historical ideal reflected both his irenic hope and his Gallican conviction that affairs of church and state were inseparable.

Here is Baudouin's own summary: "I have said that the course of universal history ought to be presented, and that its universality ought to be described according to the times, places, and events, the events being of three sorts, the state of religious, foreign, and domestic affairs, that is, of ecclesiastical, political, and military history."[42] In this "integral history" there was a threefold unity: biological, since according to Polybius it was "a body composed of many interrelated parts"; theological, corresponding to the Augustinian world-design and to the views of recent German histories, such as the chronicle of Johann Cario sponsored by Melanchthon; and aesthetic, since like the Aristotelian theory of drama "history is universal in terms of the times, places, and actions." The difference was that in the great play performed in the "amphitheater of the world" man was both actor and spectator [43] Baudouin was well aware of the subjective nature of historical investigation and interpretation. There was one, however, who might be able to escape from this epistemological liability: a philosophic scholar trained in the techniques of law and philology and committed to the ideal of a reunited and reformed Christendom. Such a man might begin to restore the unity of history (*universitas historiae*) as well.

This was only Baudouin's historiographical goal, of course, not something that had ever been achieved, even by the Magdeburg Centuriators, whose work he so much admired. The art of history as it had actually been practiced had by no means reached that level, al-

[41] Baudouin, *De Institutione*, p. 618.

[42] *Ibid.*, p. 626.

[43] *Ibid.*, pp. 599 and 742; cf. p. 601: "They are three and four times blessed who descend into this lower arena, so to say, in order to know what has been done and is being done by men. . . ."

though Baudouin had high hopes for the future. Characteristically, he saw the art of history itself in historical terms—not as a static literary genre but as a developing attitude toward the past. In particular, he recognized a transformation from "mythistory," or epic poetry, into prose, and of simple annals into narrative history. The continuity of historical writing was striking, especially in the case of Greek and Roman antiquity, where it was often quite deliberate. As for European historiography, Baudouin pointed out the succession of medieval chroniclers, "those somewhat unpolished writers . . . without pretense of formal learning but faithful to the testimony of truth," by those "lettered and learned men who adorn what the former decribe," including Flavio Biondo, Polydore Vergil, and Paolo Emilio.[44] There was a parallel progress in more properly Christian terms, too, from "ethnic" to ecclesiastical history, although for Baudouin this implied not so much the Augustinian trajectory of history as an approach to historical certainty and "integrity." Such was the design of the first and in some ways most comprehensive method of history of modern times.

From Baudouin to La Popelinière

Baudouin's book on the art of history was the first but not the only one to be published in France in the sixteenth century. Five years later it was followed—and soon overshadowed—by the still more ambitious *Method of History* by Jean Bodin, who also took his point of departure from the revival of letters associated with the magic name of Budé and in particular from legal humanism. The parallels between the books of these two men are only too obvious and will not be drawn out further here. Like Baudouin, Bodin emphasized the political value of history and the links with jurisprudence; and he demanded that history deal not only with war and politics but with ecclesiastical, economic, and even intellectual matters. Bodin's conception of history was even more "universal" and certainly more eclectic than that of Baudouin.[45]

---

[44] *Ibid.*, pp. 649 ff, 662.
[45] Most useful in this connection are J. Franklin, *Jean Bodin*; J. L. Brown, *The Methodus . . . of Jean Bodin* (Washington, 1939); E. Fournol, (work

Yet from our somewhat restricted point of view the differences between the "methods" of Bodin and Baudouin are perhaps more
striking than the resemblances. In one respect, Bodin seemed to be following the pattern of Hotman; for while he spoke warmly of the marriage of law and letters in his Toulouse oration of 1559, he soon began
to turn against many of the ideals of legal humanism. Somehow he
conceived an almost personal aversion toward those scholars who preferred to be regarded as grammarians rather than as jurists (*qui se
grammaticos malunt quam jurisconsultos haberi*) and who placed
their inferior science above justice itself.[46] According to Bodin, the
best jurists were those who combined learning, the old as well as the
new variety, with experience; and the ideal jurist would be one who
added to these a grasp of philosophy. The true successor of Alciato,
he thought, was not Cujas the philologist but Connan the system-
maker. Bodin himself complained of the absurdities in Roman law,
but he was thinking about those of a logical or legal rather than of
a historical order. So the conventional epithet "neo-Bartolist" is not
wholly inappropriate.

The result of this was that, while Bodin placed history "above all
sciences," he gave it a wholly subordinate function. It was the raw
material of the jurist, the record of the human chaos out of which a
legal philosopher could create a universal system of jurisprudence. Like
Baudouin he believed that law emerged from history (moving from a
de facto to a de jure level), but unlike Baudouin he wanted to dupli-
cate this process himself by assembling a sociological and political
science as the foundation of a new system. It was in universal history,
he was convinced, in the comprehensive study of the character and
customs of all known human societies, that one had to look for uni-

---

cited ch. IV, n. 49); A. Klempt, *Die Säkularisierung der universalhistorischen
Auffassung* (Göttingen, 1960); and above all J. Moreau-Reibel, *Jean Bodin et
le droit public comparé* (Paris, 1933), including remarks on Baudouin. More
generally, see N. W. Gilbert, *Renaissance Concepts of Method* (New York,
1960), discussing legal as well as historical "methods."

[46] Jean Bodin, *Methodus ad facilem historiarum cognitionem*, in Mesnard,
p. 109. Cf. *Oratio de instituenda in repub. juventutem* (*ibid.*, p. 17), where
he names as the chief representatives of the new jurisprudence Budé, Alciato,
and the systematist Connan.

versal law (*in historia juris universae optima pars latet*). Bodin's own
intellectual development from the *Method of History*—which in La
Popelinière's opinion was actually a "method of law"—to the *Republic*
published ten years later confirms the view that what he really wanted
was not to make a science out of history but to extract a science from
it—not to perfect history but to transcend it.[47] It was no doubt for this
very reason that the influence of Bodin's book far surpassed any other
"art of history" of the sixteenth century. Yet once again we encounter
a form of that transcendent impulse which marks history off from
philosophy and social science.

A third work in this tradition was a *Method of History* published in
1579 by a certain parlementaire and popular historian, Pierre Droit
de Gaillard. This book, too, took up the familiar theme of an "alliance
of history with other disciplines." In particular, he pointed out that
"jurisprudence emerged from history, as witness the excellent jurists
Gaius and Pomponius, discussing its origins"; and he added that "the
whole law of the Romans and other nations is nothing else than that
part of history which describes the custom and manner of carrying on
business and contracts of each people with itself as well as with foreigners." So it was, too, with theology, medicine, and other liberal
arts. "To put it in a word," he concluded, "all disciplines take their
source and origin of their principles, which we possess by nature, from
history as from an overflowing fountain."[48] History was not merely
part, it was parent of the humanist encyclopedia. Although Gaillard
seems to have derived his chief inspiration from Bodin, his attitude
resembles more closely that of Baudouin or of Le Roy. Although he
took a rather naïvely exemplaristic view of history, he dug more deeply
than any of these into the French past, and he referred to most of the
historians and jurists treated here.[49]

---

[47] Lancelot Voisin de la Popelinière, *Idee de l'histoire accomplie* (Paris,
1599), p. 29. In general, see Moreau-Reibel, *Jean Bodin*, and K. D. McRae,
"Ramist Tendencies in the Thought of Jean Bodin," *JHI*, XVI (1955), 306-23.

[48] Pierre Droit de Gaillard, *Methode qu'on doit tenir en la lecture de l'histoire*
(Paris, 1579), pp. 550, 552, echoing the "de origine juris." From Gaillard's
Latin summary (see ch. I, n. 1) "deprompta ex suis institutionibus historicis" it
appears that "method" may be equivalent to "institution." Gaillard was also the
author of an often reprinted *Chronologie* and a *Chronique ecclesiastique*.

[49] Gaillard, *Methode*, pp. 151 ff, on judicial disorder, citing Budé, Le Roy,

At the very end of the century the Huguenot historian Lancelot Voisin, Sieur de la Popelinière, published his mature reflections on the nature and function of history. This was the last and in certain ways most interesting of the French arts of history. Building on Bodin's work and yet at the same time reverting to the rhetoric of the Italian *artes*, La Popelinière presented his own version of "perfect history" (*histoire accomplie*) in a way very reminiscent of those of Baudouin (*historia perfecta*) and of Bodin (*historia consummata*). "A proper history will be a general, eloquent and judicious narrative," he wrote, "of the most notable actions of men and other occurrences, represented according to the times, places, their causes, progress and results."[50] In his view the very fact that history had to be understood in terms of times and circumstances (*selon le tems, les personnes* et *les affair[es] des hommes*) made it more reliable than either philosophy, political science (*la police*), or even theology, and so established its independence. Partly because of his obsessive desire to justify his own *History of France,* which had been condemned by his Huguenot comrades for its excessive frankness, La Popelinière was particularly insistent upon the need for accuracy and objectivity. It was not the historian's job to judge the actions of men but only to describe them faithfully. In much the same terms as his "response" to the Synod of La Rochelle years before, he argued that history should be above party and passion and yet dedicated to "the profit of human society" and to posterity.[51]

In some ways La Popelinière seemed to depart from conventional humanism. In history he detected not a universal but a national pattern and so was especially attracted to that question which, as Bodin had declared, had most disturbed historians, that of the origins of peoples.

Le Douaren, and others, and pp. 95 ff, on the Gallican church and the sale of benefices, to mention two of the topics.

[50] La Popelinière, *Idee de l'histoire*, p. 36.

[51] BN MSS, Fonds français, vol. 20797, f. 485r-63v, "Responce pour l'histoire." The parallels between this personal justification and his more systematic, published statement fourteen years later are remarkable, as I suggest in a forthcoming study of "History as a Calling: the Case La Popelinière." In general, see G. W. Sypher, "La Popelinière's *Histoire de France,*" *JHI,* XXIV (1963), 41-54, and also his dissertation (Cornell University, 1961), which includes a transcription of La Popelinière's affair (BN, MSS, Collection Dupuy, vol. 744, f. 230r-260r).

La Popelinière presented one more refutation of the theory, long since exploded, that the Franks were descended from the ancient Trojans; and he went on to offer one more "design" for a general history of France down to modern times, like the others never to be realized. He also had scant respect for the humanist "encyclopedia," which he dismissed as a disorganized "mélange of sciences." Not that La Popelinière wanted to narrow the horizons of history. On the contrary, like Bodin and Le Roy he wanted to include "the origin . . . , progress and change of all the arts and sciences,"[52] as well as matters of religion and law, both public and private; and indeed he developed the most astonishing project for a kind of general cultural anthropology to be based upon historical and geographic exploration, going beyond even the speculations of Bodin.[53] La Popelinière was hostile to the old humanist tradition mainly because he associated it with the errors of "those more attached to antiquity than to reason." He, on the other hand, was an aggressive advocate of the moderns and of the vernacular. Such was to be the orientation, too, of his ideal history.

Perhaps the most significant thing about La Popelinière's conception of history was that it was founded upon a thorough and discriminating history of history. He compiled a vast catalogue, in effect a running commentary on the reading list which Bodin had appended to his *Method*, arranged along national lines. Most interesting was his survey of French historiography, which included not only formal writers of history such as Paolo Emilio and Du Haillan, but political writers such as Seyssel and Dumoulin. None of these, of course, not even the "contemplative historian" Bodin, quite lived up to La Popelinière's exalted standards. In describing the developmental pattern of history in general, La Popelinière displayed a characteristic tendency to transform literary genres into chronological stages. "The poets," he

---

[52] La Popelinière, *Idee de l'histoire*, pp. 267 ff. The "Dessein de l'histoire nouvelle des françois" occupies pages 330-456. See G. Huppert, "The Renaissance Background of Historicism," *History and Theory*, V (1966), 48-60.

[53] See La Popelinière's letters to Scaliger (1601, 1604) in J. de Reves (ed.), *Epistres françoises . . . a Mons*r. *Joseph Juste de la Scala* (Harderwyck, 1624), pp. 151-53, 303-7, and the discussion of C. Vivanti, "Le Scoperte geografiche e gli scritti di Henri de la Popelinière," *Rivista storica italiana*, LXXIV (1962), 225-49. In general, see G. Atkinson, *Les nouveux horizons de la renaissance française* (Paris, 1935).

declared, "were the first historians." It was only after a period of "natural history," or oral tradition, he believed, and a period of fabulous history, that a nation could produce written history, in the form first of annals and finally of "continuous history," in which eloquence and philosophy were joined to the chronological narration of facts.[54] These were the four "seasons" of historiography which La Popelinère recognized and hoped to surpass with his own "new history."

It has seemed desirable to follow the course of the *ars historica* for a short distance because of its relation, tangential though it was, to legal humanism. Yet historical scholarship itself, as it should be clear by now, was considerably more sophisticated and fruitful than conventional humanist rhetoric might suggest. Certainly this is true of Baudouin, for whom the theory of history played a relatively minor role and even then was tied to a short-lived ideological enthusiasm. If his *Institution of Universal History* reflected to some extent a "transcendent impulse", this was temporary and in any case did not detract from the concreteness of his approach, which placed as much emphasis upon the richness of historical narrative as upon universal scope. For in the final analysis Baudouin was not a philosopher, but a dedicated historian, and in the last decade of his life he turned to some of the particular work of historical scholarship which his assessment had suggested. Significantly, he was drawn in particular toward medieval studies, though up to now his work in this area has received scant attention.

Medieval Studies

The failure of the Colloquy of Poissy, in which Calvin had a hand, marked the end of the irenic movement and of Baudouin's hope for a "collation of opinions." The resulting disillusionment contributed to the creation of the party of the "politiques," who became the heirs of the irenic group; but unfortunately it contributed also to the growing radicalism of the contending factions in France. From the irenic interlude no one derived much benefit, least of all Baudouin,

---

[54] La Popelinère, *Histoire des histoires*, pp. 137, 68, 33, 45, 158, 146. On French historiography, see pp. 426 ff.

who was regarded by both sides as a Lutheran interloper. Given the policy of the Guises at this time, it made him also, in the eyes of the Calvinists, a creature of the Cardinal of Lorraine. To Beza, who had been Calvin's agent in the sabotage of the Colloquy itself, Baudouin was an apostate, an "Ecebolius" who had tried to corrupt Antoine of Navarre and various German princes with the Cassandrian notions. To Hotman, who had competed with Baudouin for this very diplomatic support, Baudouin was a doctrinal chameleon who had changed faiths a half dozen times.[55] The truth is that Baudouin was, at the worst possible time, trying to maintain an Erasmian position without either the reputation—or the passivity—of Erasmus.

This time Calvin himself took charge of the prosecution of "Baudouin, whom I once loved." During the Colloquy he launched a virulent *Response to a Certain Turn-Coat Compromiser Who under Pretense of Pacifying Has Tried to Divert the True Course of the Gospel in France,* followed the next year by another pamphlet documenting his charge of betrayal by an appendix of Baudouin's old letters.[56] The old Le Douaren affair, too, was revived. Baudouin defended himself in three separate responses, the last including Hotman and Beza in his complaints. He contrasted what he had come to regard as the true Christian tradition, including Melanchthon and the early fathers, especially St Augustine, with Calvin's "new faction" and his "inhuman decrees."[57] His arguments were all in vain, of course. After

[55] Hotman, *Epistolae* (Amsterdam, 1700), p. 6 (to Bullinger, June 1556), and Beza, *Ad Francisci Balduini apostate Ecebolii convicia ... responsio* (s.l. 1563).

[56] Calvin's *Responsio ad versipellem quendam mediatorem qui pacificandi specie rectum evangelii cursum in Gallia abrumpere molitus est* (Geneva, 1561) was directed against Cassander's *De Officio viri pii,* which Baudouin had brought to France but had not, as Calvin thought, written (see letter to Beza on *1 Oct., CR,* XLVII, col. 1). The *Responsio ad Balduini convitia* (s. l. 1562), which was published by Baudouin's old friend Jean Crespin, included contributions also by Hotman and Contius and an old letter of Le Douaren. Both works appear in *CR,* XXXVII, col. 529 ff. See also Aubert, III, 226 ff.

[57] Baudouin, *Ad Leges de famosis libellis et de calumniatoribus commentarius* (Paris, 1562), comparing Calvin with the justice of the early Christian emperors, and *Responsio altera ad Joannem Calvinum* (Cologne, 1562), calling again upon the authority of Castellio, Bullinger, and Melanchthon (pp. 138-44) and referring to his recent studies of the Donatists. Baudouin kept up the

Calvin's death in 1564 Hotman and Beza kept the dispute alive. It cropped up again in the famous controversy over Hotman's *Franco-Gallia*, which will be referred to later; and later, when La Popelinière fell out with the Huguenots, one of Beza's complaints was that he had dealt too leniently with Baudouin in his *History of France*.[58] Even in the present century Baudouin, like his friend Melanchthon, has not been entirely forgiven by his former co-religionists.

After this episode Baudouin had little choice except to return to orthodoxy. Once again his candidacy for a chair, this time at the University of Valence, was blocked by the Calvinists, and Hotman was appointed instead. Baudouin himself attended the last sessions of the Council of Trent; and with the help of the Cardinal of Lorraine, who apparently had supported the irenic plan for a time, he persuaded Philip II to revoke the ban passed against him twenty years before by Charles V.[59] He continued his irenic activities in 1564 in the Netherlands, where he conferred with William of Orange, but again he was too late. In his last years Baudouin resumed his teaching of civil law at the University of Angers, and in 1568 he became *maître des requêtes* of the Duke of Anjou. He died in 1573, just after the Massacre of St Bartholomew destroyed what remained of his irenic dreams and before he could benefit from his position as advisor to the Duke of Anjou, who became Henry III in that year.

---

attack in his anonymous *Religionis et regis adversus exitiosas Calvini, Bezae, et Ottomani conjuratorum factiones defensio prima* (Paris, 1562) (*CR*, XLVI, col. 438 ff) and in his preface to his edition of Eguinaire Baron, *Opera omnia* (Paris, 1562).

[58] Theodore Beza, letter of 29 March 1581, in BN MSS, Collection Dupuy, vol. 744, f. 237^r, referring to the *Histoire de France* (see n. 25), f. 269^r, as "299," as in fact it is mispaginated in this edition. For a modern Calvinist's continued attack on Baudouin, see Doumergue, *Jean Calvin*, II, 762-75, and *Une Poignée de faux* (Lausanne, 1900), pp. 104-15.

[59] See Dareste, "Charte relatif à François Baudouin, 1563," *BSHPF*, I (1853), 147. "He thought that he would teach at Valence on a large salary," wrote Beza to Calvin about Baudouin (Aubert, III, 227), "and left [the Elector] Palatine in this hope. But warned by me, the bishop thought appropriately of Hotman and sent for him by letters." This letter is dated 25 Nov. [1561], and yet Baudouin's "conduitte par l'evêque" (though there is no extant text) is dated 19 Feb. 1562, while Hotman's not until 1 July 1563. There was also deliberation about hiring Dumoulin. See M. Fournier, "Notes et documents sur les professeurs de droit en France, IV," *NRHDFE*, XIX (1895), 202-3.

In returning to orthodox Catholicism Baudouin was not doing anything very unusual; he was not even breaking with his own values. On the contrary, he was following a rather common Gallican pattern which led many Frenchmen to prefer religious unity on a national basis, if only nominally, to a radical and destructive reformation or a hopeless ecumenical ideal. He was following, too, perhaps, the classic pattern of Newman—gravitation toward traditional religion through the study of patristics and ecclesiastical history. For this was indeed the subject of his later researches. Inspired by the obvious parallel with the Huguenots, he published a history of the "Carthaginian collation" between Catholics and Donatists, which he compared to the Colloquy of Poissy, and an edition of Optatus' account of the Donatist schism. This important work, closely related to his concern for "integral history," was carried on by his own disciple Papire Masson and later by Pierre Pithou, and so it represents perhaps the most direct link between Baudouin and medievalist scholarship.[60]

The last product of Baudouin's return to orthodoxy and his interest in history proper was his memoir on the house of Anjou, which he had been commissioned to write in 1568 and on which he was still working when he died in 1573. Here was an international theme which gave him for the first time an opportunity to put into practice some of his preachings about the content and method of history. In his youth he had composed a *Chronicle of Artois*, also in the vernacular, but this was only a conventional summary, enriched a bit through discussions of civil and customary law. The Angevin history, on the other hand, he intended to be a critical history, based on legal sources as well as chronicles, modern as well as medieval. He left only a rough outline, some disorganized notes, and one hastily written section, and yet this work affords the unusual sight of a legal humanist and meth-

---

[60] Baudouin, *Historia Carthaginiensis collationis* (Paris, 1566), still expressing the hope (prefatory letter to Jean du Tillet) that the history of the ancient church would supply examples and formulas to resolve present-day problems, and *Delibatio Africanae historiae ecclesiasticae sive Optati Milevitani . . . de Schismate donatistarum* (Paris, 1569), repeating his faith in *integra historia* (b iv). See ch. X. The man who preserved Baudouin's ideas about law and history most faithfully was Marin Liberge, especially in his *Universae juris historiae descriptio* (Poitou, 1567), and *De artibus et disciplinis* (Angers, 1592).

odizer of history turning his talents to the field of medieval studies, still largely untouched by the standards of classical scholarship.[61] The very fact that the work is unfinished, that it may be seen in the process of being created, may furnish additional insight into Baudouin's historical thinking.

Like any hired historiographer Baudouin had also to be an apologist. It was his purpose to describe the antiquity, honor, grandeur, and geographic extent of the Angevin dynasty, which had as great a claim as any family to a place in universal history. Baudouin endorsed the idea of ancestor-worship by introducing his discussion with a Ciceronian tag to the effect that ignorance of one's eminent forebears is shameful.[62] Four principal points were to be considered in Baudouin's book: the kingly status and the crowns which had been claimed by the house of Anjou; its service to the French monarchy; its military and political prowess; and its cultivation of literature and the arts. These matters would be taken up in the first two sections of Baudouin's memoirs. A third would deal with certain legal questions, mainly concerning succession, which medieval chroniclers had left obscure. In the course of collecting source material, however, Baudouin was struck by the many errors concerning this dynasty, and so he decided to devote a fourth part to clearing up these mistakes. This critique of Angevin historiography was in fact the only section completed by Baudouin before his death.

Yet despite this triteness and traditionalism, Baudouin brought to bear upon this subject all of the apparatus of humanism and the widest

---

[61] Baudouin, "Proposition d'erreur sur les Memoires d'Aniou par Fran. Balduin," BN MSS, Collection Dupuy, vol. 512, f. 6r-40r. (There are other copies in Fonds français, vol. 4437, f. 205r-220r, and vol. 5409, f. 26r-52v.) The rest of Baudouin's plan is sketched out in Fonds français, vol. 16653, f. 31r-87r (partial copy in vol. 5403, f. 23r-25r, following Du Haillan, *Sommaire Histoire d'Anjou*), "Memoires des ducs d'Anjou dressez par Messire François Balduin—lequel mourut a Paris le 24eme Octobre 1573. du College d'Arras de sa nation, et est inhumé de cloistre de Mathurins."

[62] Baudouin, "Proposition d'erreur," f. 2r-v; cf. *Chronique d'Arthois*, p. 1: "Without the communication of [history] we would be in horrible darkness and, as Cicero says, more than infants, not knowing what came before our birth or memory, without any knowledge of our ancestors or of anything that might help in the government of affairs private as well as public" (*Orator*, 120).

possible range of sources. One of the remarkable things about Baudouin's work was his insistence upon primary sources, especially in legal matters, and his preference for documentary material over histories and chronicles. He made use of inscriptions, the first being a "noble and authentic" epitaph of Hugh Capet in the *palais* which proved the relationship between the Angevins and the Capetians.[63] He examined the manuscript of an old chronicle of Anjou written "in rather good Latin" which threw some light upon the early stages of the Duchy, though on the whole Baudouin was not impressed by the medieval sense of relevance, allowing writers to neglect the most crucial religious affairs and yet report the occurrence of a comet. Baudouin took particular pride in being admitted to the royal archives and in consulting other modern archival collections. He also made the widest use of printed sources, sometimes, as in the case of Froissart, making his own emendations.[64] To this material Baudouin brought a deep knowledge of legal and genealogical questions and of chronology, by which he hoped to establish more accurately the history of the house of Anjou.

In even the best of modern historians Baudouin found it necessary to root out errors. Among French historiographers he criticized not only the credulous Nicolas Gilles but even Paolo Emilio, who had mistakenly attributed the granting of the Angevin fief to Philip Augustus because he had neglected to consult the testament of St Louis, which was in the archives. Panvinio, on the other hand, he took to task for denying the original hereditability of the duchy, for which he found evidence in the collection of Jean du Tillet, not yet published. He also criticized Biondo for his inaccurate description of the investiture of the kingdom of Naples, though he forgave this generally reliable historian on the grounds that he was no jurist. No such excuse could be offered, however, for the still more flagrant errors of Bartolus and Baldus, who, in violation of grammar and logic as well

---

[63] *Ibid.*, f. 4r.

[64] *Ibid.*, f. 5v, referring to the *Gesta consulum Andegavorum*, ed. Marchegay and Salmon (Paris, 1856), I, 65; f. 12r, to *Layettes du Trésor des chartes*, ed. Laborde (Paris, 1863), I, 54; f. 45v, to Fournier, *Statutes des universités françaises*, I, 264; and f. 15v, to Froissart, *Chroniques*, ed. S. Luce, VI (Paris, 1876), 173.

as law, argued that the kingdom of Apulia, as an ecclesiastical fief, was not subject to the law of succession.[65] He reproved Jean de Bourdigne for errors about the University of Angers, for which Baudouin had found charters dating from the late thirteenth century; Guicciardini for likening the Aragonese constitution to the Salic law; and Bodin— whom he referred to only as "an Angevin advocate who wrote on the method of history"—for praising Giucciardini.[66] Many other historians—Bonfinius, Volterranus, Lazius, Aventinus, Fazello, Colenuccio—came under fire for errors, especially genealogical and legal. No one, it seemed, had quite the right combination of talents and thoroughness to discuss adequately this family which had played so important a role in European history.

Baudouin's medievalist ventures are probably more interesting for the direction they took than for the destination they reached. Moreover, his work in this field was largely apologetic and aimed at defending the continuity of one tradition or another. With regard to the church, for example, he came to accept the principle of institutional as well as doctrinal succession. Yet this position was not entirely due to partisanship; in a sense, it was inherent in the notion of the chronological integrity of history which he developed quite independently of his ecclesiastical researches. This attitude, which he arrived at in the course of his studies in Roman law, he found still more appropriate for the study of medieval and particularly for church history. But admittedly Baudouin's approach to the legal and institutional history of medieval society was indirect, and legal humanism itself was of rather peripheral importance. In order to understand the rise of medieval studies in their proper context, it will be necessary to adopt another point of view altogether—to take leave of the philol-

[65] *Ibid.*, f. 10ʳ, referring to Gilles, *Les Chroniques et annales de France* (Paris, 1566), I, cxxxixʳ; f. 11ʳ, to Paolo Emilio, *De Rebus gestis francorum* (Paris, 1549), f. 260ᵛ; f. 6ᵛ, to Panvinio, *Romanorum principum libri* (Frankfurt, 1614), 838-42 (on Du Tillet see ch. VIII); f. 17ʳ, to Biondo, *Historiarum ab inclinatione Romanorum libri XXXI* (Basel, 1559), p. 313; and f. 34ʳ, to Bartolus, *Opera*, VIII (Venice, 1602), on Code, 2, 6, 3.

[66] *Ibid.*, f. 45ᵛ (see n. 64); f. 39ᵛ (Guicciardini, XII, ch. 6); and f. 40ᵛ. In the course of discussing the *état de question*, Baudouin takes up at least 36 historians.

ogical tradition for a time and to look more closely at the native legal traditions of the French monarchy. And there is no better place to begin than with the work of Baudouin's old friend and mentor Charles Dumoulin.

PART THREE

Medieval Traditions

CHAPTER VI

Canon Law and History: Charles Dumoulin
Finds a Gallican View of History

Nihil innovetur nisi quod traditum est.

St Cyprian, *Epistolae*, 74

IT IS WELL KNOWN that in fact the most noble, virtuous, and wise Charlemagne ... and Louis the Pious ... transmitted to you not less but equal and identical power and authority along with the same crown, and that these things are clearly indivisible and inseparable. The ancient ordinances of the said Charlemagne and Louis the Pious still exist today in the registers of your sovereign parlement and *chambre des comptes* and in many authentic books.[1]

In this declaration, made by Charles Dumoulin to Henry II in 1552, we encounter what seems to be a totally different view of history from that of the historical school of law—a view that represents the past not as a lost age to be recovered but as a living legacy to be preserved, not as antiquities but as tradition. At this point, too, we feel more directly the pressure of ideology and the shifting winds of doctrine. Yet it is only the point of view, not the target or even the techniques, that has changed. Dumoulin himself had absorbed the lessons of legal humanism, though he refused his allegiance to it. He was fully aware that the understanding of tradition, especially a corrupt or a controversial tradition, required the same methods and scholarly standards as the investigation of a bygone age. Thus Dumoulin's perspective did not contradict, it complemented that of the philologists, and it was no less significant in the shaping of modern historical scholarship.

[1] Charles Dumoulin, *Commentarius ad edictum Henrici secundi contra parvas datas et abusus curiae Romanae* (Lyon, 1552), prefatory letter to Henry II (1 Jan. 1552).

Tradition and History

One of the essential ingredients of Baudouin's "integral history" was ecclesiology; for in considering the human condition, he argued, one should not study the body and neglect the soul.[2] The Protestant Reformation aroused a passionate and a partisan interest in church history which was soon reflected in scholarship. In some ways the historical thought of the Reformation may have been an appendage of humanism, especially in the common purpose of returning to the pure sources of doctrine to furnish a model for contemporary behavior. What is more, the philological methods and epistemological assumptions of humanism were inherited by many students of church history, Catholics and Protestants alike. Yet certain basic differences must not be overlooked. The Reformation not only shifted emphasis from classical to Christian antiquity, from "profane" to "sacred" history, but drew also upon traditions independent of and alien to the humanist movement. It had to deal with very different historiographical problems and eventually to find its own perspectives.

The central historical issue of the Reformation was a problem hardly touched upon by philologists, that of "tradition."[3] Since the principal vehicle, institutional as well as intellectual, of the European tradition was the Roman church, the question had obviously to be answered through investigation of the past of the church. What was involved on the most general level was the age-old question of permanence and change, the mystical endurance of the City of God and

---

[2] Baudouin, *De Institutione*, p. 618. By far the best book is P. Polman, *L'Élément historique dans la controverse religieuse du XVIe siècle* (Gembloux, 1932); also useful are E. Menke-Glückert, *Geschichtsschreibung der Reformation und Gegenreformation* (Leipzig, 1912), and W. Nigg, *Die Kirchengeschichtsschreibung* (Munich, 1934).

[3] The only useful studies are limited to theology: A. Deneffe, *Der Traditionsbegriff* (Münster, 1931); J. Bakhuizen van den Brink, *Traditio in de Reformatie en het Katholicisme in de Zestiende Eeuw* (Amsterdam, 1952); G. Tavard, *Holy Writ or Holy Church* (New York, 1959); and Y. Congar, *La Tradition et les traditions* (Paris, 1960). More generally, see L. Willaert, *La Restauration catholique* (Paris, 1960), pp. 297 ff, and H. Jedin, *A History of the Council of Trent*, trans. E. Graf, II (Edinburgh, 1961), 52-98, as well as the discussions of Melanchthon and Luther cited below.

the conspicuous instability of its earthly incarnation. What was demanded of the investigator was not so much archeological imagination as the ability to reconstruct the earlier stages of a process still going on. How, more specifically, could one account for the fact of historical change in Christian society? What evidence might be submitted in explanation, and how could it be evaluated? What witnesses might be called, and to what extent could their testimony be trusted? And since tradition was "doctrine not written by its first author," one also had to consider problems of the transmission of ideas and the relative value of secondary sources. Consequently, that humanist topos "the faith of history" (*fides historiae* or *historica*), became an inexhaustible topic of discussion among scholars of the Reformation.[4] For these reasons it seem clear that, despite differences in perspective and in values, the study of ecclesiastical institutions also required a sense of history.

Canon law, the very embodiment of ecclesiastical tradition, was inevitably the target of scholars who wanted to come to grips with the Reformation as a historical problem. For lawyers the Decretum, together with its later appendages, constituted a book of authority, paralleling the collection of Justinian and encumbered by the same scholastic apparatus. To professional eyes, then, the *Corpus juris canonis* appeared as a vast and somewhat discordant symphony, filled with contrasting themes and unresolved conflicts.[5] From a less legalistic point of view, however, it took the form of a great gallery of

---

[4] Like other humanist formulas, such as the "new learning," *fides historiae* (see ch. II, n. 5) was taken over by religious controversialists of the Reformation, including Luther (see n. 10), Le Douaren (letter to Calvin in *Responsio ad Balduini convicia*, p. 68), Baudouin (letter to Calvin in *CR*, XXXIX, 432), and especially Dumoulin and his antagonists, as cited below. The phrase also became a major theme in seventeenth-century controversies over historical pyrrhonism, as shown by A. Momigliano, *Studies in Historiography* (New York, 1966), p. 12. The characterization of "tradition" is Bellarmine's, cited by A. Cicognani, *Canon Law,* trans. O'Hara and Brennan (Philadelphia, 1934), pp. 100-1.

[5] S. Kuttner, *Harmony from Dissonance* (Latrobe, Penna., 1960), p. 35. For present purposes the most relevant studies of canon law are S. Mochi Onory, *Fonti canonistiche dell'idea moderno dello stato* (Milan, 1951), G. Le Bras, *Institutions ecclésiastiques de la chrétienté mediévale* (Paris, 1959), and the various works of W. Ullmann.

historical monuments. What is more, canon law, like civil law, possessed certain features which were to have an important bearing upon historical thought. There was, in the first place, a fundamental distinction between "old law" (the Decretum) and "new law" (the decretals added from the late twelfth century), and second, a consistent interest in historical origins, though characteristically in the form of more or less fanciful etymologies. More important were the methodological tendencies of the canonist tradition: the emphasis on the value of first hand and written testimony, on argument from historical sources, assessing the relative merit of authorities, and, like humanism itself, on the literal interpretation of texts (*grammaticaliter et ad literam*). Anticipating the techniques of philologists, canon lawyers even developed means of determining the authenticity of documents (*de fide instrumentum*) and of detecting forgeries.[6] Finally, despite a certain compulsive *esprit de système*, canonists recognized, indeed insisted upon, the mutability of human laws, which like human history were to be regarded as relative in terms of times, places, and circumstances. There was, in short, a kind of geographical and historical relativism inherent in canon law.

Like civil law, too, canon law was undergoing a process of "historicization", a re-examination in historical terms, though without being sanctioned by anything like a "historical school." Once again the herald was Aymar du Rivail, although his *History of Pontifical Law* (1515) was more interesting for its title than for its contents.[7] Even before this (in 1512) Erasmus' and Lefèvre's friend Beatus Rhenanus had called for a revival of Christian antiquity through a critical study of Gratian's Decretum. A generation later this challenge was taken up by an equally learned but more orthodox man, Antonio Agustín,

[6] *Corpus Juris Canonici*, ed. E. Friedberg (Graz, 1959), Decretalium Gregorii IX, II, 22, 1 ("De fide instrumentum," taken from the Digest title), and Extravagantes Joannis XXII, 14, 2 ("De Verborum significatione"). On canonist method see J. Salgado, "La Méthode d'interprétation du droit en usage chez les canonistes," *Revue de l'Université d'Ottawa*, XXI (1951), 201-13, and XXII (1952), 23-35, and R. L. Poole, *Lectures on the History of the Papal Chancery* (Cambridge, 1915), pp. 143 ff.

[7] Du Rivail, *De Historia juris pontificii* (Mainz, 1530), on which see ch. IV, n. 7.

who had made important emendations of Roman law on the basis of manuscript study and who went on to apply the same techniques to canon law, though his work was not published until the next century.[8] The fact is that canon law was too contemporary and too controversial in the sixteenth century to submit to philological treatment without a struggle. Valla had opened the way to such an approach, of course, with his declamation on the Donation of Constantine, which among other things was a grammatical assault on the Decretum. But only a few men, moved by the strongest ideological compulsion, followed his lead. In this respect, Valla's true disciples were not Agustín and the Roman Correctors but Ulrich von Hutten and Martin Luther. This circumstance was to mark the course of ecclesiastical studies for the rest of the century.

The pattern for the Protestant criticism of canon law was established in 1520 by Luther, who advertized his wholesale rejection of the Romanist tradition by casting the *Corpus Juris Canonici* into the flames, itself a most traditional act. Earlier that year Luther's suspicions about canon law had been confirmed when he discovered Valla's exposé in the edition of Hutten. Explaining "Why the books of the Pope and his disciples were burned," Luther attacked not only the Donation of Constantine but all aspects of papal supremacy, especially the notion that the pope was above judgment, "from which," he added, "all misfortune has come into the world."[9] This pamphlet, he remarked prophetically, was only the beginning of the battle against the laws of the antichrist. Not of course that Luther repudiated all tradition. It was simply that he wanted to substitute his own brand, which was doctrinal rather than institutional. Nor did he deny the value of history, which he accepted as "the mother of truth" and the first door

---

[8] See F. de Zulueta, *Don Antonio Agustín* (Glasgow, 1939), and F. Maassen, *Geschichte der Quellen und der Literatur des canonischen Rechts* (Graz, 1870), I, xix-xxvi; for French contributions, J. Schulte, *Die Geschichte der Quellen und Literatur des canonischen Rechts* (Stuttgart, 1880), III, 552 ff, R. Metz, "La contribution de la France à l'étude du décret de Gratien," *Studia Gratiana*, II (Bologna, 1954), pp. 502 ff, and (pp. 679 ff) M. Reulos, "Le Décret de Gratien chez les humanistes, les Gallicans et les réformés français du XVIe siècle."

[9] Martin Luther, *Works*, ed. H. Grimm, XXXI (Philadelphia, 1957), 383-95 (trans. L. Spitz); on Luther's specific emendations see p. 265.

to the understanding of scripture (*sensus grammaticus sive historicus*). It was simply, as he wrote in his introduction to Robert Barnes' *Lives of the Popes*, the first Protestant contribution to ecclesiastical history, that he refused to recognize any conflict between the Bible and history properly understood.[10] Still, if only in a negative way, canon law figured very significantly in Luther's historical thinking.

Closer to the mainstream of Italianate humanism and at the same time more sympathetic to churchly tradition was Luther's collaborator Philip Melanchthon. Following the lead of Valla and Barbaro, Melanchthon encouraged the alliance between eloquence and philosophy (*numquam sapientia est sine elegantia*), and he joined the humanist campaign of reforming logic on the basis of, or rather through the substitution of, rhetoric.[11] Formally, Melanchthon shared Luther's fundamentalist desire for a "revived doctrine" disengaged from "human traditions"; in fact his interest in history ran much more deeply than this. The best proof of this is his promotion of history courses as part of his "reformation" of various Lutheran schools, including the University of Heidelberg, where a chair of history was established in 1557, the very year of Baudouin's arrival.[12] As for his own work, Melanchthon not only made an intensive study of the early Latin fathers but was also an enthusiastic student of German history and lectured on various medieval emperors. Naturally enough, he shared the somewhat extravagant views of his countrymen about the ancient liberty and virtue of the German tribes, and so he dismissed the

[10] Luther, "Pio lectori in Christo," in Barnes, *Vita Romanorum pontificum* (Basel, [1535]), a 5ʳ. Cf. his preface to Galeatius Capelli's history, in *Works*, XXXIV, ed. L. Spitz (Philadelphia, 1960), p. 275: "Upon thorough reflection one finds that almost all laws, art, good counsel, warning, comforting, threatening, introduction, prudence, wisdom, discretion, and all virtues well up out of the narratives and histories as from a living fountain." In general, see J. Headley, *Luther's View of Church History* (New Haven, 1963), and E. Schäfer, *Luther als Kirchenhistoriker* (Gütersloh, 1897), who points out (p. 203) the importance of canon law for Luther's knowledge of history.

[11] Philip Melanchthon, "De Studio linguae Ebraeae" (*CR*, XI, col. 875), referring to Poliziano and Pico; see ch. II, n. 61.

[12] See the excellent work of E. Scherer, *Geschichte und Kirchengeschichte an den deutschen Universitäten* (Freiburg, 1927). Among Melanchthon's disciples was David Chytraeus, whose *De Lectione historiarum* appeared in Wolf, and who gave history a status equal to that of theology; see D. Klatt, *David*

Trojan theory of Frankish origin (*sed haec fabulosa omittamus*) as a foreign invention. He also discussed certain aspects of legal history. Most famous, however, was his edition of Johann Cario's chronicle (1558), prefaced by his own encomium of history, which helped to shape the views of Baudouin.[13] For Melanchthon, too, while paying his respects to the classical view of history as a repository of examples, was most concerned with promoting the idea of universal history (*integrum corpus historiae mundi*) as it had been revived by German humanists and put into the service of Lutheranism.

The man who did most to formulate and to publicize the Protestant interpretation of eccleciastical history was Jean Calvin. Ultimately, Calvin wanted an answer to the fundamentalist question, "What was the world like in the time of Christ and the apostles?"[14] Yet he could not help being curious about what had gone wrong in the intervening centuries. So it was that canon law came to form a major theme of his work—indeed the source of his perspective. In the 1543 edition of his *Institutes of the Christian Religion* Calvin presented an account of the origin and growth of the papacy, using the Decretum as a historical source as well as a target of criticism. Like Luther and Melanchthon he saw in this process a gradual effacing of the "primitive church" through the infiltration of "human traditions." He was particularly disgusted by the various forgeries embedded in canon law,

---

Chytraeus als Geschichtslehrer und Geschichtschreiber (Rostok, 1908), p. 35. Among the first history courses in France was that taught in the Protestant College in Nîmes, where the chronicles of Sleidan and of Melanchthon (i.e., Cario) were read, according to Ménard, *Histoire civile, ecclésiastique et littéraire de la ville de Nîmes* (Nîmes, 1875), V, 179.

[13] Melanchthon, preface to *Chronica Carionis* and "Encomium Franciae" (*CR*, XII, col. 705-16, and XI, col. 387); cf. "De studiis linguae graecae," *CR*, XI, col. 862. In general, see H. Brettschneider, *Melanchthon als Historiker* (Insterburg, 1880), and above all the fundamental work of P. Fraenkel, *Testimonia Patrum* (Geneva, 1961).

[14] Jean Calvin, *Institutes de la religion chrétienne*, IV, i, 19; on canon law, IV, vii, *passim*, and on the Donation of Constantine, IV, xi, 12. About history in general Calvin tended to take a more negative view than Luther, arguing that not it but "sola scriptura" was the true "mistress of life," e.g., in his commentary on Paul's epistle to the Romans (*CR*, LXXVII, col. 86). The need for a study of Calvin's historical thought is unfortunately not met by H. Berger, *Calvins Geschichtsauffassung* (Zurich, 1955).

and in a later edition he denounced, with a wrathful rhetoric worthy of Valla himself, the attempt of Augustinus Steuchus to resurrect the Donation of Constantine. He made extensive use of Platina's standard work, though he sometimes preferred the more hostile accounts in Barnes' *Lives of the Popes,* as in the case of Gregory VII. In one essential respect, however, Calvin set himself apart from such scholars as Melanchthon and Baudouin. Although he accepted the notion of the "primitive church," he rejected their universalist ideal. Partly because of his French background, partly because of his situation in Geneva, Calvin favored religious unity on a more restricted basis. Such was the feeling of his French disciples, too, and it was to give a distinct shape to their historical thinking.

The Gallican View

Protestants and Roman Catholics were not the only ones to busy themselves with ecclesiastical history in the sixteenth century. There was a third school of thought that managed to preserve itself between those religious parties beginning to take shape in the 1540s. This was Gallicanism, which, though its position between the extremes became increasingly uncomfortable, maintained close ties with each of them. While on the one hand Gallicanism claimed to be rooted in the ancient universal church and indeed to be its chief defender, on the other hand it figured prominently in the doctrinal tradition reconstructed by Protestants. Thus, Flaccius Illyricus, compiling his authoritative *Catalogue of the Witnesses of Truth* (1556), referred not only to such imperialists as Marsiglio of Padua and to such humanist critics as Valla, but to the Gallican principles of Gerson and of the Pragmatic Sanction of Bourges.[15] They too, he argued, were part of the "true church and perpetual religion." And yet it is no less clear that Gallicanism was a self-contained and self-conscious expression of the French nation.

In the sixteenth century the Gallican church was a complex and tangled skein of rights that almost defied analysis. "Pragmatic Gallicanism," nourished by episcopal privilege and parlementary prec-

[15] Flaccius Illyricus, *Catalogus testium veritatis* (Basel, 1556), p. 833, 944, *passim,* referring also to Valla (p. 959) and Budé (p. 1025).

edent, continued to evoke nostalgia; but by the second quarter of the sixteenth century the "liberties of the Gallican church" had been transferred to the crown by the Concordat of Bologna of 1516 despite prolonged parlementary resistance.[16] This "royal Gallicanism" was encouraged by such legists as Jean Ferrault and Charles de Grassaille, who traced their own tradition back to the lawyers of Philip IV and who were faced with much the same task—to defend the monarchy against usurpation from all sides, especially from the feudal and ecclesiastical establishments. This they did by compiling lists of "regalian rights," including the so-called Gallican liberties, and by defending them on the basis of various legal and historical authorities. In the sixteenth century these legists were instrumental in creating a coherent Gallican ideology and thereby an interpretation of the legal and institutional past of the French monarchy. They played a greater part in fashioning the official image of French history than even the historiographers. This is why, once again, it is necessary to approach the field of historical scholarship by way of the lawyers.[17]

From the beginning Gallicans were unscrupulous eclectics, but most directly they were the beneficiaries—ungrateful beneficiaries, to be sure—of the sources and methods of canon law. It was the canonists, as Walter Ullmann has pointed out, who "had forged the weapons with which [the legists of Philips IV] had fought."[18] Things had not changed much by the sixteenth century, and Ferrault and Grassaille continued to rely upon canon law as well as civil law, royal

---

[16] In general, see V. Martin, *Les Origines du gallicanisme* (Paris, 1939), and J. Haller, *Papsttum und Kirchenreform* (Berlin, 1903), as well as the article in the *Dictionnaire du droit canonique*. For the sixteenth century there are no satisfactory accounts, but parts of the story are told in J. Thomas, *Le Concordat de 1516* (Paris, 1910), R. Doucet, *Etude sur le gouvernement de François Ier* (Paris, 1921), V. Martin, *Le Gallicanisme et la réforme catholique* (Paris, 1919), and F. Perrens, *L'Eglise et l'état en France sous le règne de Henri IV* (Paris, 1872).

[17] "Legist," a term which dates back to the thirteenth century (Pierre de Fontaines, *Le Conseil*, ch. 21, 37), as does "avocat" (*Etablissements de St Louis*), is conventionally, though not very precisely, applied to lawyers who wrote on the king's behalf. See W. Church, *Constitutional Thought in Sixteenth-Century France* (Cambridge, Mass., 1941), and J. Poujol, "Jean Ferrault on the King's Privileges," *SR*, V (1958), 15-26; also *infra* ch. VII and IX.

[18] Walter Ullmann, *Medieval Papalism* (London, 1949), p. 9.

legislation, and the testimony of historians to provide ammunition for the king. Like the canonists, Gallican lawyers had their own "monuments," their own curial "style," and even their own forgeries, such as the "Pragmatic Sanction of St Louis" composed in the fifteenth century.[19] Like the canonists, too, they tended to offer their proofs in the form of laborious and pedantic inventories of the past; they understood perfectly the indispensability of historical records and archival collections. In general, it was characteristic of Gallicanism that it depended more upon positive than upon divine law and that it preferred historical argument to political theory. The Gallican tradition involved a rudimentary kind of historicism which, reinforced by humanism, was to become the basis for a distinctive and comprehensive interpretation of European history.

What is more, certain sixteenth-century French scholars were beginning to look at their church with new eyes. They saw it not merely as a legal structure but as the product of a long historical development. Moved by the conflict over the Council of Pisa in 1511, for example, Jean Lemaire de Belges presented a historical sketch of schisms and councils through the ages, at one point calling upon the testimony of that "man of great literature and liberty," Lorenzo Valla, though dismissing as irrelevant his criticism of the Donation of Constantine. Out of a later Gallican crisis, that of 1551, there emerged a still more interesting work by one of the king's archivists, Jean du Tillet. The subject was familiar, the "liberties of the Gallican church," but the method was novel, for Du Tillet decided to describe these hard won privileges not according to the old scholastic arrangement but "par forme d'histoire." [20] Like canon and civil law, in short, the Gallican tradition was undergoing a process of "historicization."

---

[19] For the background of Gallican doctrine, see J. Lecler, "Qu'est-ce que les libertés de l'église gallicane?" *Recherches de science religieuse*, XXIII (1933), 385-410; G. de Lagarde, "Le 'Songe du verger' et les origines du gallicanisme," *Revue des sciences religieuses* (1934), 1-50; and the still valuable G. Hanotaux, *Essai sur les libertés de l'église gallicane* (Paris, 1888).

[20] Jean Lemaire de Belges, "Le Traicté de la différence des schismes et des conciles de l'église, et de la préeminence et utilité des conciles de la sainte Eglise Gallicane," *Œuvres*, ed. J. Stecher (Louvain, 1885), III, 232 ff. For Du Tillet, see *infra* ch. VIII, n. 40, and for later works, ch. IX, n. 41.

For Gallicans even more than for Protestants, canon law represented not only a major obstacle to reform but a key to the understanding of European history. By the mid-point of the century it had become a storm center which disturbed devoted members of the historical school of law like Baudouin as well as professional ideologues like Du Tillet. Repercussions could be heard even in popular literature, as in the mischievous chapters which Rabelais devoted to "papemanie" in his *Quart Livre* (1552). The principal contributions to the debate over canon law were summed up rather bitterly by Baudouin in his *Response of Christian Jurisconsults* of 1556.[21] First came Baudouin's immediate target, Le Douaren's *Ministers of the Holy Church and their Benefices* (1551), and then Charles Dumoulin's great commentary of 1552, which was the product not only of a royal commission but of his own *Annotations on Canon Law* of 1550. Dumoulin's book provoked a response in defense of the papal position by the Sorbonist Raymond le Roux, whom Baudouin identified as a disciple of Pierre Rebuffi, a jurist of the old school who had written a defense of tithes. This in turn was followed by a pamphlet on the *State of the Primitive Church* by Hotman, who officiously and (Baudouin charged) selfishly came to Dumoulin's rescue, and then a second response by Le Roux. Lastly came Baudouin's own book, which characteristically antagonized all parties and, as we have seen, brought the wrath of the Calvinists down upon him. Out of this pamphlet war came a reexamination not only of canon law but of a substantial part of French history.

---

[21] Baudouin, *Responsio Christianorum jurisconsultorum*, p. 7 (see ch. V, n. 20); Le Douaren, *De Sacris ecclesiae ministeriis*; Dumoulin, *Commentarius . . . contra parvas datas; In Molinaeum pro pontifice maximo, cardinalibus totaque ordine sacro, authore Remundo Rufo* and *Duplicatio in patronum Molinaei* (i.e., Hotman) in Dumoulin, *Opera omnia* (Paris, 1681), IV, 523 ff; Hotman, *De Statu primitivae ecclesiae . . . ad Remundum Rufum, ibid.*, IV, 639 ff. Baudouin also mentions *Petri Lizetii adversum pseudoevangelium haeresim libri* (Paris, 1551), and the satirical but pseudonymous reply of Beza, *Epistola magistri Benedicti Passavanti responsiva* (s. l., 1553), as well as Pierre Rebuffi, *Tractatus de decimis* (Paris, 1551). To this may be added the anonymous and unpublished *Errores aliquot selecti ex Commentariis Caroli Molinaei*, in BN MSS, Fonds latins, n. a., vol. 533. This is pursued further in my *"Fides Historiae*: Charles Dumoulin and the Gallican View of History," *Traditio*, XXII (1966), 347-402.

At the very beginning Le Douaren had stated the question in historical terms. In his preface he presented a historical sketch of canon law and its degeneration, pointing out that in France this influence was counteracted by the Gallican liberties, whose purpose was not to introduce novelties but only to preserve ancient custom (*priscorum institutionum norma*). Le Douaren's sources included not only medieval chronicles and canon law but the "monuments" of the parlement of Paris. Since the time of Charlemagne, he argued, French monarchs had many rights of ecclesiastical election and jurisdiction, arising from the secular character of the benefice and from the popular origin of election. "In France the king has the right of conferring benefices," he declared, referring to Marsiglio of Padua as well as Paolo Emilio, "whence arose that law which we call the regale." [22] As for the power of convening a council, which was a more sensitive issue at that time, Le Douaren bestowed this upon the secular ruler rather than the pope. So Calvin, too, had taught, and it is not surprising that the Sorbonne smelled heresy, forcing Le Douaren to submit a letter of justification. Yet he was not really a radical. Certainly he had little sympathy for the "utopian" church envisaged by Baudouin. He expressed hopes for ecclesiastical reform and even for a revision of canon law by Julius III. His position seemed to be that of a moderate Gallican.

This was one of the circumstances, indeed, that turned Baudouin against him, although of course personal vindictiveness also played a part. Baudouin rebuked his former colleague for moral as well as for scholarly failings, especially for not rejecting the filth (*colluvium et faecem*) of canon law—excretals (*decroutouères*) was Rabelais' equally pungent image—which, he added, holy men had consigned to the flames.[23] Bad enough to accept the Decretum, although admittedly it contained a few traces of the ancient church (*vestigia antiquitatis*), but to recognize the legitimacy of the "new law" was unpardonable.

<hr />

[22] Le Douaren, *De Sacris ecclesiae*, pp. 197 ff, 209, 250, 251. Le Douaren's so-called "Pro Libertate ecclesiae gallicanae" (*Opera*, IV, 316 ff) is merely a Latin version of a famous parlementary *arrêt* made in 1461 for the benefit of Louis XI.

[23] Baudouin, *Responsio Christianorum jurisconsultorum*, p. 21. Cf. Rabelais, *Pantagruel*, IV, 49, and Beza, *Le Passavant* (Paris, 1875), p. 49, discussing Gratian and "his latrine called the Decretum."

"By what right?" Baudouin demanded. "By what title?" And how could one seriously expect an ecclesiastical revival (*renascentem religionis lucem*) while at the same time defending the benefice (which was not a benefit, he remarked, but a sacrilege) as a divine institution. "O new breed of Protestants!" Baudouin cried. What disturbed him most was Le Douaren's treatment of history—not so much his ignorance, though this was evident enough, but his unscrupulous acceptance of the ecclesiastical corruption of recent centuries as a natural occurrence and as part of the "human condition." [24] By such complacent acceptance of the facts, it seemed to Baudouin, Le Douaren had betrayed both his profession and the cause of religious reform. His familiarity with recent history, in short, obscured his understanding of Christian antiquity. Baudouin on the other hand, preserving the humanist tendency to idealize the past, was at once more of a utopian and more of an antiquarian.

Baudouin's contribution to this pamphlet war arose from his preoccupation with the early church and the lessons which it might offer to his own age. Already he was developing his irenic views and his transcendent notion of "integral history." The controversy itself, however, ranged more widely and at the same time was more particularized. Involving the growth of ecclesiastical law and institutions, it inevitably went beyond the discussion of that pervasive theme—and dominant myth—of Protestant historiography, the "primitive church." Instead, it concentrated upon the church as a power structure analogous to other European governments, and inevitably it tended to adopt a national attitude toward this structure. If this added fuel to the fire, it also sharpened the focus. In general, this controversy helped to amplify the study of church history, which, figuring with increasing prominence in religious debates, was emerging as an independent and well-subsidized field of knowledge. One of the best illustrations of this is the work of Baudouin's old friend Charles Dumoulin, who was the principal figure, and probably the most distinguished scholar, in this preliminary skirmish for the more violent controversies of the religious wars. It is time, finally, to examine this work.

---

[24] *Ibid.*, pp. 25, 36, inquiring "if what is not good for a theologian is good for a jurist, to be more mindful of fact than of law?"

A Gallican Crisis

Charles Dumoulin, "the prince of legists," was one of the most fascinating, if not most attractive, personalities of his day. Small in stature and remarkably ugly, arrogant and compulsively argumentative, changeable in his religious views and a political outcast for much of his later life, he was nevertheless one of the most versatile scholars of the century. There was no phase of legal studies with which he was not familiar; on French customary law in particular he came to be recognized as the leading authority of modern times. A Parisian born, Dumoulin had attended the University, and although he showed little interest in the classics, he acquired enough Greek to engage in occasional etymological sport. In 1521 he took his law degree, *utriusque*, at the University of Orleans, thus escaping for the most part the new-fangled "French method" which was to claim his younger friends Baudouin and Hotman. Throughout his life he preferred the utilitarian approach of his teachers Pierre de l'Estoile and Jean Pyrrhus d'Angleberme, and this was only reinforced by the many years he spent in the municipal court (the *châtelet*) and in the parlement of Paris. It was here that he acquired his unrivalled knowledge not only of customary law and royal legislation but also of the intricacies of Gallican doctrine.[25]

Of all the influences that shaped Dumoulin's mind, the most profound was the so-called reformed religion, which by 1542 had claimed

[25] Dumoulin lacks a modern biography, but there are good short accounts in Haag and in *Dictionnaire du droit canonique*, by R. Filhol, including further bibliography. The earliest life was that by Baudouin's disciple Papire Masson, in *Elogiorum pars secunda* (Paris, 1656), p. 235. The standard account is still J. Brodeau, *La Vie de Maistre Charles Du Molin* (1654) in Dumoulin's *Opera omnia*, I; but it must be supplemented by such recent studies as J. Carbonnier, "Dumoulin à Tubingue," *Revue générale du droit*, XL (1936), 194-209, and M. Reulos, "Le Jurisconsulte Charles Dumoulin en conflit avec les églises reformées en France," *BSHPF*, C (1954) 1-12, and R. Filhol, "Dumoulin à Montbéliard (1555-1556)," *Études historiques à la mémoire de Noël Didier* (Paris, 1960), pp. 111-19, making use of some of the interesting unpublished correspondence in Basel, Universitätsbibliothek, MSS, G. I, 66, f. 101 ff, and G. II, 21, f. 104 ff. There are many other letters listed in the card files of the Amerbach correspondence; in Zurich, the Staatsarchiv as well as the Simler collection; and in the Hauptstaatsarchiv of Stuttgart.

his allegiance. This is no doubt what encouraged him to turn from feudal law, to which he had devoted most of his earlier life, to ecclesiastical studies. By this time Dumoulin's anti-Romanist bias was already formed, but his reading of the *reformatores*, including Bullinger and Melanchthon as well as Luther and Calvin, gave a sharper edge to his polemics against papal corruption and a higher color to his glorification of the "primitive church." With his usual energy he plunged into the study of canon law. In 1546 he published his famous work on usury, in which he characteristically asserted the jurisdiction of secular government and attacked canonist meddling; then he began working toward his commentary on and his edition of the *Corpus Juris Canonici*. So he was led down the treacherous path of religious controversy.[26] In other ways, too, Dumoulin had changed his middle-aged habits. He gave up his self-imposed celibacy to take a wife and later became involved in a bitter dispute with his brother over the family property. The fact that Dumoulin exchanged a contemplative for an active life so late in his career may help to explain not only his later disillusionment and paranoia but the intransigence of his religious and political opinions.

It was at the mid-point of the century, when he was fifty years old, that Dumoulin had the testing experience of his life. This was a result of the famous Gallican crisis in which Henry II, under the urging of his more radical advisors, was almost led to follow the schismatic road of Henry VIII. In November 1550 Julius III had recalled the Council of Trent, and the king had responded to this unfriendly act with the traditional threat of a national council. By the following August relations were broken off between France and the church. As in the days of the Great Schism, an embargo was placed upon currency bound for Rome. "Money is said to be the ornament of peace and the sinews of war," ran the edict enregistered (in Jean du Tillet's hand)

---

[26] This *Sommaire livre analytique des contrats, usures . . .*, Dumoulin's translation of the Latin original, was an early vernacular classic (*Opera*, II, 334 ff). See the discussions of this revolutionary work by W. Tauber, *Molinaeus' Geldschuldlehre* (Jena, 1928), and M. Le Goff, *Dumoulin et le prêt à intérêt* (Bordeaux, 1905). On Dumoulin's conflict with his brother, see *Inventaire des registres des insinuations du Châtelet de Paris, règnes de François Ier et de Henri II*, ed. E. Campardon and A. Tuetey (Paris, 1906), p. 399.

by the parlement on September 7, and for this reason civil law strictly and under pain of punishment forbids the shipping of money not only to enemies but also to barbarians and to foreigners."[27] There was even talk of the traditional "withdrawal of obedience," for which Du Tillet had begun to collect Gallican precedents. It did not, however, go beyond talk. In the end Henry was too cautious and too hostile to the radical party to go as far as outright schism. In February 1552, thanks partly to the peacemaking efforts of the Cardinal of Tournon, a reconciliation was arrived at, and so the crisis spent itself.

It was Dumoulin's great misfortune to be drawn into these dangerous waters. Turning his polemical talents and his knowledge of canon law to account, he composed a pyrotechnical advertisement for Henry II's edict of 1550 directed against the predating and selling of benefices. This *Commentary on the Edict of Henry II against the Little Dates and Abuses of the Court of Rome*, commissioned by the king himself, was more than just another attack on papal usurpation; it was a critical study of ecclesiastical history from earliest times down to the sixteenth century, with particular emphasis upon the more sensational episodes of the Gallican tradition. Many of the radical views expressed in this book appeared also in the revised edition of his annotations on canon law and in his brief history of the French monarchy, written in this period. Dumoulin's book, which created a sensation in Switzerland as well as in France, was to become a classic of Gallicanism.[28]

Unfortunately, Dumoulin himself derived little profit from this *succès de scandale*. He had wanted to play the role of royal champion,

---

[27] The edict may be seen in G. Ribier (ed.), *Lettres et memoires d'estat* (Paris, 1666), II, 343-46, with other documents relating to the crisis, as well as in Isambert, XIII, 211-15. See L. Romier, *Les Origines politiques des guerres de religion* (Paris, 1913), I, 258 ff, H. O. Evennett, *The Cardinal of Lorraine*, pp. 34 ff, and L. Pastor, *History of the Popes*, ed. R. Kerry (London, 1951), XIII, 101 ff.

[28] The version used here is *Les Commentaires analytiques sur l'edit des petites dates*, Dumoulin's own translation, in *Opera*, IV, 417 ff; the edict itself may also be found in A. Fontanon (ed.), *Les Edicts et ordonnances des roys de France* (Paris, 1580), II, and Isambert, XIII, 164-73. On the reaction in Switzerland, see *Histoire particulière de la court du Roy Henry II*, in *Archives curieuses de l'histoire de France*, sér. 1, ed. Cimber and Danjou (Paris, 1835), III, 289 (here attributed to Claude de l'Aubespine), from BN MSS Français, vol. 2831, f. 189 (Col. Dupuy, vol. 86, ff. 15-16).

but with the king's reversal he found himself a scapegoat instead. He was exactly in the position of Rabelais: his book was banned, and he was indicted for heresy by the Sorbonne. At the same time he lacked the protection against the "papemanes" enjoyed by Rabelais. Too proud to recant ("considering my rank of doctor"), Dumoulin could do nothing except enter an *appel comme d'abus* against the papal inquisitor. This could not save him from the king, however, and in May he was forced to defend himself before the parlement. He held out as long as possible, but before his last hearing he yielded to his lawyer's instinct. He fled—to the "very great regret" of his inquisitors.[29] Like Luther, although he had taken his stand on conscience, he had no wish to be a martyr.

Where could he turn? First he went to Basel and then returned to Paris, in hopes of a royal pardon. His welcome was something less than cordial, and in various letters to Calvin and Bullinger he described his "persecutions," including the ransacking of his house and the loss of his books.[30] The next stop, Lyons, he also found infested with his enemies, especially the Cardinal of Tournon. Thus, like so many other reform-minded Frenchmen before him, he turned to Geneva. On the way he stopped in Lausanne to pay a visit to Hotman, who the next year was to write a pamphlet on Dumoulin's behalf. Dumoulin did not find a home in Geneva either. He was too independent, perhaps too old, to become anybody's disciple, especially Calvin's; and in the spring of 1553 he moved on again, this time to Germany, where he had other protestant friends, including his for-

[29] Dumoulin, *Les petites dates*, pp. 380 ff. The proceedings against Dumoulin (1 May - 2 July 1552) appear in BN MSS, Collection Dupuy, vol. 488, ff. 7-12 (copy from Archives nationales, X 1ᵃ, 1572, ff. 86, 121, 144, 236, 239); see my *"Fides Historiae,"* pp. 399-402. Cf. J. Plattard, *La Vie de François Rabelais* (Paris, 1928), pp. 204, 214 ff, and for the proceedings against Rabelais' *Quart livre*, see the edition of his works by Marty-Laveaux (Paris, 1873), III, 420-21.

[30] Letter to Calvin, 12 Apr. 1552, and to Bullinger, 14 Oct. (*CR*, XLII, col. 310-12 and 387-92), telling of his hopes from German princes. Tournon, who had commissioned one response to Dumoulin's *Les petites dates*, was the negotiator chiefly responsible for the reconciliation between France and the papacy beginning the previous February (Ribier, *Lettres et memoires*, II, 382-86).

mer client Philip of Hesse. He turned down an offer to teach at Strasbourg, the same position to be occupied successively by Baudouin and
Hotman, and accepted an invitation to come to the University of
Tübingen. Once again he became a center of controversy, having resumed his favorite topic, the spreading poison of popery, in his inaugural lecture.[31] His views were too strong for his Lutheran colleagues and for the Duke of Württemberg, who wanted to stay on
good terms with the Emperor and who called Dumoulin to account
in August 1555. Even Calvin had advised him, as he later advised
Hotman, to behave more diplomatically, but it was to no avail. Instead,
Dumoulin decided to flee this new "Egypt" and left without even
being able to get Baudouin appointed as his successor. He continued
to search for a position which would guarantee him liberty of conscience as well as a salary in keeping with his rank, but most of all
he sought help in obtaining permission to return to Paris.

Dumoulin's "Germanic exile" left a deep impression on his work,
but it by no means taught him moderation or even caution. Until his
death in 1566 he passed through one storm after another. Misfortune
followed him to Strasbourg, Montbéliard, Dôle, and Besançon, and he
succeeded at last in alienating the Calvinists, too. By 1557 he was at
last back in Paris, restored to royal favor, and working again on his
Gallican projects.[32] Like Baudouin—and partly in consultation with

---

[31] Dumoulin, *Solemnis oratio ... de sacra theologia et legum imperialium
dignitate, differentia, convenientia, corruptione et restitutione* (*Opera*, V, 4 ff).
That Dumoulin had been recommended by Vergerio appears in *Briefwechsel
zwischen Christoph Herzog von Württemberg und Petrus Paulus Vergerius*,
ed. Kausler and Schott (Stuttgart, 1875), p. 63. Dumoulin gave his inaugural
18 Dec. 1553 and by March was already complaining about the "papists" (to
Calvin, *CR*, XLIII, col. 86, and to Bullinger, Zurich, Zentralbibliothek, MSS,
S. 81, f. 89ʳ); and on 4 Sept. he told Bullinger of his plans to leave and of his
unsuccessful attempts to get Baudouin appointed. Dumoulin's affirmation to
the Duke and his denial of any intention of stirring up trouble appears in
Zurich, MSS, S. 82, f. 155ʳ. See also A. Bouvier, *Henri Bullinger* (Zurich,
1940), and Carbonnier, "Dumoulin à Tubingue."

[32] Besides the letters to Calvin in *CR* and to the King of Navarre (*Opera*,
III, 4), see "Deux lettres inédites de Charles Dumoulin à Amerbach," ed.
Dareste, *Revue de législation et de jurisprudence*, III (1852), 136-46. During
this crucial year 1555 Dumoulin saw much of Baudouin, in Strasbourg as well
as Montbéliard, and wrote favorably about him to Calvin, while recalling with
some distaste (13 Dec. 1555) the "grammarian Hotman" who "adorned himself

him—he turned against the Genevan church because it was beginning to seem no less "foreign" and "seditious" than that of Rome. His antagonism had been aroused by his bizarre experiences in Montbéliard, where he had been imprisoned (though it was largely his own fault) and apparently abandoned by the reformers; but it was confirmed by the disorders succeeding the death of Henry II and leading up to the religious wars. By 1563 he wanted to disassociate himself entirely from such "evil and illicit liberty." [33] After one of his books was burned publically in Geneva, Dumoulin formulated his charges more systematically: the Calvinist ministers wanted "to enrich themselves by exactions from the people of France . . . , to usurp ecclesiastical and secular jurisdiction . . . , and what is worse . . . to overthrow the government of the kingdom of France." They were not reformers, they were rebels.

None of this implied, however, that Dumoulin had changed his attitude toward Romanism, which was also taking a new and aggressive form in these years. In 1564, in fact, Dumoulin had published two seminal pamphlets against ultramontanism on precisely the same grounds as those on which he had attacked Calvinism. One was aimed at the "new sect" of Jesuits, who had "established a new religion against all the ancient canons, including the conciliar ones . . . , against the *arrêts* of the supreme court of the parlement of Paris . . . , against the common good . . . and against public law." [34] The second dealt

---

with my feathers," referring to his work on usury; see ch. V, n. 19. See also Filhol, "Dumoulin à Montbéliard"; P. Pialat, *Dumoulin à l'Université de Dôle 1555-1556* (Dôle, 1844); J. Duquesne, *Les Débuts de l'enseignement du droit à Strasbourg au XVIe siècle* (Strasbourg, 1922); U. Robert, *L'Enseignement à Besançon* (Besançon, 1900); and L. Febvre, *Philip II et la Franche-Comté* (Paris, 1911), pp. 479-80. In Nov. 1557 Dumoulin received royal pardon (Isambert, XIII, 502), and by the next July he is seen back at work on customary law, according to a letter to Nicolas Pithou, in *BSHPF*, XI (1862), 266.

[33] Dumoulin, *Apologie contre un livret . . .* (Lyon, 1563), p. 20, and "Articles . . . contre les Ministres de la Religion Pretendue Reformee" (*Opera*, V, 621). See Reulos, "Le Jurisconsulte Charles Dumoulin"; A. Cartier, " 'La deffense civile et militaire des innocens et de l'Eglise de Christ,' et l' 'Apologie de Charles Dumoulin,' 1563," *Revue des livres anciens*, II (1917), 200-4; and especially R. M. Kingdon, *Geneva and the French Protestant Movement 1564-1572* (Geneva, 1967), pp. 138-48.

[34] Dumoulin, *Consultation . . . sur l'utilité ou les inconveniens de la nou-*

with the "heretical and schismatical" decrees of the Council (or rather the "conciliabulum") of Trent, which might "in no way be received into the kingdom of France, since it would be against the sovereignty of the king and the rights of his crown and the authority of his edicts." Later on this tract was to be very popular with the politiques, but once again Dumoulin had chosen an unfortunate time to express his opinions. He was imprisoned and released only on his promise to keep silent on political matters. This time death, which came the next year, guaranteed that he would keep his word.

Dumoulin may have been, as the Calvinists regarded him, a "fantastic spirit." He was also an arrogant one—"I who yield to no man," he is supposed to have said, "and who can be taught by no man"— and undoubtedly more single-minded than he seemed to his contemporaries.[35] If he was vacillating in his religious affiliations, he was always faithful to his profession and to his royalist convictions. What Ernest Renan remarked about Guillaume de Nogaret, that "to serve the king was his only motto," applies equally well to Dumoulin, who liked to compare his efforts to those of Pierre de Cugnières.[36] His allegiance to the legist tradition appears most conspicuously in his annotated editions of the *Style of Parlement*, the works of Philip Decius, and Ferrault's book on the regalian rights. It was this legacy, in combination with an intense and systematic anti-Romanism, that led Dumoulin to fashion what may be taken as a model of sixteenth-century

---

velle secte . . . des Jesuites (s. l. n. d.), pp. 1-4, and *Conseil sur le faict du Concile de Trente* (Lyon, 1564), p. 1, which later became an "arsenal" for the politiques, according to V. Martin, *Le Gallicanisme et la réforme catholique*, p. 73. Cf. H. Jedin, *Das Konzil von Trient, Ein Ueberblick ueber die Erforschung seiner Geschichte* (Rome, 1948), pp. 67-69. For the record of the proceedings against him, see E. Maugis, *Histoire du parlement de Paris* (Paris, 1914), II, 281 ff. A copy of the *arrêt* of condemnation and of his release on 7 July 1565 may be found in BN MSS Col. Dupuy, vol. 694, f. 137ʳ. Dumoulin's *Conseil* also appears in *Mémoires de Condé* (London, 1743), V, 81-129.

[35] Masson, *Caroli Molinaei vita*, p. 239, and *Histoire ecclésiastique des églises réformées au royaume de France*, ed. P. Verron (Toulouse, 1882), II, 397. That Dumoulin died a Catholic appears in *Épitaphes du vieux Paris*, I (Paris, 1890), p. 192.

[36] Ernest Renan, *Études sur la politique religieuse du règne de Philippe le bel* (Paris, 1899), p. 247.

Gallicanism. If his enemies, the curialists, were *plus catholique que le pape,* Dumoulin was *plus gallican que le roi.* This was at once his tragedy and the source of his historical vision.

Ecclesiastical History

While Baudouin was pursuing his irenic ideals and his theories of universal history, Dumoulin was assembling one of the most radical interpretations of royal Gallicanism and of national monarchy of modern times. He worked out his views in the course of a lifetime's study of French institutions, from his great *Treatise on Fiefs* of 1539 to his general commentary on all the customs of France, completed and published in the year of his death. Dumoulin's program rested upon a threefold ideal: the unity and self-sufficiency of French law, of the French monarchy, and of the Gallican church—or, to use a slogan already popular in the sixteenth century, *une foi, une loi, un roi.*[37] Each part of this formula represents a defense of one major rival of the crown, that is, the papacy, the feudal establishment, and the Hapsburg empire. Each was supported by an organistic conception that had theological as well as philosophical sources, and each drew strength from a single, all-pervasive historical myth, the archetypal figure of Charlemagne. For it was Charlemagne who had legitimized feudal custom, who had established the primacy of the "French" monarchy, and who had provided the most fundamental Gallican precedents. On every level—legal, political, ecclesiastical, and perhaps cultural as well—he symbolized national unity. If Charlemagne had not existed, the Gallicans would have had to invent him. In a sense, some critics might argue, they did invent him.

Dumoulin's program of "integral Gallicanism" was threefold in terms not only of the principal institutional concerns of the monarchy but also of his simultaneous roles as feudist, as royal legist, and as canonist. As for feudal law (which will be taken up in the next

[37] In Dumoulin's day this formula was already traditional, and one of his contemporaries, Claude de Guyot, regarded it as "the symbol and device which the good city of Paris ... has carried from antiquity," according to N. Weiss, *La Chambre ardente* (Paris, 1889), p. 157. On analogous canonist and civilian formulas (*unum corpus ecclesiae; unum jus, unum imperium; debet esse unus rex*), see Mochi Onory, *Fonti canonistiche,* pp. 220, 243, 166.

chapter), Dumoulin recommended the creation of a uniform code based mainly upon the customary law of Paris, thus anticipating the "anti-Tribonianist" program of Hotman. In fact his "Oration on the union and concord of the customs of France" (1546) become a manifesto of the movement to reform customary law led by another old friend, the first president of the parlement of Paris, Christofle de Thou.[38] In his capacity as legist Dumoulin hoped to extend the principles of unity and uniformity into the sphere of public law, and he was at great pains to deny the validity of such "foreign" influences as Roman law. As a canonist, finally, he undertook to undermine the formidable ideology of the Roman church and to provide a coherent formulation of the accumulated prerogatives of the crown. Such were the principal sources of Dumoulin's Gallican view of history.

One of the most remarkable features of Dumoulin's thought was his consistent attachment to a historical point of view. He was deeply read in contemporary historical writing, Italian and German as well as French; and he was particularly critical of intentional bias, as for example appeared in the work of such "popish" historians as Vincent of Beauvais and even Biondo and Platina and in the chroniclers of St Denis, whose benefices inclined them unduly toward the church. Of all the guarantees against such distortion the best was adherence to original sources, by which Dumoulin meant archival and legal rather than literary sources. He recognized the value of ancient history, too, as in his study of usury, in which he made full use of the achievements of Barbaro and Budé. "In order to understand as a whole the origin of our present-day rents," he wrote, "it is expedient to enter a bit into history and to present the usage of the ancients. . . ."[39] He much ad-

---

[38] Dumoulin, "Oratio de concordia et unione consuetudinum Franciae," (*Opera*, II, 690-92). General assessments of Dumoulin's work include F. Olivier-Martin, *L'Esprit de tradition et l'esprit critique ou novateur dans les œuvres de Dumoulin* (Paris, 1908); G. Meyer, *Charles Dumoulin, ein führender französischer Rechtsgelehrter* (Nürnberg, 1956); F. Gamillscheg, *Der Einfluss Dumoulins auf die Entwicklung des Kollisionsrecht* (Berlin, 1955); Aubépin, "De l'influence de Dumoulin sur la législation française," *Revue critique de législation et de jurisprudence*, III (1853), 603-25, IV (1854), 27-44, V (1854), 32-62; W. Church, *Constitutional Thought in Sixteenth-Century France*; and works cited in the next chapter.
[39] Dumoulin, *Sommaire livre des contrats* (*Opera*, II, 336).

mired the work of Budé and Alciato in the restoration of Roman law (*ad juris civilis repurgationem*), and in his own editions he tried to emend in humanist fashion so that "the form of the ancient manuscript would arise out of the ancient text itself.[40] Dumoulin, too, deplored the ignorance of the "scholastic doctors" and contrasted his own method, which was based on "all the arts and sciences," to the indecisive dialectic of Gratian and Accursius.

Yet Dumoulin's historicism was not that of the great philologists. It is true that he adopted a literal mode of interpretation and emended on the basis of style, but this was not inconsistent with the methods of medieval jurists who had no interest in classical scholarship. He accepted humanist techniques, but he attached quite as much importance to practical experience and characterized his method as "analytical" rather than grammatical. When faced with a legal problem, his first question was apt to be "What is the origin?" but again this was quite compatible with his professional training. Dumoulin's Latin, too, fell harshly on the ears of classical scholars, and his interest in Roman law was utilitarian. On the whole, although his discussions of French law have often been compared to Cujas' observations on civil law, he had little use for the peddlers of pure philology, less even than Hotman. The source of Dumoulin's historical point of view was rather that complex of medieval legal traditions which absorbed his professional energies: the Bartolist school of civil and feudal law and the canonist tradition, especially as shaped by Gallicans and as reshaped by Protestants. As a "neo-Bartolist," he combined a lawyer's present-mindedness with an antiquary's perspective, transcending the pragmatism of the one and the pedantry of the other.[41] As a Gallican, he combined a legist's concern with legitimacy with a reformer's nostal-

---

[40] Dumoulin, introduction (1549) to *Stylus parlamenti* (on which see the critical edition of F. Aubert), letter to Franciscus Montolanaeus, and preface (1546) to *De Eo quod interest*, in *Opera*, II, 408, vii, and 7. Dumoulin's use of manuscripts was shown by Baluze in his edition of *Capitularia regum Francorum*, I (Paris, 1780), 32.

[41] Not only modern scholars but one of Dumoulin's own contemporaries placed him in "the chamber . . . of the Italian Bartolus": Étienne Pasquier, *Recherches de la France* (Paris, 1633), p. 902. Bodin, on the other hand, placed him in that genus of jurists (including humanists such as Connan as well as Bartolists such as Tiraqueau) who combined practical experience with academic

gia for ancient purity. To his sense of history, in short, he added a sense of tradition.

Canon law was one of Dumoulin's points of departure as well as one of his primary targets. He attacked to plunder as well as to demolish it. His basic objection was that the canonist standard of judgment was provided not by scripture but by the papal chancery (*non secundum evangelium sed secundum stilum papae*). By ignoring elective rights they violated the ancient constitution of the church (*contra antiques canones et normam primitivae ecclesiae et constitutiones imperiales*).[42] In general, the canonists were ignorant not only of law but of history. What was worse, they had a compulsive attachment to anachronism and forgery, which Dumoulin, like Valla, took a malicious pleasure in exposing. Besides the notorious Donation of Constantine, he rejected the "fable" of St Peter's twenty-five year residence in Rome and the report of a council before the time of Clovis—which, he suggested, "some popish monks, with their customary madness, ascribed to earlier times to give luster and authority to their false and superstitious inventions."[43] Dumoulin's annotations on canon law are covered with labels marked "fabricated by Palea." His experiences in the parlement only confirmed his conviction that forgery (*crimen falsi*) was the priestly crime par excellence and had infected the whole Romanist interpretation of history.

"By their fruits you shall know them" was a favorite maxim of

knowledge, though denying him the highest rank reserved for philosophers: preface to *Methodus* (Mesnard, p. 108).

[42] Dumoulin, *Annotationes ad jus canonicum*, "In Decretum," D. 55, c. 3 (*Opera*, IV, 10); cf. D. 88, Palea 2 (p. 20), referring to the principle of *sola scriptura* and to "true religion, which is not to be mixed with the water of human traditions." Like Budé though for different reasons, Dumoulin thought that the true tradition of France was not Roman but Greek (*Livre des contrats*, p. 336).

[43] *Ibid.*, C. 13, Q. 2, c. 7 (*Opera*, IV, 39), and *Les petites dates*, p. 373. Following Erasmus, he rejected the suppositious sermons of St Augustine and the "apostolic canons," D. 22, Q. 4, c. 50 and D. 16, c. 1 (p. 53, 4), surmising that "the style is that of Gregory the Great." On the Donation of Constantine see D. 96, c. 4, Palea 13 (p. 22); "palea falso conficta" is an ubiquitous label in the *Annotationes*. In this work, too, the phrase *fides historiae* frequently appears, in the sense not only of historical truth but also of textual authenticity; e.g., T. 22, c. 6 ("De fide instrumentum") (p. 114).

Dumoulin.[44] This test made it obvious to him that the church was the product of purely "human tradition," if not of the devil himself. In his account of church history, then, it was natural for him to select as secondary sources the most radical and offensive critics of ecclesiastical institutions: imperialists such as Piero della Vigna, Marsiglio of Padua, and William of Ockham; conciliarists such as Dietrich of Niem and Cardinal Zabarella; Gallicans such as Jean Gerson and Pierre d'Ailly; the legists of Philip IV, including those represented in the *Somnium Viridarii*; and such historians as Platina, Valla, and even Machiavelli, who "depicted marvelously well the origin, rise, and growth of the papacy and the ruses of the pope by which this was achieved."[45] Needless to say, Dumoulin also rehearsed the familiar complaints of generations of reformers about dispensations, reservations, indulgences, "traffic in benefices," the infiltration of "bankers of simoniacal heresy," as well as the "little dates."[46] At worst these were frauds, at best "new inventions" which violated both law and history.

In general, it was Dumoulin's thesis that the fruits of ecclesiastical tradition were idolatry and avarice. He divided the process of degeneration into four stages, corresponding to the four grades of "divine law" recognized by the canonists themselves. First came the Bible itself, then the subsequent elaboration and perversion by theologians, next the body of canon law, and finally the rise of such diabolical sects as the Dominicans, the Franciscans, and their brothers in iniquity. The fifth stage, he hoped, would be a return to the true tradition. The restoration of letters and law and the work of Erasmus as well as certain reformers seemed to point to such a happy revival.[47] Turning more specifically to ecclesiastical institutions, Dumoulin dis-

---

[44] *Ibid.*, D. 40, c. 6 (*Opera*, IV, 8). Besides identifying the pope with antichrist, Dumoulin brought up the old legend of "Pope Joan" (*Les petites dates*, p. 454), which was to be discredited shortly by Panvinio.

[45] Dumoulin, *Les petites dates*, p. 464.

[46] *Ibid.*, pp. 511-13. The "little dates," he explains (p. 400), is the practice of predating petitions to be registered in the papal chancery.

[47] Dumoulin, *De Sacra theologia* (*Opera*, V, 38 ff). Cf. Calvin, *Institutes*, IV, 8, 18, and Bullinger, *De Origine erroris* (Zurich, 1548), pp. 63 ff. According to Dumoulin, idolatry was the chief cause of the fall of Rome (*Les petites dates*, p. 440).

tinguished two aspects of this process of corruption: the feudalization of the episcopate, "as if it were a right of office belonging to the title-holder after the fashion of secular offices"; and the pursuit of papal monarchy with the pope acting as "universal chief, raised above the bishops in the manner of a king or an emperor." [48] To these the troubles of the present age could be traced quite directly. Such was the pattern of church history.

How had this come about? Dumoulin realized that the disease had spread through all the members of the church, but like his Protestant mentors he was convinced that it was basically a disorder of the head, *de motu proprio*. The growth of canon law, the proliferation of church offices, the endless search for new sources of revenue: it was the "Roman church which is the source and parent of all these evils." [49] Dumoulin's first steps, then, were to deny that the *primatus* of the papacy was of ancient origin and that the ecclesiastical hierarchy had any scriptural authority. "Obedience to the purer primitive church and to ancient history," he declared, 'show to be false what this monk [Gratian], who moves heaven and earth on behalf of papal power, has tried to do." [50] Yet upon this basis, and in violation of the principles of civil law, the doctrine of the canonists was erected. It was in Dumoulin's own lifetime that the pest of popery reached its climax. "In May 1552," he lamented, "the Sorbonicians were seen publicly in Paris, like hired and sworn soldiers of the pope, trying by the clamor of their sermons to persuade the people that for their salvation they must believe and do all that the pope commanded." [51] Dumoulin was not the first, nor would he be the last, to see history as a vast drama reaching its climax in the scene in which he himself played a crucial role.

The trouble had begun, it seems, with Leo I, who first laid claim

[48] Dumoulin, *Les petites dates*, p. 451; cf. *Annotationes*, "In Decretum," C. 16, Q. 7, c. 9 and C. 22, Q. 5, c. 17 (*Opera*, IV, 47, 51).

[49] *Ibid.*, p. 394; *Annotationes*, "In Decretales" (Boniface VIII), T. 4, c. 24 (*Opera*, IV, 227). Cf. Calvin, *Institutes*, IV, x, 15, and Rabelais, *Pantagruel*, IV, 53.

[50] Dumoulin, *Annationes*, "In Decretum," D. 97 (*Opera*, IV, 22). Cf. Calvin, *Institutes*, IV, vi.

[51] Dumoulin, *Les petites dates*, p. 473.

to kingly power. Then, with the decline of the Carolingian empire, the popes "little by little began to usurp the churches of France and Germany, setting up in opposition many fables, such as the Donation of Constantine. . . ."[52] The villains of this early period were those three "horrible monsters," Benedict IX, Sylvester III, and Gregory VI, and more particularly that incarnation of Antichrist, Hildebrand, who tried to abolish the regale and who issued that "satanic bull" absolving subjects from their allegiance to the emperor. Through the efforts of Innocent III, who claimed feudal jurisdiction over several European sovereigns and multiplied the number of priests and monks, the hierarchy was placed upon a solid foundation, thus permitting the poison of popery to spread throughout Europe. This work was furthered by the canonist and "grand usurpateur" Gregory IX and above all by Boniface VIII, who, filling his Unam Sanctam "full of heresies and blasphemies," became the nemesis of the French monarchy. "In 300 years," Dumoulin concluded, "by their ambition and subtle artifices and by their priests and monks, ministers of iniquity . . . , they have established sovereignty over all churches, not only the Italian, German, Spanish, and English, but also the Gallican."[53] For this perverted universalism Dumoulin had nothing but loathing.

Responses from the Sorbonists were not long in coming. Two of these were by Raymond le Roux, and another was commissioned by Dumoulin's enemy, the Cardinal of Tournon, but never published. Both authors came to grips with Dumoulin on his own terrain, that of historical argument. The truth of history (*fides historiae*), they held, demonstrated both the liberty of the church and the primacy of the papacy. The anonymous writer charged Dumoulin with sedition as well as the Lutheran desire of burning the books of canon law.[54] More systematically, Le Roux tried to rescue ecclesiastical tradition by showing that the principal institutions of the church were of ancient, in some cases of pre-Christian, origin. He found Dumoulin's method

[52] *Ibid.*, pp. 448 ff. Cf. Calvin, *Institutes*, IV, ix, 12, and Rabelais, *Pantagruel*, IV, 50.

[53] *Ibid.*, pp. 428, 494.

[54] *Errores Caroli Molinaei*, f. 11ʳ, 18ʳ. These responses are discussed more fully in my "*Fides Historiae*," pp. 379-86.

intolerably literal-minded and marred by a confusion of words and things, as if tracing terminology, such as the pope's "principatus," were the same thing as tracing historical development. (It was precisely on this issue, the application of philology to history, that Hotman attacked Le Roux.) What is more, in spite of his ostentatious love of antiquity, Dumoulin seemed quite uncrititcal in his use of sources and failed to distinguish between early and later authorities. On the other hand, Le Roux complained, he was unreasonably skeptical about tradition, "as if everything were made of fraud and lies." [55] Even the Donation of Constantine, Le Roux thought, although its historicity might be questioned, should be regarded as valid through long custom (the *praescriptio longae temporis*). How could Dumoulin, who after all was a lawyer, not a grammarian, deny these arguments? [56]

The answer is simply that Dumoulin never considered identifying doctrinal and institutional tradition, that is, the true church with ecclesiastical organization. So he found it impossible to understand "those rebels who prefer the tradition . . . of the pope and his curia not only to the crown and government of France but to the word of God." [57] Here Dumoulin reveals his dual allegiance and the key to his interpretation of history. This was the national church, the point of intersection between human and divine tradition.

---

[55] Raymond Le Roux, *Pro pontifice maximo*, pp. 566, 625, and 546: "We are obliged to apply to the ancients because Dumoulin does not admit all witnesses, and if we choose more recent ones, he might not accept them . . ."; and yet Dumoulin himself, Le Roux complained, relied upon such unreliable authors as Marsiglio of Padua and Machiavelli and cited others, such as Gerson and Erasmus, out of context.

[56] *Ibid.*, p. 534: "For to grammarians belongs the art of discourse, to jurisconsults things and the law of persons, things, and actions." "Custom is the master of words." Not only the papacy but the whole hierarchy, he argued, was "most ancient," even if its terminology was not.

[57] Dumoulin, *La Premiere partie du Traicté de l'origine, progrez, et excellence du royaume et monarchie des françois, et couronne de France* (*Opera*, II, 1034), taken from Dumoulin's own Latin. This Gallican tract, published in 1561 but obviously the product of the Gallican crisis ten years before, constitutes Dumoulin's only contribution to historiography properly speaking except for the introduction to his commentary on the custom of Paris discussed in the next chapter. Cf. *Les petites dates*, pp. 417-18.

National History

Dumoulin was not a historian by design, but in the course of his Gallican propagandizing he was led to make a comprehensive reassessment of the French past. What is more significant, his professional concerns guaranteed that this reassessment would not be limited to the dynastic and military subjects treated by historiographers but would encompass legal, institutional, and social aspects of history. The shift of emphasis encouraged by Dumoulin and other legists, analogous to that encouraged by legal humanists, had a profound but seldom appreciated effect upon historical studies. This is why an examination of his work seems to be particularly appropriate for an understanding of modern historical scholarship.

Dumoulin's point of view was, in a most fundamental sense, that of a historicist. Yet it was ideology and not philology that produced this view. In the first place. Dumoulin took great pains to establish the legal independence, which is to say the historical individuality, of the French monarchy. This institutional uniqueness was manifested in several ways: in the assembly of estates, which made France, like England, a mixed monarchy (*monarchia mixta; monarchie mixtionee*); in the parlement of Paris, despite its sad decline in the sixteenth century; in the provincial customs, which reflected French character in the most direct fashion; in "the most ancient, perpetual, and inviolate Salic law," which, sanctioned by the "natural law" of blood succession, gave stability to the monarchy; and above all in the Gallican church and the royal privileges derived from it.[58] In the second place, Dumoulin assumed that the excellence of the French monarchy was a function of its antiquity, which he calculated to be 1,632 years, unequalled by any except perhaps the Jewish nation. Of course, Dumoulin's lawyer's mind required not only the antiquity but the continuous existence of the cause he had chosen to defend, and he never failed to insist that legitimacy, like history itself, was a living thing. "It is necessary to recall these noble antiquities," he remarked to the king in defense of his historical approach, "not to attribute to you new authority, which is integrally the same as that exercized by your predecessors,

[58] Dumoulin, *Traicté de l'origine*, p. 1036.

but to maintain and prove that it has existed at all times."[59]

One of the clearest indications of political continuity was the Gallican tradition itself. This tradition Dumoulin represented as a kind of countervailing power which paralleled and to some extent offset the usurpations of the Roman church. "For it is no new thing that the kings of France have made laws and statutes concerning ecclesiastical affairs, especially the abuses and excesses of churchmen, including bishops and popes." One had only to think of the precedents established by Charlemagne. From him the French king derived the right both of electing his bishops (*jus eligendi, jus ordinandi*) and of reforming his church. Dumoulin seemed to suggest that Charlemagne, who had called councils, administered his clergy, and in general maintained "the pure word of God," was not only the first effective Gallican ruler but the first Protestant prince.[60]

This tradition was preserved, though with some difficulty, by the Capetian dynasty, which was the direct successor of the Carolingian (*la vraye continuation du vray et ancien regne*). Thus "Louis IX, following his predecessors and the ancient holy canons, passed a law in 1228 concerning the new establishments and preventions of the court of Rome . . . , which ordinance was obviously made for the liberty of the Gallican church."[61] Dumoulin also praised the seminal acts of Philip IV, including the embargo on funds to Rome, which set a precedent for later such acts, most recently by Henry II in 1551, and the *appel comme d'abus*, which he regarded as a kind of general antidote for curialist encroachments and which he himself resorted to in 1552. Still more fundamental were the precedents established during France's "withdrawal of obedience" and the conciliar period, culminating in the Pragmatic Sanction of Bourges.[62] From a legal point of view these Gallican liberties seemed to reflect the ancient constitution of the monarchy, a myth analogous to that of the "primitive

---

[59] Dumoulin, introduction to *Les petites dates*.

[60] Dumoulin, *In Regulas cancellariae*, XVIII, 98 (*Opera*, IV, 43).

[61] Dumoulin, *Traicté de l'origine*, p. 1041.

[62] Dumoulin, *Annotationes*, "In Decretales" (Gregory IX), L. II, T. 28, c. 7 (*Opera*, IV, 122), and on the withdrawal of obedience *Les petites dates*, p. 428. See R. Génestal, *Les Origines de l'appel comme d'abus* (Paris, 1951), arguing that it was not of ancient origin, as Dumoulin believed, but basically from the Pragmatic Sanction of Bourges.

church." In practical terms, however, Dumoulin represented them as a gradual accumulation of several centuries, and so in spite of himself he contributed to the secularization of ecclesiastical history.

In his long-winded and legal-minded fashion Dumoulin was working toward a conception of history based upon the principle of nationality. Given the popular basis of power, only the nation could be legitimate; given the national basis of culture, only the nation could be an "intelligible field of study." For this reason Dumoulin could not support the irenic program promoted by Baudouin, not to speak of the Calvinist international to which Hotman gave his allegiance. For this reason, too, he sympathized with the ideals of vernacular humanism and composed several of his works to promote national culture (*reipublicae Franciae ornandae causa; pour le bien et honneur du peuple françois*). Above all, he repudiated ultramontanism as the most flagrant subversion of nationality and of divine law. "In human things," he declared, "the most perfect piety is love of country, that is, of the people toward their prince, and similarly of the prince toward his people." [63] Dumoulin was referring, of course, to the more permanent of the "king's two bodies," his public person, which symbolized the unity of the French monarchy. Anything that detracted from this unity, any disparagement of the cultural or institutional integrity of France, was at once an act of aggression and a violation of history. It was upon such a set of values that the faith and intelligibility of history was to be based.

Dumoulin's views became much more popular after his death than they had ever been in his lifetime. During the last stages of the religious wars and during the Gallican revival sponsored by Henry IV, they were disseminated by politiques and radical Huguenots alike. Thus Dumoulin's old friend Hotman, in his *Brutish Thunderbolt* written on behalf of Henry of Navarre and the Prince of Condé after their excommunication in 1585, returned to the familiar charges of the fundamentally subversive character of canon law and its incorrigible penchant for fraud and forgery.[64] So, hardly less forcefully, did more

---

[63] Dumoulin, *Les petites dates*, p. 421.
[64] Hotman, *Brutum fulmen* (s. 1, 1587), pp. 87, 110, 128 ff. Hotman's correspondence with Navarre has been published by P. J. Blok in *Archives du*

responsible writers like Etienne Pasquier and the brothers Pithou. By this time, however, the substance of the Gallican tradition and its critique of Romanism had already been absorbed into historical scholarship. What for Dumoulin had been a means of magnifying the image of the French monarchy had become a perspective from which more open-minded scholars were beginning to reconstruct the general history of French society.

Musée Teylor, sér. 2, XII (1911), 204 ff. The *Hottomannia* in this Haarlem library (no shelf mark) contains also unpublished letters of Jean Hotman.

CHAPTER VII

Feudal Law and History: The Legists
Investigate the History of Institutions

Le roi ne tient nullui fors de Dieu et de lui.

Etablissements de St Louis, 1, 1, 78

WHOEVER CONSIDERS our fine laws, such as the Salic, the privileges of the Gallican church, the authority of kings limited by laws which they themselves made, the *appel comme d'abus* against prelates, the establishment of the peers of France, the courts of the parlement, the secret, privy and great councils . . ., fiefs, *regalia*, and many other institutions, will confess that the government of this monarchy owes nothing to the government of Rome.[1]

This inventory offered by the royal historiographer Du Haillan may be taken as a commonplace of French historical thought in the later sixteenth century as well as a reflection of the official image of the monarchy. His point was that while classical scholarship might furnish a methodology, it could never furnish an ideology for the interpretation of the French nation. In general, the statement represented an awareness of one of the essential aspects of Renaissance historicism, that ultimately every society had to be understood in terms of its own character and development. Yet again this was an attitude, at once narrowing and fruitful, that owed at least as much to legal studies as to historiography. It was from such a point of view that Dumoulin had investigated ecclesiastical institutions; it was from such a point of view that, in advance of historians, he and other legists would investigate the secular institutions of feudal society as well.

[1] Bernard de Girard, Sieur du Haillan, *De l'Estat et succez des affaires de France* (Paris, 1619), "au roy . . . Henry III" (1580).

Origins of Feudalism

One of the most remarkable features of the historical school of law
was the growing fascination with medieval institutions, feudal as well
as ecclesiastical. What for Budé and Alciato had been of contingent
interest became a central concern of their younger disciples. "If we are
French, English, German, Spanish, or Italian," wrote Baudouin, "we
must not, in discussing ourselves, he ignorant of the history of the
Franks, Angles, Saxons, Goths, and Lombards." For this purpose he
recommended the study not merely of medieval chronicles, which were
largely irrelevant even when they were trustworthy, but collections of
legal sources. Nor was it enough simply to follow the career of Roman
law. "In that miserable devastation of lands," he pointed out, "there
emerged in the place of written law those customs which we call
fiefs."[2] Only through the examination of customs (*consuetudines*),
which classical jurists themselves had recognized as a distinct form
of law, could a modern observer hope to understand the nature of
feudal society. This marks not only a vital link between the European
middle ages and classical antiquity, but one of the most troublesome
issues of sixteenth-century historical scholarship.

The customary place to begin was the so-called *Book of Fiefs*. Appended to the corpus of civil law, this curious work was actually a
twelfth-century mélange of imperial constitutions, Milanese statutory
law, and northern Italian jurisprudence, usually attributed to Obertus
de Orto, perhaps in collaboration with Girardus Niger. From the beginning, this collection of feudal customs (*consuetudines feudorum*)
had been the target of commentary and controversy. Between the fourteenth and sixteenth centuries jurists argued over the authority and
authenticity of this work, compared feudal and civil law, and debated
whether the provenance of feudal custom was Roman or barbarian.
Characteristically, they never reached agreement, but they did assemble
and criticize important evidence. By the sixteenth century there was
not only a flood of commentaries on the subject but also several historiographical surveys. In 1438 Jacopo Alvarotto counted over forty
commentaries "super feudis," and by the later sixteenth century the

---

[2] Baudouin, *De Institutione*, p. 623, and *Praefata de jure civile*, p. 12.

number must have more than doubled.[3] The topic was so popular that it attracted even humanists, including Budé, Alciato, Zasius, and Cujas, who produced the first critical edition of the *Book of Fiefs*.

The most valuable contributions, however, were made neither by the humanists nor by the Bartolists but by certain French legists, who were not bound by the presuppositions of civil lawyers and, more important, who brought a wider range of evidence and experience to bear upon the question. Their source material included that complex of French customary laws which, according to a thirteenth-century jurist, were "so diverse that one cannot find in all of France two chatellanies using the same custom."[4] By the sixteenth century there were still over 700 individual customs which continued to resist efforts of reform but which supplied feudists with endless material for discussion. They had even received a certain illumination from humanist scholarship. Such pioneering commentators as Barthélemy de Chasseneuz, André Tiraqueau, Nicolas Bohier, and Jean Pyrrhus d'Angleberme had little interest in the philological method, but they did make important and original contributions to the comparative and historical study of medieval law.[5] They were the direct predecessors of Dumoulin, in whom the feudist tradition reached its fruition.

[3] Jacopo Alvarotto, *Lectura in usus feudorum* (Frankfurt, 1570), "proemium." The most complete survey up to the mid-sixteenth century was provided by Marino Freccia, *De subfeudis baronum et investitum feudorum* (Venice, 1579), ending with the work of Baudouin. A contemporary bibliography of feudist scholarship, as well as that of canonists, civilians, and historians of every description, may be found in Conrad Gesner's *Bibliotheca universalis*, II (Zurich, 1548).

[4] Philippe de Beaumanoir, cited by Louis le Caron, *Pandectes du droict françois* (Lyon, 1596), p. 388. In particular, see F. Olivier-Martin, *Histoire de la coutume de la prévôté et vicomté de Paris* (Paris, 1922); R. Filhol, *Le Premier Président Christofle de Thou et la réformation des coutumes* (Paris, 1937); J. Van Kan, *Les Efforts de codification en France* (Paris, 1929); and J. Dawson, "The Codification of the French Customs," *Michigan Law Review*, XXXVIII (1940), 765-800.

[5] The best treatment for present purposes is J. Bréjon, *André Tiraqueau (1488-1558)* (Paris, 1937), who suggests (p. iii) that "Tiraqueau teaches us that the historical school was largely prefaced by Bartolus and his disciples.... It is necessary to investigate law through its monuments, but also through its interpreters." It is interesting that Tiraqueau, a precursor of Dumoulin, was was also one of the judges who condemned him in 1552 (BN MSS, Collection Dupuy, vol. 488, ff. 7-12).

THE TREE OF FRENCH GOVERN-
MENT (Charles de Figon, *Discours des estats
et offices*, Paris, 1579)

What was the origin of feudal law? This was a kind of question that intrigued jurists of all schools of thought, but medieval scholars meant something different by it than humanists did. They were thinking not of historical beginnings but of sources or, if they were philosophically inclined, of causes. In general, the question of feudal origins went back at least to the fourteenth century, in particular to the conventional rubric "On the origin of feudal law" (*De origine juris feudorum*), established on the analogy of the famous Digest title "On the origin of law." The usual answer (the *communis opinio*) was what I have called the Romanist thesis. This was inevitable since no good imperialist would dare deny that the *Book of Fiefs* was a legitimate part (the *decima collatio*) of Roman law, as shown by the inclusion of legislation of various emperors. This collection was both authentic and universal, argued Baldus, who called also upon the authority of canon law and other doctors of law. The clinching argument was the etymology repeated by every jurist from Obertus to Dumoulin and beyond, whether they knew better or not, that " 'fief' is said to come from 'fidelity' or 'faith.' " [6] A Latin derivation was enough to convince most jurists of an ancient origin.

It may seem curious that, to begin with at least, humanists agreed with the Bartolists in accepting the Romanist thesis. The reason was that they also wanted to maintain a link with antiquity, and they were too intimidated by the values of classicism to have absorbed the deeper lesson that the philological method was not restricted to Latin and Greek. This was the case not only with Budé, Alciato, and Zasius, but with Haloander and even Cujas, who, though he was aware of the difficulties of the Romanist thesis, could find no more satisfactory solution. One of the presumed authors of the *Book of Fiefs*, in fact, had referred to feudal law as ancient (*jus antiquissimum*). It was Cujas' opinion that feudal law was an outgrowth of certain precarial

---

[6] Baldus, *Opus aureum . . . super feudis* (Venice, 1516), f. 2ʳ, citing *Consuetudines feudorum*, II, 3, in K. Lehmann, *Das langobardische Lehnrecht* (Göttingen, 1896), p. 119. The best study is by Savigny's disciple E. A. Laspeyres, *Über die Entstehung und älteste Bearbeitung der Libri feudorum* (Berlin, 1830). Many medieval and humanist commentaries on feudal law may be found in *Tractatus*, X. The subject is more fully analyzed in my "*De Origine Feudorum:* The Beginnings of an Historical Problem," *Speculum*, XXXIX (1964), 207-28.

tenures (such as the *procuratores* and *actores*) which in the course of time became hereditary and acquired "the new and foreign names of vassals, *leudes*, or feudatories."[7] This is similar to the argument of Chasseneuz that fief was simply a modern term (*mutato nomine*) for the military land grants (*praedium stipendiarium*).[8] In general, there was a single assumption underlying the Romanist thesis, whatever form it took, that feudalism was a kind of organization common to various societies at different periods of time and that it was passed on by "imitation."

Yet from the beginning there had been a minority opinion which opposed the Romanist thesis on historical grounds. To at least a few readers it seemed clear that the *Book of Fiefs* was not Roman at all but only a barbarous appendage (*nec lex sed faex*). This is what Petrarch implied when he demanded that Roman law be purged of its medieval accretions, and this is what jurists meant when they doubted that the collection was "authentic" or at least that it had more than local validity. The crucial historical argument was supplied by the fourteenth-century feudist Andrea de Isernia, who doubted "whether fief and vassal are new names [*nova nomina*] or are contained in Roman law."[9] In the next century Claude de Seyssel, who regarded Andrea as the best of his predecessors, pointed to the rudeness and impurity (*rusticitas obscaenitasque*) of the style of the *Book of Fiefs*. "It is obvious," he concluded, "that fiefs were wholly unknown to ancient jurists and only came to be used by later men."[10] It was from this nominalist standpoint—the insistence upon a literal interpretation of terms—that the Romanist thesis came under fire in the sixteenth century.

[7] Jacques Cujas, *In Libros quinque feudorum*, in *Opera*, X, 832. See the discussion of J. G. A. Pocock, *The Ancient Constitution and the Feudal Law* (Cambridge, 1957).

[8] Barthélemy de Chasseneuz, *Consuetudines ducatus Burgundiae* (Paris, 1548), f. 99r.

[9] Andrea de Isernia, *In Usu feudorum commentaria* (Naples, 1571), f. 6r. Even in the thirteenth century Jacopo de Ardizone (*Summa feudorum*, in *Tractatus*, X, part I, f. 225v) admitted that "nothing about vassal or fief can be found in Roman law."

[10] Claude de Seyssel, *Speculum feudorum* (Basel, 1566), p. 1. This was intended to support Seyssel's basic argument, common to French jurists, that "those who do not recognize the emperor are not bound by these laws."

Humanist arguments were vulnerable for much the same reason. Thus the feudist Angleberme rejected Budé's opinion as anachronistic and offered merely "for the sake of purer speech."[11] This criticism was reinforced by the realization that feudal law, especially in France, was too diverse to possess such a simple ancestry, and by the recollection that Roman law itself had resulted not from "imitation" but from the elaboration of native custom. "It is doubtful," admitted Le Douaren, "that [feudal] law takes its origin from the law of the Romans." Lelio Torelli, the first editor of the Florentine manuscript of the Digest, had expressed similar doubts about the views of Budé and Zasius.[12] Joining in the chorus of criticism, too, was François Connan, the distinguished friend of Le Douaren, Hotman, and Calvin. On the basis of Caesar's testimony and the Celtic derivation of the word "vassal," Connan offered the curious counterproposal that feudal law was a creation of the ancient Gauls.[13] This Gallic thesis, which was one illustration of the interest in Gallic antiquity fashionable in the mid-sixteenth century, was never widely accepted, although it persisted in scholarship until the nineteenth century. But it did indicate the attitude which scholars were adopting toward the problem of feudal origins: that it had to be resolved through a philological method and in terms of the history of European society.

Dumoulin the Feudist

The man who did most to discredit the naïve Romanist theory of feudal origins was that arch-Gallican Charles Dumoulin, using ammunition provided by humanists and Bartolists as well as his own researches. His *Treatise on Fiefs*, which first appeared in 1539 and again twenty-five years later in an expanded form, was the first comprehensive and critical history of feudalism. The humanist aspect of

---

[11] Jean Pyrrhus d'Angleberme, *Consuetudines Aurelianae*, in *Opuscula* (Paris, 1517), f. II^v, referring to Budé, *Annotationes*, f. 146^r (see ch. III, n. 62).

[12] Le Douaren, *Commentarius in consuetudines feudorum*, p. 137, and Torelli, *De Militiis* (*Tractatus*, X, part I, f. 323^v).

[13] François Connan, *Commentariorum juris civilis libri* X (Naples, 1724), II, ix, 65 (p. 116).

this work is shown in Dumoulin's use of a philological method, the more traditional side in the form of the book itself, which tended to follow conventional scholastic rubrics, though not conventional scholastic conclusions. From the Bartolist school, too, Dumoulin derived habits which were to be taken over by historians and antiquaries, that is, introducing his analyses by criticisms of earlier authorities, the historiographical *état de question* as it were, and founding his discussion upon precise references to the primary sources.

In his critique of "the origin of fiefs" Dumoulin spared neither Bartolists, such as Baldus and Lucas de Penna, nor humanists, such as Budé and Alciato. In general he aligned himself with the revisionist school, including Andrea de Isernia and his own teacher Angleberme. "Those who derived the invention and origin of fiefs from Roman law," he declared, "show a great ignorance of antiquity and produce futile conjectures." [14] In this respect Lucas de Penna who had identified the feudal contract with the *stipendiaria* of Roman law, was no more guilty than Zasius, who assumed a connection between vassalage and the ancient clientele, an institution which was obsolete three centuries before Justinian and in any case involved no military obligation. Even Budé, whom Dumoulin honored as "the glory of all France," as the man who "restored the elegance of laws after more than 800 years," had erred in this matter; and Dumoulin repeated the charge of Angleberme that he had derived vassalage from the ancient *patrocinium* simply "for the sake of purer speech," although the monuments were obviously filled with "Gothic" language.[15] In this way Dumoulin turned the weapons of philology against their own creators.

Dumoulin's own conclusion in which he paid formal respect to the opinion of Andrea de Isernia, was founded upon the soundest philological basis. This was, in brief, "that in all of Roman law there ap-

---

[14] Dumoulin, *Commentarii in Parisienses ... consuetudines*, in *Opera*, I ("De Fiefs"), 3-4 (p. 1). The *Prima pars* of this commentary on the coutume of Paris appeared in 1539.

[15] *Ibid.*, I, 23-25 (p. 6), referring to Budé, *Annotationes*, f. 146r, and Zasius, *In usus feudorum epitome* (Lyon, 1556), p. 3. On the other hand Dumoulin's rival Pierre Rebuffi (*Feudorum declaratio*, in *Tractatus*, I, part 1, f. 300v) commended Budé because he "restored to the Latin language ... this barbaric term fiefs."

pears no word of fief or vassal . . . , neither in the Pandects nor in the Code nor in the constitutions of Justinian . . . ," nor, Dumoulin added, in any of the histories. For this reason he agreed absolutely with Angleberme that "feudal law is most recent, originating neither with the jurists nor with the ancient emperors of the Romans but was introduced afterwards as custom." Dumoulin thus endorsed a view that was to have the greatest significance for the historical study of institutions, that laws had to be understood not as an expression of abstract reason or conscious imitation but as a gradual development from specific custom.

As for the "ultramontane book of fiefs" itself, Dumoulin followed the tradition of the French legists in rejecting its "authenticity," which was to say its authority. He dismissed the "colorful arguments" of Baldus, who had defended its validity on the grounds of acceptance by canon law and of general consent. This was nonsense, Dumoulin retorted, if only "because of the notorious irregularity of feudal customs." So also was the widely held view that the *Book of Fiefs* was the "tenth collection" of imperial authentics. In the place of this anachronistic thesis Dumoulin offered a "new opinion" that

this book has the force neither of law nor of custom . . . because it was apparently compiled by Obertus de Orto, who was a lawyer or *pragmaticus* of the Milanese court . . . , a private person having the public authority neither of a prince nor of the people. . . . It is clear that Obertus had no power to decide at what court or to what place a custom belonged . . . or to judge the force of a law or custom. . . .[16]

Not that it would make any difference to a Frenchman anyway, for not only the Lombard custom, Dumoulin concluded, but "even the imperial constitutions may be considered local law since at that time the empire itself was limited and local." Here again Dumoulin was assuming the orthodox posture of the French legist, rejecting the notion that any part of the emperor's law, whether feudal or civil, had force in France.

In general, it was Dumoulin's conviction that feudalism was basically a product of French—which of course he did not separate from

---

[16] *Ibid.*, I, 100 (p. 21).

Frankish—tradition. This, too, was in keeping with legist doctrine, which always argued from the jurisdiction of Charlemagne. The Lombard kingdom itself had been incorporated into the Carolingian empire, recalled Bohier, who used this fact to reinforce French claims in northern Italy.[17] But Dumoulin went beyond this merely legal point:

I have learned that the authors of fiefs were the kings of the Franks, reigning in eastern Franconia even before the birth of Christ. . . . I have seen the ancient records of the donation of Childebert, son of the Frankish king Clovis, to the monastery of St-Germain-des-Prés, near the city and house in which I write . . ., made before the time of Justinian the great, who never had jurisdiction in Gaul. . . . This is the true origin of fiefs.[18]

It was, of course, only the beginning of a long and complicated story.

These Franks conceded in fief the occupied lands of the frontier in return for recognition, an oath of fealty, the promise of certain military duties for the fief, renewal of investiture, and other conditions. . . . Whence it was introduced into Gaul . . ., then Lombardy, the two Sicilies, Apulia, and many other regions. . . .

So from these "Francigermani," as Dumoulin called them, feudal institutions had been inherited by modern European society.

As usual, Dumoulin's arguments were not wholly disinterested. Besides hoping to add further luster to the French monarchy, he intended to assert the superiority, or at least the special significance, of French customary law. In particular, it was part of his program of legal reform to establish the Parisian custom, which like Tiraqueau he regarded as supreme in French society (*caput omnium hujus regni et totius etiam Belgicae Galliae consuetudinum*), as the basis of common law and eventually of a unified legal system. "The French are one people," Dumoulin argued, "and therefore should have one law." [19] But this law should conform to their own usages, and so Dumoulin objected to the practice of resorting to Milanese custom (*non est recurrendum ad usus feudorum compilates per Obertum . . . sed . . . ad jus commune*). In this way Dumoulin was led to anticipate the modern

---

[17] Nicolas Bohier, *Leges Longobardorum* (Lyon, 1512), f. iii^r.
[18] Dumoulin, *Commentarii*, I, 13 (p. 5).
[19] Dumoulin, *Oratio de concordia*, p. 812.

view that the most representative form of feudalism appeared not in Lombardy but in northern France.

In the later sixteenth century Dumoulin's thesis became something of a "common opinion," at least among French feudists and historians. René Choppin, who composed his own commentary on the Parisian custom, repeated not only Dumoulin's arguments about the origin of fiefs but his specific evidence.[20] Another of Dumoulin's successors was Louis le Caron, who had studied with Baudouin at the University of Bourges before turning to the study of French law. He agreed that long before the Lombards "fiefs [and] . . . vassalage were known and used in France, having arisen from benefices and recompenses which kings and great lords gave to warriors who had followed them in their victories in Gaul. . . ." What is more, Le Caron contradicted the conventional etymology of the fief which even Cujas and Dumoulin had accepted, explaining that "fief or *feudum* or *beneficium* . . . were barbaric and known in Italy only after the Lombards descended from Germany . . . , so that it should not be derived from or denoted by the Latin term *fides* or *foedus* or *fidelitas*, but rather from a German word, which some have *faida* or *feed*, which means emnity, hostility, or war." [21] Here we can see philology joining history in questioning the authority of a major source of medieval law.

It was fitting that the final link in this chain of argument should have been made by Dumoulin's former friend Hotman, who seemed compelled to push every idea to its extreme. The traditional conception of the *Francigermani* he transformed into the chauvinistic image of the *Francogalli*, and he attacked the Romanist thesis as simply one more aspect of that hydra-headed enemy, ultramontanism. Repeating the arguments of Dumoulin and rejecting those of Cujas, Hotman denied any parallel with Roman tenures, which had no military basis. He also accepted the Germanic derivation of the fief, and then went on to propose what was to become the standard explanation of the origin of vassalage, that it was descended from the *comitatus* de-

[20] René Choppin, *Commentaire sur les coustumes . . . de Paris* (Paris, 1662), p. 35.
[21] Louis le Caron, *Responses et decisions du droict françois* (Paris, 1637), p. 93.

scribed by Tacitus.[22] In general, Hotman was convinced that feudal institutions were autochthonous and that, contrasting sharply with the universalist and authoritarian tradition of Rome, they exhibited pronounced local variations wherever they had taken root. It was in this way that the foundations were laid for what can only be regarded as a Germanist interpretation of history.

For most historians, of course, Hotman had gone too far. What he offered was not a picture but a caricature of French history. And how, after all, could one deny altogether the influence of Roman organization? This was why many scholars continued to favor the notion of some connection between feudalism and the society of the late empire. Thus Forcadel, although he admitted that "with respect to origins . . . feudal customs are not to be attributed to written law," still made use of Roman analogies.[23] Etienne Pasquier's friend Jean de Basmaison reverted to the view of Alciato and Zasius that the Roman *stipendiaria* were the principal source of fiefs, but he qualified this by admitting that the "elegant name" itself was modern and referred to unwritten customs which differed not only from nation to nation but from province to province.[24] This was the opinion, too, of Dumoulin's rival Guy Coquille and of a number of historians whom we shall encounter. In general, it was a compromise between the naïve Romanist theory of cultural imitation and the equally naïve Germanist theory of racial inheritance. It made use of, without being a slave to, philological argument, and it was flexible enough to allow for the manifold heritage of feudal society. While the extreme Romanist and Germanist theses continued to operate as ideological poles, historical scholarship was coming to occupy a middle ground which encompassed both this Romanist opinion and the moderate—and not wholly irreconcilable—view of Dumoulin.

---

[22] *Ad Disputationem de feudis* (1573) (*Operum*, II, col. 807), referring (e.g., col. 813) to "our ancient Franco-Gauls." He had discussed this question eleven years before, in *Observationum liber secundus* (Basel, 1561), pp. 12-19, and had remarked on the "Gothic" language but had not yet arrived at his Germanist opinion.

[23] Étienne Forcadel, *De Feudis commentarius* (Hanover, 1603), p. 5.

[24] Jean de Basmaison, *De l'origine des fiefs et riere fiefs* (1579) (Paris, 1611), f. 7ʳ, and Coquille, *Les Coustumes de Nivernois* (Paris, 1610), p. 92.

The Legist Tradition

The debate over feudal law was carried on within the context of a broader discussion of the nature and provenance of European institutions, in which the central issue was the monarchy itself. In France the terms of this discussion were, inevitably, set by the royal legists, who carried out much of the work of gathering and interpreting the evidence. As they defended the monarchy against the encroachments of the ecclesiastical establishment, so they defended it against the claims of the feudal establishment and of the emperor; as they provided an account of the growth of Gallicanism, so they provided an account of the growth of secular institutions. Essentially, the purpose of the legists was to preserve an old tradition, or at least to find ancient excuses for modern policies, but they carried this out in an increasingly sophisticated and critical fashion and with a certain awareness of history and the nature of society. At the same time they retained the legal apparatus and the accumulated stock of questions and answers, the memory of past successes and failures, of their tradition. For good or for ill, French historical scholarship never quite effaced the view of medieval history shaped by these professional ideologists.

By the sixteenth century the legist tradition was so conventionalized —so cumulative and, in a manner of speaking, so corporate—that any one of a number of individual propagandists might be taken as representative. The last and most comprehensive survey of legist doctrine before the work of Dumoulin was Charles de Grassaille's *Regalia of France*, which appeared in 1538. In this inventory of royal prerogatives, twenty of the "jura" being ecclesiastical and twenty secular in character, Grassaille laid a scholarly foundation as broad as his purpose was narrow. He drew not only upon his immediate predecessors, including Jean Ferrault, Barthélemy de Chasseneuz, Nicolas Bohier, and Jean Lemaire de Belges, but also upon civil, canon, and feudal law, jurists of every school, and historians of every description. In short he showed familiarity with all of the raw materials for medieval institutional history which were in published form.

The official image of French history as it appeared in Grassaille's work was less legalistic and more human than might be supposed, for he took pride in the good fortune and cultural achievements as well as in the political form of the monarchy. France had always been a promoter of learning (*doctrinae genatrix*), he argued, referring to the *studium* of Paris and, like Dumoulin, misattributing it to Charlemagne.[25] France was also a promoter of the legal profession, and here Grassaille paid tribute to his own tradition and to the parlement of Paris which had nurtured it. What is most remarkable about Grassaille's discussion of these subjects is his awareness of the underlying factors of economics and geography. He attached enough importance to national wealth to include it among the *regalia* as a necessary condition of political power and cultivation of the civilized arts, especially of literature and jurisprudence. He pointed out the significance of environment, too, in the shaping of national character. Chasseneuz had gone still further by elaborating this assumption into a general theory of the relation between geography (the *climata*) and national differences.[26] Thus, anticipating the more systematic work of Bodin, the legists placed their analysis of political power in a social and physical context.

Like the humanists the legists were interested in the problem of national origins, but of course they could not allow themselves the same scholarly license. Even if Grassaille had shared Paolo Emilio's suspicions, for example, he could not have publicly rejected the theory that the Franks were descended from the Trojan hero Francus. Yet this did not prevent him from emphasizing the Germanic heritage of France (*saltum ex genere Germanorum*) and disparaging the Roman. Inevitably, he repeated the old etymology associating the French with the term "free" (*Franci, id est, liberi*), that is, exempt from Roman taxes.[27] Above all, Grassaille exalted Charlemagne, who furnished an inexhaustible supply of precedents—and legends—of fundamental importance for the king's business. In particular, Grassaille recalled, it was through Charlemagne that the French king could claim a share

---

[25] Charles de Grassaille, *Regalium Franciae libri duo* (Paris, 1545), p. 198.

[26] *Ibid.*, p. 195; cf. Chasseneuz, *Catalogus gloriae mundi* (Geneva, 1617), pp. 470 ff.

[27] *Ibid.*, p. 11.

in the majesty of empire. Among other privileges deriving from this source, the king claimed the right to be a candidate for empire, he was "above all kings" and even "vicar of Christ in his kingdom," he "recognized no superior in temporal things," and he administered his own church (*motu proprio regis*). In short, to use the most famous formula of all, he was "emperor in his kingdom."[28] It is most significant that, while this aspect of French kingship was Carolingian in origin and established on historical grounds, it was expressed in formulas of canonist devising.

The basic principle around which these time-honored formulas revolved was the "translation of empire" (*translatio imperii*), which was also of canonist origin. Ultimately, the explanation for the transference of the empire from the Greeks to the Germans in the person of Charlemagne was the Biblical principle that "God transfers kingdoms from one people to another because of injustice, injuries, blasphemies, and other evils."[29] But beyond this there was little agreement among lawyers and historians. "Translatio est magna altercatio," remarked Chasseneuz; and this was particularly true in the sixteenth century when the old conflict between France and the empire was intensified by the clash between the Valois and the Hapsburg. The French legists did not deny that there had been subsequent translations from the Franks to the Lombards and finally to the "Teutons," but they would not admit that this derogated in any way from the imperial claims of the "third race" of French kings. "From this translation," Chasseneuz declared, "the imperial power has always remained with the French . . . , from which it may be said that the king

[28] *Ibid.*, pp. 2, 51, 225, 36. Cf. Chasseneuz, *Catalogus*, pp. 236 ff, and Ferrault, *Privilegia regni Franciae*, in Dumoulin (ed.), *Stilus supremae curiae parlamenti.* In general, see P. Schramm, *Der König von Frankreich* (Weimar, 1960), pp. 252 ff; and Mochi Onory, *Fonti canonistiche*, pp. 96 ff, 155 ff; and G. Post, *Studies in Medieval Legal Thought* (Princeton, 1964), pp. 434 ff. The "no superior" formula is from Innocent III, *Per Venerabilem* (Decretales Gregorii IX, L. IV, T. 17, c. 8), in *Migne*, CCXIV, col. 1132.

[29] Grassaille, *Regalium Franciae*, p. 10, and Chasseneuz, *Catalogus*, p. 240 and 482. In general, see the study of W. Goez, *Translatio Imperii* (Tübingen, 1958), which however is limited to Germany, and F. Ercole, *Da Bartolo all'Althusio* (Florence, 1932), pp. 52 ff. Cf. *Daniel*, 2 : 21, and *Liber ecclesiastici*, X, 8.

of France is above all kings . . . [and] is another emperor." By virtue of this heritage and of his title, traceable at least to Pepin, of "most Christian," Grassaille argued that he was equal in status to the ancient Roman emperors.[30]

Yet if the legists were efficient in appropriating features of imperial majesty for their own sovereign, they were still more insistent upon the independence of France from this same imperial authority. No Roman emperor, said Grassaille, not even Antoninus or Justinian, had ever been a truly universal lord *(dominus mundi)*. He referred in particular to the principle, commonly held by "citramontane jurists," as Chasseneuz observed, that "there have been many countries and nations not subject to the empire."[31] It was this "common opinion," rather than any special breadth of vision, that furnished the principal grounds for Bodin's famous rejection of the old idea of Four World Monarchies. The immediate conclusion drawn by legists, however, was that French society had no place for Roman law, still less for the *Book of Fiefs*. French courts recognized neither donations nor testamentary successions made according to civil or canon law or by foreign notaries, said Grassaille, and the Roman *patria potestas* was rejected in France "because all men are free."[32] In general, as Ferrault had stipulated, there had been a "reception" of Roman law but no "subjection" to it. Or, as Grassaille and Dumoulin put it, it was accepted as a rational standard but not as legal authority. This too was, if only implicitly, a historical argument.

Here is a point that has never been sufficiently emphasized: the most striking thing about the legists of the sixteenth century was not their use of Roman law, as has so often been said, but their insistence upon the primacy of native traditions. In fact, there was a reaction

[30] Grassaille, *Regalium Franciae*, p. 96. See J. de Pange, *Le Roi très chrétien* (Paris, 1949).

[31] *Ibid.*, p. 67, and Chasseneuz, *Catalogus*, p. 231. Cf. *Pragmatico Sanctio glossata per Cosmo Guymier* (Lyon, 1548), f. 1ʳ: "The Franks were never subject to the emperor in temporal matters, as is shown by the old histories."

[32] Grassaille, *Regalium Franciae*, p. 96; cf. p. 67: "The seventh great law of the most Christian King . . . is that he is not subject to the laws of the Roman emperors or jurisconsults"; and (p. 7) "Similarly, the laws or *consuetudines feudorum* have no place in France." It was also upon the medieval tradition exemplified by these arguments that Hotman built his *Anti-Tribonian*.

against Romanist influence in favor of feudal law which, though it grew out of the antagonism between France and the empire dating back to the thirteenth century, was reinforced by the conflicts of the sixteenth century. The kingship, while it might be decorated with Romanist formulas, was in fact defined not by analogy with the imperium but in terms of its individual prerogatives, that is, by those regalia which had been accumulated over a long period of time in response to specific problems that had arisen. The king of France may have been "emperor in his kingdom" but, as Chasseneuz summed it up, he had "many rights and privileges which no other prince possessed." [33]The French monarchy, then, was the product of a unique historical experience; the French king was bound to no past but his own, and this past was obviously not classical but feudal. What is more, in order to gather and to document these unique marks of sovereignty, historical scholarship was clearly much more important that Roman law or political theory.

Besides innumerable particular rights of a feudal or ecclesiastical character (Chasseneuz counted 208 *jura regalia*), the legists placed special emphasis upon two "fundamental laws" which set the French monarchy apart from other governments. One of these was the so-called Salic law, which was still attributed to the legendary Pharamond but which, according to Grassaille, was validated in any case by custom (*ex longaeva consuetudine*) and by the natural superiority of males (*dignior in rebus publicis*). "Women do not succeed to a fief," he said, repeating an old feudist formula, "much less to a kingdom." [34] History was filled with examples of female incompetence which had threatened the political continuity of France, and with the regency of Catherine de' Medici history seemed to be repeating itself. No wonder

[33] Chasseneuz, *Catalogus*, p. 241.

[34] Grassaille, *Regalium Franciae*, pp. 164 ff; cf. Angleberme, *De Lege salica* (in Forcadel, *De Feudis*, pp. 100 ff). The Salic law was likened to civil law by Masson, *Annalium libri quatuor* (Paris, 1577), p. 42; to the *lex regia* by Le Caron, *Pandectes du droict français*, p. 9. In general, see A. Lemaire, *Les Lois fondamentales de la monarchie française d'après les théoriciens de l'ancien régime* (Paris, 1907); R. Giesey, *The Juristic Basis of Dynastic Right to the French Throne* (American Philosophical Society, *Transactions*, LI, 5, 1961); and J. M. Potter, "The Development and Significance of the Salic Law of the French," *English Historical Review*, LII (1937), 235-53.

the Salic law was regarded by many legists and historians as the life-principle of the monarchy—the *lex regia* if not the *jus civile* of France. In 1593 it was officially declared a "fundamental law."

Finally, there was the rule of government by counsel and consent, which legists also construed as a source of kingly power, as a "prerogative" rather than as a "constitutional" limitation in a modern sense. For most of them, however, this fundamental law was associated not with the antiquated assembly of estates but with the sovereign court which was their own ideological home and which they graced with tributes that fell little short of idolatry. "The king of France and no other holds the parlement" ran the twelfth regale of Grassaille, who referred also to the panegyrical tract of Bohier.[35] Equal in status to the Roman senate (as Budé had also argued), the parlement of Paris was at the same time a unique institution with its own tradition and "style." As to the problem of its origin, etymology offered little help since the term "parlamentum" was much too general—unless one accepted the facetious derivation, "the peers' lament," suggested by Grassaille. Most legists agreed that there were antecedents in the Carolingian assemblies, but in practical terms they were content to accept the judgment of historians, such as Gaguin and Paolo Emilio, who traced the parlement back to the fixing of the royal court, probably by Philip IV, in the late thirteenth or early fourteenth century. In that form it became a bulwark against feudal and ecclesiastical usurpation.

It will not do to exaggerate the history-mindedness of legists like Grassaille. Admittedly, they were mouthpieces of the monarchy and quite uncritical in matters touching the interests or the prestige of the crown. Yet their work reflects more clearly than that of the historians the ideological underpinnings of historical scholarship and the major rubrics of the newly established field of institutional history. They contributed substantially to the transmission of legal methods, for-

---

[35] Grassaille, *Regalium Franciae*, pp. 111 ff, and Bohier, *Tractatus de auctoritate magni concilii et parlamentorum Franciae*, in *Stilus parlamenti* (Paris, 1542), f. cxxvi^v-cxxxv^r. There are other works of this sort which belong on the fringes of institutional history, such as J. Montaigne, "De Auctoritate et praeeminentia magni concilii et parlamentorum" (*Tractatus*, XVI), and E. Bourg, *Solium regis . . . in suprema curia parlamenti Parisiensis* (Lyon, 1550).

mulas, and problems into the study of history proper. During the period of the civil wars in France this convergence of the legist tradition and historiography helped to bring about a profound change in historical scholarship.

The Germanist Thesis

Irresistably, the interpretation of legal and institutional history came to reflect the ideological divisions of the religious conflict. Just as the French monarchy was caught between the fires of ultramontane Catholicism and radical Protestantism in the later sixteenth century, so French scholarship found itself trapped between the extremes of Romanism and Germanism. There was, it is true, some attempt to find a Gallican compromise in scholarship as well as in politics. At first it seemed that this might be found in the heritage of ancient Gaul, for which there was a wave of literary and antiquarian enthusiasm at mid-century that attracted both historians, such as the young Pasquier, and jurists, such as Connan.[36] For the most part, however, the *gaulois* thesis had a literary rather than a scholarly significance. French scholars, especially those with Protestant sympathies, turned increasingly to the Germanic side of their inheritance as a means of establishing national identity.

As might be expected, their views were quite derivative. As Frenchmen of an earlier generation had plundered the work of Italian scholars, so Frenchmen of the later sixteenth century plundered the work of Germans, humanists as well as Protestants. In the books of such historians as Beatus Rhenanus, Albert Krantz, Johann Cario, and Johann Sleidan, they found a ready-made and sharply defined ideology. This "Germanism," whose locus classicus was the recently discovered *Germania* of Tacitus, provided perhaps for the first time a plausible alternative to the intimidating Romanist scheme of history. Out of commentaries on Tacitus and interpretations of certain medieval chroniclers, such as Jordanes and Paul the deacon, and of legal codes, especially the Salic law, there emerged a number of themes most attractive to reform-minded scholars: the antiquity and in-

[36] See ch. X, n. 49 and 53. Among the promoters of this Celtic revival were Forcadel, Ramus, Robert Ceneau, Postel, and Guillaume du Bellay.

dependent origin of Germanic society; the indigenous nature of Ger-- man culture, especially as indicated by philological evidence; the simplicity and purity of German morals ("the Germans are not usurers"); the racial integrity of the Germans ("unmixed," said Tacitus); and above all the distinctive freedom of the Germanic tribes, embodied in the very name of the Franks.[37] While German authors associated these virtues with the empire or with individual princes, Frenchmen began to claim a share of this tradition for their king, who as a collateral descendant of Charlemagne was an heir of the "Franci-Germani." Such themes colored, if they did not shape, French historical thinking in the later sixteenth century.

The beginning of the infusion—or infection—of French scholarship by Germanism may be seen in the work of Dumoulin. Inspired by his Protestant enthusiasm, Dumoulin's favorable view of Germanic culture was given substance by extensive reading in German historians and by his legal work on behalf of Philip of Hesse, and it was confirmed by his "Germanic exile" beginning in 1553.[38] (For many young Frenchmen, it may be remarked, the German, or Swiss, voyage was replacing the Italian voyage as an essential step in their education.) It is clear that Dumoulin's ideas were generated in the heat of ideological combat and shaped by intense political and religious pressures; the fact that his major professional concerns—feudal, canon, and civil law—were by their very nature controversial further ex-

---

[37] Besides Beatus Rhenanus, *In P. Cornelium Tacitum Annotationes* (Lyon, 1542), see the collection of Schardius, *Historicorum opus*, vol. I, *Germaniae illustrationem continet* (Basel, 1574), containing numerous celebrations of Germany and glosses on Tacitus' *Germania*, including that of Melanchthon. Discussions of this subject include P. Joachimsen, "Tacitus im deutschen Humanismus," *Neue Jahrbücher für das klassische Altertum*, XXVII (1911), 697-717; H. Tiedemann, *Tacitus und das Nationalbewusstsein der deutschen Humanisten* (Berlin, 1913); R. Buschmann, *Das Bewusstsein der deutschen Geschichte bei den deutschen Humanisten* (Göttingen, 1930); E. Etter, *Tacitus in der Geistesgeschichte des 16. und 17. Jahrhunderts* (Basel, 1966); and E. Hölzle, *Die Idee einer altgermanischen Freiheit vor Montesquieu* (*Historische Zeitschrift*, Beiheft V, 1925).

[38] Dumoulin, *Consilia quatuor* (Paris, 1552), p. 71, remarking on the "holy and ancient friendship between Germany and France." Cf. *Conseil du Concile de Trente*, p. 2: "These two great monarchies of France and Germany . . ., which in Charlemagne's time were but a single monarchy . . ., have always been allied and bound together. . . ."

aggerated his opinions. Yet partisanship is precisely what gave vitality and direction, if not complete reliability, to his investigations and sustained him in his prodigious scholarly efforts. If his purpose was to find a "usable past" for the French monarchy, his achievement was to open up new resources for the study of medieval institutions.

In general, what Dumoulin accomplished was a kind of transvaluation of values through the rehabilitation of "barbarism." He insisted upon the indigenous and nonclassical character of French traditions, not only feudal and monarchical but (as described in the previous chapter) ecclesiastical. He fortified his congenital anti-Romanist prejudice with notions of Germanic virtue and joined the "liberties of the Gallican church" to those of the Germanic tribes. He contrasted the confused but uncorrupted customary law (*jus consuetudinarium*) of France with the abstract and authoritarian character of Roman law. This was one reason for insisting that feudal law was a product of Germanic custom and had no relations with Rome in either a linguistic or an institutional sense. This was so with many royal offices, too, such as the *mareschal*. In general, Dumoulin confessed, "I regard myself as an enthusiast for the Frankish name and for the nobility, dignity, and virtue of the ancient Franks, but I have been led to this conclusion by judgment rather than by emotion."[39] In Germanism, then, Dumoulin found a treasury of ideas and attitudes to counteract the manifold evils of Romanism, imperial as as well as papal.

Once again, as with Gallicanism, the vital link between ancient ideals and the present-day monarchy was Charlemagne. The translation of empire came to him not as king of the Germans but as king of the Franks, and his dominion included most of Europe. The emperor Otto, on the other hand, had a much more restricted territory and was the beneficiary of a more modest transference of power (the *translatio ad Saxones*). "All German writers," Dumoulin argued, "not only simple chroniclers but also famous doctors of law and theology like Philip Melanchthon, believe that the empire was translated from the French to the Saxon princes not by the death of Conrad I of

---

[39] Dumoulin, letter to Montmorency (*Opera*, III, 807), discussing that favorite etymological example, the *mareschal*.

the east Franks but by his cession.[40] Moreover, through the "Salic law, the most ancient, perpetual, and inviolable law of the crown of France," the French king could claim a more direct descent from the Carolingians than the merely elected German emperors. Like Melanchthon and Calvin, Dumoulin was careful to join his program with a permanent and doctrinal, in this case legal, tradition having its origins in an idealized antiquity.

But the imperial heritage of the French monarchy by no means implied a direct connection with classical antiquity, and here Dumoulin was in complete agreement with the legists. "The Franks," he repeated, "were never subject to the empire." Consequently, Roman law had no place in France except as a rational standard (*non ratione imperii sed rationis imperio*). In this context, of course, Dumoulin did not scruple to call upon Innocent III, who testified that "the king of France recognizes no superior in temporal things."[41] Like all the legists, Dumoulin used imperialist arguments up to the point where they derogated from the king's power; then he slipped comfortably into the formulas of canon law. But his ultimate justification was unquestionably the native Germanic, that is, the Franci-Germanic and feudal, traditions of the monarchy.

From Dumoulin to Hotman

As usual, it fell to Hotman to push the Germanist thesis to its extreme, if not completely into the realm of fantasy. His interpretation of history, like Dumoulin's, was basically a function of his reform program and a variation on the familiar Protestant theme of a return to a pure and native tradition, but he lacked Dumoulin's breadth of view. The enemy Hotman identified in the most brutal terms: it was Italy, all that it stood for and all that it tried to export, including canon law, Catherine de' Medici, the influence of Machiavelli, and the swarms of benefice-hunting and tax-collecting *fuorusciti*. "All taxes . . . ," Hotman complained in Lyons, "are in the hands of Italian publicans." Such complaints echo through all the Huguenot

---

[40] Dumoulin, *Commentarii*, I, 52 (p. 12).
[41] *Ibid.*, I, 28 (p. 8), and *Annotationes*, p. 176.

pamphlets of this period, contrasting the 'Italiens francisquez,' in the phrase of Nicolas Barnaud, with the 'bons politiques . . . , nouveaux reformateurs," who tried to preserve French traditions.[42] The sources of corruption in French society, according to Hotman, were foreign vices that ranged from avarice to idolatry and from Ciceronianism to sodomy. Added to this was the disarray caused by the remnants of Roman law.

Both in temperament and in training Hotman resembled Dumoulin, whom he had known since the age of sixteen and whom he had perhaps introduced to Calvin. He welcomed Dumoulin to Lausanne after his flight from Paris in 1552 and the next year, as we have seen, rose to his defense against Le Roux.[43] Like Dumoulin, too, Hotman was drawn irresistibly into ecclesiastical politics, especially after his appointment to teach law at Strasbourg in 1556 and with the political conditions that prevented his return to France. He continued to be Calvin's agent and informant; at the same time he extended his Protestant contacts, especially among the Marian exiles in Strasbourg and then among the German princes. By 1558 he had already grown to hate the Guises, particularly the Cardinal of Lorraine, who two years later was to be the target of his sensational *Tiger of France*.[44] For this and other polemics written on behalf of the conspirators of Amboise, including perhaps the first history of this

[42] Hotman, *Matagonis de Matagonibus* (s. 1., 1575), p. 19. Barnaud, *Le Miroir des françois* (Paris, 1581), pp. 31, 291. In the reform of education Barnaud encouraged teaching (p. 202) "the German language because it is with this nation that we negotiate and visit the most." On the large anti-Machiavellian literature see A. Cherel, *La pensée de Machiavel en France* (Paris, 1935), and W. Kaegi, *Historische Meditationen*, I (Zürich, 1942), 121-81; also L. Clement, *Henri Estienne et son œuvre français* (Paris, 1898), and C. Lenient, *La Satire en France* (Paris, 1886).

[43] Letter of Dumoulin to Bullinger, 14 Oct. 1552 (*CR*, XL, col. 392); see ch. VI, n. 21 and 30, and ch. IV. Again, see the various publications of R. Dareste and H. Vuillemier, "Le Séjour de Hotman à Lausanne (1) 1549-1555," *Bulletin du bibliophile et du bibliothécaire* (1901), 125-29.

[44] Hotman, letter to Calvin, 7 March 1558 (*CR*, XLV, col. 84). See Charles Reade (ed.), *Le Tigre de 1560* (Paris, 1875); Baudouin (anonymously), *Religionis et regis defensio* (*CR*, XLVI, col. 453 ff); and Dareste, "François Hotman et la conjuration d'Amboise," *Bibliothèque de l'École des chartes*, sér. 3, V (1854), 360-75. The *Histoire du Tumulte d'Amboise* is in *Mémoires de Condé*, I, 320 ff.

fiasco, Baudouin wanted Hotman's title to be not "master of requests" (an honor bestowed by the king of Navarre) but "master of pamphlets." It was in the course of this propagandizing for the "malcontents" that Hotman received his real introduction to the issues of French political and legal traditions. Like Dumoulin, he was strongly affected by his friendship with—and his employment by—German Protestant princes at this time. Although he continued to teach civil law, he never ceased to be available as legal counsel, propagandist, diplomat, and intriguer for the Huguenot cause. This was the source not only of his personal misfortunes but of his interpretation of history.

The Massacre of St Bartholomew was not only the central event, it was the confirming experience of Hotman's life. He himself, forewarned by the first attempt on Coligny's life in the summer of 1572, escaped from Bourges with the help of his students. "By the providence, mercy, and clemency of God," he wrote from Geneva in October, 'I have been delivered from the hands of assassins the likes of whom no age has suffered." [45] "Machiavelli's holiday," an entertainment which he did not doubt was planned by Catherine de' Medici, encouraged him to complete his reassessment of French history from that Germanist point of view to which he had been led by his political bias and by his studies in feudal law. Such was the purpose of his *Franco-Gallia*, which appeared the next year along with his life of Coligny, commissioned by the admiral's widow, and his *French Fury,* an account of the Massacre. The book was both an attempt to describe and a plea to restore the "ancient constitution" (*vetus Galliae institutum*) whose partisans in France, the "politiques" (*politici*), were by now advocating the calling of the Estates General. [46] Hotman might regard his book as "the history of a fact"—and in-

[45] Hotman, letters to Bullinger (Zürich, Zentralbibliothek, MS, S. 127, f. 47r) and to A. Sulzer, 3 Oct. 1572, in L. Ehinger, "Franz Hotman, ein französischer Gelehrter, Staatsman und Publizist des XVI. Jahrhunderts," *Beiträge zur vaterlandischen Geschichte*, XIV (1896), 116. Cf. N. Weiss, "La Saint Barthélemy," *BSHPF*, XLIII (1894), 431.

[46] Hotman to Gualter, 7 Dec. 1573 and 27 Apr. 1574, Zürich, Zentralbibliothek, MSS, F. 39, ff 198r and 196r. See also "Lettre inédite de Jacqueline d'Autremont veuve de l'amiral Coligny à François Hotman, 1573," *BSHPF,* VI (1858), 28-29.

deed he had a claim to the office of royal historiographer—but the orthodox party was bound to see it as seditious propaganda on behalf of "mixed monarchy."[47]

The interest of this book, in which Hotman threw caution and some of his scholarly standards to the wind, is not really in its contribution to historical scholarship but in defining the outer limits of historical interpretation. It provoked one of the most garish literary quarrels of the century. In response to Hotman's *"Franco-Gallic"* thesis another alumnus of the historical school of law proposed a contradictory "Italo-Gallic" thesis. This was Papire Masson, a protégé both of the Cardinal of Lorraine and of Hotman's old nemesis Baudouin, whom Masson had just succeeded at the University of Angers and whose biography he had just written. In a sense, then, this response may be taken as a revival of the controversy over the Colloquy of Poissy a decade before. Masson was actually a first-rate historian, but in this debate he was, like Hotman, more successful in trading insults than information. Besides ridiculing Hotman's bad Latin, incorrect German, and impossible Spanish (referring to the famous Aragonese oath cited by Hotman), he accused Hotman of sedition and placed him in the company of the "epicurean" Rabelais and that "prince of atheists" Henri Estienne, whose life of Catherine de' Medici seconded the views of Hotman.[48] As always, Hotman had the last word with this wretch who emerged "not from paradise but from

---

[47] Hotman, *Epistolae* (Amsterdam, 1700), p. 49. One attack was by the historiographer François de Belleforest, *Les Grandes Annales et histoire generale de France* (Paris, 1579), prefatory letter to Henry III. The innumerable discussions of Hotman include D. Smith, "François Hotman," *Scottish Historical Review*, XIII (1915-16), 328-65; E. Blocaille, *Étude sur François Hotman. La Franco-Gallia* (Dijon, 1902); and B. Reynolds, *Proponents of Limited Monarchy in Sixteenth-Century France* (New York, 1931). More generally, see G. Weill, *Les Théories sur le pouvoir royal en France pendant les guerres de religion* (Paris, 1891); R. Schnur, *Die französischen Juristen im konfessionellen Bürgerkrieg des 16. Jahrhunderts* (Berlin, 1962); and the fundamental work of V. de Caprariis, *Propaganda e pensiero politica in Francia durante le guerre di religione (1559-1572)* (Naples, 1959).

[48] Matharel, *Ad Franc. Hotomani Franco-Galliam . . . responsio* (Paris, 1575), p. 155. In his prefatory "judicium" Masson claimed "Cujas most truly to have said that Hotman's writings deserved the lash." Cf. Masson, *Responsio ad maledicta Hotomani* (Paris, 1575), remarking (f. 5r), "I am the disciple of

the *palais* of Paris, which however is the paradise of lawyers." He labeled Masson a "cuckolded Jesuit" who deserved no better than his master "Ecebolius-Baudouin."[49]

This quixotic "battle of two humanisms" was not very edifying, but it was not wholly unproductive. It served to provoke further investigations into the French past as well as to define the poles of historical interpretation which had emerged during the religious wars. Masson's position was simple and conventional. He rejected the fable of Trojan origins, but he was not convinced that the French were Germanic in origin, nor did he accept Hotman's subordination of the parlement to the Estates General. What he offered, in essence, was a rather orthodox Gallican interpretation of history with emphasis upon the Latin heritage of France.

Hotman's interpretation, on the other hand, was a caricature of certain Germanist and Protestant attitudes supported by an impressive, but indiscriminate and often irrelevant, collection of legal and historical texts. Through Italian influence, he believed, France had become a land of tyranny and tribute, of idolatry and litigation (*regnum rabularium*; *royaume de plaiderie*), and Paris an "Italo-gallic Sodom and Gomorrha." Still worse was the invasion of the courts and law schools by cival law, which Hotman had denounced earlier in his *Anti-Tribonian*.[50] Hotman rejected the authority of Roman law

Baudouin. . . . What in this name makes you tremble?" In the *Discours merveilleux de la vie, actions et deportemens de la royne Catharine de Medicis* (Paris, 1663), attributed to Estienne, the remark is made (p. 7) that "the majority of Florentines, as those who have broken bread with them say, bother themselves little with their conscience, wishing to seem but not to be religious, as one of their leading politicians Machiavelli advises his prince. . . ." Cf. Innocent Gentillet's *Discours sur les moyens de bien gouverner et maintenir en bonne paix un royaume . . . contre Nicolas Machiavel Florentine* (s. l., 1576), addressing the "truly French": "French government once thrived on ancient custom; now, alas, it goes to ruin with Italian people and practices." This subject is pursued further in my forthcoming "Murd'rous Machiavel in France."

[49] Hotman, *Matagonis de Matagonibus*, p. 3. Cf. *Monitoriale adversus Italogalliam . . . Matharelli* (s. l., 1575), and *Strigil Papiri Massoni . . . Jesuitae excucullati* (s. l., 1575). The definitive account of this controversy is P. Ronzy, *Un Humaniste italianisant, Papire Masson (1554-1611)* (Paris, 1924), which is also one of the best studies of sixteenth-century scholarship.

[50] Hotman, *Franco-Gallia* (Frankfurt, 1665), p. 319. As in his *Anti-Tribonian* (see ch. IV, n. 51) he had condemned the use of Latin in the courts, so here

not only on anti-Tribonianist grounds, but on the precedent of the famous ordinance of Philip IV which, incorporating the University of Orleans and prohibiting the study of civil law at Paris, stipulated that France was to be ruled only by customary law, to which civil law was related as the liberal arts to theology. The only remedy for the evils of civil law was to restore the ancient customs of the Franks, who were distinguished by the purity of their morals, the simplicity of their laws, by their "mixed" constitution, and above all by their exemption from Roman taxation. As Aventinus had said, the Franks were synonymous with freedom (*die freien Francken, hoc est liberi franci*).[51] In short, what Calvin had done for the "primitive church" Hotman proposed to do for the "ancient constitution" of France. In Hotman's view, it seems, history had become a quest for lost innocence.

"The Franco-Gallic king is not absolute," Hotman declared, "but is circumscribed by certain laws."[52] In his discussion of the fundamental laws (*leges regias*), however, Hotman went far beyond the legists. For him the agency of counsel and consent was not the parlement, which he regarded as a hotbed of chicanery and corruption because of its long involvement in ecclesiastical affairs, but the "great council," that is, the Estates General, which he derived from the oldest Germanic assemblies and affected to trace through all three races of

---

(p. 23) he commended the edict of Francis I requiring the use of French in civil suits; cf. *Commentaire de Maistre Charles du Molin sur l'ordonnance du grand Roy François en l'annee 1539* (Paris, 1637), p. 141. Hotman's criticisms of canon law appear most clearly in his *Brutum fulmen* (s. l. n. d.), directed against Sixtus V's condemnation of Henry of Navarre, referring to the critique of the Donation of Constantine (p. 129), but Cusanus' rather than Valla's! Cf. letter to Amerbach, 5 Feb. 1577, Basel, Universitätsbibliothek, MSS, G. II, 19, f. 184r.

[51] Hotman, *Franco-Gallia*, pp. 52-53, following up his rejection of the Trojan theory of Frankish origins (p. 51). The "Germanist" character of Hotman's thought was recognized by both Maitland, *English Law and the Renaissance* (Cambridge, 1901), p. 58, and Figgis, *Political Thought from Gerson to Grotius* (Cambridge, 1916), p. 173, as well as E. Hölzle, *Die Idee einer altgermanischen Freiheit*, and the review by P. Harsin, "La Parrain d'une école germaniste," *Revue des sciences politiques*, XLIX (1926), 607-22.

[52] *Ibid.*, pp. 283 ff; cf. pp. 115 ff on the Salic law. Ralph Giesey has prepared a "variorum edition" of the *Franco-Gallia*, indicating the substantial changes made in the later versions.

French kings. Reaching still further into Germanic tradition (Tacitus), he even suggested the elective character of the French monarchy, though later he retracted this view when his patron, Henry of Navarre, became heir apparent to the throne in 1584. Hotman also favored the exclusion of women from the throne, but anticipating the modern view, he regarded this rule as the product of feudal custom rather than the Salic law, which was anachronistic and in any case applied to private, not public succession.

"No question has more disturbed historians," Jean Bodin had written, "than that of the origins of people."[53] This problem, too, Hotman approached from a Germanist point of view. Hotman gave serious attention only to the Franks since the Gauls had been reduced by the Romans to servitude, legal and fiscal as well as political. On the issue of their genealogy Hotman took his lead entirely from German scholarship. In humanist circles the theory of Trojan origins had long been discredited. As early as 1507 Heinrich Bebel, commenting upon a favorite text from Tacitus, offered a "demonstration that the Germans were indigenous"; and this view was taken up, with less eloquence but more documentation, by such scholars as Albert Krantz, Beatus Rhenanus, and Melanchthon.[54] Thence it had passed on to a later generation of French historians, who had the same incentive for adopting it, that is, disassociation from Italian culture. Even Paolo Emilio had his doubts, though he was too cautious to express them publicly. Jean du Tillet was more explicit, but his great *Collection* had not yet appeared when Hotman was writing. So it was through Hotman that the exposé of the Trojan theory became widely known in French scholarship, though it by no means died out in popular literature.

These are a few of the more conspicuous features of that Germanist paradigm which Hotman, better than any other writer, represents. Obviously, the value of this attitude was largely negative: that is, it

---

[53] Jean Bodin, *Methodus* (Mesnard, p. 230).

[54] Heinrich Bebel, "Oratio ad Maximilianum I Caesarem de ejus atque Germaniae laudibus" (in Schardius, pp. 221-242); Krantz, *Wandalia* (Cologne, 1519), c iv[v]; Beatus Rhenanus, *Rerum Germanicarum libri tres* (Basel, 1551), p. 27 ff; and for Melanchthon, ch. VI, n. 13. For the French critics see G. Huppert, "The Trojan Franks and their Critics," *SR*, XII (1965), 227-41.

operated as a corrective to the more flagrant errors arising from a classicist bias. Just as obviously, Germanism had weaknesses of its own which more cautious historians than Hotman would have to correct.

Institutional History

From the bright land of philology we have wandered a long way into the battlegrounds of religious and political controversy. Yet such an itinerary seems necessary if the world of sixteenth-century historical scholarship is to be seen in all its color and complexity. The two most outrageous combatants, Dumoulin and Hotman, were certainly not models of disinterested research, but they were pioneering investigators and promoters of that manifold merger of legal and historical studies which occurred in the later sixteenth century. They also serve as sensitive indicators of the ideological undercurrents in the great stream of scholarship which religious parties and European powers were trying to harness for their own ends. It would be a mistake to dismiss this unwholesome aspect of the history of history, for what David Douglas remarked about English scholars of the next century, that "the positive achievements of the age in medieval scholarship would never have been attained had the scholars not been urged to their work by motives derived from religious conviction," [55] is still more appropriate for their sixteenth-century predecessors. Nor has medieval scholarship ever quite outgrown the effects of its original polemical environment.

But Dumoulin and Hotman gave new life to history in a more important way than simply putting it to practical use. Because of the many-sided character of their learning, which was interdisciplinary as well as international, they were able to place the study of law and institutions into a European context and to employ a rudimentary kind of comparative method. How else, after all, could the complexities of feudal society be understood? What is more, they did not limit them-

---

[55] David Douglas, *English Scholars 1660-1730* (London, 1951), pp. 19-20. "History nourishes polemic and polemic nourishes history," wrote G. Lebras, *Historie du droit et des institutions de l'église* (Paris, 1955), p. 9, about the beginnings of the history of the church and of canon law.

selves to the grand themes of political philosophy but delved also into private law and the problems created by the plurality of European customs. They considered, too, the relation between law and public morality, and they examined in concrete terms the manifestations of national character. In this way they seem to illustrate the remark of Walter Ullmann that "by viewing law as a social phenomenon medieval jurisprudence was forced to elucidate some basic principles relating to human society, and was thus led to consider topics which, under modern conditions, would be dealt with, not by the lawyer, but by the sociologist."[56] Building upon old traditions, Dumoulin in particular helped to bring a kind of sociological sophistication to the study of history.

What remained was for this concern for the texture of history to be introduced into historiography itself. In fact, such a convergence was already taking place. Partly, this was the result of a growing interest of historians in legal scholarship, but more particularly it was through an extension of the legist tradition that pointed to a kind of "historicization" already evident in other branches of legal scholarship. This took the form of a new type of publication that began to appear in the second half of the sixteenth century—handbooks devoted to the systematic, historical analysis of French institutions.

The first representative of this new legal genre was a treatise on the *Origin of Dignities, Magistrates, Offices and Estates of the Kingdom of France* (1551) by the jurist Vincent de la Loupe, author also of a commentary on Tacitus. Like Grassaille, La Loupe gave pride of place to the "royal majesty," but then he launched into a detailed survey of the whole institutional structure of the monarchy from the parlement of Paris and the Estates General to the *trésorier des chartes* and the lowliest *secrétaires.* More critical than the legists, he did not hesitate to reprimand Nicolas Gilles for assigning a Trojan origin to the peers of France and Gaguin for tracing them back to the Carolingians. Nor did he show sympathy for the notion of the Trojan origin of the Franks, "as they boast."[57] Etymological evidence pointed

---

[56] Walter Ullmann, *The Medieval Idea of Law as Represented by Lucas de Penna* (London, 1946), p. 163.

[57] Vincent de la Loupe, *Origine des dignitez, magistratz, offices et estats du*

rather to a Germanist thesis. "As for me," he concluded, "I do not doubt that most French words have come from the German," though he warned that "all etymologies of Frankish words are difficult because they have been so corrupted by time." Like Dumoulin he cited the word *mareschal*, which on the authority of Beatus Rhenanus he related to a German word (*marca*) meaning horse, a derivation he much preferred to that of Budé, who mistakenly associated the meaning of horse with the second syllable (*juges a cheval*).[58] A trivial point, perhaps, but it illustrates the growing Germanist orientation of French scholars.

Among the successors to La Loupe's pioneering book were Jean Duret's *Harmony and Comparison of Roman Magistrates with French Officers* (1574) and Charles de Figon's *Discourse on the Estates and Offices of France* (1579). Duret's work, a veritable encyclopedia of sixteenth-century French administration, quite consciously followed Grassaille's formulation of the *regalia*, but it showed also the influence of legal humanism, especially in the admiring references to Budé and Le Douaren and to those "two great luminaries of ancient and modern jurisprudence," Cujas and Hotman. In spite of his title Duret was concerned less with comparing than with contrasting Roman institutions; and rejecting the Trojan theory, he located the "ancient liberty" of the kingdom mainly in its Germanic traditions.[59] Figon discarded classical analogies altogether and described the growth and proliferation of French institutions as a coherent native development, diagrammed as a great tree on which his text was an extensive commentary.[60] While these works retained the panegyrical tone of legists'

---

royaume de France, in *Archives curieuses de l'histoire de France*, sér. 2, IV (Paris, 1838), pp. 377 ff. On La Loupe see *Catalogue des actes de François*, VIII, 732, and Aubert, I, 39.

[58] *Ibid.*, p. 409.

[59] Jean Duret, *L'Harmonie et conference des magistrats Romains avec les officiers françois, tant laiz, que ecclesiastiques* (Lyon, 1574), f. 65[r]. Among other works in comparative law may be mentioned René Choppin, *De Domanio Franciae Libri III* (Paris, 1572); and La Popelinière, *L'Amiral de France* (Paris, 1584); and Pierre Ayrault, *De l'ordre et instruction judiciaire, dont les ancient Grecs et Romains ont usé en accusations publiques. Conferé a l'usage de nostre France* (Paris, 1576). See ch. X, n. 15.

[60] Charles de Figon, *Discours des estats et offices . . . de France* (Paris, 1579).

tracts, formally they tried to place the study of government and administration in a historical context.

The most illustrious work of this sort was Du Haillan's *State and
Success of the Affairs of France*, which appeared in 1570. This book
also represents the most direct link with historical writing, since the
next year Du Haillan became, in succession to Hotman, royal historiographer. In general, Du Haillan's work (to which we shall return in the next chapter) constitutes the most useful summary of the
state of French scholarship at the height of the civil wars. Besides
manuscripts and medieval chronicles, his sources included the whole
range of writers under discussion in this book: Gaguin, Paolo Emilio,
Claude de Seyssel, La Loupe, Bodin, Le Roy, Choppin, Masson, La
Popelinière, Pasquier, Fauchet, and Vignier. Du Haillan concluded,

But the work that has served me best is the fine and laborious book of
Jean du Tillet, secretary of the king and greffier of his parlement, in
which, with incredible pains, admirable diligence and control of diffuse
material, he collected all the precious papers, monuments and titles
found in the courts of the parlement, *chambre des comptes* and other
public places, and charters of the kingdom. Long before this work was
published I took from it things which appear in the third and fourth
parts of my book, which in many places may serve as a summary of his.[61]

This marks not only the culmination of the legist tradition but the
appearance of another aspect of legal studies which was essential for
the understanding of medieval history. For in the royal archives, some
historians were beginning to suspect, one might find the most valuable
of all sources of historical information.

[61] Du Haillan, *Estat et succez*, "Preface aux lecteurs." Cf. the still fuller
statement of Du Haillan's debts in the "Preface aux lecteurs," *Histoire de
France* (Paris, 1619), I.

CHAPTER VIII

The Archives and History: Jean du Tillet
Makes an Inventory of History

> Comme il ne soit chose plus necessaire ... a
> l'intelligence et conduitte de tous nos affaires
> d'estat ... que ... l'on ait moyen de reprendre
> et reveoir les choses passees ..., pour ceste
> cause eust esté anciennement ordonné ... le
> *tresor de noz chartes.* ...
>
> Francis I, letter of 12 June 1539

"THE FRAGILITY and weakness of human nature, prone to lapse of
memory, are said to have led our predecessors through the art of
writing to compose letters, charters, registers, and various kinds of
books, lest those things that arose in time should perish with time."[1]
These words, expressing at once an awareness of "devouring time"
and a reverence for ancient monuments, were set down in the fourteenth century not by a humanist but by a practical-minded keeper of
the king's archives. These are themes that run through the whole
history of the archivist tradition. Although the emphasis is upon
preservation rather than restoration and upon the compilation of useful books (*libri utiles*) rather than histories, the parallel with humanism is unmistakable. Yet it was not until the sixteenth century
that the potential of this tradition for historical scholarship was
realized. This was very largely the work of one man, who combined
the roles of archivist, advocate, and antiquary, and who more or less

---

[1] Gérard de Montaigu, preface to his *Inventaire*, BN MSS, Fonds latins,
vol. 1090.

inadvertently became one of the best historians of the century. This versatile scholar, Jean du Tillet, represents still another point of intersection between law and history in the sixteenth century.

The Archivist Tradition

One of Baudouin's most fruitful suggestions was that scholars would find some of their most indispensable sources of information in archival collections. "Of these," he added, "the noblest and fullest will be . . . the records of the kingdom of France and the court of the parlement of Paris."[2] In fact, these records had long been cited for specific purposes by legists and historians, and as we have seen, Budé and Dumoulin made extensive use of such material. There had also been published collections and commentaries, such as the one made by Dumoulin's enemy Pierre Rebuffi.[3] Yet in 1561, when Baudouin made his suggestion, it remained true that the archives constituted an untapped source for legal and institutional history. At that very time, however, men were working to remedy this defect—those men, at least, who were fortunate enough to gain access to state secrets (*arcana imperii*). Once again the result was not only to give impetus to the rising wave of antiquarian enthusiasm but to add further fuel to the political and religious controversies of that generation.

The archives, as lawyers and historians alike realized, practically embodied the public memory of the monarchy. In general, as Seyssel wrote, "Everything would be uncertain if our ancestors had not left us the memory of genealogies, testaments, contracts, judgments, laws, statutes, and other human actions. . . ."[4] For many scholars the model for such a collection was offered by ancient Rome. It was in the context of a discussion of the Roman *scrinium,* for example, that Budé had celebrated the royal archives, which he regarded as an institution

---

[2] Baudouin, *De Institutione*, p. 653, though unfortunately, as La Popelinière complained (*Idee de l'histoire*, p. 256), they were closed to the public.

[3] Pierre Rebuffi, *Commentarii in constitutiones seu ordinationes regias* (Lyon, 1554), in his preface applying the "translation" idea (from Greece to Rome to France) to laws.

[4] Claude de Seyssel, "Proheme" to his translation of Xenophon (Paris, 1529).

essential for any civilized nation.[5] But it was from the papacy, whose archives constituted one of the most powerful weapons in the arsenal of the curia, that European governments had learned the practical necessity of keeping legal records. In order to act, a prince required a precedent; in order to expand, a government needed a title, or at least an excuse. This is what Francis I meant when he remarked euphemistically upon the importance of "having a way of reviewing past events . . . for the elucidation of future difficulties."[6] Walter Ullmann has spoken of "the transmission of papal ideology through the vehicle of the archives"; much the same might be said of Gallicanism and the French archives.[7] The defenses of Gallican liberties and royal prerogatives were little more than lists of precedents, buttressed by legal and historical texts but deriving their authority mainly from royal edicts or titles preserved in the archives. The need to have such authorities at hand and conveniently classified was the motive for most sixteenth-century collections, notably those made by the two well-known legal humanists Barnabé Brisson and Louis le Caron, as well as for the work of Du Tillet.[8]

In France the archives date from the twelfth century. The story was often told how Philip Augustus, having lost his fiscal records in a battle with Richard I of England, decided to establish a *greffe* for his public acts. This *trésor des chartes*, transferred by St Louis to a building adjoining the Sainte-Chapelle within easy reach of the advocates of the *palais*, grew as rapidly as the monarchy itself. There was already a well-established archivist tradition by the four-

---

[5] Budé, *Annotationes*, f. 66ᵛ (Digest, 1, 16, 9), representing "the perpetual genius of this kingdom."

[6] Cited by L. Dessalles, *Le Trésor des chartes* (Paris, 1844), pp. 91-92.

[7] Walter Ullmann, *Principles of Government and Politics in the Middle Ages* (London, 1961), pp. 24-25.

[8] Le Caron, *Les Pandectes ou Digests du droit françois* (Lyon, 1596), and Brisson, *Code du Roy Henry III de France* (Paris, 1587). In *Responses et decisions du droict françois* (Paris, 1637), p. 8, Le Caron described his combination of legal and historical motives in this way: "Antiquity and ancient monuments have always had more faith and authority, as in histories, annals, the witnesses and authorities of the most famous authors, charters, titles, investitures . . ., inscriptions on tombs and supulchres, and other such information."

teenth century, when Philip IV created the office of *garde des chartes*. This function was performed first by Pierre d'Etampes and later, more illustriously, by Gérard de Montaigu (1371-91), who compiled the first comprehensive inventory of the archives.[9] Quite separate were the archives of the parlement of Paris, though down to the fourteenth century they were sometimes administered by the same man, who served as *greffier* of the parlement as well as *garde des chartes*. The parlementary collection had started in 1254 with the rolls of *Olim* compiled by Jean de Montluçon, and it continued throughout the old regime.[10] The *trésor des chartes*, on the other hand, became a dead archive in 1568, when Michel de l'Hôpital created a *garde des chartes* for his chancery. Toward the end of the civil wars the *trésor des chartes*, still the ideological storehouse of the kingdom, passed into the hands of the *procureur général*, beginning with Pierre Pithou, who was also the first historian of these archives.

If the royal archives reflected the growth of the monarchy, they reflected also the disarray of feudal government. In the fourteenth century Gérard de Montaigu had complained that "the confusion and disorder of letters, arranged separately and not consecutively ... disturbs the minds of investigators ... while impeding and nullifying the suit or negotiation which was the purpose of the investigation."[11] Despite several attempts to "reform" the archives, the situation had hardly changed by the sixteenth century. Guillaume Budé's father, for

[9] The history of the *trésor des chartes* begins with Pierre Pithou's "Tresor des chartes du roi," BN MSS, Collection Dupuy, vol. 233, f. 98 ff, written in 1586 (see next chapter), and then Pierre Dupuy, "Le tresor des chartes du roi, et la charge du tresorier et garde dudit tresor," in his *Traictez touchant les droits du roi treschrestien* (Paris, 1655), making ample use of Pithou's essay. There was an earlier but very summary account in Duret, *Harmonie et conference*, f. 126. More recent studies include H. Bordier, *Les Archives de la France* (Paris, 1855); C. V. Langlois and H. Stein, *Les Archives de l'histoire de France* (Paris, 1855); p. 16; H. F. de Laborde, "La Constitution du trésor des chartes," *Layettes du trésor des chartes*, I (Paris, 1866), and "Les inventaires du trésor des chartes dressés par Gérard du Montaigu," *Notes et extraits des manuscrits de la Bibliothèque nationale*, XXXVI (1895), 545-98, and most complete, L. Dessalles, *Le Trésor des chartes*.

[10] See E. Boutaric's preface to *Actes du parlement de Paris*, in Laborde, *Inventaires et documents* (Paris, 1863), I, 1254-99, and F. Lot and R. Fawtier, *Histoire des institutions françaises*, II, *Institutions royales* (Paris, 1958), p. 95.

[11] Bordier, *Les Archives de la France*, p. 140.

example, was ordered by Louis XI in 1474 to compile an inventory and was apparently dismissed temporarily for his failure to do so. An inventory was finally completed by Guillaume's brother (Dreux II) in 1500, but throughout the administration of his nephew Jean Budé (1525-38) the archives remained in a state of chaos.[12] Guillaume himself testified to the difficulty of using the documents. Another campaign of reform was inspired by the complaints of Francis I in 1539 that "many things are not inventoried, and things inventoried are all mixed together, and the old inventories are so illegible and defective in substance that it is impossible to use the titles."[13] But this, too, was in vain. Throughout the long administration of Sebastian le Rouillyé and the short one of Christofle de Thou, whose "reforming" activities were devoted to the French customs, practically nothing was done to clear up the confusion.

Such was the task which Jean du Tillet inherited when, in addition to his regular job as keeper of the parlementary *greffe*, he was commissioned by Francis II to reorganize the royal archives.[14] "To our beloved and faithful protonotary and *greffier* in our court of the parlement of Paris, Master Jean du Tillet . . . ," runs this commission:

we have been well and truly advised that the charters, titles, notices, and other important papers in our *trésor des chartes* are in such confusion that . . . it is troublesome and difficult to find them, so that even if they exist, much time is lost, which may greatly prejudice our affairs. . . . Moreover, since most of the said . . . papers have been effaced, they can be read only with the greatest difficulty because of the age of the script, and it is to be feared that, through time which consumes all, they will become and remain useless . . ., which would be the greatest imaginable loss to our successors. To prevent this, therefore, we have ordered everything to be enrolled in good registers with a well-organized index and classification, in order to find more easily and quickly the said registers when the need arises.

[12] Pithou, f. 98^v; Dupuy, p. 1009; and Dessalles, p. 79. The "antien Inventaire" of Dreux Budé's collaborator Jacques Louet is BN MSS, Fonds latins, vol. 9042.

[13] Dessalles, *Le Trésor des chartes*, p. 91.

[14] A copy of this commission (dated 12 May 1562 though granted by Francis II) will be found in BN MSS, Fonds français, n. a., vol. 20256, f. 55^v, published in H. Omont, "Jean du Tillet et le trésor des chartes (1562)," *Bulletin de la Société de l'histoire de Paris*, XXXI (1904), 79-81; also pub-

This plan was altogether typical of the perennial attempts to reform
the archives. If it had succeeded, it would have been a great benefit
to historians as well as to lawyers. Unfortunately, Jean du Tillet did
no better than his predecessors; in one way, in fact, he made matters
worse. Even before this commission he had been ransacking both the
royal and the parlementary collections. "M. du Tillet gained entrance
into the archives to examine and to borrow whatever he needed,"
lamented one of his successors, "and this he did with such abandon
that the titles he used were not replaced and many were kept by him
and lost...." [15] But if Du Tillet failed to reform the archives, he
unquestionably made better use of the material. What he could not
borrow he copied, and by the outset of the civil wars he had collected
a great treasury of documents which served not only to lighten the
burden of the legist but also to open up new resources for the historian. What was novel about Du Tillet's *Collection of the Kings of
France* was that, although it was intended to be a set of "useful
books" in the archivist tradition, it came in fact to be regarded as one
of the most valuable historical works of the century. It will be worth-
while to inquire further into the genesis of this collection.

Two Scholars

"Never have citizens had a more exact knowledge of our law and of
our Frankish and Gallic antiquities." [16] So wrote the historian Jacques-
Auguste de Thou, whose father and brother each held the office of
garde des chartes, about the brothers Du Tillet. Born in the early years
of the sixteenth century of a noble and Gallican family, both were
given the name Jean; and to the further confusion of biographers,

---

lished, but mistakenly ascribed to Francis I, in *Catalogue des actes de François
Ier*, VII, p. 453, and in A. Boislisle, "Jean du Tillet et le trésor des chartes,"
Société de l'histoire de France, *Annuaire-Bulletin* (1873), 106-11.

[15] Dupuy, *Traitez*, p. 1011. Brisson also made such borrowings, according
to J. J. Scaliger, *Epistolae* (Leiden, 1627), p. 198. In general, see L. Delisle,
Cabinet des manuscrits de la Bibliothèque impériale (Paris, 1868), I, 285, and
H. Leclercq, *Dom Mabillon* (Paris, 1953), I, 158.

[16] De Thou, IV, 334. Much of this discussion is based upon my "Jean du
Tillet, Archivist and Antiquary," *Journal of Modern History*, XXXVIII
(1966), 337-54.

both died in 1570, six weeks apart. The elder Jean du Tillet inherited both his father's title, Sieur de la Bussière, and his office, *greffier civil* of the parlement of Paris, which he held for almost half a century. After 1521 his name appears frequently in legal documents both in his capacity of "protonotary and secretary of the king" and in various suits before the parlement, including a dispute with another brother, Sèraphin, over the office itself.[17] He was a busy man. There was little royal legislation that did not pass under his eye. By midcentury he had risen high in the counsels of the king, and he was beginning to be drawn into Gallican politics.

Better known in scholarly circles was the younger Jean, who was also a successful officeholder, becoming bishop of Saint Brieux (1553) and then of Meaux (1564-70). He was another one of these disoriented Gallicans who at first sympathized with radical reform but then, more fearful of schism than of ultramontanism, returned to orthodoxy and even attended the Council of Trent in its last sessions. Like Baudouin, who had followed much the same road, Du Tillet displayed his political sympathies in his historical scholarship. Inspired by the obvious parallel with the Huguenots, he compiled an account of the Albigensian Crusade based on archival documents, acquired no doubt through his brother. The most popular of his works was a universal chronicle which followed the Eusebian pattern, though refurbished by modern scholarship, including the works of Biondo, Paolo Emilio, Gaguin, and Polydore Vergil.[18] It was as a philologist,

---

[17] "Provision de l'office de protonotaire et greffier civil du Parlement de Paris, en faveur de Jean du Tillet, sur la résignation de Séraphin du Tillet, son père. Dijon, 6 juin 1521," *Catalogue des actes de François Ier*, I, 249-50; and "Proces entre Séraphin du Tillet et Jean du Tillet, frères, touchant l'office de greffier civil . . ., mars 1526," I, 494; see also index. In general, information about the Du Tillets may be found in *Dictionnaire de la noblesse* and in G. de Rubercy, "Les du Tillet, seigneurs de la Bussière (Loiret)," Académie de Saint-Croix d'Orléans, *Lectures et mémoires*, VI (1891), 477-541. See also R. Calderini De-Marchi, *Jacopo Corbinelli et les érudits français* (Milan, 1914), p. 188. Another brother, Louis, was an early adherent of Calvin; see *Correspondance française de Calvin avec Louis du Tillet*, ed. A. Crottet (Lausanne, 1850).

[18] Jean du Tillet, *De Regibus Francorum*, published in the 1539 and later editions of Paolo Emilio's *De Rebus gestis Francorum*; an expanded French version appears in the *Recueil* (see n. 21). The *Sommaire de l'histoire de la*

however, that he achieved greatest distinction. "To the study of our history," De Thou remarked, "he added the knowledge of language and a great familiarity with Roman law and all of ecclesiastical antiquity." [19] His works included the edition of the fragment of Ulpian on which Cujas' earliest book had been based, one of the first collections of the canons and decrees of the early church, a collection of Carolingian capitularies, and another of Frankish laws which included the *editio princeps* of the Salic law.[20] The latter furnished perhaps the closest link with the work of his brother, whose *Collection* begins with a discussion of Frankish origins and laws. In general, the Bishop's publications of early Frankish antiquities form a neat complement to the *greffier*'s collection of more recent records.

While the Bishop was visiting the major libraries of the kingdom, the *greffier* was leading the more exacting, if somewhat more precarious, life of the chief archivist of the parlement of Paris.[21] His first

---

guerre faicte contre les heretiques Albigeois, extraict du tresor des chartes (Paris, 1576) was published posthumously by his nephew Elie du Tillet.

[19] De Thou, IV, 334. The only work about the bishop is C. H. Turner, *Jean du Tillet: A Neglected Scholar of the Sixteenth Century* (Oxford, 1905), merely a bibliography of his published writings.

[20] Du Tillet, *Libelli seu decreta a Clodoveo et Childeberto prius aedita ac postremo a Carole lucide emendata, auctaque plurimum* (s. l. n. d.), published sometime between 1549 and 1557; *Opus illustrissimi et excellentissimi seu spectabilis viri, Caroli Magni . . .* (s. l., 1549); and *Apostolorum et sanctorum conciliorum decreta* (Paris, 1540). His contributions to legal humanism were *Tituli ex corpore Ulpiani* (Paris, 1549), and *E Libris constitutionum Theodosii* (Paris, 1550). Another publication, later criticized by Bellarmine, was *Evangelium Hebraicum Matthaei* (Paris, 1555), on which see H. J. Schonfield, *An Old Hebrew Text of St. Matthew's Gospel* (Edinburgh, 1927), pp. 3-4. Finally, it was Du Tillet's manuscript of Optatus that was edited, successively, by Baudouin, Masson, and Pierre Pithou.

[21] The elder Du Tillet's major work, collected from his manuscripts and published posthumously by his nephew, had at least eight editions: 1577 and 1578 as *Les Mémoires et recherches*; 1580, 1586-88, 1602, 1602, 1607, and 1618 as *Recueil des roys de France, leur couronne et maison*. The edition used here (Paris, 1607), the most complete, had three separately paginated parts, which will be cited as *Recueil* I, II, or III: first the "Recueil des roys": second a "Recueil des rangs des grands de France" with "To. II contenant les guerres et traictez de paix, trefves et alliances d'entre des rois de France et d'Angleterre"; third the bishop's *Chronique* followed by the *greffier*'s "Memoire et advis . . . sur les libertez de l'Eglise gallicane" and related documents, including Pithou's Gallican compilations (see next chapter). There are several manuscript

involvement in high politics came during the Gallican crisis of 1551, and at first he found himself on the same side as Dumoulin. It was no doubt at this time that he began gathering precedents for a possible "withdrawal of obedience." In De Thou's opinion, the edict of September, which prohibited the export of gold to Rome and called upon the precedents of Philip IV and St Louis, was issued "at the instigation of or at least on the advice of Du Tillet."[22] Undeniably, it was registered in his hand. But the next spring, as we have seen, the king reversed his policy. Du Tillet himself, who had not made Dumoulin's mistake of publicizing his views, seems to have escaped retribution. He was embarrassed by the episode, however, or at least sobered. When he made his next venture into politics ten years later, he had joined his brother in the camp of conservative Gallicans.

In general terms this is not hard to understand. Du Tillet was too close to the center of power to follow his own conscience, and like Dumoulin he came to believe that "heresy was an inseparable companion of sedition."[23] His Huguenot enemies, however, told a somewhat more sinister story, involving direct pressure from, if not corruption by, the Catholic party, especially in the person of that bogeyman of Calvinists, the Cardinal of Lorraine. "Searching the ancient registers of the parlement of Paris," wrote La Planche, "Du Tillet began to examine them and, finding them worthy of memory, by neglect or ignorance forgotten by historians, proposed to make a collection to serve posterity."[24] This sort of material could be inflam-

---

copies: BN MSS, Fonds français, vols. 2847-49, 2854, 2859, 5000, 6491 and a beautiful illuminated copy, Geneva, Bibliothèque publique et universitaire, MSS Français, 84.

[22] De Thou, I, 667. The edict itself may be found in *Recueil*, III, 375-76 (and see ch. VI, n. 27). In general, see L. Romier, *Les Origines politiques des guerres de religion*, I, 269, and H. O. Evennett, *The Cardinal of Lorraine*, pp. 34-44.

[23] BN MSS, Fonds français, vol. 17318, f. 79ʳ ("Du crime de leze maiesté par le Sʳ du Tillet").

[24] L. Regnier de la Planche, *Histoire de l'estat de France*, ed. P. Buchon (Paris, 1836), p. 269. Other sources for this affair include Pierre de la Place, *Commentaires de l'estat de la religion et republique* (included in the same volume), and La Popelinière, *Histoire de France*, f. 286ʳ. None are sympathetic, and Du Tillet himself attacked the "impudent calumny" of the "imposter" La Place (*Recueil*, I, 277-78). There is an excellent critical account in Bayle.

matory, as the Gallican crisis had shown, but through the influence of Anne de Montmorency, Du Tillet was given the opportunity of defending his project before the king. Just as Du Tillet had his books spread out on a table, "the Cardinal of Lorraine entered, glanced at them . . . and began to find fault with this fine enterprise of Du Tillet, going so far as to accuse him before the king of disloyalty and the desire to publish royal secrets. . . ." Besides the fact that this was classified material, in La Planche's view, the Cardinal feared that such researches might undermine his own privileges. Afterwards, however, "the Cardinal, having these books examined by scholars in his service . . . , decided that these labors might be of great use to him. . . ." Thus Du Tillet, who "feared for his life, his possessions, and his estates," was conscripted by the Guises. No doubt this is an exaggeration which distorts the political realities of the situation. Still, it is hard to avoid De Thou's judgment that he "could not write with complete freedom." [25]

The specific question to which Du Tillet addressed himself was the very delicate constitutional problem posed by the death of Henry II in 1559. Had the legitimate heir, the 15-year-old Francis II, attained his "age of discretion," or would it be necessary, as stipulated by civil law, to wait another ten years? Or to put it in practical terms, would power fall to the Guises, who possessed the person of the young king, or to the princes of the blood, meaning the king of Navarre? On the basis of his unsurpassed knowledge of French history—and needless to say his political commitments—Du Tillet undertook to provide a documented answer to this question, thus becoming involved in the same controversy in which Hotman, the principal, if anonymous, spokesman for the Huguenots, had been initiated into the issues of French constitutional history. Du Tillet's first pamphlet was attacked by the Huguenots, who confused him with his brother the bishop; and so later that year (1560) he composed a second work against the "rebels" of Amboise, whose leader, La Renaudie, happened to be his personal enemy. His work acquired legal authority when L'Hôpital inserted it in the collection of royal ordinances.

[25] De Thou, II, 697.

In these two classic tracts "on the majority of the king" Du Tillet, drawing his support from the legist tradition, rejected the authority of Roman law and asserted the priority of feudal custom. "According to the laws of France in the provinces of customary law," he argued, "the age of minority is not determined by Roman constitutions." [26] Instead, he referred to a famous ordinance of Charles V in 1374 which set the age of reason at fifteen. It was Du Tillet's position, in short, that the native tradition of the monarchy was not Roman (the *pays du droit écrit*) but Germanic (*pays du droit coutumier*). So he found it natural to refer to Tacitus' *Germania*, which noted the barbarian practice of giving high office to youths. On the other hand, Du Tillet rejected the "rebel" demand for a regency under the princes of the blood and a meeting of the Estates General, warning that this assembly was a consultative, not a sovereign organ. Above all, he upheld the public law of the monarchy, and he criticized his opponents for using such unreliable sources as the chronicles of St Denis. "The said rebels," he argued, "should be ashamed of opposing to the truth of charters, sealed and dated, a passage from the said annals . . ., full of fables and inventions of the *palais*." [27] The true and authentic tradition of the monarchy, he concluded, resided in the royal archives.

Whether or not Du Tillet really sold his pen, as the Huguenots claimed, he never deserted the Gallican tradition, though he may well have had trouble in locating it politically during the struggles under-lying the religious wars. What is more, his contributions to historical scholarship tended in the long run to reinforce the position of such "rebels" as Hotman, since it confirmed their belief in the indigenous

[26] Du Tillet, *Pour la majorité du roi treschrestien contre les escrits des rebelles* (Paris, 1560), p. 10; cf. *Recueil*, I, 277. Copies of this and the second tract may be found in BN MSS, Fonds français, vols. 17299 and 23659, and in Collection Dupuy, vol. 290. Michel de l'Hôpital had the work inserted in the collection of royal ordinances: *Ordonnances des roys de France de la troisième race*, VI (1741), 26-32. On Du Tillet's conflict with La Renaudie, see H. Naef, *La Conjuration d'Amboise et Genève* (Geneva, 1921), pp. 33 ff.

[27] Du Tillet, *Pour l'entiere majorité du roy treschrestien contre le legitime conseil malicieusement inventé par les rebelles* (Paris, 1560), f. c 3r. This and the other tract are published also in Dupuy, *Traicté de la majorité de nos rois* (Paris, 1655), pp. 317-47. The "legitime conseil," together with Du Tillet's first tract, is in *Mémoires de Condé* (London, 1743), I, 437 ff.

nature of French institutions. In any case, although Du Tillet's view of history may have been dominated by national sentiment and official ideology, he really lacked Hotman's fierce and obsessive partisanship. In practice, he had the temperament of a scholar, not a reformer, and even his archives he looked at through the eyes of an antiquary, not an advocate. Spending so much of his life among these monuments of the French past, he came to be impressed more with their commemorative than with their pragmatic value. This was the true source of his life's work, the *Collection of the Kings of France*, which he had essentially completed before the civil wars but which only appeared six years after his death.

Royal Antiquary

Jean du Tillet has been regarded as one of the founders of the historical school of French law.[28] It was his purpose, indeed, to do for French law and institutions what legal humanists, including his own brother, were doing for Roman law. He has been regarded also as one of the most distinguished historians of the century, and it is true that his *Collection* deserves to be placed in the tradition of official French historiography. Finally, his work gave him a certain claim to a place in the tradition of royal legists. But from any of these points of view, it is clear that Du Tillet brought ususual gifts and training to his researches. The main reason for this was his unique professional pedigree.

As administrator of the parlementary *greffe*, Du Tillet was not only a direct descendent of those *greffiers* of the parlement who had been transferred from the king's notarial staff in the fourteenth century, he was also a collateral descendent of those first archivists who managed the *trésor des chartes* through the chancery. By 1562 he had a staff of at least fourteen clerks and four notaries, although he continued to prepare many of the transcripts himself.[29] His job—registering and preserving parlementary *arrêts*, minutes, and other records—had by then, through the inflationary effects of religious and

---

[28] Lemaire, *Les Lois fondamentales*, p. 82.
[29] E. Maugis, *Histoire du parlement de Paris* (Paris, 1913), I, pp. xvii-xviii.

political controversy, become monumental in more than one sense. His manuscript remains, scattered through the libraries of Paris, attest to his assiduity and throw some light upon the *greffier*'s particular duties. He compiled genealogies, lists of ceremonial precedences, and accounts of ceremonies; he drew up briefs for the king's various territorial claims, including Roussillon, Cerdagne, Savoy, Nice, Metz, Toul, and Verdun; he discussed, always in terms of legal precedent, appanages and all of the principal offices of the monarchy; he wrote a detailed monograph on the development of lese majesty; he documented the course of Anglo-French diplomatic relations from the eleventh century; and he gathered material to demonstrate the liberties of the Gallican church.[30] While he performed in a rather specialized fashion the function of a royal legist, he was able to offer much fuller documentation and exhaustive "inventories" of pertinent archival material. Here, then, was the raw material for his *Collection*.

How did Du Tillet look upon his antiquarian calling? Here is his report to Francis II:

Having by great effort and expense, since being installed in office, visited the countless registers of your parlement, searched libraries, and by permission of the late king your father (whom God absolve) having entered your *trésor des chartes* . . . I undertook to organize, in the form of histories and according to reigns, all the controversies of this third dynasty with its neighbors, the domain of the crown by provinces, the laws and ordinances since the Salic by volumes and reigns and, by separate collections, what pertains to the royal person and house, and the ancient form of government of the three estates and the orders of justice in the kingdom, and the changes which have occurred.[31]

Thus his purpose was both legalistic, to attain a "knowledge of prec-

---

[30] On genealogies, e.g., BN MSS, Fonds français, vols. 2850, 2859; on *rangs et preseances*, vols. 4315, 4318, 10901, n. a. 9751; on territorial rights, vols. 4363, 18563-64 (and Collection Dupuy, vol. 96); on lese majesty, vol. 17318; on appanages, vols. 4502, 6615; on English relations, vols. 2853, 2855-58, 4997, 10831. Du Tillet also left letters scattered throughout the Fonds français, all listed in the manuscript catalogues of the Bibliothèque Nationale. See H. Pinoteau, "Quelques réflexions sur l'œuvre de Jean du Tillet et la symbolique royale française," *Archives héraldiques suisses*, LXX (1956), 2-25, and R. Giesey, *The Royal Funeral Ceremony in Renaissance France* (Geneva, 1960).

[31] Du Tillet, *Recueil*, I, preface; also BN MSS, Fonds français, vol. 5000.

edent," and historical, "to represent the past as in a mirror . . . in order to make use of a thousand years of experience." On the whole, Du Tillet was not much impressed with the literary tastes of humanism and admittedly took few pains to cultivate his own style. It was enough for him to add to the stock of historical erudition and to contribute to "the science of good and bad governments."

Yet Du Tillet's method had much in common with that of the legal humanists. He displayed a highly developed sense of historical relativity, and he distinguished carefully between laws still valid and those which had become obsolete. To Henry II he explained the distinction in this way:

From King Philip I until your reign, Sire, there have been a multitude of ordinances, and yet only a few of them are available and none before King Hugh Capet. . . . To the first of these it is not desirable to grant authority because of their age, except to serve the history of the ancient government of states then subject to your empire. . . . But others since Philip I, although they were useful in their time, I consider worthier of suppression than of publication, the instability of human things having turned the world about and made injurious what used to be profitable. . . .[32]

Even as a royal official, then, Du Tillet recognized his antiquarian function. From the beginning—Du Tillet voiced the traditional complaint—"France had loved arms better than letters," and it was the business of the modern scholar to rescue events and institutions from oblivion.

In his investigations Du Tillet made full use of medieval chronicles, but the major purpose of his *Collection* was to make available to the public the archival resources of France which reached back into the twelfth century, especially the *trésor des chartes*, the registers of the parlement, and the *chambre des comptes*. His "inventories" were arranged according to individual kings (mainly genealogical), the principal noble families, and the major institutions of the monarchy, from the crown itself through the whole hierarchy of offices underlying

[32] BN MSS, Fonds français, vol. 17294, f. 215ʳ ("Discours sur la loy salique"), apparently an early draft of "Des anciens loix des françois," in *Recueil*, I, 9.

it. They included such documents as marriage treaties, testaments, letters, ordinances, feudal contracts, commissions, *arrêts* of the parlement, legitimations, donations, legal judgments, privileges, treaties of peace, papal bulls, dispensations, indulgences, and diplomatic instructions. The book furnished the means, in fact, for a complete rewriting of French history.

Preoccupation with archival sources reinforced one basic feature of Du Tillet's historical thought which he shared with the legists, namely, his belief in the indigenous nature of French institutions and society. Surrounded as he was by the relics of feudalism, he turned naturally not to classical parallels or to romantic legends of the Gauls but rather to the Germanic heritage of France. Although he had no sympathy with the Protestants, Du Tillet deserves to be placed, along with Dumoulin and Hotman, among the earliest of the "Germanists." He was probably the first French scholar to reject outright the Trojan theory, and he made no attempt to disguise either his ideological motives or his source of inspiration. "Those who have written that the French were really German by origin have done them more honor than those who have made them issue from the Trojans, since honor is due only to virtue," Du Tillet declared, "for there is no nation which has suffered less corruption in its good manners than the German, which today would still be the best if it were unified."[33] He loved to emphasize the traditional hostility of Frank and Roman— "the Romans triumphed many times over the Germans without vanquishing them"—and, like all the legists, to contrast the rigidity of Roman institutions with German liberty.

Yet Du Tillet, who had an unusual knowledge of barbaric tongues as well as a familiarity with contemporary German scholarship, tried to establish his Germanist thesis upon solid historical and philological grounds. His point of departure was the standard group of texts celebrating Germanic virtue, including Tacitus, Jordanes, the prelude to the Salic law (which his brother had edited and put to similar use in his chronicle) and, among the moderns, Beatus Rhenanus and Althamer. Once again etymology seemed to offer the best proof of

---

[33] Du Tillet, *Recueil*, I, 1. See ch. VII, n. 54.

the Germanic origin of French institutions. As examples, Du Tillet pointed to the mayor of the palace (*"meyer du palais,* from a low German word meaning superintendent, later through corruption of language called *maire* or *maistre du palais"*) and to that favorite exhibit of historians, the marshal of France ("a word from the old low German, in which *march* means . . . horse and *schal* servant or officer").[34] As for feudal law, Du Tillet would not trace it further back than to the Lombards, adding that the fief did not become hereditary until the age of the Capetians, and noting the barbarian habit of taking the family name from territorial holdings, which was the reverse of the Roman practice.[35] In general, the character of customary law, which was the creation not of princes but of the people and so was not subject to legislation, showed both its Germanic origin and, in terms of social character, "the conformity of the French with the Germans."

The link between these liberty-loving Franks and the modern French (*franci* or *françois* served to designate either) was the second "race" of kings, the Charliens or Carolingians. The French inherited not only the virtues of barbarism but the political traditions of Rome from Charlemagne, who was, as the bishop Du Tillet put it, "the architect of the western empire, which was divided into two crowns, the Germanic and the Gallic."[36] What is more, according to the greffier, "Charlemagne belonged more to France than to Germany," and so did the hereditary monarchy which the Capetians received from him. It was not at all uncommon, Du Tillet went on to show from archival sources, for Capetian kings to be styled "emperor," which in fact was the most revered title next to that of "most Christian." The first text offered by Du Tillet in support of these imperialist arguments was the canonist formula from the bull of Innocent III, that "the king recognized no superior in temporal things," a copy of which was preserved in the registers of the parlement. Among other valuable items were the bulls of Clement V annulling the acts of Boniface VIII against Philip IV, and the "Deliberation" of Pierre Dubois, which

---

[34] *Ibid.,* I, 5; cf. p. 386.
[35] *Ibid.,* I, 9.
[36] Preface to *Libri Carolini,* in *Migne,* XCVII, 989; and *Recueil,* I, 250.

would finally be published in the next century by Du Tillet's successor Pierre Dupuy.[37]

The major point of Du Tillet's argument, however, was not the similarity of French kingship to the Roman *imperium* but rather its superiority. His conviction that the French monarchy was unique and its traditions self-sufficient was most clearly illustrated by the native formula, taken from the *Establishments of St Louis,* that "the king holds from God and himself and no other." One consequence of this was that the king was bound by feudal and not by "the emperor's law," and here Du Tillet referred to the famous ordinance of Philip IV (1312), which stipulated that "this kingdom is ruled by customs and not by written law," and that while civil law might be taught in the universities except that of Paris, it was not to be received into the kingdom. On this issue Du Tillet was in complete agreement with Hotman, Dumoulin, and the whole legist tradition. It is clear that what one historian has called "juridical nationalism," while it may have reached a peak in the sixteenth century, had its roots deep in medieval society.[38]

It was in the vast accumulation of regalian rights that the uniqueness and the continuity of the monarchy was best illustrated. "In this crown," wrote Du Tillet, rehearsing the litany of the legists, "there are certain flowers which stand for royal prerogatives and rights belonging to it alone, as the jurist Baldus remarked."[39] In the *trésor des chartes* in particular, he added, there were countless testimonies to this dignity, a bibliography of which Du Tillet appended to his discussion. The most celebrated of these flowers (*fleurons*; *lilia*) was the Salic law, but Du Tillet denied the conventional attribution to "Pharamond," since there was no evidence that this legendary king even entered Gaul, while on the other hand there were obvious traces of Christianity in the code itself. In general, Du Tillet was seldom a victim of that temptation, so irresistible to legists, to exaggerate the antiquity of institutions in order to enhance their

---

[37] Du Tillet, *Recueil*, III, 274.

[38] See Caprariis, *Propaganda*, p. 50, and V. Piano Mortari, *Diritto romano e diritto nazionale in Francia nel secolo XVI* (Milan, 1962), pp. 79 ff.

[39] Du Tillet, *Recueil*, I, 253; cf. ch. VI, n. 33.

authority. He attached too much importance to particular texts to succumb to this weakness.

Perhaps the most conspicuous signs of political vitality were the liberties of the Gallican church, a subject to which Du Tillet devoted a pioneering essay "in the form of history." [40] These ecclesiastical privileges had their roots, he thought, in the title "most Christian king" as well as in numerous Carolingian precedents, such as the calling of national synods and legislating in matters of doctrine and discipline, best exemplified by the *Caroline Books* published by his brother. Once again Du Tillet concluded that these "ancient liberties" were Germanic rather than Roman in origin, and he traced them back to the proprietary and feudal rights of the Frankish kings, who had always enjoyed the *congé d'élire* and who had established the cathedral churches of France. Out of this tradition, he continued, came the withdrawal of obedience, the acts of the University of Paris and the parlement, and the achievements of the conciliar period which culminated in the Pragmatic Sanction of Bourges. This Gallican thesis, which was to be pursued in legal monographs over the next two generations, was also to play an increasingly significant part in historiography.

Finally and most elaborately, Du Tillet illustrated the autonomy and continuity of French political tradition by means of historical commentary on the major institutions and offices of the monarchy. His work resembled those handbooks of institutional history mentioned earlier except that he was concerned more with documentation than analysis. The continuing political force of French law was maintained in particular by the parlement of Paris, whose officers, he remarked, customarily wore red instead of black at royal funerals to symbolize the perpetuity of French government. Among other important organs of the body politic were the twelve peers (which Du Tillet granted only a Capetian, not a Carolingian, origin), the *conseil privé*, the marshal, the admiral, and the governors, each of which he provided with its own chronologically arranged inventory.[41] In these various ways Du Tillet built up his major theses: the individuality

---

[40] *Ibid.*, III, 273-81.
[41] *Ibid.*, I, 362 ff.

of French constitutional structure, the uniqueness of French historical development, the antiquity and superiority of French kingship. From every point of view—legal, historical, ecclesiastical, social—France was declared independent of classical antiquity. And so, of course, was French historical scholarship.

From Du Tillet to Du Haillan

The effect of the archives in general and of Du Tillet's book in particular on historical scholarship in the last quarter of the sixteenth century was remarkable. One of the most conspicuous illustrations of this was, as was noticed before, the work of Du Haillan, who published his *State and Success of the Affairs of France* in 1570, the year of Du Tillet's death. Bernard Girard, Sieur du Haillan, was born in Bordeaux in 1535 and had close ties with two famous local families, the Montaignes and the Noailles. The latter he served for several years on various diplomatic missions and with their help found a place in the service of the house of Anjou. He must have been commissioned to write a history of this dynasty at about the same time as Baudouin, and whether or not he made use of Baudouin's "Proposition d'erreurs," he offered a similar critique of the "fables and lies" which plagued Angevin history.[42] Then in 1571 Du Haillan received an appointment as historiographer of the king and five years later, when his patron had become Henry III, published the first edition of his *History of France*.[43]

---

[42] Du Haillan, *Histoire sommaire des comtes et ducs d'Aniou*, in *Estats et succez* (Paris, 1570), pp. 145 ff; manuscript copy in BN MSS, Fonds français, vol. 5403, f. 1ʳ-22ᵛ, just proceeding copy of Baudouin's notes toward his own unfinished history of Anjou (see ch. V, n. 61).

[43] The only useful study is P. Bonnefon, "L'Historien du Haillan," *Revue d'histoire littéraire de la France*, XV (1908), 453-92, including a number of letters; other letters in Feuillet de Conches, *Causeries d'un curieux*, III (Paris, 1864), 133 ff. See also Caprariis, *Propaganda*, Lemaire, *Les Lois fondamentales*, and the estimates of Fueter and A. Thierry, *Dix ans d'études historiques* (Paris, 1883), p. 353, calling him "the father of French history." One of Du Haillan's commissions is in BN MSS, Fonds français, vol. 25730, f. 589ʳ, cited by P. M. Bondois, "Henri III et l'historiographe du Haillan," *Revue d'histoire littéraire de la France*, XXX (1930), 507-9.

At this time the standard work was still Paolo Emilio's *Deeds of the French* (1516), which was superior to Robert Gaguin's *Compendium* in more than a literary way. Besides being more critical, it was based upon much wider reading in modern authors and researches in the byways of philology, epigraphy, and social and institutional history, though admittedly the conventional dynastic and military focus was retained.[44] After the death of Paolo Emilio (1529) the historiographical tradition suffered a notorious decline and had little to offer beyond a few undistinguished continuations. Of his immediate successors the most active was Guillaume du Bellay, and his work was dismissed as intolerably thin and credulous by such critics as La Popelinière and Hotman, who himself held the office of royal historiographer for a time.[45] Pierre Paschal marked a further decline in this office, to which he was appointed in 1554 by the Cardinal of Lorraine. His inactivity and his classicist excesses made him a standing joke with the Pléiade and with such contemporary historians as Le Roy, Pasquier, and Pithou.[46] It may not be saying much, then, to call Du Haillan the best historian after Paolo Emilio.

In general, Du Haillan's purpose was the same as that of his humanist predecessors. It was to celebrate the "fortune and virtue" of France, which he thought had too long been obscured by that of Rome. Though built upon the ruins of the empire, the French monarchy had established its own pattern from the beginning. Following Seyssel, Du Haillan distinguished four stages in the development of France: infancy and adolescence under the Merovingians, maturity under the Carolingians, and decline under the Capetians. Like Seyssel, too, he tried to show the unique and indigenous character of the

[44] The best analysis is K. Davies, *Late XVth Century French Historiography, as exemplified in the* Compendium *of Robert Gaguin and the* De Rebus Gestis *of Paulus Aemilius* (Edinburgh, unpubl. diss., 1954). See also the article "Histoire" by E. Roche in *Dictionnaire des lettres françaises, Le Seizième siècle* (Paris, 1951).

[45] Guillaume du Bellay, *Epitome de l'antiquité des Gaules et de France* (Paris, 1556). Cf. Hotman, *Franco-Gallia*, p. 30, and La Popelinière, *Idee de l'histoire*, p. 449. See also V. L. Bourrilly, *Guillaume du Bellay, Seigneur de Langey, 1491-1543* (Paris, 1905).

[46] Bonnefon, *Pierre de Paschal, historiographe du roi (1522-1565)* (Paris, 1883), and Pierre de Nolhac, *Ronsard et l'humanisme* (Paris, 1921), p. 326.

"grand monarchy of France" in terms of the three "bridles," that is, religion, justice, and police. If he did not positively endorse the Franco-Gallic interpretation of Hotman, at least he repudiated "certain bold authors . . . who have written that it is treasonable to say that the state of France is composed of three constitutional divisions" (*choses publiques*).[47] Not that such "constitutionalist" enthusiasm prevented Du Haillan from celebrating the regalian rights so dear to the hearts of the legists. In fact, these "marks of sovereignty," together with the three bridles, furnished the principal rubrics for Du Haillan's detailed discussion of the institutions of French government.

Du Haillan deplored Romanist influence in any form, whether the "chicanery" of the papal curia which had begun infiltrating France in the fourteenth century, or the oppression of civil law which had been introduced into the universities even earlier. In France the function of civil law was based not upon authority, he recalled, but on utility (*par coustume non par domination; ne pour authorité, ains seulement pour la raison*), and even then only in the south.[48] Du Haillan also denied the Roman origin of feudalism, a problem which had "caused so many large volumes to be written." In his opinion, the Lombards were the "first inventors" of fiefs, which were later introduced into French society and eventually, after the example of the Capetian monarchy itself, made hereditary.[49] Like other institutions of modern France, Du Haillan assumed, feudal law was the product of custom—of the peculiar experience and problems of French history.

Although basically a popularizer, Du Haillan had certain claims to originality. Besides writing the first French history in the vernacular, he did not hesitate to depart from Paolo Emilio's plan when it suited his purpose. What is more, he boasted, "I have said with unprecedented boldness many things that no one before me has wanted or dared to say. . . . For I have rejected such common opinions as the

---

[47] Du Haillan, *Estat et succez* (1619 ed.), f. 2ʳ, 170ʳ. Cf. Louis le Roy, "Les Monarchiques," in *Exhortation aux françois*, f. 120ᵛ, and S. Champier, *De Monarchia ac triplici imperio* (Lyon, 1537), ch. 4, as well as Seyssel, *La Monarchie de France*, ed. J. Poujol (Paris, 1961), p. 108.

[48] *Ibid.*, f. 189ʳ.

[49] *Ibid.*, f. 236ʳ. Cf. *Histoire de France*, p. 201.

coming of Pharamond into France, the attribution of the Salic law to
him, the creation of the peers of France by Charlemagne, and other
points."[50] From this it becomes clear why he was so generous in his
praise of Du Tillet, who had anticipated him in each of these instances. Like Hotman, moreover, Du Haillan rejected any connection
between the prohibition of female succession to the throne and the
original Salic law. "It is old enough," he added, "being derived from
such a great antiquity as the death of Louis IX in 1314. . . . At that
time Philip V put forth this 'Salic law,' of which no one had heard
before." Similarly, he attributed the peers of France to the Capetians
and recognized that the parlement of Paris, at least in its modern
form, was a creation of Philip IV. Finally, he dismissed the Trojan
story as a myth (*une fable, non une vraye histoire*), although he did
not take this position publically until after the publication of Hotman's and Du Tillet's critiques.[51] On some points he retained conventional views, such as the attribution of the University of Paris to
Charlemagne. For the most part, however, he was more critical than
either the legists or the official historians, from whom he derived
much of his inspiration.

Many of the attitudes associated with professional historians of
more recent times Du Haillan displayed in abundance. To a very large
degree this was due to his discovery of Du Tillet's work, which occurred sometime between the first (1570) and second (1580) editions
of his *State and Success*. Between the first (1576) and second (1584)
editions of his *History of France*, moreover, he worked "night and
day" in search of original sources. In language much like Du Tillet's
he tells us of the great difficulty and expense of assembling manuscript sources (*livres, tiltres, chartes, memoires, enchartemens et autres
monumens qu'il fault avoir pour le bastiment d'un si grand ouvrage*).[52]
These erudite labors reinforced his conviction that history, "the avenger

[50] Du Haillan, *Promesse et desseing de l'histoire de France*, f. 13ʳ. Cf.
Histoire de France, pp. 10, 147, and *Estat et succez*, f. 12ʳ, 226ʳ.

[51] Du Haillan, *Estat et succez*, f. 11ᵛ, and *Histoire de France*, "Discours de
l'etymologie et origine des francs et francons" (unpaginated), obviously dependent upon Du Tillet.

[52] Du Haillan, *Promesse et desseing*, 2ᵛ, and the prefaces of both the *Estat
et succez* and the *Histoire de France*.

of truth and the mother of philosophy," was an independent discipline and had parted company with the humanities. According to Du Haillan, history was superior both to rhetoric, which he did not regard as particularly devoted to truth, and to poetry, which offered "too much pleasure with little utility."[53] In this unintentionally revealing remark Du Haillan indicated one of the more unfortunate results of the transformation of history from an art into a science—and one of the more insidious effects of legal studies.

About conventional historiography in the later sixteenth century there is little to say except that it continued to be a genre more responsive to propaganda and popular taste than to scholarship. Paolo Emilio's book continued to be published as well as to serve as a pattern for all historiographers. This includes Papire Masson as well as Du Haillan's prolific friend François de Belleforest and the Huguenot Jean de Serres, who sponsored an irenic plan similar to that of Baudouin after publishing his best-selling *Inventory of French history*.[54] In the seventeenth century, too, the most notable thing about the tradition of official historiography was its intellectual sterility.

The archivist tradition, on the other hand, continued a vigorous and creative existence in the later sixteenth century. It was carried on, indeed, by a scholar considerably more distinguished than Du Tillet or any of his predecessors. This was Pierre Pithou, who took over the administration of the *trésor des chartes* in the last years of his life (1594-96) when he became *procureur général* of Henry IV. In his medieval studies he showed much the same mixture of practical and antiquarian motives as Du Tillet. He possessed many of the works of both the bishop and the greffier, and he relied extensively on their scholarship, though just how much it is no longer possible to determine. Pithou adopted the same method, too. "He made extracts by

[53] Du Haillan's more general evaluations of history appear in the dedicatory epistles "au roy" of these two books. Here he presents a variation on the Ciceronian topos, *utilitas non voluptas* (*Brutus*, 128).

[54] See C. Dardier, Jean de Serres, historiographe du roi...," *Revue historique*, XXII (1883), 291-328, and XXIII, 28-76, and A. Gambier, *Jean de Serres, historiographe de France sous Henri IV* (Lyon, 1873); also C. Vivanti, *Lotta politica e pace religiosa in Francia fra cinque e seicento* (Turin, 1963), pp. 246 ff.

title and by topic," his biographer tells us, "of royal ordinances, ancient as well as modern, of the parlement and of the *chambre des comptes* and other sources which he was able to recover, and also of all the customs and statutes of the kingdom and the surrounding provinces."[55] Since he was also a leading member of the historical school of Roman law, Pithou exhibits even more fully than Du Haillan the manifold ingredients of French historical scholarship. With his work and that of certain colleagues engaged in the same enterprise, we return finally to the mainstream of philology and to its merger with the study of medieval history.

---

[55] A. Loisel, *Vie de M. Pierre Pithou*, in *Divers opuscules*, ed. C. Joly (Paris, 1652), pp. 258-59.

PART FOUR

Historical Scholarship

CHAPTER IX

The Historical School of French Law:
Pierre Pithou Introduces Philology
into Medieval Studies

Philologia ... olim ornatrix, hodie instauratrix
atque interpolatrix.

Budé, *De Philologia*

THOSE OF OUR AGE who have worked and who work still to rescue from
the shades of oblivion the writings of the ancient Greeks and Romans
and to embellish them with examples and annotations, have deserved
well of the sciences and are no less praiseworthy than are, in their own
way, those who publish new books. Following their example, French
patriots ought to devote themselves to searching for and restoring the
ancient books of their language for its decoration.

These words were set down in 1596 by a man who was a disciple
both of Baudouin and of Cujas and at least a peripheral member of
the Pléiade—who was, in other words, both a legal humanist and a
vernacular humanist. The point of view of Louis le Caron, here ad-
vertising his edition of the *Grand Coutumier of France*, reflects not
only the convergence of legal scholarship with linguistic nationalism
but also one of the fundamental motives of medieval studies. The
study of vernacular and vulgar Latin texts in the light of philology
and with the inducement of national enthusiasm represents one of
the most enduring achievements of sixteenth-century scholarship. To
this achievement no one contributed more—or more variously—than

---

[1] Louis le Caron, *Le Grand Coustumier de France* (Paris, 1598), prefatory
letter to his son.

Pierre Pithou. The fact that his work has direct ties with every major scholarly tradition discussed in this book makes an examination of it here all the more appropriate.

A Society of Antiquaries

At mid-century French society seemed to be passing through a kind of identity crisis both in politics and in learning. Steering between the Roman Scylla and the Genevan Charybdis, the monarchy needed some kind of ideological compass. In general, it fell to historians to find the national bearings by throwing new light upon the French past. A new generation of scholars, brought up on the classics but weary of Italian cultural hegemony, began to seek their own vision of the French "genius," as Budé had called it.[2] Although they were philologists as well as patriots and as devoted to the muses as they were to the monarchy, they were able to overcome the lingering embarrassment at their "barbarous" heritage and to disengage the method of the new learning from its Italianate context. Their independent attitude came all the more easily since they were not only men of letters but also men of law, and so brought to their work the habits and scruples of the legist tradition. They combined, in short, the ideological commitment of Dumoulin with the scholarly standards of Cujas. It was their fate, moreover, to carry out the investigation and interpretation of French history at the very time that religious conflict was shaking the foundations of the French monarchy and foreign powers were threatening its very existence.

These men were identified by more than a common purpose and a common experience; they belonged to a new and quite self-conscious intellectual class which, defined more by professional function than by social status, was taking shape in the sixteenth century. Independent of the universities and inclined toward use of the vernacular, this learned élite owed its existence largely to two circumstances: the emergence of the magistracy as an officially privileged group (*noblesse*

---

[2] Budé, *De Asse*, "praefatio," f. 104ᵛ. See E. Kantorowicz, *The King's Two Bodies*, p. 79, on the representation of national "genius."

Non opus ut quæras Cuius Cuiatius hic sit:
Natus Parnasso, natus in orbe viget. *ff.*

JACQUES CUJAS (T. de Bry, *Icones et
effigies virorum doctorum*) Courtesy of the
Bibliothèque Nationale, Paris

de robe), and the invention of printing, which brought in its wake a new vocation best described as public enlightenment. Its growth may be measured not only by the number and nature of published books but also by the increase of private libraries.[3] Naturally attracted to controversy but covetous as well of scholarly renown, these cultivated advocates divided their attention between the ideological needs of the monarchy and the growing public appetite for learning of all sorts. Not that they saw any contradiction between apologetics and erudition: on the contrary, they were confident that by promoting national consciousness through historical and literary publications they were contributing also to the strength and glory of the monarchy. Their dual function—and dual origin—helps to account for the curious blend of propaganda and pedantry that went into the making of their historical work.

It is significant that the growth of historical scholarship in France had such a firm social as well as an intellectual basis. Nor did this pass unnoticed at the time. In fact, it was precisely to define this new class and to record its accomplishments that La Croix du Maine compiled his *de viris illustribus* of French scholarship. This pioneering bibliographer and amateur of (other people's) learning explained the purpose of his *French Libraries* (1587) to Henry III in this way: first, he wanted to make the acquaintance of his many learned contemporaries, "the majority of whom," he reminded the king, "are employed in your service", and second, he wanted to publicize the great honor which they were bringing to France.[4] While noting the pursuit of classical studies, La Croix gave pride of place to the vernacular. He counted three thousand French authors, substantially more than any other nation (Italy, he claimed, could boast only three hundred). Ridden with inaccuracies and overembellished with superlatives, this work nevertheless revealed the growing self-consciousness of the intelligensia in France.

---

[3] The increase of lawyers' libraries, as compared with those of prelates, is shown by L. Febvre and H. Martin, *L'Apparition du livre* (Paris, 1958), pp. 398 ff; see also R. Doucet, *Les Bibliothèques parisiennes au XVIe siècle* (Paris, 1956).

[4] La Croix du Maine, *Les Bibliothèques françoises*, ed. R. de Juvigny (Paris, 1772), "Épistre au ... Henry III."

At the end of the century a more original scholar, Antoine Loisel, expressed this self-consciousness still more pointedly in his *Dialogue of the Advocates*, which he modelled on Cicero's *Brutus* and named in honor of his friend and colleague Étienne Pasquier.[5] This book celebrated a somewhat more restricted group, the order of the royal legists—"so stable," Ste.-Beuve remarked, "so courageous and even heroic,"—which constituted much of the strength of the *politique* party.[5] These *gens de robe* traced their pedigree back not only to the lawyers of the Last Capetians, beginning especially with Pierre de Cugnières, to whom Dumoulin had proudly compared himself, but also to the grander tradition of the Roman orators. In the course of describing this legist tradition, Loisel showed off the philological methods which he and his friends, including the principal speakers in the dialogue, Pasquier and François Pithou, had derived from their humanist training in the universities. Thus, Loisel revealed the two-fold source of that "historical school of the parlement of Paris" which, inspired by legal humanism, was turning from the naïve defense of royalism to the critical examination of French history.[6] It was from this learned branch of the legist order, indeed, that the first generation of French antiquaries emerged.

In the antiquarian renaissance of the later sixteenth century—repercussion of the "historical revolution" achieved several generations before—the leading figures were Pierre and François Pithou, Loisel, Pasquier, Claude Fauchet, Louis le Caron, and one or two others. These *érudits du roi* formed a sort of scholarly Pléiade whose artistry was too restricted, whose tastes were too prosaic, and whose learning was too weighty for them to reach the literary magnitude of their friends in Ronsard's poetic circle. Yet these sister groups overlapped

---

[5] *Pasquier, ou dialogue des advocats du parlement de Paris*, ed. M. Dupin (Paris, 1844), pp. 14 ff. Cf. Sainte-Beuve, "Étienne Pasquier" (Lundi, 6 Jan. 1851).

[6] F. von Bezold, "Zur Entstehungsgeschichte der historischen Methodik," *Aus Mittelalter und Renaissance* (Munich, 1918), p. 373. See also the classic article of G. Monod, "Du progrès des études historiques en France depuis le XVIe siècle," *Revue historique*, I (1876), 5-38, and on the legal class in general, R. Delachenal, *Histoire des avocats au parlement de Paris 1300-1600* (Paris, 1885), and M. Rousselet, *Histoire de la magistrature française* (Paris, 1957).

in various ways. Not only did these men all try their hand at poetry, but Pasquier and Le Caron could claim membership in the "brigade" which fought for vernacular culture during the middle years of the century, an episode which later would figure prominently in the pioneering histories of literature written by Pasquier himself and by Fauchet.[7] In general, the principal concern of both groups was the "defense and illustration" of French civilization.

Like the poetic Pléiade, too, Pasquier and his colleagues, even as they celebrated the splendors of French culture, drew inspiration from classical scholarship, especially from the historical school of Roman law. They were all trained in civil law and were converts to the cause of legal humanism. In their eyes one man stood above all others as an exemplary scholar: Jacques Cujas, with whom all of them (except for Fauchet) had studied and corresponded. Budé they honored as a titan of philology; Cujas they worshipped almost as a god, especially when his "divine work," the *Observations and Emendations,* began to appear in 1556.[8] As a godfather to French historical scholarship Cujas followed the work of his students with interest and sympathy. Yet these "Cujacians," while they continued to study Roman law, were never intimidated by their master's legendary query, "What has this to do with the pretorian edict?" (Neither, strictly speaking, was he). They were more likely to ask what the pretorian edict had to do with France. What is more significant, none of these men followed Cujas into academic careers; in some cases they positively shunned university chairs. Instead, they became lawyers and administrators. As such they drew upon pragmatic as well as philological traditions, and their work retained some of the marks of each.

There are good reasons for considering these men as a more or less unified group, as a kind of unchartered society of antiquaries. Not only did they share a common education, common professional standards, and common scholarly goals, but they also maintained close

[7] Étienne Pasquier, *Recherches de la France* (Paris, 1633), VII, 7 (p. 616), including also Beza and adding, "I compare this brigade to those who stand in the vanguard of a battle."

[8] See ch. IV, n. 59. That Cujas was not entirely above polemic was shown by his anonymous *Pro Io. Monlucio ... adversus Zachariae Furnesteri defensio* (s. l., 1575), written against a (pseudonymous) tract by Hotman's friend Doneau.

personal relations. They dedicated books to one another, paid mutual visits, and met at various social gatherings, whether in Parisian salons such as those of the De Thous and of the Dupuys, or at the provincial *grands jours*.[9] In contrast to the lonely pioneers of the previous generation, they practiced what amounted to cooperative scholarship, as a reading of their abundant correspondence makes clear. Pithou, the profoundest scholar of the lot, was a constant source of inspiration and information to his contemporaries. He offered scholarly counsel and books from his great family library to Cujas, Loisel, Fauchet, and other members of his circle, including De Thou, Barnabé Brisson, Nicolas Vignier, and the younger Scaliger, and to such foreign scholars as Bonifacius Amerbach, Josias Simler, Theodore Zwinger, Isaac Casaubon, and William Camden. Pasquier was still more communicative. To Cujas he offered his reflections on language and problems of translation, to La Croix du Maine suggestions about whom to include in his *French Libraries*, to Fauchet advice about his public behavior and help in regaining his office in the *chambre des comptes,* and to Pithou and Loisel news of war and politics as well as discussions of various legal questions. Indeed, Pasquier's correspondence, appropriately dedicated to Loisel, is one of the most concrete manifestations of the connections and coherence of this group and its scholarly enterprises.

By the outbreak of the religious wars all of these men had finished their educations, entered upon their professional careers, and begun their researches. Pasquier had been among the very first auditors (in 1546) of Baudouin and Hotman and (in 1547) of Cujas, whose acquaintance he renewed a dozen years later; and in 1557 he began to venture into the wilderness of "French antiquities." Even earlier Fauchet, whose scholarship is sometimes hard to distinguish from Pasquier's, had begun his "first essays," including critical estimates of

---

[9] A classic example of this was the salon of Mesdames des Roches, which Pasquier visited in 1579 during the *grands jours* of Poitiers along with Loisel, Choppin, and Brisson, and which he described to Pithou in *Les Lettres* (Paris, 1622), VI, 7 (I, 161). On the Parisian circles at the end of the century, reflected in Loisel's *Pasquier,* see M. Pattison, *Isaac Casaubon 1559-1614* (London, 1875), pp. 128-31. And see the next chapter, ns. 3 and 4.

various medieval historians.[10] By this time, too, public attention had been called to their mutual friend Louis le Caron, who planned to honor both of them in his *Dialogues* of 1556. Le Caron was a graduate of the law school of the University of Bourges, where he had sided with Baudouin against the "partisans of Le Douaren" and had finally become disgusted at the abandonment of scholarship for squabbling. Attracted to the investigation of early law, he published an edition of Zasius' catalogue of Roman laws and, in the wake of Baudouin's pioneering work, a reconstruction of the Twelve Tables.[11] Afterward he, too, turned increasingly to medieval studies. He may be encountered as a student of feudal law (following Dumoulin as a commentator on the Parisian custom), as an editor of medieval texts, and as an analyst of various problems of institutional history.

In the meantime, Antoine Loisel and Pierre Pithou were busy studying law with Cujas, whom they followed from Bourges to Valence in 1557, when he became another victim of the faction. A native of Beauvais, Loisel had previously studied with Adrien Turnèbe and Ramus at the University of Paris, where he probably made the acquaintance of Pasquier, before coming into contact with Cujas at Toulouse. In 1555, having accompanied Cujas to Bourges, he met

[10] J. Espiner-Scott, *Documents concernant la vie et les œuvres de Claude Fauchet* (Paris, 1938). See also her principal thesis, *Claude Fauchet, sa vie, son œuvre* (Paris, 1938), as well as various articles in *Humanisme et Renaissance*, VI (1939), 352-60 (comparing his work to Pasquier's), 546-55, and VII (1940), 233-38. Next to Ronzy, *Papire Masson*, this work provides the best introduction to medieval studies in sixteenth-century France, though there are some observations in N. Edelman, *Attitudes of Seventeenth-Century France toward the Middle Ages* (New York, 1946), and W. Evans, *L'Historien Mézeray* (Paris, 1930). On the great libraries and manuscript collections, see L. Delisle, *Le Cabinet des manuscrits de la Bibliothèque Impériale* (Paris, 1868), I.

[11] Le Caron, *Les Dialogues* (Paris, 1556), was to have included in Book II "Pasquier, ou l'Orateur," and "Fauchet, ou de la utilité qu'apporte la cognoissance des choses naturelles." Le Caron's *Ad Leges duodecem tabularum* follows the essay of Baudouin (see ch. V, n. 5) in *Tractatus*, I, f. 268^r-271^v; his edition of Zasius' work is *Catalogus legum antiquarum* (Paris, 1555). In general, see A. Digard, "Études sur les jurisconsultes du seizième siècle. Louis le Caron, dit Charondas," *RHDFE*, VII (1861), 177 ff, and L. Pinvert, "Louis le Caron, dit Charondas (1536-1613)," *Revue de la Renaissance*, II (1902), 1-9, 69-76, 181-88.

Pithou, who henceforth was to be his closest friend and collaborator.[12] The two young men worked under the direction of Cujas for almost five years and took their degrees in 1559 at the University of Valence. The next year they settled in Paris, Loisel arriving the very day when the lawyer Anne du Bourg was executed, and for a time they shared the same house. Both entered the *barreau,* of which Pasquier and Fauchet had long been members, and both continued their scholarly investigations. For over thirty years their "sacred friendship" and their "common bond of studies" remained intact.[13] This period, just spanning the wars of religion, also coincides with the heroic age of historical scholarship in France.

A Medievalist in the Making

Of all these men Pierre Pithou was the one who carried on most faithfully and fruitfully the great tradition of philology. Patterning his work after that of Cujas, he was less interested in writing history than in collecting and editing material and in working out problems of a monographic character. Yet like most of his contemporaries who were active lawyers, he could not avoid being drawn into religious controversy, and partly for this reason his work provides a good illustration of the shift from classical to medieval studies in this period. His prodigious labors, which became the basis for the more celebrated achievements of the next century, form the most impressive link between the historical school of law and the critical study of French antiquities.

Pierre Pithou was the best-known member of an erudite family of Troyes.[14] His father, also named Pierre, who had studied law with

[12] A most valuable study is M. Reulos, *Étude sur l'esprit, les sources et la méthode des Institutes coutumières d'Antoine Loisel* (Paris, 1935). See also "Vie de M. Antoine Loisel" by C. Joly in his edition of Loisel's *Divers opuscules* (Paris, 1652).

[13] Pierre Pithou, *Adversariorum subsecivorum libri II,* prefatory letter to Loisel, in *Opera sacra, juridica, historica, miscellanea* (Paris, 1609), p. 345.

[14] The first biography was Loisel's own "Vie de M. Pierre Pithou" in *Divers opuscules,* pp. 255-75. Most complete is Grosley, *Vie de Pierre Pithou* (Paris, 1756), but it should be supplemented by L. de Rosanbo, "Pierre Pithou," *Revue du seizième siècle,* XV (1928), 279-305; XVI (1929), 301-30. There is a contemporary eulogy by Masson in *Elogiorum pars secunda* (Paris, 1656).

Christofle de Thou and perhaps with Dumoulin at the University of Orleans, was responsible both for founding the family library, one of the arsenals of sixteenth century scholarship, and for enlisting his sons in the cause of philology. He sent Pierre to the University of Paris to study with Turnèbe and Ramus and encouraged him to concentrate his legal reading not on the Gloss but upon the Digest itself, in the humanist edition of Gregory Haloander. In view of this heritage and in view of his encounter with Cujas and Loisel in 1555, it is not surprising that Pithou fell in love with classical studies. Even when launched upon his legal career, as Loisel reported with some awe, he kept his heroic habits of nocturnal study. The fruits of these early researches appeared in 1564 and were dedicated to Loisel. These *Adversaria* had the form, or rather the formlessness, of the conventional humanist miscellany, similar to Cujas' own *Observations and Emendations*, but ranging more widely. Already Pithou had expanded his interests to include feudal institutions as well as Roman law and classical literature.

For Pithou a quiet life of study was not to be. His social status guaranteed him professional advancement and prevented exclusive devotion to his books. His conversion to Protestantism, coming after the outbreak of the second war in 1567, made it impossible for him even to follow his career in peace. He retired from Paris, where the legal profession retained a strict orthodoxy, first to Troyes, then to Basel, where he was welcomed by Amerbach. Yet neither travel nor the fortunes of war dulled his antiquarian enthusiasm. In 1566 Cujas had published, with the aid of a manuscript supplied by Loisel, a critical edition of the Theodosian code; and five years later Pithou supplemented this with an edition of imperial novels (beginning with Theodosius), which he drew from the manuscript riches of his father's library and which, naturally, he dedicated to Cujas. Like other legal humanists, he conceived a fascination for inscriptions, and the collecting habit which he picked up in Switzerland he later carried over into his medieval studies. What is perhaps most significant about

---

p. 321. Especially valuable for the Pithou library are J. Boivin, *Petri Pithoei vita* (Paris, 1711), pp. 65 ff, and the catalogue published by the Troyes library, *Les Richesses de la Bibliothèque de Troyes* (1951).

these years as an émigré, Pithou became attached to the field of history proper. During his residence in Basel, he produced editions of Paul the Deacon and Otto of Freising, dedicating the first to his publisher Amerbach and the second again to Cujas. These volumes may be regarded as preparatory to the great collection of medieval chronicles which Pithou was to issue twenty years later.

Like Baudouin, though in rather more practical terms, Pithou believed that history and law should establish more cordial relations. "The ancient laws of the Franks, the Goths, and the Lombards are closely connected to the histories of those nations . . . ," he remarked; "I have much material of this sort."[15] His claim was borne out by several later publications, including his edition of the Visigothic laws (1578) and his collection of Carolingian capitularies (1588). This alliance of law and history was sanctioned in his investigations of his own province, which resulted both in a commentary on the customs of Troyes and in his *Memoirs of the Counts of Champagne and Brie.* In this book, submitted as usual to Cujas' scrutiny, Pithou discussed such problems as the origin of the "vassal," which he recognized to be Celtic, and of the "advocate," which (like Loisel, who followed the argument in his *Dialogue of the Advocates*) he linked neither to the "advocati" of Theodosius nor to the Germanic "vogt" but to the medieval "clamatores."[16] In general, the work established Pithou as one of the leading authorities in France on medieval history.

By this time Pithou had not only expanded his perspective, he had formulated his historical method. His attitude, though unconventional

---

[15] Pithou, *Historiae miscellae a Paulo Aquilegiensi diacono primum collectae* (Basel, 1569), prefatory letter to Amerbach; the other work of this period is *Ottonis Episcopi Frisengensis . . . Chronicon* (Basel, 1569). On his epigraphical activities see T. Mommsen's account in *Berichte über die Verhandlunger des königlich sächsischen Gesellschaft der Wissenschaften zu Leipzig*, Phil.-hist. Classe, IV (1852), 278-82, from the Simmler collection in Zürich. There are other examples in BN MSS, Collection Dupuy, vol. 449, f. 62ᵛ ff.

[16] Pithou, *Le Premier libre des memoires des comtes hereditaires de Champagne et Brie*, in *Opera*, pp. 457-510, and also in *Les Coustumes du baillage de Troyes en Champagne* (Troyes, 1609). Cf. L. Pigeotte, *Manuscrite autographe du Commentaire de Pierre Pithou sur la coutume de Troyes* (Troyes, 1872), and also the critical remarks of Arbois de Jubainville, *Histoire . . . de Champagne* (Paris, 1859), I, v-vi. All the prefaces to Pithou's editions appear in *Opera*, pp. 700 ff (mispaginated).

in the emphasis on post-classical sources, was hardly revolutionary. It reflected the practice of modern German historians, of whom Pithou was a careful student, as well as that of Cujas. In order to understand Gallic and Germanic society, he assumed, one had to take into account medieval views (*posteriorum temporum memoria*) as well as the testimony of Caesar and Tacitus. Just as legal scholars could not afford to restrict themselves only to the purest and most polished authorities, so historians could not avoid sifting through the unclean deposits of later times (*non tantum legum et constitutionum, sed a historiarum fece coenoque haurire cogimur*).[17] While deploring the ignorance of medieval observers and their remoteness from public affairs (*affaires d'estat, qui sont le principal sujet de l'histoire*), he was thankful that the revival of letters sponsored by Francis I had made it possible for modern scholars to amend these faults.[18] To Pithou, in short, the historian was not a mere compiler, a "scissors-and-paste" writer, but a critical scholar, a philologist who had to penetrate beneath the surface of chronicles and contemporary histories, an antiquary who had to seek out other, sometimes nonliterary, sources of information and build upon them.

Pithou's career took another turn in 1572, when he decided to return to the orthodox faith of his family. His shifting interests, especially his studies in early Christian literature, may have contributed to this, but there is little doubt what prompted his decision at this time: it was the events of St Bartholomew's day. A letter written earlier that year to his brother Nicolas about the unrest in Paris shows that he was aware of the danger of living in the capital.[19] Yet in August there he was, staying in a Calvinist household. When the Massacre began, rioters entered the house and killed several of the inhabitants. Awakened by the noise, Pithou barely had time to put on his shirt and escape by the roof. He took refuge with his friend Nicolas Lefèvre, then with Loisel, who had not endangered his career with radical opinions. Loisel not only saved his life but retrieved a

---

[17] Pithou, preface to his edition of Paulus Diaconus.
[18] Pithou, *Mémoires . . . de Champagne* (*Opera*, p. 458).
[19] BN MSS, Collection Dupuy, vol. 700, f. 57ʳ; also in Grosely, *Pierre Pithou*, I, 149.

precious manuscript which he had discovered a couple of years before in the library of St Denis, the so-called *Comparison of the Mosaic and Roman Laws*, which Pithou had shown to Cujas, Le Caron, Scaliger, and others, and which he was to publish in 1574. He wanted to dedicate it to Loisel, but his friend diplomatically suggested instead the first president of the parlement of Paris, Christofle de Thou. Appropriately, Pithou rewarded Lefèvre with the dedication of his edition of Salvianus, who in his time had also witnessed the tragic consequences of religious controversy.

The year 1572 was as crucial for historical as it was for political thought, but it did not affect every scholar in the same way. Some, like Cujas, emerged shaken and cautious; some, like Hotman, emerged more belligerent than ever; others, including Pithou's old teacher Ramus, did not emerge at all. Pithou and Loisel, on the other hand, seemed to acquire a heightened sense of responsibility and a willingness to enlist their learning in the cause of political unity. They became valued supporters of the party of the "politiques," as they were now being called. It was only natural that their scholarly work should reflect this program, both in its breadth of view and in its national tone.

The Legist

Within a year after the Massacre Pithou and Loisel assumed important administrative posts for the first time. Refusing Cujas' invitation to come to Valence, Pithou became *bailli* of Tonnerre, while Loisel succeeded Barnabé Brisson as advocate to the Duke of Alençon, whom he advised on the proposed English marriage. In 1576 Loisel delivered a series of orations in celebration of the peace of that year named after his patron ("Monsieur"), singling out as the fruits of this peace the reformation of justice and education and applauding in particular the idea of establishing a humanist college of Alençon.[21]

---

[20] Pithou, *Mosaycarum et Romanarum legum collatio*, in *Opera*, pp. 1 ff. See the critical edition of M. Hyamson (London, 1913), introduction, pp. xiv-xlix, and Loisel, *Vie de M. Pierre Pithou* (*Divers opuscules*, p. 261).

[21] Antoine Loisel, *Remonstrance faicte a l'eschiquier d'Alençon* (s. l., 2 Nov 1576).

Pithou, though he was busy with legal duties, began a more enduring contribution. He compiled a commentary on the Ordinance of Blois (1579), which was a veritable code of legislation reflecting the demands of the Estates General of 1576 and designed to implement the pacification. This was the first step in Pithou's examination of that familiar topic, treated by so many of his colleagues, "the liberties of the Gallican church." [22] So this great ordinance, which led also to Brisson's famous *Code of Henry III*, inspired what was to become the classic, if not the official, summary of Gallican doctrine.

At the same time Pithou and Loisel were given a chance to participate more directly in the Gallican program of pacification and reform taken over by the politiques. Partly as a result of the Peace of Monsieur, new courts including Protestant as well as Catholic officers (*chambres mi-partis*) were to be attached to the parlement. To one of these, the chamber of justice of Guyenne, Pithou and Loisel were assigned as *procureur du roi* and *avocat du roi* respectively. Although Pithou still found time to visit local libraries and to take notes on all kinds of antiquities, he had to bear much of the burden of administration and correspondence.[23] Loisel, on the other hand, was charged with the dispensation of eloquence rather than learning, and again he delivered remonstrances on behalf of peace and justice. The antiquarian habit was evidently upon him, too, and he compared his and Pithou's roles to those of the Carolingian *missi dominici*. In general, both were sympathetic to the kind of Gallicanism associated with Michel de l'Hôpital, whose epigrams Pithou found time to edit in 1585. Indeed, in one harangue entitled "Amnesty" (dedicated to a sympathetic local notable, Michel de Montaigne) Loisel prescribed the same Gallican formula which L'Hôpital had recommended: the old device "of our fathers and ancestors, that is, to live under one God, one King, one faith, one law." [24]

---

[22] Collection Dupuy, vol. 422, especially f. 76ʳ-78ʳ (also Fonds français, vol. 13801); published in Loisel, *Divers opuscules*, pp. 345-52. The ordinance is in Isambert, XIV, 430 ff.

[23] Collection Dupuy, vols. 219-220, *passim*. See Loisel, *Vie de Pithou*, p. 263, and in general, R. Doucet, *Les Institutions de la France au XVIe siècle* (Paris, 1948), I, 215-16.

[24] Loisel, *La Guyenne* (Paris, 1605), p. 99. Cf. pp. 131-32, dedication of

Politically, of course, they were doomed to disappointment at this time, especially since their program was tied to the person as well as to the estate of the king. With the death of Alençon and the failure of the two-party court in 1584, Pithou and Loisel left Guyenne, the one returning to his *bailliage* in Tonnerre, the other to become advocate of the queen Mother. In the summer of 1586, when the parlement was mutinously but vainly opposing Henry III's revocation of the pacification edicts, they were appointed substitutes in the offices of *procureur* and *avocat général* in order to expedite a number of venal edicts of that year. In these uneasy weeks Pithou appealed to the parlement for financial as well as moral support. "My lords, our misfortunes are such that they can neither be avoided nor overcome by words . . . ; the necessity which presses upon us is clear, and the duty we owe our prince and our country obliges us to refuse nothing that may bring relief." [25] At the same time he and Loisel began to feel a certain vicarious unpopularity. Verses composed on the occasion of their appointment attacked the king for delegating his charge to such wretches. "Since two Henries already occupy the throne with you," the pamphlet concluded, "you are with good reason called 'Henry III.' " [26] No wonder that Pithou, who had married in 1579 and started a family, preferred to retire to Troyes. Thus he escaped imprisonment and possibly the tragic fate of his friend Brisson, whom he had warned about the dangers of Parisian politics.

Pithou was deeply disturbed by the civil—they were no longer merely religious—wars, which he compared to the fratricidal conflicts of Rome under Sulla. [27] The anarchy in Paris, the dispersal of the parlement, the disrespect for kingship, the scenes of horror he witnessed in his own Champagne, some chronicled by his brother, led him, like many of his contemporaries, to brood about the decline and fall of states in general. But the discouraging prospect only made him

---

another harangue ("Homonoee," 1594) to Pithou. Pithou's preparations for the 1585 edition of L'Hôpital's *Poemata* appear in Collection Dupuy, vol. 901.

[25] Collection Dupuy, vol. 728, f. 99r.

[26] L'Estoile (Henry III), p. 468; cf. p. 454, referring to the appointments of Pithou and Loisel, and p. 451, to the mutiny of their predecessors.

[27] Collection Dupuy, vol. 838, f. 142r.

work the harder. Besides continuing his manifold scholarly projects, he contributed to the notorious *Satyre Menippée*, an anonymous attack upon the League by several legists, including his old friend Jacques Gillot; and working with his brother François, he composed a defense of the French clergy's right to absolve Henry IV and so to clear the way for his conversion to Catholicism.[28] Whatever his faults as a practical politician, Pithou's faith in the Gallican ideal was unswerving.

With the triumph of this ideal in 1594, Pithou received his reward. Restoring the parlement in March of that year, Henry IV appointed Pithou his *procureur général* and Loisel his *avocat général*.[29] In general, his job was the usual one of the royal legists since the thirteenth century, to defend the privileges of the king against both feudal and ecclesiastical usurpation by appeal to precedent and principle, which most often meant to history. It was a job which allowed Pithou to play a leading role in that Gallican revival sponsored by the king and the politiques. It was a job, too, for which he had been preparing himself for most of his adult life. The office not only required him to make use of his vast knowledge of the sources of French history, it also encouraged him to add to it. The royal archives, on which he was already something of an authority, were part of his charge. He also took an interest in the royal library and was instrumental in having the books of Catherine transferred there. Pithou had found the ideal position for a bibliophile—a man who, as Scaliger remarked, "could smell a book as a dog his bone"—and for an omnivorous scholar who had come to be regarded as "the Varro of France."[30]

[28] *La Satyre Menippée*, ed. C. Reade (Paris, n. d.), to which Pithou's contribution was probably the harangue of M. D'Aubray (according to his brother François, *Scaligerana*, II, 496), and *Memoire par lequel il est prouvé que le Roy Henry IIII. Peut estre canoniquement et legitimement absous d'heresie par les Evesques de son Royaume*, in Loisel, *Divers opuscules*, pp. 427 ff. Nicolas Pithou's *Histoire ecclesiastique de l'Église prétendue réformée de la ville de Troyes* ... (Collection Dupuy, vol. 698) has been published in part by C. Recordon as *Le Protestantisme en Champagne* (Paris, 1863).

[29] Letters patent of 27 March 1594 in Isambert, XV, 85. See Le Prince, *Essai historique sur la bibliothèque du roi* (Paris, 1782), p. 36.

[30] *Scaligerana*, I, 507, adding that (unlike his brother François) he lent books to everyone.

Tragically, he did not enjoy this position for long. In 1596, in the midst of countless projects, Pithou died at Nogent, "a loss affecting not merely a single town or city of France," wrote his friend De Thou, but the whole world of scholarship.[31] Like Budé, Pithou was a many-sided and many-skilled investigator whose public life gave impetus and direction to his scholarly work. Humanist ideals infused with national devotion, archeological enthusiasm steered by ancestor-worship, literary tastes weighted down with legal learning: these were the sources of Pithou's love of history. Sometimes his Gallican bias seemed to overwhelm his dedication to philology, and it was very nearly true, as he wrote in his testament, that "my *patria* has absorbed all my affection."[32] Yet if he shifted his interests, he nevertheless kept faith with the ideals of Cujas; he merely translated them into modern terms. More than a lawyer with literary leanings, more than a philologist caught in politics, Pithou was the most fully equipped historian of the century. He was the complete antiquary—in his day the most exciting of callings.

It was unfortunate that Pithou did not live to finish his work, still more unfortunate that he never took the time to write a book of general import. Yet he felt instinctively—and surely with reason—that his was an age to accumulate and to restore "monuments" rather than to compose works of synthesis. Like Lord Acton three centuries later, he shunned the task of large-scale interpretation. Instead, like Acton, he left massive manuscript remains which, if nothing else, provide later observers with an unusual opportunity of looking over the shoulder of a pioneering historian in the preliminary stages of his researches. In conjunction with his published books, these chips from Pithou's workship—transcripts, notes, outlines, first drafts—may offer insight not only into one man's expedition into the terra incognita of medieval history but also into the origins of a new field of scholarship.[33]

[31] De Thou, I, 234; cf. Grosely, *Pierre Pithou*, II, 13 ff.

[32] Collection Dupuy, f. 139ʳ, and Grosely, *Pierre Pithou*, II, 93.

[33] In general, see S. Solente, "Les Manuscrits des Dupuy à la Bibliothèque Nationale," *Bibliothèque de l'École des Chartes*, LXXXVIII (1927), 177-250, and the indispensable L. Dorez, *Catalogue de la collection Dupuy* (Paris, 1928), following very closely the catalogue of Dupuy (Fonds français, n. a.,

The Antiquary

Pithou's learning was as wide as his training was diverse. In keeping with his humanist tastes and Gallican methods, he was a through researcher, a compulsive note-taker; and these habits were reinforced by an inexhaustible, though somewhat indiscriminate, curiosity. His manuscripts, which through the De Thou and Dupuy families made their way into the royal library, are filled with notes on his reading, especially of jurists and historians, and his travels, including facts and impressions about the Swiss and Italian cities he visited and about various regions of France (Perigord, Bordeaux, Burgundy) to which his duties took him. Local history fascinated him; he sought out manuscripts, charters, inscriptions of churches and monasteries, and later commissioned friends, especially Lefèvre, to assist him in this work. He developed diplomatic as well as paleographic skills, and at one point we find him trying his hand at copying Merovingian script.[34] Like Loisel and Pasquier, he liked to collect not only classical quotations but also old French proverbs, which he regarded as a kind of folk wisdom comparable to customary law.

At the same time, in the course of his official duties, Pithou followed the procedures of Du Tillet, on whose work he quite obviously built and whose collected materials he used. He made inventories of documents and extracts from the registers of the parlement. Likewise, as a follower of Dumoulin, he made legal and historical comments on French customary law. If as a philologist he tended to pile up examples and comparisons, as a legist he was obliged to accumulate precedents and "proofs," and as a feudist to make comparisons between the customs of Troyes and Paris and other feudal law. In all of these roles—as the protégé of Cujas and as the beneficiary of Du Tillet and Dumoulin—he was committed to the view that knowledge was possible only through the intensive study of the particular, that an understanding of human behavior had to be established on the basis of

vol. 5714), which however covers but 800 of the 1,000 volumes. Of this great treasury, which has material on many of the authors discussed here, 64 volumes have to do with Pithou.

[34] Collection Dupuy, vol. 222, f. 13ʳ. The correspondence with Lefèvre, twenty odd letters, appears in vol. 700, f. 62ʳ-88ʳ.

primary and especially unpublished sources.

Throughout his busy career Pithou had always found the time for his philological pursuits. He was always on the alert for unknown manuscripts, and periodically he issued editions of classical works. Most famous, perhaps, was his *Pervigilium Veneris* (1577), based upon a manuscript (*codex Thuanus*) discovered by him and corrected with the help of friends, especially Scaliger—and indeed this "sick poem," referring to the state of the text, needed all the help it could get.[35] Later he published works of Quintilian, Juvenal, Perseus, Petronius, and, just before his death, Phaedrus. He also conceived an ambitious plan for a new edition of Roman law, which was to be based on the most recent scholarship. For the Digest, he explained to his brother Nicolas, he would use not only the Florentine manuscript but also the paratitles of Cujas.[36] For the *Book of Fiefs*, too, he would follow Cujas' work, though with corrections. Pithou never lost his interest in legal humanism, though he did not live to see the appearance of his edition.

Pithou's contributions to medieval studies were still more substantial. Inevitably, his researches into French law and history were functions of his legal duties, but this circumstance, if it warped his interpretation, did not obstruct his search for material. From a lawyer's perspective the French monarchy could be regarded as a vast corporate complex—a network of personal, feudal, ecclesiastical, commercial, and professional relationships. All facets of this complex interested him, though mainly from the standpoint of public authority. It was the king's interests he had in mind, for example, when he made extracts from the registers of the parlement of Toulouse and from an unidentified "old book" in Bordeaux during his commission to Guyenne.[37] This was his reason, too, for collecting material and

[35] Collection Dupuy, vol. 395, with notes by Scaliger and Pithou. Cf. letter of 2 June 1578 in Collection Dupuy, vol. 496, f. 178r, also in Scaliger's *Lettres françaises*, ed. P. Tamizey de Larroque (Paris, 1881), p. 78. For a complete list of Pithou's editorial publications, see the catalogue of the Bibliothèque Nationale.

[36] Collection Dupuy, vol. 688, f. 48r, and Grosely, *Pierre Pithou*, I, pp. 174-77.

[37] Collection Dupuy, vols. 219, f. 70r ff, and 220, f. 29r. As before, these are only samples.

compiling bibliographies on such topics as the regale, the *dîme,* the *cas royaux,* the minority of the king, the title "most Christian," and especially the boundaries (*limites*) of various provinces. In this work he was assisted by his brother François, who later carried it on by himself. In general, it is hard to tell where the antiquarian activities of the Pithous leave off and their official duties begin—if indeed such a distinction is valid at all.

As a member in good standing of the order of royal legists, Pithou looked with great suspicion upon the feudal establishment, which had played so dubious a part in the civil wars. In his view it was an antiquated obstacle to monarchy which should be kept within prescribed and if possible uniform limits. One way to resist the centrifugal tendencies of feudalism was by attacking it at the roots, that is, through the reformation, ultimately the unification, of French customs. This was the aim of the movement inaugurated by Christofle de Thou in 1555 as well as such systematic works as Dumoulin's commentaries and Loisel's *Customary Institutes,* which was the product of almost half a century of legal experience and research practically identical with Pithou's. The movement was promoted directly both by Pithou, who had followed Dumoulin in commenting on the Parisian custom and who assisted in the reformation of the custom of Sedan in 1567, and by Loisel, who represented the clergy in the reformation of the Parisian custom in 1580.[38] The ideal of social unity underlying this movement was a convenient assumption, it may be noticed, not only for the king's advocates but for the historians of the monarchy.

In the service of Henry IV Pithou continued to promote this ideal. He was called upon, for example, to resist the "new customs" of Lorraine published in 1594 by Duke Charles, who was eventually to be charged with lese majesty. In the matter of feudal allegiance "his highness" had indeed princely ambitions. What was intolerable, he carried his pretensions over into Bar, which he held from the king, as well as the imperial fief of Lorraine. After a detailed examination of the *coutume,* Pithou charged that "he remains as sovereign in Bar as you are in the rest of your kingdom, unless you are content with

[38] F. Olivier-Martin, *Histoire de la coutume . . .de Paris,* I, 113, and Grosely, *Pierre Pithou,* I, 115.

mere lip service." The law stipulated—and history proved—otherwise. "He is the vassal of the king by reason of Bar . . . ," Pithou concluded, "and so as your *procureur général,* I have done discreetly what I know to be necessary in such a case."[39] It was with such an attitude, too, that Pithou made his interpretations of feudal institutions.

A more formidable obstacle for the French nation—and a more popular target for the legists—was the papal monarchy. The king's ecclesiastical privileges had concerned Pithou since his original reaction to the Council of Trent, on which he had been collecting notes since at least 1563. In his commentary on the Ordinance of Blois (1579), Pithou recalled that the French king had always held councils and reformed his own church.[40] Like Dumoulin, whom he may have known personally as well as professionally, he looked upon the *appel comme d'abus* as a general remedy for papal usurpation. He was interested enough in Dumoulin's consultation against the Tridentine decrees to copy out the documents concerning his interrogation by the parlement, which were inserted, Pithou added, among the articles of the Council of Trent. During the 1580s, when the seditious implications of ultramontanism were impressed more clearly on him, Pithou began to collect material for a broader defense of the Gallican liberties. On the basis of the famous edict concerning the "little dates" he argued that "the bulls of popes Pius IV and V could not be received in France because they confiscated the fruits of benefices for their own use." Pithou became an authority on political writings, imperialist as well as Gallican, against the papacy; but much more important for his purposes were the historians of medieval and modern times, of whom he had an exhaustive knowledge. As usual, his most original and substantial work was accumulating specific proofs of the

---

[39] Collection Dupuy, vol. 492, f. 89r. See *Coutumes générales du duché de Lorraine* (Nancy, 1770), pp. 132 ff (Estates of Nancy, 1 March 1594), and Isembert, XV, 93 *(arrêt* of 6 June 1595, charging the Duke with lese majesty).

[40] Collection Dupuy, vol. 422, f. 29r, and Loisel, *Divers opuscules,* p. 346. Pithou's notes on the Council of Trent are preserved in Collection Dupuy, vol. 357, f. 298r-301v; cf. vol. 493, f. 194r, where he refers to the edict on the "little dates." From vol. 691, f. 136r, it appears that Pithou collaborated with Dumoulin on a case.

king's rights—fiscal, legal, and administrative—over various churches and monasteries and over the French clergy in general. For Pithou, as for Dumoulin and Du Tillet, Gallicanism was not a theory but a concrete and continuous tradition.

Pithou might well have poured his learning into a history of the French church as Pasquier did. Instead, because of his office and the needs of Henry IV, he compressed it into a brief and rather dogmatic survey of that perennial topic, which so many of his friends were writing about in these years, the "liberties of the Gallican church." Yet this little pamphlet turned out to be the most durable and influential, at least in political terms, of all his works.[41] It consisted of eighty-three items, mainly restrictions on papal power, substantiated by historical references and organized around two basic propositions: that the pope enjoyed no temporal authority in France, and that his spiritual jurisdiction was limited by the ancient councils and canons recognized by the French monarchy. Besides the treatise itself, Pithou published a collection of conciliar precedents, consisting primarily of edicts passed during the Great Schism, including that of February 18, 1407, which Victor Martin once called "the birth certificate of Gallicanism."[42] He began to collect voluminous "proofs" in support of the Gallican liberties, including those of the Gallican crisis of the

[41] Pithou, *Les Libertez de l'eglise gallicane* (Paris, 1594), re-edited many times, e. g., in Du Tillet's *Recueil* (see ch. VIII, n. 21). There is even an English version in Crozer Theological Seminary, *Historical Leaflet*, no. 7 (1911). See J. Lecler, "Qu'est-ce les libertés de l'église gallicane?" *Recherches des sciences réligieuses*, XXIII (1933), 385-410; the article in the *Dictionnaire du droit canonique*; and the bibliography cited by L. Willaert, *Après le concile de Trent, La Restauration catholique (1563-1648)* (Paris, 1960), p. 367. Other works on this topic are noted by J. le Long, *Bibliothèque historique de la France* (Paris, 1771), I, 469 ff.

[42] Victor Martin, *Les Origines du gallicanism*, I, 38. Pithou's collection was *Ecclesiae Gallicanae in schismate statu* (Paris, 1594), also reprinted in Du Tillet's *Recueil* and probably making use of Du Tillet's researches. The "Preuves des libertez de l'Église Gallicane" are collected in BN MSS Fonds français, n. a. vols. 7121-7136. This material was published by Pierre Dupuy, *Traitez des droits et libertez de l'eglise gallicane* (Paris, 1639), remarking that "these proofs left by the author have until now been suppressed." In general, see G. Demante, "Histoire de la publication des livres de Pierre Dupuy sur les libertés de l'église gallicane," *Bibliothèque de l'école des chartes*, V (1843-44), 585-606, and Delisle, *Cabinet des manuscrits*, I, 422.

mid-sixteenth century, which formed the basis for Pierre Dupuy's great collection of the next century. In all of this work it is clear that Pithou himself was building upon the work of his own predecessor Du Tillet.

At the same time Pithou was drawn increasingly to Christian antiquity and to medieval Europe, and he began working also upon an edition of canon law.[43] This work, for which Pithou provided an introductory survey of the sources as well as critical notes on the text, was published posthumously by his brother François. As for ecclesiastical history, Pithou completed the work of Baudouin and Masson on the text of Optatus. Theology, too, came to interest him, and he considered the possibility of publishing an edition of the early Gallican fathers. In his last years he even entered into the field of Biblical criticism and the history of dogma. Finally, at the time of his death, he was working on a collection of the canons of the early councils, which his brother again took over, though never finished. In general, no scholar of that age, with the possible exceptions of Scaliger and Casaubon, neither of whom was burdened with public office, had so wide a range of competence.

The direction of Pithou's interests and the requirements of his legal work led him into another and still less-explored field, the history of institutions and offices. His earliest studies concerned the antiquities, legal and ecclesiastical, of his native province. In the 1580s he began collecting materials for a history of the parlement of Paris, as well as those of Bordeaux and Toulouse, and he made extensive extracts from the registers for this purpose. He assembled material also on the *chambres des comptes* and various offices, such as the chancellor and the *greffiers*—subjects which his friends Pasquier and Fauchet, among others, had begun to investigate. Most interesting, perhaps, was his work on the history of the *trésor des chartes*, which he traced from the beginning down to his own immediate predeces-

---

[43] *Corpus Juris Canonici*, ed. Pierre and François Pithou (Paris, 1637), making use of both Catholic and Protestant histories, e. g., Baronius and the Magdeburg Centuriators, as well as canonist sources. See F. Maasen, *Geschichte der Quellen und der Literatur des canonischen Rechts* (Graz, 1870), I, xxxvi-ix. The best summary of Pithou's later work is still in Grosely, *Pierre Pithou*.

sors Du Tillet and Christofle de Thou. His unpublished treatise on this formed the basis of later studies, beginning with that of Pierre Dupuy, the inheritor of his manscripts.[44] These are only a few of the subjects which attracted Pithou's curiosity.

If Pithou's scholarship was placed in the service of the monarchy, he by no means allowed his royalist obligations to distort his humanist ideals. This is shown most clearly in what was the most significant of all his historical publications, that is, his pioneering collection of medieval chronicles—*textes pour servir à l'histoire de France*. These *Histories of the French* included letters and capitularies as well as eleven medieval chronicles, some printed for the first time. "It was our intention," Pithou explained, "to contribute to our *patria* and to posterity not only histories but laws and synods, especially those which until now have suffered from the ravages of time."[45] The effects of this book were profound. "An excellent book!" exclaimed Scaliger; "If you could see my copy, you would know how I have worked it over." So did Casaubon, as may be seen from his copy, now preserved in the British Museum.[46] Like other works of Pithou, it became the foundation for—to some extent a model for—the more comprehensive and more celebrated labors of the seventeenth century. The significance of his researches, and those of his colleagues, has been too little appreciated since the eighteenth century. He deserves a place in the great tradition of French scholarship including such figures as Mabillon, Migne, and Leopold Delisle. If Pithou represents the culmination of Renaissance philology, in another sense he should be recognized as one of the founding fathers of medieval studies.

---

[44] Collection Dupuy, vol. 233, f. 98ʳ ff (see ch. VIII, n. 9). Notes on other offices may be found, e. g., in vols. 141, 219, 225, and 235.

[45] Pithou, *Annalium et historiae Francorum ab anno Christi DCCVIII ad ann. DCCCCXC* ... (Paris, 1588) and the second edition, *Historiae Francorum ab anno Christi DCCC ad ann. MCCLXXXV* ... (Frankfurt, 1596), "praefatio." A previously unpublished continuation of this preface (Collection Dupuy, vol. 688, f. 17ʳ) was printed by Grosely, I, 293-99.

[46] *Scaligerana*, I, 506. Casaubon's copy of the *Annales* (1594) is in the British Museum (shelf mark, 1058. b. 12.).

Pithou's Circle

The range and depth of Pithou's scholarship is reflected not only in his publications and manuscript remains but also in his remarkable circle of acquaintances, which included many of the great figures of late sixteenth-century philology. At the top of the list, of course, was Jacques Cujas, the man from whom he derived his historical method and his scholarly goals. Throughout the religious wars the two men remained friends, exchanging books, gossip, and serious criticism. The principal topic, naturally, was Roman law, especially Cujas' preparations for his various editions. To Cujas Pithou opened his library and supplied him with much valuable manuscript material, while for his part Cujas showed a growing interest in medieval studies and clearly regarded Pithou as his first disciple. Not only did he offer Pithou a teaching post at the University of Valence (probably in 1574), but he begged him to come and share his house—"You shall want for nothing," he promised[47]—and eventually he chose Pithou to be his literary executor.

In 1571 one of Cujas' brightest students, destined ultimately, in fact, to outshine the master, wrote to Pithou to borrow a copy of Fulvio Orsini's collection of inscriptions, and he remained a faithful correspondent for the last quarter century of Pithou's life. This was Joseph Justus Scaliger, the greatest of all philologists, whose monumental *Emendations of Chronology* was one of the major contributions to historical scholarship of the century. A better Greek scholar than Pithou and already launched into the study of Semitic languages, Scaliger was one of the few persons who could talk to Pithou on equal, in some cases superior, terms. Scaliger offered corrections for the edition of the *Pervigilium Veneris*, for example, and later he was able to give Pithou a remarkable lesson in historical criticism. He showed why the pseudo-Ciceronian "Consolatio" (forged in the later sixteenth century, probably by Carlo Sigonio) could not be accepted as authentic.[48] Yet Scaliger respected Pithou's work and like Casau-

---

[47] Pithou, letter of 15 August 1574 (?) in Collection Dupuy, vol. 700, f. 12[r]. This is one of twenty-seven unpublished letters from Cujas to Pithou (ff. 1[r]-40[r]), dealing largely with scholarly topics.

[48] J. J. Scaliger, letter of 31 August 1583 in Collection Dupuy, vol. 496,

bon, another of Pithou's correspondents, recognized Pithou's superiority in the field of medieval studies.

Of Pithou's other correspondents the best known was Jacques-Auguste de Thou, who also profited from Pithou's counsel and his library, part of which he eventually inherited. Although a proud man and later a peerless historian of contemporary Europe, De Thou showed quite a different face to men like Pithou and Scaliger, and he expressed a certain chagrin at his scholarly deficiencies. "M. de Thou," remarked Pithou's sharp-tongued younger brother, "is not learned outside of poetry and eloquence." Yet his own historical labors stemmed from the same enthusiasm for learning that animated the philologists of this generation. A different sort was Nicolas Lefèvre, who not only helped to save Pithou's life in 1572 but afterwards spent much effort collecting material for Pithou, visiting libraries, checking catalogues, and sending along scholarly news. Pithou received similar aid from François Roaldès, successor of Cujas at Valence who was interested in local history as well as the classics, and François Juret, who was a specialist in early Christian literature.[49] But in general, Pithou gave more than he received, as illustrated by his correspondence with Claude Fauchet, who presented him with a long list of questions about French history, and Nicolas Vignier, who in his work on Frankish origins admitted his debt to Pithou.[50] In

---

f. 187[r], and *Lettres françaises*, p. 154. Of the twenty-eight letters from Scaliger (ff. 171[r]-204[r]) twenty-three have been published in this edition. See also "Lettres inédites de Cujas et de Scaliger," *NRHDFE*, XL (1917), 403-24.

[49] In Collection Dupuy, vol. 700: thirty letters from François Juret (ff. 119[r]-158[r]); twenty-one from Nicolas Lefèvre (ff. 62[r]-93[r]) and another in vol. 490, f. 183[r]; and ten from François Roaldès (ff. 46[r]-56[r]), also in Roaldès, *Discours de la vigne*, ed. P. Tamizey de Larroque (Bordeaux, 1886), appendix. In vol. 838 there is also an extensive correspondence between Pithou and Jacques-Auguste de Thou, of which the latter's only has been published in *Choix de lettres françoises* (Paris, 1877). The significance of the Collection Dupuy for De Thou has been detailed by S. Kinser, *The Works of Jacques-Auguste de Thou* (The Hague, 1966), pp. 329-36. There are other letters from Pithou in the Zentralbibliothek of Zürich (10 to J. Simler) and in the Universitäts-bibiliothek of Basel (fifteen to Amerbach and two to Zwinger), and many more from his brother François, who seems to have acted as a purchasing agent for Amerbach. There are also a few published letters to Pithou in the old collections of letters of Scaliger, Casaubon, and Lipsius.

[50] Collection Dupuy, vol. 700, ff. 99[r]-118[r], contains eighteen letters from

medieval history, at least, Pithou was widely regarded as a final court of appeal.

Beyond doubt Pithou's closest collaborator and most faithful disciple was his brother François, whose career, as Cujas was pleased to note, seemed to take the same course as that of Pierre. François, too, began as an orthodox humanist and, because of patriotism and professional duties, turned increasingly to medieval history. Like Pierre he distributed his talents over the fields of classical literature, Roman, canon, and feudal law, and was engaged in both research and polemic on behalf of the monarchy. Like Pierre, too, François became a Calvinist and spent several years traveling in Switzerland and Germany, though he did not surrender his Protestant sympathies quite so readily.[51] Inferior to his brother in scholarship and political success, François seems to have been a stronger personality. Pierre himself became upset by his independent attitude while he was studying law at the University of Valence. Cujas, then François' teacher, came to the younger man's defense: "It is merely his youth that is restless and uncertain . . . , but time will remedy this because on the whole he is a fine and virtuous young man."[52] In later years jealousy, as François seems to suggest, threatened to separate the brothers, and at one point Lefèvre interceded. If the *Pithoeana* can be accepted, François was immensely vain and critical of almost all his contemporaries, except for Cujas and Scaliger.

Yet in spite of such differences François carried on his brother's work with great competence and fidelity, and it is sometimes hard

Vignier, beginning at about the time of the publication of his great *Bibliotheque Historiale* (Paris, 1587), remarking (f. 100r), "I submit it all to your judgment and discretion, asking you to be the father and patron." Fauchet's letter (vol. 490, f. 178r), published by Espiner-Scott (*Documents*, pp. 199-201), consists of twenty-two minute questions about early French history and ends by inquiring about the publication of Vignier's book. It may be added, since it has never been noticed, that one of Pithou's first clients was François Hotman, who was trying to recover his French fief at the time (letter of Hotman to Henri de Mesmes, 1 Jan. 1566, BN MSS, Fonds latins, vol. 10327, f. 143r).

[51] See Arbois de Jubainville, "Certificat donné à François Pithou par le recteur de l'Académie de Bâle, 13 mai 1573," *RHDFE*, II (1856), 178-79.

[52] Pithou, letter of 21 May 1576 (?), Collection Dupuy, vol. 700, f. 36r.

to distinguish between their labors. If François' edition of imperial novels (1576), dedicated to Pierre, was the result of independent study, his anonymous "Letter of a François," written for Henry of Navarre against Spanish pretensions, obviously leaned upon the materials Pierre was collecting for his treatise on the Gallican liberties.[53] Toward the study of the past in general, François took the same attitude as Pierre. He recommended the reading of ecclesiastical history above the fathers, and he emphasized the mutual dependence of law and history. "When you read a constitution or a decretal . . . ," he remarked elsewhere, "it is always necessary to see in history what was significant at that time." Among François' best works were his glossary to Pierre's collection of capitularies and his own annotated edition of the Salic law. For this work, he boasted, later ages would look upon him as a magician.[54] (Certainly, he was respected as a pioneer in the study of one of the most difficult of all medieval texts.) He continued to add to the Pithou library and to collect notes on the various interests of the king. He died in 1621, the last of this generation of antiquaries.

As for Pithou's old friend Loisel, he lived for another twenty years, pursuing the same scholarly objectives. Like Pithou, he had remained in contact with Cujas and had given him assistance, furnishing him, for example, with a manuscript for his edition of the Theodosian Code (1566). Loisel, too, was interested in institutional history, and made important investigations of the University of Paris, which also attracted the attention of Pithou and later Pasquier.[55]

---

[53] This *Lettre d'un François, sur certain discours faict n'agueres, pour la preseance du roi d'Hespagne,* printed with *Un traicté, de la grandeur, droits, preeminences, et prerogatives des roys et du royaume de France* (s. l., 1587) is a conventional Gallican pamphlet, based upon a wide range of legal and historical sources. Later in a letter to De Thou (Collection Dupuy, vol. 838, f. 135ʳ) he expressed his apprehension about publishing his Gallican materials and recalled the fate of Dumoulin. In another letter of 18 Nov. 1612 (f. 139ʳ) we see him hoping for a privilege for the vast "prouve des libertez de l'eglise gallicane—dressés par Monsieur Pithou mon frere . . .," but this did not appear until Dupuy took the initiative in 1639, and even then it caused a great stir. See n. 42.

[54] *Scaligerana,* II, 491.

[55] Loisel, *De l'Université de Paris* (Paris, 1587). His discussions of the Salic law and other legal topics appear in the *Divers opuscules.*

Except for polemical and rhetorical works, however, he published little, although he continued to collect material on civil, customary, and ecclesiastical law. It was only after Pithou's death that his major books appeared. Besides his biography of Pierre and his *Dialogue of the Advocate*, he published his great *Customary Institutes*, which was at least forty years in the making and which was based upon the same sort of omnivorous reading in literature as well as law as the work of Pithou.[56] Loisel's masterpiece was a compilation of the usages and proverbs which embodied French custom and perhaps national character as well. Like Pithou, Loisel also studied the antiquities of his own province and in 1616, just a year before his death, published his *Memoirs of Beauvais*.

This leaves the last and best of Pithou's (and Loisel's) friends, who ranged still more widely, though perhaps a bit more superficially, over the field of medieval studies. Étienne Pasquier, however, more fortunate than Pithou, was able to carry his monumental researches into his extreme old age. He and Loisel continued to exchange letters on various legal questions and on the delights of retirement. Pasquier had returned to his youthful interest in civil law, on which he was engaged in writing a commentary, and he discussed with Loisel the similarities and differences between Roman and French law. For his part, Loisel pretended to be converted to a cause which Pasquier had been urging upon him for many years, that is, the promotion of the vernacular:

> As, approaching the end, the old become young,
> So I substitute French for the old Latin tongue.[57]

In his *Dialogue,* in which Pasquier and François Pithou were the main speakers, Loisel celebrated not only the legist tradition, which he and Pithou had served so well, but also the scholarly enterprise which all

[56] Loisel, *Institutes coustumieres*, ed. M. Reulos (Paris, 1935) and *Mémoires ... de Beauvais et Beauvaisis* (Paris, 1617), both based upon the widest range of unpublished legal and historical material. Among other things Loisel was an amateur numismatist, as appears in Collection Dupuy, vol 667, f. 116^r.

[57] *Épitre d'Antoine Loisel à son ami Étienne Pasquier*, ed. A. Sorel (Arras, n. d.). In general, see E. Charvet, *Les dernières années de Antoine Loisel* (Beauvais, 1880).

of these men had undertaken a half-century before. It is appropriate that this crucial work should be named in honour of the best-known of this group, Pasquier. For if Pierre Pithou represents the scholarly level attained by this generation, Pasquier was the man who did most to transmit to posterity the findings of this scholarship and its significance.

CHAPTER X

The Rise of Medievalism: Etienne Pasquier Searches for a National Past

Nova res novum vocabulum flagitat.

Valla, *In Barptolomaeum Facium Ligurem invectiva*

"AS FOR ME, I have set myself to study the antiquities of France, and for this reason I have called my book the 'researches.' The enterprise is a great labor which requires the scanning of many old books. If you have anything on the subject, you would do me a great kindness by sending it to me."[1] This confession, made by Pasquier to Jacques Cujas in the late 1550s, may not be quite as dramatic as Gibbon's account of the decision he took while musing among the ruins of Rome; and yet, overlooking the bibliographical naïveté, it does have a comparable significance. For here we may see the launching of one of the most original and ambitious enterprises of Renaissance scholarship. It was fitting that the greatest of sixteenth-century historians, who himself owed so much to the historical school of law, should have begun by an appeal to the greatest of the legal humanists, though of course Pasquier's investigations ranged far more widely than those of Cujas. His book, almost sixty years in the making, was a compendium of monographs on all facets of French culture—an *Encyclopedia* if not a *Principia* of sixteenth-century historical thought. In its form, its self-consciousness, and its critical spirit it bore a remarkable resemblance to the "essays" of Pasquier's more famous friend, who likewise devoted his life to the investigation of a subject

[1] Pasquier, *Les Lettres* (Paris, 1619), II, 6 (I, 86).

close to the hearts of humanists. Pasquier, carrying on his own quest for self-knowledge, was indeed "the Montaigne of history."[2]

The Historian

Pasquier's aim was to write a "modern history." By this he did not mean conventional narrative, which smacked rather of pedantry than historical illumination (*plus de l'ombre des escholles que de la lumiere de l'histoire*). He meant the investigation of specific problems on the basis of first-hand evidence (*authoritez anciennes*), and his models were not historians like Livy or Paolo Emilio but philologists like Varro or Cujas.[3] His subject was the antiquities (*anciennetez*) and above all the government of France (*le faict de nostre police*). In this he included not only laws and institutions but also language and literature and certain "notable examples" neglected by chroniclers.

Pasquier had studied Roman law under several masters, including Baudouin, Hotman, Cujas, and Alciato, and by 1549 he had begun his legal career in the parlement of Paris. Yet unlike most of his colleagues, Pasquier was first impelled to the study of history by literary rather than legal motives. Like Budé, but with a wider perspective, he traced his intellectual pedigree back to the great Italian humanists. Petrach—whom Budé had ignored—had opened up the way while still living in an "age of barbarism," and he had been followed by such champions of classicism as Valla, Poggio, and especially Poliziano. Growing out of and at the same time transcending this tradition was the vernacularist movement. It was to this party, Pasquier told his old Greek teacher Turnèbe, that he had given his allegiance. To

---

[2] H. Baudrillart, *Étienne Pasquier, écrivain politique* (Paris, 1863), p. 25.

[3] Pasquier, *Les Recherches de la France* (Paris, 1633), I, introduction (p. 1). For the editions of this work see D. Thickett, *Bibliographie des œuvres d'Estienne Pasquier* (Geneva, 1956). The most useful studies are P. Bouteiller, "Un Historien du XVIe siècle, Étienne Pasquier," *BHR*, VI (1945), 19-27, and *Étienne Pasquier, sa vie et ses recherches sur l'orgainsation civile française* (Nogent-le-Rotrou, 1943); R. Bütler, *Nationales und universales Denken im Werke Étienne Pasquiers* (Basel, 1948); V. de Caprariis, *Propaganda*, I, 257 ff; A. Lemaire, *Les Lois fondamentales*, p. 86; and G. Huppert, "Naissance de l'histoire de France: les 'Recherches' d'Estienne Pasquier," *Annales*, XXIII (1968), 69-105, and especially his *The Idea of Perfect History* (Urbana, 1969), which also discusses Bodin, La Popelinière, Le Roy, and Vignier, though in a somewhat different context than the present work.

be French, he added, was to be "frank and free"—that is, of classical influence.[4] He displayed this independence not only in his *Researches* but also in his poems, his pamphlets, and his letters, which in his dedication to Loisel he contrasted specifically with the Latin epistles of such authors as Poliziano and Budé. According to Budé, French was not really fit for much except such vulgar subjects as the hunt; Pasquier wanted to welcome it also into law, history, and philosophy. By celebrating national culture in this explicit way, Pasquier practiced what Budé had only preached.

Unfortunately, like many another university graduate overstuffed with learning and opinions, Pasquier was a better critic and observer than he was an artist. Unable to emulate Montaigne, he could appreciate his wisdom and point out the provincialisms in his prose. Unable to emulate Ronsard, he could admire the ingenuity of his work and begin to place it in historical context.[5] In general, he found it hard to forget the habits of philology, and again like Budé he leaned more to lexicography than to literature. It became his mission to do for the vernacular what "in our times Erasmus, Budé, and Alciato" had been doing for the classical languages. "My imagination declining with age," he confessed to Pithou, "I began to investigate the antiquities of France, wherein I have had some small success."[6] So, after his marriage to one of his rich clients and after an illness that forced him to retire for a few months, he set to work on the Gallic and Frankish origins of French society; and in 1560 he published

---

[4] Pasquier, *Lettres*, I, 2 (I, 6, to Turnèbe, 1552), and I, 1 (I, 1, to Loisel, Jan. 1886); cf. *Recherches*, IX, 29 (p. 857). Budé had written letters in French but had declined to publish them. In general, see M. J. Moore, *Estienne Pasquier, historien de la poésie et de la langue françaises* (Poitiers, 1934); K. Voigt, *Estienne Pasquiers Stellung zur Pléiade* (Leipzig, 1902); L. Feugère, "Vie d'Étienne Pasquier" in his edition of *Œuvres choisies d'Étienne Pasquier* (Paris, 1849), I, vii-ccxxxviii; and D. Thickett, *The Letters of Étienne Pasquier* (unpubl. diss., London University, 1950). Some of Pasquier's letters have been edited critically with valuable annotations by D. Thickett: *Choix des lettres sur la littérature, la langue et la traduction* (Geneva, 1956) and *Lettres historiques pour les années 1556-1594* (Geneva, 1966); a third volume is in preparation.

[5] Pasquier, *Lettres*, II, 7 (I, 25, to Ronsard), and XVIII, 1 (II, 517).

[6] *Ibid.*, VIII, 1 (I, 497).

the first book of his *Researches of France*, dedicating it to the Cardinal of Lorraine. For the graces of poetry he substituted the faith of history (*foy historiale*), or rather, since he later became a pioneering historian of French language and literature, he managed to combine the two in a most original fashion.

Pasquier's second impulse came from his profession, to which he returned in 1560. In his view the *gens de justice* constituted practically a fourth estate, and he ranked the vocation of law just below that of religion.[7] What is more, his political conscience had been awakened by the disorders which followed the death of Henry II. As may be seen in his anonymous exhortation for peace in 1561, he looked with equal suspicion upon the "Romans" and the "Protestants." Like Baudouin, he set great store by the Colloquy of Poissy, in which his former friend Beza played such a negative role. It is not surprising that in the second book of his *Researches*, published in 1565, he should turn to the institutions of the French monarchy, especially to the parlement of Paris, which was not only his ideological home but, as the meeting ground between kingship and people, the basis of "all the grandeur of France."[8] Here Pasquier took up the familiar theme of the fortune and virtue (*conseil*) of France and predictably, decided that the latter was the more significant. This pioneering essay on the councils and offices of medieval France was widely used, or plundered, as Pasquier preferred to think, by historians of this generation. Although his essays continued to grow, fear of further plagiarism prevented him from publishing other parts of this book for over thirty years.

The natural drift of Pasquier's interests was accelerated by an episode which was as crucial for his professional as for his scholarly career. In 1564 he was chosen to represent the University of Paris in

[7] *Ibid.*, IX, 6 (I, 533).

[8] Pasquier, *Recherches*, II, 2 (p. 42). Cf. his *Exhortation aux princes* (1561) in *Écrits politiques*, ed. D. Thickett (Geneva, 1566), where Pasquier's authorship (denied on ideological grounds by Caprariis, *Propaganda*, p. 152, and Lecler, *Histoire de la tolérance*, II, 43) has been established beyond reasonable doubt. See also D. Thickett, "Estienne Pasquier and his part in the Struggle for Tolerance," *Aspects de la propaganda réligieuse* (Geneva, 1957), pp. 377-402. The ambiguities in Pasquier's position illustrate again the classic confusion of Gallicanism in the period of religious conflict.

its suit against the Jesuit order, which for over a decade had been seeking to establish a college in the city. Years before, Pasquier had learned much about the order from Loyola's companion, Pasquier Brouez, one of the leading Jesuits in France; and in his plea in 1565, which he printed in later editions of the *Researches*, he expressed the hope that "Pasquier" would be the name not only of the "first founder" but of the "first extirpator" of this sect.[9] It did not quite turn out this way. Yet if the plea was unsuccessful, it did further Pasquier's legal career, and it made him one of the most dedicated foes of this particular brand of ultramontanism for the next half-century. What is more relevant, it led him, in his third book, into a deeper investigation of the ecclesiastical institutions of France. In fact, he admitted, his dissertation on the Gallican tradition was basically "a summary of my plea." Naturally, his anti-Romanist views and his prescription for religious settlement spilled over into his researches. To a certain degree, then, Pasquier's interpretation of history, like Baudouin's and Dumoulin's, hinged upon, or at least was colored by, a stirring event in which he happened to become involved.

Pasquier's historical studies were profoundly affected by the civil wars, of which he was a close observer and, in his letters, one of the most reliable reporters. This generation of strife suggested to him a vast drama in five acts. "Mon Dieu!" he cried, "How I should like some Christian Livy among us to show with a bold pen how God has demonstrated His hidden power against the foresight of men."[10] Later he offered more specific advice to Jean de Serres, one of the claimants to this title. To the clash of extremes, "papist" against

---

[9] *Ibid.*, III, 43 (p. 320); cf. *Lettres*, IV, 24 (I, 259-66) and XXI, 1 (II, 626), and the account in De Thou, III, 543-44. See also P. Feret, "L'Université de Paris et les Jésuites dans la seconde moitié du XVIe siècle," *Revue des questions historiques*, XXXIII (1899), 455-97; F. Michaux, "Étienne Pasquier et les Jésuites," *Revue d'histoire littéraire de la France*, XXXIII (1926), 87-97, including certain critical annotations, made about 1607-13, in a copy of Pasquier's *Recherches* (Paris, 1607); and J. M. Prat, *Maldonat et l'Université de Paris au XVIe siècle* (Paris, 1856), pp. 108 ff. An "Advis de quelques célèbres Advocats en faveur de l'Université de Paris contre les Jésuites" (24 Mar. 1564), signed by Pasquier and others, was sent to Geneva (Bibliothèque publique et universitaire, MSS français, vol. 406, ff. 5r-7r).

[10] Pasquier, *Lettres*, IV, 14 (I, 216); X, 6 (I, 265); and XV, 18 (II, 211-16, to De Serres).

"Huguenot," Pasquier attributed all the ills of modern France, comparing it to the struggles of Guelph and Ghibelline and the Wars of the Roses. His own remedy was "to take refuge in the ancient principle of the Gallican church." For Pasquier as for Loisel, this meant living "united in one king, one faith, one law"; but bitter experience led him to set his sights lower.[11] The most he hoped for was a kind of peaceful coexistence, guaranteed by a mutual abstention from entangling alliances, and even in this he was disappointed. In general, the lessons of the religious wars gave Pasquier a sense of tragedy as well as a sense of history. Like Montaigne, he grew increasingly relativistic and aware of historical change.

The denouement of the drama witnessed by Pasquier came with the crisis of 1588. Attending the Estates General of Blois, he wrote to Pithou, "I fear that all these orations are, like the swan's song, the prognostic of our monarchy's ruin."[12] By this time Pasquier had attained the dignity of *avocat général* in the *chambre des comptes*, but he backed the parlement in its opposition to the League. In 1589 he joined the king and the government in Tours, and he shifted his allegiance to Henry IV immediately after the death of Henry III. In an anonymous pamphlet he attacked the "assassins" of his old friend Brisson, who had been executed by the League in 1591—hanged with a sign designating him "chief of the heretics and politiques."[13] He rejoiced at the restoration of Henry IV and at the appointment of Pithou and Loisel to high office, and he soon joined them in Paris. Although he did not cease his legal and polemical activities, he was at last able to return to his *Researches*, of which he published six more books in 1596. He retired from his office in 1604 and continued to work on his masterpiece until his death in 1615. Six years later this book, the greatest monument to sixteenth-century French historical scholarship, appeared in its final form.

[11] *Ibid.*, VI, 1 (I, 154, to Sainte-Marthe), and *Écrits politiques*, p. 40.

[12] *Ibid.*, XIII, 7 (II, 50, to Pithou); cf. *Advis au roy* (1588) in *Écrits politiques*, pp. 99 ff.

[13] *Ibid.*, XVII, 1 (II, 306, to Sainte-Marthe). Cf. L'Estoile (Henry IV), I, 137, and P. Gambier, *Le Président Barnabé Brisson* (Paris, 1957). *Lettres*, XV, 3 (II, 192), is a joint letter to Pithou and Loisel "at the parlement reestablished in Paris."

Like Pithou, Pasquier had a large circle of correspondents—patrons, friends, supplicants, satellites—and of course it included many of the same people. Among these was his chief rival Claude Fauchet, a year younger and also a native Parisian. The two men probably met in 1550, when Fauchet was just back from Orleans with his law degree, and when Pasquier was starting out in practice.[14] Fauchet, too, attained high office—president of the *cour des monnaies*, a position which he lost and then, with the help of Pasquier, recovered after the civil wars. Their researches had begun at about the same time and followed a remarkably similar, though largely independent, course. Both were on friendly terms with the Pléiade, both contributed to the defense of the Gallican liberties, and both wrote on the history of French institutions, language, and literature. Fauchet's treatises on these subjects were published before, though in most cases they were written after, the corresponding sections of Pasquier's *Researches,* and a comparison of the two is unavoidable. As a historian, especially in his *French Antiquities,* Fauchet was at once more thorough and more conventional, partly because he was not so deeply involved in contemporary politics. In general, Pasquier was the more original of the two and more concerned with the history of law and institutions.

Another of Pasquier's correspondents was Pierre Ayrault, who had been a pupil of Cujas as well as a friend of Baudouin and Pithou. With Pasquier he shared a deep aversion for the Jesuits, who in 1586 had accepted his son René without parental consent. As they had subverted the state, he charged, so they were subverting the family. But between these two advocates, who had known each other since youth, there were still closer ties. In 1568 Ayrault sent Pasquier his "Angevin fruits," that is, his *Judicial Order and Instruction,* a work as remarkable for its comparative approach as for its erudition. The similarity between Ayrault's and Pasquier's views appears not only in this book but in his *Origin and Authority of Judgments,* and especially in an early essay called "The Variety and Mutation of Laws."[15]

---

[14] *Ibid.,* XIV, 14 (II, 180). See J. G. Espiner-Scott, *Claude Fauchet,* pp. 66 ff, and especially, "Claude Fauchet et Etienne Pasquier," *HR,* VI (1939), 352-60.

[15] *Ibid.,* XI, 7 (I, 695-96); see ch. VII, n. 59. Baudouin is mentioned as a

These works showed Ayrault as a scholar with a great distrust for the static formulas of conventional law and with a strong bent for an historical approach. Even more conspicuously than Pasquier and Le Caron, he illustrates the attitude of relativism, geographic as well as historical, which was becoming so common among jurists during the civil wars.

The work of these men—and that of Pithou's circle discussed previously—cannot be entirely disengaged from Pasquier's, which indeed it may serve to enhance and in some respects to amplify. After all, they were all committed to the same ambitious enterprise, which was nothing less than to recreate the past of French society and culture; and they worked in such close cooperation—and competition—that it is often useless to try to assign priority for particular discoveries or conclusions. It is almost better to regard their achievements, like those of the legists, as a corporate product. Yet in this constellation of scholars Pasquier was clearly the leading light. More consciously than the others, he understood that the job was one of synthesis, of putting together the disparate and disjointed efforts of several generations of scholarship. He understood, too, who his true predecessors were: not the historians but the philologists, especially the legal humanists (*docteurs humanistes*, he called them), and the legists (*avocats du roi*). He shared the linguistic presumptions and critical methods of the one, and the professional habits and national commitments of the other. These were the principal forces that shaped the image of French history which appears in Pasquier's *Researches* and, more dimly, in the work of his colleagues.

History of Language

In the beginning—for Pasquier as for Valla, Budé, and other devotees of philology—was the word: sooner or later all of Pasquier's thoughts

---

fellow *maître des requêtes* in the *hôtel* of Anjou by Ayrault, *Plaidoyers et arrests, opuscules et divers traictez* (Paris, 1615), p. 85. On Ayrault, besides the works cited in Cioranesco, see the article in *Dictionnaire de biographie française*. Other correspondents of Pasquier encountered in this book include Pithou, Loisel, Brisson, De Thou, Choppin, La Croix du Maine, Basmaison, De Serres, Juret, Pibrac, Postel and Ramus.

about human history seemed to return to his conception of language. He, too, was an amateur lexicographer and often cast his analyses in the form of commentaries on particular terms or phrases. Although he did not neglect interesting or instructive stories, he was much more concerned with the symbolic world of man's creation. The specific object of his search was the genius of France—*esprit* was his word— and ultimately he found the most concrete manifestation of this in the discourse of men. Consciously or not, therefore, he preserved the epistemological premises of scholarship which Valla had expressed so pointedly and which had become an integral part of historical method. Yet Pasquier had a much deeper awareness of the variety and instability of language. "Everyone believes that the vulgar language of his own time is most perfect," he remarked, "and everyone is deceived in this." What is more, Pasquier admitted, language was the source of most disputes, misunderstandings, and even heresies.[16] Like positive law, he thought, it seemed to be the product not of reason but of a "vague and fluctuating opinion." To Pasquier, as to Budé, this was a depressing idea, but it is precisely why he attached so much importance to philology. It was in language, he assumed, that the substance of human reality was best revealed.

Like his humanist forebears, Pasquier found the concept of style of fundamental significance for the study of human culture, although again his vernacularist orientation led him to transcend the conventions of classical scholarship. To him style was not merely a standard of taste or even a tool of analysis but also a means of identifying the peculiarities of local and national character.

Languages normally coincide with the disposition of our spirits in particular as well as in general. For if you inquire into the particular, you will not easily find a man brusk in manner who is not so in speech as well, and few melancholy persons who do not speak sadly. So with the general: among the French you see the cautious Norman guarded also in his speech; and the other hand the open Gascon speaking freely ...; the arrogant Spaniard creating a proud and ceremonious vernacular; the

---

[16] Pasquier, *Recherches*, VIII, 3 (p. 684); cf. *Lettres*, X, 1 (I, 598). In general, see my "Legal Humanism and the Sense of History," *SR*, XIII (1966), 184-99.

Germans, deprived of luxury, a very rude language; and the Italians, having degenerated from ancient Roman virtue . . ., a soft and effeminate vernacular.

It was an axiom of Pasquier's historical thought, in short, that human culture was the product not of a universal logos but of a Tower of Babel. If he expressed this in the popular terms of medio-geographical lore, it was grounded in the experience of language, and it offered a concrete means of investigating cultural variation.

For Pasquier style was not only an expression of social character, it was also an indicator of historical change. On the lowest level this meant simply the appearance of new terms, a process which he regarded as both natural and necessary. "In my time," he remarked, "I have seen come into use many words not sanctioned by our predecessors [*devanciers*]; perhaps the word *devancier* itself." [18] The term *avant-propos*, to take a trivial example, he found to have been introduced by his friend Le Caron. Like Budé, Pasquier looked with more distrust upon anachronisms or foreign imports than neologisms. So he chided Loisel for the excessive classical embellishments in his orations, comparing his style to the pseudo-antique Sainte-Chapelle, and with Henri Estienne he objected to the Italianizing of the French language as unnatural.

"As all things human," Louis le Roy once remarked, languages have a beginning, progress . . ., corruption, end." [19] A commonplace observation, no doubt, and yet it acquired new meaning with the growing interest in comparative and historical linguistics by such men as Pasquier, Estienne, Du Bellay, and Fauchet. Pasquier himself was aware not only of the temporal mutability of language but also of the curious problems of intermixture. In general, he recognized two kinds of change. "The first . . . originates in our character, such that according to the diversity of the times . . . languages change by accumulated deposit. . . . Besides this mutation, there is another which some call

---

[17] *Ibid.*, VIII, 1 (p. 675).

[18] *Recherches*, VIII, 3 (p. 682). Cf. ch. IV, n. 42.

[19] Le Roy, *Vicissitude des choses*, p. 47. Like Pasquier, Le Roy was fascinated with problems of translation and with what Leo Spitzer has called "historical semantics."

corruption, when a nation is subjugated by force of arms."[20] This opinion was seconded by Fauchet, who had in mind the examples of the Gauls and the Franks. The most significant cause of mutation, in his view, "comes from the change of lordship or location, as when a people is forced to accept a new master in their land and to live under new laws." There is at least an implication here that linguistic purity was a function of national independence.

Pasquier's sense of the mutability of language, derived from philological tradition, was intensified by his life-long interest in the problems of translation. He moved a great distance from the conventional belief of Leonardo Bruni that "nothing can be said in Greek that cannot be said in Latin."[21] Not only did he deny that classical Latin was the best of all possible media, he suggested that there could be no single permanent standard. In a letter to Cujas he illustrated the fact of linguistic change by referring to an old translation of the Code, which Loisel had borrowed and showed to Cujas. Although such translations were well enough done according to the sense of their age (*selon la portee de leurs siecles*), he argued, they were bound to lose much of their value. "One's language changes gradually in such a way that it is as if one had bought a new coat and does not want to wear the old one."[22] Even the ancients had been aware of this. In general, according to the scheme of Crinito adopted by Pasquier, Latin itself had passed through four or five stages ending in "decadent" Italian. "I do not doubt," Pasquier added, "that the same has happened to our French, which has assumed different forms according to the diversity of the ages."[23]

This process was not reversible, of course, but Pasquier was happy to find that in his age the French language was reaching the height

[20] Pasquier, *Recherches*, VIII, 1 (p. 675). Cf. Fauchet, *Recueil de l'origine de la langue et poesie françoise*, in *Œuvres* (Paris, 1610), f. 534ᵛ (also in the critical edition of Espiner-Scott).

[21] Leonardo Bruni, "De Interpretatione recta," *Humanistisch-philosophische Schriften*, ed. H. Baron (Leipzig, 1928), p. 95. The significance of this genre for the history of ideas was pointed out by Wilhelm Dilthey in his fundamental study, "Die Entstehung der Hermaneutik," in *Gesammelte Schriften*, V, 334.

[22] Pasquier, *Lettres*, II, 6 (I, 84-85).

[23] Pasquier, *Recherches*, VIII, 3 (p. 680); cf. ch. II, n. 68.

of its powers. As early as the fourteenth century it had begun "to cast off its ancient crudity," as could be seen not only in the scholarly prose of Nicolas Oresme but in the registers of the *chambre des comptes*. A century and more after this, in the writing of Commines and Seyssel, it found "a purity which was beginning to approximate that of our own day." Pasquier agreed with Du Bellay that "it was impossible to equal the ancients in their languages."[24] He even admitted that French, which developed under a monarchical form of government, lacked the plenitude of Latin, which had grown to serve the forensic needs of a republic; but French, which was still in its youthful vigor, was clearly superior in other respects. Pasquier's interpretation of the history of language inevitably placed him in the party of the moderns. This was another way, of course, of declaring the superiority of French culture in general.

Underlying Pasquier's conception of language was an assumption, which Valla and Budé had also made, that there were analogies and presumably connections between verbal discourse and the visual arts (as recognized by the classical topos, *ut pictura poesis*), and beyond that with law and even public morality. This was inherent in Le Roy's grand thesis (suggested by Budé) of a universal "concurrence of arms and letters," which he tried to document in his *Vicissitude of Things*. It was inherent, too, in the old notion of a "translation of studies" accompanying the "translation of empire," a view which was still popular in the sixteenth century, although in a characteristically expanded form. As Gaillard wrote, "Among our kings Charlemagne was not more a lover of arms than a promoter of letters, which, having originated among the Hebrews, thence came to the Ethiopians and Egyptions, next to the Lydians and Chaldeans, then to the Greeks, Romans, Arabs, French, Germans, English, Poles. . . ."[25] Pasquier

---

[24] Joachim du Bellay, *La Défense et illustration de la langue française*, ed. L. Séché (Paris, 1905), ch. XI; cf. Pasquier, *Lettres*, I, 2 (I, 6), repeating many of the same arguments.

[25] Gaillard, *Methode*, p. 235. This popular topos, best known in the lines of Chrétien de Troyes (*Cligés*, 27 ff), appeared also in the preface to the *Grans croniques de France, dites croniques de S. Denis* (Paris, 1835), I, 4-5, though in the more restricted medieval form: "In the city of Athens philosophy formerly resided and in Greece the flower of chivalry; from Greece they came to

himself, who was critical of the various legends surrounding Charlemagne, did not indulge in speculation about this grand old myth; but it is evident that he adopted, at least as a working hypothesis, the notion of a vital connection between cultural phenomena and the political condition of a nation. It is this notion that accounts for the constancy of Pasquier's purpose and, if only in his own mind, the organic form of his *Researches*. It accounts also for the fact that he came closer than anyone to realizing La Popelinière's ideal of including "the origin, progress, and change of the arts and sciences" as well as the organization of society, though as usual his contributions were concrete rather than formal.[26] They emerge most clearly in the correlations which he found between language and the subject which most occupied him—the institutions and social structure of the French monarchy.

History of Law

Laws are subject to the same kind of change as language, though with graver consequences. The anachronisms and anomalies of Roman law were quite as familiar to Pasquier as to Cujas. He pointed to the increase of princely power, for example, though he dismissed Ulpian's famous formula of absolutism (*quod principi placuit legis habet vigorem*) as an uncharacteristic piece of flattery designed for the emperor, to the striking conflicts of judicial opinion (the *responsa prudentum*), and to the uneven influence of Christian doctrine. Tribonian, of course, had only made things worse; and according to Pasquier, "The Digest is a *pesle-mesle* of jurists . . . , the Code a *pesle-mesle* of disconnected ordinances."[27] In general, the Byzantine collection illustrated not only the degeneration of Roman jurisprudence but also the corruption of Latin elegance. Then as today, declared

---

Rome; from Rome they came to France, where God grant they shall long remain." See the discussions of E. Gilson, *Les Idées et les lettres* (Paris, 1932), pp. 183-85; E. Curtius, *European Literature and the Latin Middle Ages*, trans. W. Trask (New York, 1948), pp. 384-85; and P. Renucci, *L'Aventure de l'humanisme au moyen âge* (Paris, 1953), pp. 134 ff.

[26] La Popelinière, *Idee de l'histoire*, pp. 269 ff.

[27] Pasquier, *Lettres*, XIX, 12 (II, 516). There is a much more extended discussion in his *Interprétation des Institutes de Justinian*, ed. M. le duc Pasquier (Paris, 1847), I, 26 ff.

Le Caron, whose views were quite in accord with Pasquier's, Justinian's collection "generated contradictory and repugnant interpretations and thereby a labyrinth of litigation."[28] Here again sounds the anti-Tribonianist theme. "It is impossible to say," concluded Pasquier, "how many faces the laws of Rome have taken according to the diversity of the times."[29]

These are the words of a conventional legal humanist. What really interested Pasquier, however, was the after-life of Roman law—not its value as a source for ancient history but its posthumous effects upon modern European society. Since the Roman conquest, he wrote, "we in France form [our laws] in a generally Roman spirit," at least in the provinces of written law.[30] Yet it was mainly through the universities that ancient Roman law was "naturalized" in France, and Pasquier claimed to be the first to describe this phenomenon. In much the same way as contemporary scholars, he divided the modern study of civil law into three stages. First came the "glossators," including the reputed founding father, Irnerius, and Placentinus, who introduced civil law into France. Although Montpellier was the first center, leadership was soon taken over by the universities of Orleans and Toulouse, especially after the teaching of civil law was forbidden in Paris. Next were the "doctors of law," or "scribentes" (so-called because of their productivity), including Placentinus' disciple Accursius, Guillaume Durandus, Bartolus, and a whole school of "Italian doctors," whose output staggered Pasquier.[31] He marvelled at the famous collection published in Venice in 1583, containing twenty-five volumes, each larger than the Code with its accompanying gloss. The methods of this "Bartholiste" school were adopted by all the law faculties in France, which Pasquier went on to survey one by one. Finally, in his own century there arose the "new jurisprudence" founded by the "humanist doctors."

[28] Le Caron, *Pandectes du droit françois,* f. 35ᵛ.
[29] Pasquier, *Interprétation des Institutes,* I, 481.
[30] *Ibid.,* I, 64, though he pointed out (p. 30) that the principal "sources" of French law were the ordinances, the customs, and the *arrêts* of the parlement, while Roman law formally provided only certain useful maxims. Cf. *Lettres,* XIX, 15 (II, 523).
[31] *Recherches,* IX, 34-41 (pp. 881-910), referring to *Tractatus.*

Although Pasquier was unusually conscious of the continuing influence of Justinian's legislation before the twelfth century, he repeated the "fairy tale" (as Haskins was to call it) of the miraculous recovery of a unique manuscript of the Digest by the Pisans in their capture of Amalfi. After Pisa itself was taken by Florence in 1406, this manuscript of the "Pandects," as it was now called, found its way into the library of the Medici. It was the study of this monument that brought about the "third age" of modern jurisprudence dominated by that great triumvirate of Budé, Alciato, and Zasius, and the later scholars who "followed with great honor the trail of our Budé." Of these, Pasquier added, the greatest was Cujas. Presenting a list of his friends and colleagues who belonged in this school, including Le Caron and Ayrault, Pasquier concluded with satisfaction that "the true center of this new jurisprudence is our France."[32]

The consensus of Pasquier and his colleagues was that the effects of written law in France had been profound and, on the whole, pernicious. This opinion reflected both the humanist prejudices against scholastic jurisprudence and the legist suspicions of the "emperor's law." Most disturbing were the absolutist tendencies of Roman law, and while Pasquier did not want to deny that in a sense the prince was above the law (*legibus solutus*), he insisted that it was "not necessary to take this phrase cruelly."[33] "Not what pleases the prince," was Ayrault's emendation, "but what best and lawfully pleases the prince." Roman private law, too, had distasteful features. Like Hotman, Pasquier contrasted the patriarchal power (*patria potestas*) and preference for testamentary succession with the French concern for the integrity of family property, the Roman penchant for litigation with the simplicity of French custom. Here the favorite image was St Louis personally dispensing justice beneath the oaks in Vincennes. "The subtlety of Roman law has so changed and corrupted the simplicity of ancient French law," Le Caron charged, "that it only produces new suits and diverse interpretations of Roman law."[34] More

[32] *Ibid.*, IX, 39 (pp. 900-2).
[33] Pasquier, *Interprétation des Institutes*, I, 26. Cf. Ayrault, *De Origine et auctoritate rerum judicatum* (Paris, 1573), a 7ᵛ.
[34] Le Caron, *Pandectes du droit françois*, f. 11ᵛ, citing the famous line of Juvenal (Satire VII, 148), "Gallia ... nutricula causidicorum. ..."

than a lament for lost purity, this evaluation of Roman law became a basic principle of the interpretation of French history in the later middle ages.

How had French society become infected with this alien tradition in modern times? Like most French jurists, not caring to distinguish carefully between civil and canon law, Pasquier placed more blame upon the ecclesiastical courts than upon the universities. The real culprit (*la source premiere de tous maux*) was the Avignonese papacy, which had brought with it those twin scourges, political absolutism and judicial anarchy. In a letter to Choppin, he referred to the famous verse of Pibrac for a condemnation of those canonist formulas of arbitrary rule (*plenitude potestatis* and *de motu proprio*). The latter idea in particular (*propre mouvement*), which involved arbitrary transference of jurisdiction, Pasquier attacked as "not a French but an Italian invention which we owe to the Roman curialists who came to live in the city of Avignon."[35] "It is from there that we have learned chicanery," declared Loisel, and in L'Hôpital's experience this was "the opinion of most modern historians, Italian as well as French."[36] So, according to Pasquier, who "hated nothing more than chicanery," the fortunes of France were once again linked with those of Italy. Out of the Babylonian Captivity there emerged a continuous stream of complaints about the venality of offices and of justice, about unnecessary litigation, and about encroachments upon the estate of the king. By the sixteenth century it could again be said that France was "the nursing mother of solicitors," if not that surrealistic land of the *chicanous* derided by Rabelais.

A number of irresistible pressures—the Gallican tradition, the passions generated by the religious wars, and his own polemical enthusiasms—confirmed Pasquier in his opinion. The ultramontane thrust of the papacy, carrying with it a wave of Italian office-seekers and propagandists, seemed in some ways to recreate the conditions of the fourteenth century. The symbol as well as the scapegoat of this in-

---

[35] Pasquier, *Lettres*, VI, 2 (I, 363-65), and Pibrac, *Les Quatrains* (Bern, 1642), XCIII. Cf. *Recherches*, III, 14 (p. 208 ff), and II, 4 (p. 60).

[36] Loisel, *Pasquier*, p. 37; and L'Hôpital, *Traité de la réformation de la justice* (Paris, 1825), I, 321.

vasion was the Jesuit order, on which Pasquier had cut his legal teeth, and from which he derived his most profound insight into the crisis of his age. Like Dumoulin, whom he much admired, Pasquier found the Roman and the Reformed parties equally guilty. But ultimately, it seemed, Loyola's error was more dangerous than Luther's. "In 1565," he recalled with some satisfaction, "it occurred to me to say that the Jesuits would open the door to troubles in France between Roman and French Catholics. . . . Later I saw that the Jesuits, who were the prime instigators of our troubles in 1585, had not given the lie to my prediction." [37] Having discussed the origins of the Jesuits in his plea of 1565, Pasquier returned to a more systematic and up-to-date attack in his *Jesuits' Catechism* of 1602 and then again four years later in his *Researches*, for which he was reviled as a Huguenot and a "libertine."

But of course the Jesuits were, to Pasquier, merely part of a larger Romanist syndrome—one strand in a vast pattern of aggression, in which he found places also for the Tridentine decrees, the *fuorusciti*, the fallacies of "Machiavellianism," [38] and papal policy on behalf of the League. One did not have to be a "rebel" like Hotman to accept this diagnosis; it attracted loyal Gallicans as well. In Pasquier's eyes Italian villainy was all of a piece—the shadow cast by a great cultural edifice quite alien to Frenchmen. But Pasquier's anti-Italian prejudices, which continually lurk just beyond his purview of history, did not answer the essential questions: what was the pattern and what was the provenance of French culture?

[37] Pasquier, *Recherches*, III, 44 (p. 315). Cf. *Catechisme des Jesuites* (Paris, 1602), which appeared anonymously and was translated the same year into English. The best-known reply to Pasquier was Garasse's *Les Recherches des recherches* (Paris, 1622), which stigmatized Pasquier (p. 126) as "a libertine, which means a Huguenot and a half," and also as a *gaulois*.

[38] "Machiavelizer" and "Machiavelliste" are words applied by Pasquier, e.g., *Lettres*, IX, 7 (I, 540), notably to the Jesuits or, as in *Lettres*, XII, 9 (I, 827), to the Catholic League. See Caprariis, *Propaganda*, pp. 286 ff. According to Warburg, this is the earliest usage.

History of Culture

Pasquier's mission as a historian was to establish the independence of French tradition on all levels, but it was in the fields of law and language that the configurations of French culture emerged most clearly. The most conspicuous illustration of this was in Pasquier's contribution to the old Ciceronianist controversy, which by his time had a vernacular as well as a classical side. Everyone remembered how Erasmus had ridiculed those pedants, Italians for the most part, who blindly applied a classical vocabulary to contemporary society and institutions. In just this way, indeed in Erasmus' very words, Du Bellay rebuked those who "fondly dream of the conscript fathers, the tribunes . . . and all of ancient Rome." [39] This was precisely the point Pasquier pressed upon the classicist Turnèbe:

> I suggest to you that since the Romans were under a popular government and we are under a monarchy . . ., our administration has nothing in common with theirs. For these words "senate," "senator," "consul," "tribune" . . . which are taken from a democracy . . . cause us, while speaking French, to Latinize. I mean that they do not contribute to the edification of the French, not brought up according to the laws and manners of the Romans.[40]

A more legalistic version of this argument was expressed by Le Caron: "One should not compare French magistrates and their jurisdictions to the laws and manners of the Romans . . . any more than the interpretations, sentences, and decisions of the [Roman] jurists should be accepted as law in France." [41]

These views, in close accord with Hotman's anti-Tribonianism, resulted from the convergence of humanism and the doctrine of the legists and pointed clearly to the growing national orientation of historical thought. "It is high time," Pasquier wrote Brisson, congratulating him on his *Code of Henry III,* "that we rid ourselves of that stupid notion . . . by which we trample under foot the true and

---

[39] Du Bellay, *La Défense et illustration,* ch. XI. Cf. Erasmus, *Ciceronianus,* in *Opera omnia* (Leiden, 1703), I, col. 992. See ch. II, n. 37.

[40] Pasquier, *Lettres,* XI, 6 (I, 689-90, to Turnèbe).

[41] Le Caron, *Pandectes du droit françois,* p. 17.

primitive laws of France and reduce all our judgments to those of the Romans. . . . God wished to separate us from Italy by a high thrust of mountains, so He separated us in all things, in manners, in laws, character, humors." [42] This was the ultimate source of the principle that, as Le Caron put it to Charles IX, "you are subject to the laws neither of the Greeks nor of the Romans, and your magistrates do not apply them except in so far as they find them reasonable." This warning could easily be rephrased for the benefit of historians, and so Le Caron did in another place: "Frenchmen, you have enough examples in your history without searching those of the Greeks and the Romans." [43] This is an appropriate epitaph for Pasquier's *Researches*.

It was Pasquier's conviction that, despite the infiltrations of Romanism, there remained in French society native traditions more vital and more deeply rooted. Even in the provinces of written law, he argued, Roman law was "common law" not in the sense of having more general validity than specific customs, as the Bartolists held, but as a last resort in the absence of any customary rule. Much superior, he thought, was the practice in the provinces of customary law, where social context was a prime consideration. "Since customs were formed gradually in each province according to the diversity of our characters," Pasquier explained, "it seems appropriate in case of obscurity or doubt to have recourse to people close to us, who by their proximity would seem to conform to [*symbolisent*] our manners and character and so to our customs." [44] In one sense this reflected the old principle of territoriality (*locus regit actum*) enforcing local jurisdiction; more significantly it illustrated the view, common to French lawyers and historians, that law was an expression of as well as a means of controlling social behavior. From a historical point of view, laws were not a gift of God or a product of reason but an outgrowth of custom.

[42] Pasquier, *Lettres*, IX, 1 (I, 515-16, to Brisson), going on, in anti-Tribonianist fashion, to particularize the differences between Roman and French private law. Cf. *Interprétation des Institutes*, I, 490 ff.

[43] Le Caron, *Responses et decisions, avant-propos*, and *Panegyrique . . . au roy Charles VIIII* (Paris, 1566), f. d 3ʳ.

[44] Pasquier, *Lettres*, IX, 1 (I, 522), and XIX, 15 (II, 527). "Experience has shown," remarked Le Caron (*Responses et decisions*, p. 34), "that . . . custom is the corrector of laws" (*usus legum corrector*).

What lies at the root of this argument is not only an understanding of the vagaries of feudal law but also a profound realization of the geographic relativity of laws and customs. "The diversity of laws is due to the diversity of manners which arises in people according to the diversity of regions and environment [*air*]," wrote Pasquier, "and just as a doctor changes the remedy for patients with regard to countries, ages, and complexions, so the wise legislator acts toward the people he governs." [45] So Christofle de Thou had reputedly done in his campaign to reform customs, which was carried out not by royal fiat but by consent of the local estates. In a work dedicated to De Thou, Ayrault compared the legislator to a painter, who tried to make his creation resemble nature. Climate and environment were as important as reason itself. "In republics," he remarked elsewhere, "one does not always consider what is just in itself, but the state, which preserves itself here in one way, there in another." [46] From here it is not far to the kind of moral relativism seen in Montaigne or Le Roy, who, considering the troubles of the civil wars, lamented that "what is good in one time is bad in another, what is respected in one religion is scorned in another, what is holy here is profane there. . . ." Yet he, too, sought a rational, or at least an empirical, explanation. "Let us understand the difference of things," he demanded, "in terms of the differences of places." [47] Such was the basis of that crude social

---

[45] *Ibid.*, XIX, 7 (II, 465). Pasquier was also a student of English law, for it was he who showed his copy of Littleton to the unappreciative Hotman (*Commentarius de verbis feudalibus*, in *Operum*, II, 913).

[46] Pierre Ayrault, "Discours de la nature, varieté, et mutation des loix," in F. Grimaudet, *Paraphrase du droict de retraict lignager* (Paris, 1567), f. bb iv^v; also f. aa ii^r: "Men live in all countries but not by the same food and nourishment; likewise there is no place where they are not ruled and policed by laws, constitutions, and customs, but not by the same or similar laws or customs; and what is more, with regard to atmosphere [*aër*], which fills all things . . ., this also is not in all countries as soft, subtle . . . and composed equally of the four seasons as it is in our France or under some other climate." Even this, he added (f. a iii^r) is subject to a kind of translation: "by this vicissitude, commutation, and conversion of all things, including republics and languages, the atmosphere itself, in a manner of speaking, is transported from one place to another, changing its habitat." Cf. *De l'Ordre et instruction judiciaire* (Paris, 1576), f. 29^r.

[47] Le Roy, *Des Différences et troubles*, p. 21, and *Vicissitude des choses*, f. 15^r.

science which he and Bodin toyed with and which Montesquieu developed systematically. But these ideas were at least as useful, it would seem, for historical scholarship.

The fundamental trait of Pasquier's historical thinking and that of his confreres was not their adherence to a particular theory or ideology but their total commitment to the values of quantitative erudition. Whatever might be appropriate for an understanding of nature, human culture was accessible only through concrete investigation of specific texts and monuments. An understanding of law, as of language, came only after laborious experience (*usus docendi magister*); for in historical terms, as Ayrault argued, law was not a manifestation of reason but the accumulation of many human judgments (*res judicatae*).[48] Valla's mottos, therefore—back to the sources, back to particular things—they put into practice with a vengeance. Like Valla, too, Pasquier and his friends had an ingrained distrust of philosophic categories, of the short-cuts and blind alleys of scholasticism. As a consequence, though they were not entirely conscious of it, they operated in terms of their own kind of "anti-philosophy," which justified their labors, or at least allowed them to go about their work undisturbed.

The Spirit of France

In order to grasp the individuality of French society it was not enough, of course, simply to invoke the impressionistic formulas of ancient geography, astrology, and medicine. Ultimately, the character of France stemmed from its unique origin and the peculiar trajectory of its fortune. On the question of origins, Pasquier at first attached primary significance to the Celtic antecedents of French culture. At this time, moved by the Celtic renaissance that marked the middle years of the century, Pasquier seemed to be as concerned with literary honor as with historical knowledge. Taking off from Du Bellay's *Defense and Illustration*, he sought to show that the ancient Gauls were in no sense "barbarians," nor were they unstable (*leger*) in

---

[48] Ayrault, *De Origine et auctoritate rerum judicatum*, f. a 4ᵛ, *passim*. See the discussion of R. Filhol, *Le Premier Président Christofle de Thou*, pp. 127 ff; also ch. IV, n. 56.

character. He took great pleasure in opposing the authority of Caesar to the opinions of Livy and of such contemporary writers as Crinito and Paolo Emilio, who, though a national historian of France, was solicitous neither of national honor (*la gloire de son pays*) nor of historical truth (*la verité historiale*).[49] In particular, Pasquier showed how the Gauls had anticipated modern parlements and even the provincial sessions (*les grands jours*). Although they had been careless about leaving a record of their accomplishments, they had, quite independently of Greece and Rome, cultivated good letters from ancient times.

Complementing the Celtic heritage was that of the Franks, whose legacy Pasquier came increasingly to appreciate, although he never became a "Germanist" like Hotman. While at first he suggested that the Franks were drawn southward by a Gallic fate (*induit par une destinee gauloise*), he never agreed with Connan that the Franks were related to the Gauls. Nor did it take him long to reject the theory of Trojan origins, which lacked all positive substantiation and was only too patently a literary fabrication. In any case, the Germanic origin of the Franks could be shown through their similarity with Tacitus' ancient Germans and, still more satisfactorily, through philological evidence based upon place and family names and such characteristic offices as the "mareschal." The major contribution of the Franks to modern French character is indicated by their name, derived "from the liberty and franchise which they showed in their spirits."[50] Here Pasquier was repeating arguments long familiar to German historians and increasingly popular among French scholars of his own generation, including Du Tillet, Hotman, and his friends Fauchet and "the learned Nicolas Vignier."

[49] Pasquier, *Recherches*, I, 2-4 (pp. 6-15); cf. Du Bellay, *La Défense et illustration*, ch. II. Petrarch also complained of the *gallica levitas* (see Simone, *Il Rinascimento francese*, p. 14). See G. de Bremond d'Ars, "Un Gaulois de la renaissance, Étienne Pasquier," *Revue des deux mondes*, 1888 (no. 3), pp. 177-202. There is no study of this Celtic renaissance, though there are some observations in H. Gillot, *La Querelle des anciens et des modernes en France* (Paris, 1914), pp. 132 ff. See ch. VIII, n. 36.

[50] Pasquier, *Recherches*, I, 6 (p. 17) and 14 (p. 37). Cf. Vignier, *Traicté de l'estat et origine des anciens françois* (Troyes, 1582) and La Popelinière, *Idee de l'histoire*, pp. 401 ff ("Le Dessein de l'histoire nouvelle des françois").

On the whole, Pasquier did not take much stock in questions of ultimate origins. Rather than speculate about prehistory he preferred to describe the various national groups that had gone into the making of French society. Fauchet, too, would rather "leave aside these remote matters, fabulous because of their antiquity," although he did, very apologetically, include certain philological digressions in order to throw light upon problems of origins.[51] Vignier devoted a whole monograph to a criticism of the Trojan thesis, but his main concern was to establish, on the foundations laid by the great work of Scaliger, a sound chronology of general history.[52] These men all agreed in shunning speculation, which meant any discussion not tied to material proof. The principal difference was that Pasquier, while he tended to distribute his analyses along a roughly chronological line, really went on to study, in Acton's famous words, "problems not periods." This is at once the merit and the novelty of his work.

One vexing problem was the Salic law, which became a particularly sensitive issue, in historical as well as political terms, in the last years of the civil wars. Pasquier began by discarding the various far-fetched etymologies of the term "Salic" and "terra salica" which had wide currency at this time: that of Guillaume Postel, who suggested that it arose from a misreading of "Gallic"; that of Robert Ceneau, who took it from the French "sale"; that of Seyssel (in fact, the anonymous treatise of 1464 on the Salic law), deriving it from "sel", metaphorically "sapience"; that of certain medieval chroniclers, who related it to Pharamond's counselor Salogast, mentioned in the prelude to the law; and several others.[53] Such medieval word-sport was far from dead in the sixteenth century. Instead, Pasquier contented him-

---

[51] Claude Fauchet, *Antiquitez gauloises ou françoises*, I, 2 (*Œuvres*, f. 3ᵛ).

[52] Nicolas Vignier, *Bibliotheque historiale* (Paris, 1587), I, preface, expressing his gratitude to the Pithous, Fauchet, and Scaliger, especially for his *Opus de emendatione temporum* (Paris, 1583). Chronology fascinated many scholars of this generation; e.g., Brisson, "Du commencement de l'an entre les anciens peuples mieux policiez," *Trois discours* (Paris, 1609).

[53] Pasquier, *Recherches*, II, 17 (p. 138). Cf. Postel, *La Loy salique* (Paris, 1552), ch. 7; even the Venetian ambassador spoke of the "legge gallica o salica," *Relazioni degli ambasciatori veneto al senato*, ed. E. Alberi (Venice, 1839), I, 232. See the summary also in Brantôme, *Des Dames*, ed. Lalanne (Paris, 1875), VIII, 49.

self with the view of Paolo Emilio, who linked the term with the "Salian" Franks mentioned by Ammianus Marcellinus. As for Pharamond himself, Pasquier realized, like Du Tillet, that he had never actually entered France. Was he the author of the law? In Fauchet's opinion, this was probable, although obviously it had been corrected by a Christian king, probably Clovis. More critical was Le Caron, who argued, as Dumoulin had for the *Book of Fiefs*, that the collection had been made by a private person. But again, it was not Pasquier's habit to enter into such conjectures, even with the support of reason and authority, if he did not also have historical evidence.

Examining the growth of feudal society in general, Pasquier went back to the voluminous opinions of the jurists. Even modern scholarship, he realized, had no easy answers. "Concerning the origin of fiefs," he recited, "some attribute the first source to the Franks, some to the Burgundians, Lombards, and other peoples of Germany. . . . Others," he continued, referring specifically to Budé and Zasius, "seeking to banish barbarism from their discourse, attribute the invention to the earliest Romans, and others, to gratify our own country, to the Gauls" (that is, Connan).[55] Pasquier himself, partly because he saw that feudalism was not restricted to France, was attracted to the moderate Romanist thesis, that fiefs were related to the *militiae*, the grants of land given to soldiers settled on the frontiers of the empire. The relationship was indirect, of course; the Frankish kings bestowed their "benefices" simply in imitation of the Roman emperors. But some connection seemed plausible in view of the fact that the Franks adopted so many Latin terms. Still, Pasquier admitted, the question was not closed. It was much easier to trace the later stages of feudal organization and its gradual subordination to the crown.

Fauchet's discussion of the problem seems even more thorough and more sophisticated. Much in the fashion of contemporary medievalists, he distinguished between the feudal organization of modern France, which he would not trace much further back than to Hugh Capet,

[54] *Ibid.*, I, 7 (p. 24). Cf. Fauchet, *Antiquitez gauloises*, f. 43^r, and Le Caron, *Pandectes du droit françois*, p. 7.

[55] *Ibid.*, II, 15 (pp. 120-21).

and feudal institutions in a more general sense, in which he saw a social pattern that transcended nationality. "They are mistaken who consider fiefs to be an invention of the Lombards," he wrote, perhaps twenty years after Pasquier, "for it is certain that there have always been lands pledged to more powerful kingdoms and communities in return for military service." Such practices may be found in the law of nations, he added, and in antiquity going back to the times of the Medes and the Persians. "And it is not impossible," he added, "that these first feudatories had subordinates obligated to them like our sub-vassals."[56] To some extent such a sociological generalization may represent a surrender to the "transcendent impulse." Yet in practical terms it signified merely a hypothesis of comparative history, for it in no way blunted Fauchet's particular analysis of specifically European feudalism. On the contrary, it illustrated the richer awareness and deeper perspective which he had attained.

In contrast with the previous generation of scholars, Pasquier, Fauchet, and their colleagues became increasingly wary of attributing an exaggerated antiquity to any modern institution. This was the fallacy not only of Romanists but also of enthusiastic French historians. "It is a common thing," Loisel remarked, "for our chroniclers, when they do not know the source of some fine old institution, to attribute it to Charlemagne."[57] Such was the case with the peers of France. To this Pasquier objected on the grounds that the hereditary principle did not come into practice until the time of the Capetians. Such, too, was the case with the University of Paris, because of the interpretation which historians had placed upon certain remarks of Einhard. As early as 1565 Pasquier questioned this attribution. In his last years he took up the subject in greater detail and argued that the university had its legal origin in the charter of Philip Augustus, although in a less technical sense it could be traced back to the time of Louis VII.[58] Again it is clear that Pasquier preferred to tie his discussions to

---

[56] Fauchet, *Origines des dignitez et magistrats de France* (1584) (*Œuvres*, f. 497r). Cf. the discussion in ch. VII.

[57] Loisel, *De l'Université de Paris*, f. 3r.

[58] Pasquier, *Recherches*, IX, 3-7 (pp. 798-812); cf. his plea against the Jesuits in 1564, III, 43 (p. 316).

specific written evidence, which indeed he presented in great abundance, with the additional novelty of including translations.

The second book of Pasquier's *Researches*, where he took up these problems of the Salic law and of feudalism, showed an improvement over the first in both knowledge and judgment. His growing familiarity with documentary and archival sources is most conspicuous in his accounts of the offices and organs of French government, which is the principal subject of this book. Pride of place naturally went to Pasquier's own tradition, located in the magistracy and the parlement of Paris, which he traced "according to the diversity of times and seasons" down to his own day. Like most legists he accepted the Carolingian *placita* as "the primitive origin and institution of the parlements."[59] Yet he realized that the formative period of the modern parlement was the thirteenth century, especially the reign of Philip IV, whose edict of 1307 he took as most crucial. Other products of this period were the *chambre des comptes*, in which Pasquier later served as *avocat du roi*, and the Estates General. His estimate of this assembly, which he contrasted sharply with the councils of the church, was not affected by the propaganda of the religious wars. Like recent historians, he was sure that the Estates operated not to limit but to strengthen the monarchy, if only because its finances in fact grew steadily.[60] But of course there was a darker side to this institutional growth of the fourteenth century, for it was just at this time that those lamented "longueurs et chicaneries" began to infest French judicial practice.

An equally prominent feature of this age was the establishment of the liberties of the Gallican church, and to this subject Pasquier devoted most of his third book. In general, his position was indistinguishable from that of Pithou, whom indeed he claims to have assisted. He recognized three (corresponding to Pithou's two) fundamental principles: first, that the pope had no power of excommunication in France; second, that the king was wholly independent in temporal matters; and third, that the pope was subordinate to a

---

[59] *Ibid.*, II, 2 (p. 44). Cf. G. Ducoudray, *Les Origines du parlement de Paris* (Paris, 1902), p. 66, and ch. VII, n. 35.
[60] *Ibid.*, II, 7 (pp. 81-87).

general council. Not, of course, that Pasquier pretended to be original in this pronouncement. "Who teaches this lesson?" he asked—and answered, "Jean du Tillet. Was he perhaps a secret Huguenot? By no means; he was their formal and declared foe." [61] Nor did Pasquier have any fear of sounding unorthodox, for like Fauchet he was writing not as a theologian but as a historian. In any case, he believed, his view was in accord with the early councils and, at least in France, was embedded in ecclesiastical tradition.

As usual, Pasquier preferred to submit his results not as a theory of ecclesiastical organization but as an analysis of a series of problems —in this case revolving around the interplay between the French and the papal monarchies. So he followed the procedure not of Pithou (who, of course, had a more practical purpose in mind) but of Du Tillet and of Fauchet. He traced the Gallican liberties from "the middle age of our church," that is, from Merovingian times, down to his own strife-filled age, once again "according to the changes of times and of reigns." [62] He accorded separate treatment to such institutions as the regale and the *appel comme d'abus*, and again he showed discrimination in assessing their age and significance. The first of these, which was linked to the investiture controversy, had Merovingian roots; the second dated only from the reign of Louis XI, although the notion of judicial remedy against ecclesiastical usurpation had been suggested by the fourteenth century jurist Pierre de Cugnières, whom Loisel regarded as the first *avocat du roi*. Like Fauchet, who as usual concentrated on the very early period, Pasquier did not pretend to be doing more than summarizing a time-honored tradition that had been well defended by several generations of lawyers.

With the archetypal conflict of Philip IV and Boniface VIII, Pasquier's detailed treatment begins and continues through the conciliar period. Here, too, he takes up the great tradition of royal legists which

[61] *Ibid.*, III, 17 (p. 219); cf. III, 9 (p. 186).
[62] *Ibid.*, III, 8-41 (pp. 178-311). Cf. Fauchet, "Traicté des libertez de l'eglise gallicane," in *Œuvres* (unpaginated, following f. 532ᵛ), remarking that "Pierre de Cugnières, the *Defensor Pacis*, the *Songe du Verger,* the acts of the Council of Constance and Basel, Jean Lemaire de Belge . . ., Dumoulin on the little dates will satisfy you more than I."

had begun with such royalist champions as Cugnières and Guillaume de Nogaret and which more recently had been carried on by Dumoulin, Du Tillet, and himself. Through this school the Gallican ideology had been preserved and extended—and finally incorporated into historical scholarship. The most seminal of periods was that of the Great Schism, when, as in Pasquier's own day, the monarchy had to maneuver between the extremes of a corrupt papacy and, in the persons of Wycliffe and Hus, who "cried out against the traditions of the church," heresy. Pasquier singled out for special mention the writings of the great Gallican doctors, Gerson and D'Ailly, and the famous ordinance of 1406 which Du Tillet had also seized upon. Nor did he try to disguise his conciliarist sympathies. "The grandest and most solemn council that has been held since the middle age of Christianity," he told a friend, "is, I think, that of Constance."[63] Out of this finally emerged the conciliar acts and the Pragmatic Sanction of Bourges, which summed up the Gallican rights fought for during the previous half-century. The Concordat of 1516 did not change these liberties, he added; it simply "incorporated them with the majesty of the king."

In this way, Pasquier concluded, "the Gallican church was built up during a long period of time." His basic argument was identical with that of Dumoulin, whom indeed he cited with reverence (the *Little Dates* as well as the *Treatise on Fiefs*); and it rested upon an examination of canon law, which Pasquier regarded as a priestly imitation of Roman law. The liberties of the Gallican church, which originally had been at one with Rome, were "most ancient." If certain Gallican institutions were modern creations, this was only to counterbalance the pernicious innovations of the papal curia and a clergy disposed to avarice and chicanery. This ancient Gallican tradition contrasted most sharply with the "new sects" of the Jesuits, and the Huguenots, which had brought such disaster to France. Returning to this subject over forty years after he began, Pasquier was happy to report the restoration of a Gallican monarchy, though the Jesuit menace still remained. Writing the history of Gallicanism was, for him, both the celebration of national tradition and the promotion of

[63] *Ibid.*, III, 26 (p. 251).

political and social reform. In Pasquier's historical thought, then, there was a significant blending of the themes of tradition and of scholarly restoration—of the legist and the humanist points of view.

As Pasquier placed Gallicanism in historical perspective, so he placed the humanist revival in historical perspective.[64] In France the new learning was associated most closely with the University of Paris, which also happened to be the major repository of Gallican doctrine. Here again Pasquier was led to revise the conventional Italianate view of the revival of learning, believing as he did that, in France at least, "good letters" made their appearance in the twelfth century in the persons of Peter Abelard, St Bernard, Peter Comester, and others. Pasquier discussed each of the faculties and the establishment of colleges in this "university," as it began to be called in the reign of Philip Augustus, which was to be the model for other such institutions, such as Frederick II's school in Naples. In more recent times the University of Paris came to house the first printing press in France and so to promote the revival of Latin eloquence, especially in those "two first champions" in the battle against barbarism, Valla and Poggio. In the sixteenth century, finally, the university became a major center of classical scholarship through the royal professorships established in the "faculty of humanity." The "director of this company," he added, was Guillaume Budé, whose letter to Longueil of 1520 Pasquier cited as proof that Budé inspired the foundation of the trilingual college.[64] Of these professors, he believed, the most distinguished were his own teachers Ramus and Turnèbe.

It was to this beloved subject that Pasquier devoted his last efforts. Once again, as in his discussions of the French government and of the Gallican church, Pasquier's scholarly analysis reached its climax in his own experiences. To these Pasquier always, like Montaigne, returned sooner or later. It is this factor, together with his single-minded quest for the spirit of France, that gives coherence to the *Researches of France*. This—even more than the encyclopedic range of interest and the rich intellectual heritage, which after all Pasquier shared with Pithou and others—is why Pasquier's work illustrates, more fully than that of any other author, the nature of Renaissance

[64] *Ibid.*, IX, 18 (p. 832).

historical scholarship. It falls short of the best accomplishments in philology, in historical narrative, and in the philosophy of history; but it offers a matchless, indeed a unique, synthesis of all of these traditions. In the largest perspective it appears as one of the first and most distinguished achievements of European historicism.

CHAPTER XI

Conclusion: Toward a New Design of History

... i grandi frantumi dell'antichità, inutili finor
alla scienza perche erano gracuti squallidi,
tronchi e slogati, arrecano de' grand lumi,
tersi, composti ed allocati ne' luoghi loro.

Vico, *La Nuova Scienza*, 357

No ONE HAS EXPRESSED the conditions of historicism better than Erich
Auerbach.[1] According to his formulation, these are

when people realize that epochs and societies are not to be judged in
terms of a pattern concept of what is desirable absolutely but rather in
every case in terms of their own premises; when people reckon among
such premises not only natural factors like climate and soil but also the
intellectual and historical factors; when, in other words, they come to
develop a sense of historical dynamics, of the incomparability of historical phenomena, so that each epoch appears as a whole whose character
is reflected in each of its manifestations; when, finally, they accept the
conviction that the meaning of events cannot be grasped in abstract and
general forms of cognition and that the material needed to understand
it must not be sought in the upper strata of society and in major political
events but also in art, economy, material and intellectual culture, in the
depths of the workday world and its men and women, because it is only
there that one can grasp what is unique, what is animated by inner
forces, and what, in both a more concrete and more profound sense, is
universally valid. . . .

In practice if not in theory, these conditions were approximated by
the humanist tradition in general, from Valla to Vico and beyond,

---

[1] Auerbach, *Mimesis, the Representation of Reality in Western Literature*,
trans. W. Trask (Princeton, 1953), p. 391.

and in particular by that phase of it treated in this book. Like Auerbach's own views, moreover, they were attained above all through researches into and reflections upon language.

The Science of History

To inquire into the origins of any human creation is neither to define nor to justify it, but it is a question that, in one form or another, the historian is obliged to ask. In the search for the origins of historicism itself, it has been necessary to explore certain parts of that "crumbling Roman road from the antique to the modern world,"[2] especially the traditions of civil and canon law. Most directly, however, historicism must be traced to the humanists of the Renaissance, who themselves were obsessed with the problem of "origins." At the very least it may be concluded that humanism, or rather that scholarly aspect of humanism which for five centuries European scholars have called philology, created the most basic attitudes which have gone into the making of historicism. It established a point of view dependent upon the study of things in terms of time, place, and circumstances. It provided a "historical" method and certain concepts, such as those of style and anachronism, essential for the interpretation of cultural history. Most important, humanism created a scholarly tradition which preserved and elaborated these ideas and passed them on to modern scholarship.

Yet crucial as was the impact of Italian humanism, it was only by casting off the cultural hegemony of Rome that philology could establish itself as a science—and historicism as an independent force. In this reduction of classicism from an absolute standard to a model of historical experience, the work of French scholars was most significant. Their Gallican convictions prevented them from identifying history with the classical tradition while their humanist interests led them to doubt that the Christian world-plan was sufficient. Thus, Bodin rejected the old notion of the four world monarchies, and Le Roy admitted many non-Western civilizations into his view of universal history. More generally, Baudouin defined the arena of human

[2] E. R. Curtius, *European Literature and the Latin Middle Ages*, trans. W. Trask (New York, 1953), p. 19.

history as the whole sphere of human activity (*res humanae*), which he marked off carefully from the great "amphitheater" of nature (*res naturales*). In the former, he pointed out, man was a performer (*actor*) as well as an observer (*spectator*) and critic (*judex* or *interpres*), and he left no doubt that this epistemological distinction rendered the human "academy" the more admirable.[3] On just these grounds— the distinction between the world of man's making (*factum*) and that of God's making (*verum*)—Vico was later to define the historian's field of inquiry. On these grounds, too, such modern authors as Troeltsch and Croce have defined "historicism."

The Renaissance revolt against classicism, of course, found more concrete expression. Besides those twin theories, the "translation of empire" and the "translation of studies," it took the form of various quarrels between ancients and moderns and between Romans and "barbarians." In France, where ancient and modern Rome were looked upon with equal suspicion, these issues converged to form a basic theme of historical thought. "Cicero said that Rome could not be vanquished by arms nor Greece by letters," observed one of Budé's contemporaries, "but ... he was Italian and suspect in this matter, for ... if Italy was once invincible, now she is surpassable in manners and other later achievements."[4] This remark illustrates one of the motives not only of vernacular humanism but of anti-Tribonianism and more generally of the defense and illustration of modern French culture. At the same time this modernist argument was tempered by a deep sense of historical relativism. As Valla and Budé had excused medieval scholars on the grounds that their errors were the product rather of the age than of the men, so Le Roy admitted that the ancients "knew all that it was possible for them to know in their time."[5]

A still more striking example of the growing perspective of sixteenth-century scholarship was the "historicizing" of various disciplines. This was conspicuous in the study of laws and institutions and

---

[3] Baudouin, *De Institutione historiae universae*, pp. 599 and 742, the opening and closing statements of the book. Almost the same language is used by Johann Grynaeus in his *De Historia in universum* (Zürich, Zentralbibliothek, MS. B. 130).

[4] Symphorien Champier, *La Nef des princes* (Lyon, 1502), f. XXᵛ.

[5] Le Roy, *Vicissitude des choses*, pp. 121-22.

of history itself. Indeed, in such works as Polydore Vergil's *Inventors of Things* and Christophe Milieu's *Writing the Universal History of Things*, as well as Le Roy's *Vicissitude of Things*, history may be seen replacing hierarchy as a means of organizing the humanist encyclopedia itself. But it is important to note that such "historicization" was not limited to the recasting of knowledge in chronological form. It also involved an awareness of the growth of human creations from a primitive to a sophisticated stage, from infancy to maturity, perhaps from there to senility, although this was by no means a predetermined process. In language the trajectory was from barbarism—"every word was once a barbarism," as Erasmus suggested[6]—to elegance. In jurisprudence it was from simple custom to a multiplicity of written laws, perhaps to a code. Similarly, history moved from fable to folklore, that is, poetry, to a truthful and instructive narrative. Here again we can see the germ of one of the basic concepts of Vico's "new science" and perhaps of Niebuhr's views of prehistory.

The search for a comprehensive "method of history" in the sixteenth century was important in a formal rather than a practical sense. Undoubtedly this movement helped to dignify history and to give it a measure of independence. On the other hand, in the attempt to transform history into an organized science, scholars ran the risk of confining historical investigation within a closed system ruled by more or less fixed categories and laws. Such was clearly the tendency of Bodin's—as it would be of Vico's and Montesquieu's—conception of universal law. Such, to some extent, was the tendency of the Renaissance ideal of universal history. It was, of course, a noble ideal. By nature, as Daniel Heinsius said, man "would be free from the limits of time and space. . . . He would gather into one focus the immeasurably great vastness of ages and generations. . . . History renders man contemporary with the universe."[7] But if attained, this transcendent ideal would seem to mark the end as well as the fulfillment of history.

In fact, many French scholars were aware of this. Baudouin for one, despite his irenic dreams, regarded universal history not as a

---

[6] *Ciceronianus* (*Opera*, I, col. 996).

[7] Heinsius, *The Value of History*, trans. G. Robinson (Cambridge, Mass., 1943), pp. 10-11.

suprahistorical abstraction but as a complex and richly textured story of many societies and ages. The purpose of his "method," indeed, was to enrich the substance of history through the addition of legal, institutional, and implicitly social studies. A still more elaborate ideal was set forth in La Popelinière's "design for a new history of the French," which extended the jurisdiction of history over all facets of man's public life.[8] What is more, both he and Baudouin assumed that universal history ultimately consisted of the individual histories of many nations with different characters and different destinies. Like Vico, they understood that the world of humanity and of Christendom was also the world of the *gentes.* If history was really to furnish self-knowledge, it had to rest upon a relatively narrow national basis and upon relatively tedious areas of research. This has been at once the strength and the weakness of historicism.

The Historical Imagination

Clio has always been a two-faced muse. If Herodotus was the father of history, he was also the father of lies; and if history is philosophy teaching by example, it may also be a dreary story of human folly and misfortune. It is, alternately, a nightmare from which we must awake or a vision of God's design; it is full of deceit or the education of the human race; it is the embodiment of reaction or the means of liberation. In the sixteenth century, too, such antinomies were common. Not long after Gaillard had called history the fountain of all disciplines, Charles de la Ruelle denounced it in conventional skeptical fashion as the fountain of all error.[9] Catholic authors could equate history with ecclesiastical tradition, while Protestant opponents identified it with a lost age of innocence. And while Pasquier devoted his life to the recollection of things past, Galileo was devising a mathematical philosophy which would purportedly render such knowledge

---

[8] La Popelinière, *Idee de l'histoire*, pp. 358 ff, translated by G. Huppert in *History and Theory*, V (1966), 59-60.

[9] Charles de la Ruelle, *Succincts adversaires ... contre l'histoire et professeurs d'icelle* (Poitiers, 1574). Cf. Henry Cornelius Agrippa, *De Incertitudine et vanitate scientiarum declamatio invectus* (Cologne, 1537), ch. 5.

useless. In four centuries or more, it may seem, the terms of these debates have hardly changed.

There is no point in denying the ambiguity and even duplicity of Renaissance historical thought. In historiography more than anywhere else, as Eliade has suggested, myth is preserved or recreated; and this is only too obvious in sixteenth-century historical scholarship.[10] In celebrating and magnifying the principle of nationality, for example, especially in a naïve Celtic or Germanist form, French historians were in a sense reverting to tribalism and the ancestral myths associated with it. Ronsard might deny that the poet and the historian had anything in common, but in reality his *Franciade* appealed to much the same audience, and played upon the same sentimental traditions as the writings of his friends Belleforest, Du Haillan, and Pasquier.[11] The theory of Trojan origins, various Carolingian legends, the Germanic derivation of the estates and other councils, and the idealized "ancient constitution" and "fundamental laws" were mythical views that maintained and even, in the seventeenth century, increased their popularity. The *Kulturkampf* of the civil wars, while it gave incentive for a fresh examination of French traditions, intensified the nationalist and anti-Italian bias of French scholars. "What is all history but the praise of Rome?" Petrarch had asked; who was Charlemagne but a European king "whom by the cognomen 'the great' barbarous people dare to raise to the level of Pompey and Caesar"?[12] The first principle of the French design of history was a total inversion of this. It did not at first seem calculated to broaden the horizons or to sharpen the critical sense of historians.

In the seventeenth century the shortcomings of historical scholarship became painfully obvious. Born out of ideological conflict and set in the framework of a prescientific world view, the Renaissance "science" of history could hardly compete with the new philosophy that cast all in doubt—that regarded language not as an expression

---

[10] Eliade, *Myth and Reality* (New York, 1963), pp. 113 ff.

[11] Ronsard's epic was based upon annals (preface of 1587), while Belleforest in his *Les Grandes Annales...* (Paris, 1579), did not hesitate to cite the *Franciade*.

[12] Cited in T. E. Mommsen, *Medieval and Renaissance Studies* (Ithaca, 1959), pp. 122 and 120.

of reality but as a mask hiding it and history not as a treasury to be preserved but as a prison to be escaped from. The uneasy alliance between the academy and the forum further compromised historical method; for the radically critical and extravagantly antiquarian attitude of humanism, especially legal humanism, had been seriously undermined by the conservative and utilitarian approach of practicing jurists and official ideologists. Nor did Renaissance historical scholarship produce an authentic masterpiece, that is, a work that combined erudition with literary merit and intelligent organization, to exhibit its achievements. Unsystematic, eclectic, often controversial, history was particularly vulnerable to the attacks of Pyrrhonists in the seventeenth century. In the wake of the great flood of scientific achievement of that period, sixteenth-century historical scholarship might indeed seem antediluvian.

For all the talk among Pasquier's contemporaries about a new design of history, then, it may seem that what they produced was rather a patchwork than a paradigm. Moreover, the tradition of historical scholarship in the seventeenth century was as tenuous as it was duplicitous, prodigious in quantity but surviving mainly on the level of a somewhat disoriented "normal science." Pithou, whose work consisted mainly in collecting and criticizing, had his successors in men like Mézeray, Duchesne, and the Dupuys; but Pasquier's ideals were not seriously pursued. The interplay between philology and religious controversy continued to inform historical investigation, but in the eyes of many secular-minded men this tended further to discredit historical studies. Techniques of cooperative research—correspondence, "conversations," and scholarly voyages of discovery— became still more effective, so that the seventeenth century became the first age of historical societies and "great historical enterprises"; but the gap between raw erudition and a shaping intelligence became wider than ever.[13] Voltaire's "new history" was notoriously hostile to the unenlightened pedantry of his monkish and even humanist predecessors, while Gibbon, though he made use of the work of the Renaissance philologists, did not much share their interest in institutional and cultural history. Baudouin's true successors were Savigny

[13] See D. Knowles, *Great Historical Enterprises* (London, 1963), p. 41.

and Mommsen, it may be concluded, as Pasquier's were Thierry and
Fustel de Coulanges.

Yet it is as unfair—and as unenlightening—to judge the achievement of French scholarship in this heroic age according to twentieth-
century standards as it would be to judge those of Kepler or Harvey.
Their work should be assessed in terms not only of their results or
the extent of their direct influence but also of the questions they
thought of asking and of the means they devised to answer them.
They exhibited, to a fault, that "mental cross-fertilization between
different disciplines" [14] which Koestler has declared essential for critical as well as creative thought; and despite the intolerance of their
age, they exercised their critical faculties with a recklessness that in-
vited, and often received, official censure. Indeed, every one of the
legends mentioned above was rejected by Pasquier and his colleagues.
If French historians labored under a somewhat oppressive Gallican
bias, they took an increasingly tolerant and relativistic view of history.
If nationality was a myth, it was in some respects preferable to the
grander myth of Roman universalism, which violated legal and linguistic sensibilities as well as historical sense. They were even capable
of creating new myths, such as that of the absolute malignancy of
the Jesuits, but this did not prevent them from attaining a broad
appreciation for the Roman as well as Celtic and Germanic elements
of French civilization. And their immersion in medieval legal traditions tended to enrich historical scholarship by bringing a greater
familiarity with the problems of ecclesiastical politics, national rivalries, and feudal society. In general, distressed by the catastrophes of
their age and distrustful of scholarly as well as philosophic and
theological dogma, they concerned themselves more with the substance than with the shape of history. In the end, perhaps, their significance for European thought rests precisely upon the eclectic and
unsystematic character of their scholarship.

Yet Pasquier and his co-workers had a distinctive vision of the
world even if they did not give it explicit formulation. For them history was, in practice and in theory, an autonomous discipline, a mode
of thinking that was independent of, though it could be applied to,

[14] Koestler, *Act of Creation* (New York, 1964), p. 230.

any form of human behavior. They had a sense of the interconnectedness of cultural phenomena, but they preferred to show this by concrete analogies between language, law, and other arts of civilization. What is more, their investigations, even when they originated in political necessity, seemed to gather a momentum and create a rationale of their own. Man made himself and could only come to understand himself through the study of the products of his mind and of his society. According to one of Pasquier's friends, who was well aware of the cultural as well as the biological implications of the observation, "Human eyes perceive things only through the forms of their understandings."[15] If philosophers affected to seize upon reality directly, the proper study of historians was the "human condition" itself in its cultural context. Here is the true significance of Renaissance historicism, that it raised—some might say lowered—the pursuit of self-knowledge to the level of human history.

[15] Montaigne, "Apologie de Raimond Sebond."

INDEX